The Rocky Mountain PLANT GUIDE

George Oxford Miller

Cover and book design by Jonathan Norberg
Edited by Brett Ortler, Ritchey Halphen, and Jenna Barron
Proofread by Emily Beaumont
Maps created by Jonathan Norberg

10 9 8 7 6 5 4 3 2 1

The Rocky Mountain Plant Guide

Published by Adventure Publications
An imprint of AdventureKEEN
310 Garfield Street South
Cambridge, Minnesota 55008
(800) 678-7006
www.adventurepublications.net

Printed in China
Cataloging-in-Publication data is available from the Library of Congress
ISBN 978-1-64755-325-8 (pbk.); ISBN 978-1-64755-326-5 (ebook)

TABLE OF CONTENTS

DEDICATION

Dedicated to my wife, Carole Price, whose abiding love fills my life with joy every day.

ACKNOWLEDGMENTS

I want to thank my editor, Brett Ortler, and the crew at Adventure Publications for giving me the opportunity to express my passion and awe for the wonders of nature through words and photography. Their artistic book design and layout have allowed me to author 13 beautifully produced books and guides that I hope will inspire readers to love, understand, and appreciate the beauty and hidden miracles waiting to be discovered in even the smallest flower. Henry David Thoreau famously said, "In wildness is the preservation of the world," and I know no better way to experience and embrace that wildness than in a wildflower.

O Friend!

In the garden of thy heart, plant naught by the rose of love.

-Bahá'u'lláh, founder of the Bahaí Faith

INTRODUCTION

As North America's 3,000-mile-long spine (4,828 km), the Rocky Mountains span the continent from New Mexico to northern Canada. Bordered by broad plateaus and plains, the mastiffs rise abruptly from the surrounding plains, creating a vertical difference of up to 7,000 feet (2,134 m). With towering peaks, rugged slopes, deep canyons, and broad intermountain valleys, the mountains are the most dramatic–and dynamic–landscape features of New Mexico, Colorado, Utah, Wyoming, Montana, Idaho, and northern Washington, as well as Alberta and British Columbia in Canada.

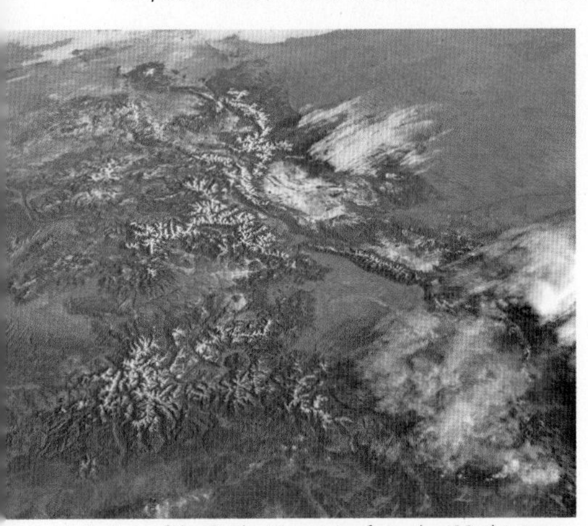

A Portion of the Rocky Mountains from the ISS; this image shows the Front Range and the San Juan Range. *Photo credit: NASA/ESA/ISS Crew*

With thousands of peaks towering above timberline, and 58 above 14,000 feet (4,570 m), the north-south geological wall reaches into the atmosphere and siphons moisture carried by the prevailing winds from the Pacific to the west and the Great Plains to the east. With vast watersheds, the great rivers born in the Rockies water the West and irrigate the farmlands that feed America. From the Continental Divide, which follows the sinuous ridgelines of the crest of the continent, the Colombia and Fraser Rivers and their tributaries flow into the Pacific; the Colorado River into the Gulf of California; the Rio Grande into the Gulf of Mexico; and the Arkansas, Platte, and Missouri recharge the Mississippi River. Rivers from the Triple Divide in Glacier National Park also wind across the plains of Canada to the Hudson Bay, while a number of rivers rising in the Canadian Rockies flow north to the Arctic Ocean.

Born of fire and shaped by ice, the Rocky Mountains began their journey to the sky 80 million years ago. At that time, an inland sea dissected the western half of the continent from the Arctic to Mexico, covering the footprint of today's Rockies. Pacific tectonic plates, creeping east millimeter by millimeter, crashed into the North American continental plate and wedged their way underneath the lighter landmass. These tectonic forces uplifted and contorted the continental land mass. Over the next 15 million years, they created coastal and interior mountains, uplifted vast plateaus, and down dropped what are now intermountain basins.

The forces of the colliding subterranean plate wrinkled the surface to create the Canadian Rockies and uplifted a 20,000-foot-high plateau in the western United States. The Rockies of the US we see today began their transformation from plateau to towering peaks 65 million years ago. Wind, rain, erosion, and the rock-crushing forces of countless, mile-thick glaciations carved the plateau like a master sculptor. The relentless forces of ice chiseled jagged peaks, gouged broad valleys to the bedrock, and bulldozed thousands of feet of pulverized gravel and sand into valleys and intermountain basins. Water cut deep canyons, eroded slopes, and covered the plains below with a mile-deep layer of soil and rock aggregate.

The result of eons of random, chaotic destruction across this continent-spanning landscape created the majesty and magic of the Rocky Mountains. The scenic beauty, unmatched variety of wild creatures big and small, and vast diversity of plant life from towering forests to dazzling mountain meadows combine to inspire, challenge, and stretch the human imagination to its limits. Elevations vary from near sea level to well above timberline, moisture gradients from semi-desert to lush mountain slopes drenched with rainfall and snowpacks, and exposures varying from chilled northern slopes, broiling southern slopes, and sun-radiated, wind-whipped arctic tundra. With such diversity, the Rockies harbor a plethora of life zones, habitats, and micro-niches, each packed like treasure chests with the wonders of nature.

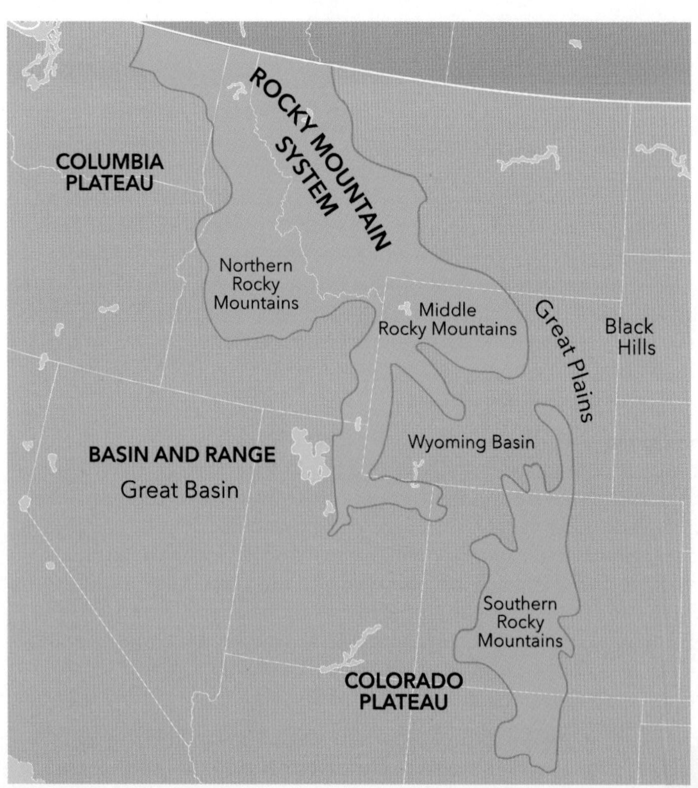

THE REGIONS

The Rocky Mountains are not one continuous, homogenous range formed at the same time by the same processes. The more than 100 separate ranges can be divided into the Northern and Canadian Rockies, Middle Rockies, and Southern Rockies, separated by plateaus and basins. Each region has its own distinct topography, geology, and ecosystems. Within each region, altitude, precipitation, and exposure create broad, well-defined life or bio zones with numerous unique habitats and vegetative associations, or communities, of plants.

Northern and Canadian Rockies

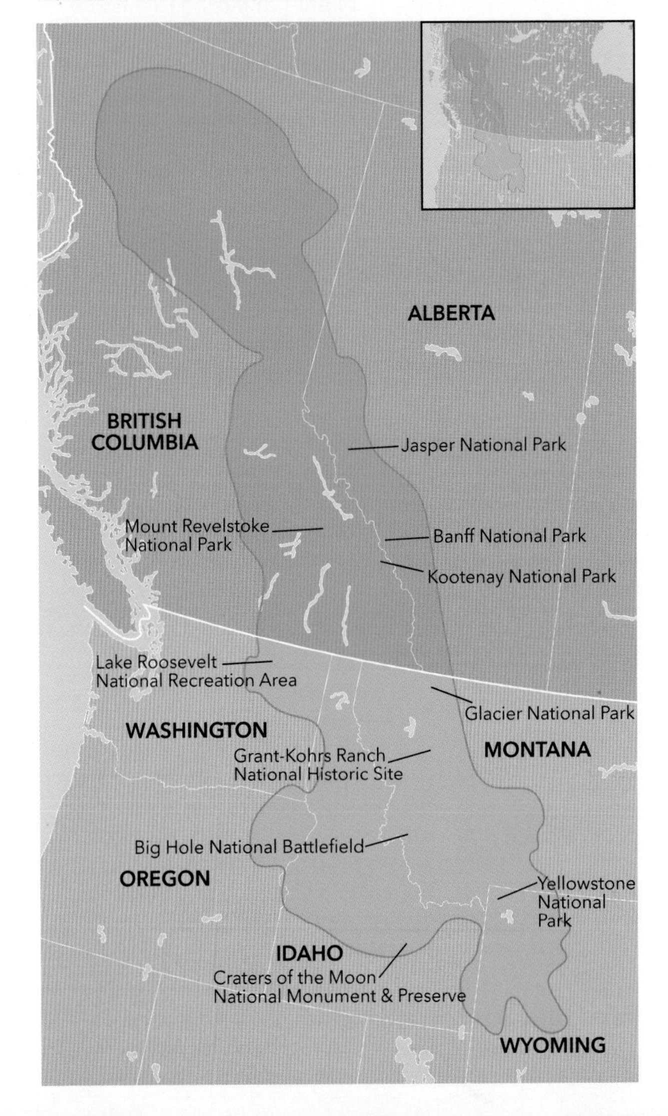

Wenkchemna Peak in the Canadian Rockies

Running through Montana, Idaho, and northeastern Washington into Alberta and British Columbia, the Northern and Canadian Rockies rise from about 1,000 feet (305 m) in Idaho to 12,972 feet (3,954 m) atop Mount Robson in British Columbia. The majestic Canadian Rockies, straddling the border of Alberta and British Columbia, boast 50 peaks over 11,000 feet high (3,354 m). Glacier National Park in Montana has 150 peaks that exceed 8,000 feet (2,438 m), and a half dozen over 10,000 feet (3,048 m). Treeline begins at about 6,500 feet (1,980 m).

Glacier National Park, Montana

Glacier National Park, as well as Banff and Jasper National Parks in Canada, preserve some of the best examples of the rapidly disappearing glaciers that once dominated the Rockies. Though only a few can still be seen on distant slopes in Glacier, Banff and Jasper contain the Columbia Icefield. Covering 125 square miles (325 sq. km) and reaching 1,200 feet deep (365 m), the icefield feeds six named glaciers, including the easily accessible, 4-mile long (6.5 km) Athabasca Glacier. Currently, the massive glacier retreats 16 feet per year (1.5 km) and has lost half its volume in the last 125 years. For perspective, the Columbia Icefield formed 230,000 years ago, or 100,000 years before modern humans, *Homo sapiens,* began migrating from Africa.

Athabasca Glacier, Columbia Icefield, Canada

While the Columbia Icefield receives 24 feet of snowfall a year (7 m), precipitation across the Northern Rockies averages from 100 inches (2.5 m) at high elevations to 10 inches (4 cm) in low valleys and shrublands. Because of rain shadow effects that trap moist Pacific winds, the western slopes tend to be wetter and warmer; the eastern slopes, more influenced by Arctic air masses, are cloudier, colder, and drier.

Vegetative zones extend from low-land sagebrush steppe going west and Great Plains grasslands to the east, to dry montane forests of lower slopes and valleys, moist montane forests along streams, lush subalpine coniferous forests, and alpine tundra. The

Pacific maritime climate influence supports four conifers not found elsewhere in the Rockies: Western Hemlock, Mountain Hemlock, Western Red Cedar, and Pacific Yew.

Middle Rockies

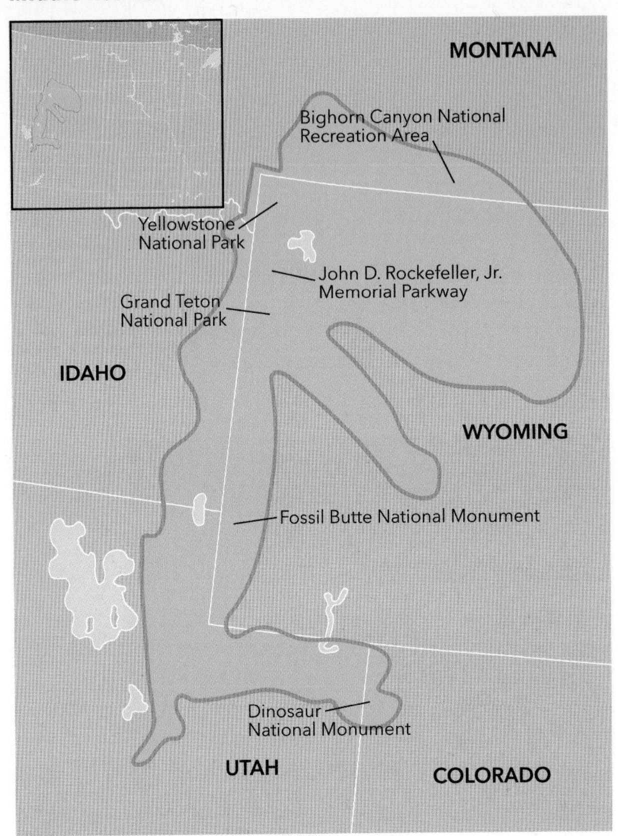

The Grand Tetons in Grand Teton National Park

Spanning sections of Wyoming, Idaho, Utah, and Montana, this cluster of mountain ranges, all formed separately, is surrounded by a sea of sagebrush and grasslands. The down-dropped Wyoming Basin and uplifted high deserts of the Colorado Plateau border the two southern extensions, the Snake River Plain and the Basin and Range Province converge to the west, and the Great Plains grasslands lap against the eastern edge.

With jagged peaks, breathtaking scenery, and spectacular flora and fauna, the region is best known for Yellowstone National Park and its magma hotspot, the bend in the Earth's mantle that fuels the amazing geysers and other thermal features. Yellowstone, along with the adjacent Grand Teton National Park, lie at the heart of the Greater Yellowstone Ecosystem, which encompasses much of the Middle Rockies. At 22 million acres, it is one of the largest remaining intact temperate-zone ecosystems on the planet, and one of the most scenic. Dramatically, the Teton Range, with Grand Teton at 13,775 feet (4,200 m), abruptly thrusts up 7,000 feet (2,132 m) from the valley grasslands with no intervening foothills.

The varied life zones from sagebrush scrublands, through conifer forests, to alpine tundra, harbor a great biodiversity of wildflowers, trees, and shrubs. From mid-June to late August, meadows, slopes, valleys, and alpine tundra burst into bloom with a rainbow array of buckwheats, arnicas, columbines, lupines, and penstemons. The Chief Joseph Scenic Highway (HWY 296), between Cody and Cooke City and on to Mammoth Hot Springs, climbs from sagebrush-grasslands through montane and subalpine forests, with dependable, spectacular wildflower displays.

Southern Rockies

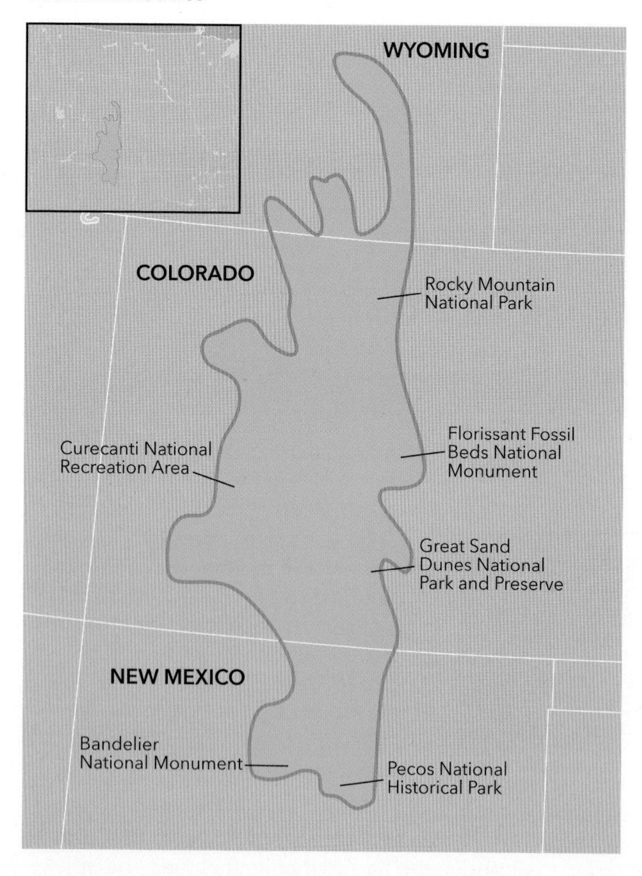

The rugged Southern Rockies encompass ranges in northern New Mexico, all the mountains in Colorado, and three prongs that extend into southern Wyoming. This rugged region has 58 peaks that exceed 14,000 feet (4,267 m), 647 that exceed 13,000 feet (3,962 m), and the 30 highest peaks in the Rockies. The tallest, Mount Elbert, reaches 14,440 feet (4,401 m) into the Colorado skies.

Hallowell Park Meadow, RMNP

The towering ranges are bordered by the arid shrublands of the Colorado Plateau to the west, the intermountain sagebrush of the Wyoming Basin to the north, and the Great Plains grasslands to the east. Mountain parklands, expansive valleys of sagebrush and grasslands above 9,000 feet (2,743 m), are filled with thousands of feet of infill bulldozed into place by past glaciers.

With Rocky Mountain National Park as the crown jewel and dozens of other national and state parks, forests, and wilderness areas, the Southern Rockies are world renowned for spectacular scenery, outdoor recreation, and wildflower displays. With sagebrush steppes and grasslands giving away to pinyon-juniper foothills, mixed conifer montane forests, subalpine spruce-fir forests, and spectacular alpine blooms, the Southern Rockies harbors the greatest diversity of wildflowers in the mountain west. The meadows and slopes of the San Juan Mountains in southern Colorado receive honorable mention on lists of the top 50 wildflower hotspots in the world.

LIFE ZONES

With a 3,000-mile (4,828 km) north–south latitudinal change and elevations varying from 1,000 to 14,000 feet (305–4,268 m), the Rocky Mountains encompass a patchwork mosaic of vegetation zones from semi-desert to alpine tundra. For every 1,000-foot (305 m) gain in elevation up a mountain slope, the temperature drops 3 degrees Fahrenheit (1.7 °C), and precipitation increases about 4 inches (10 cm).

The vegetation community of any one area depends on a number of factors, including elevation; average annual precipitation and temperature; number of growing days; soil type and depth; and even the frequency of rains, floods, winds, and fires. At any single location, the abiotic factors with the greatest influence are moisture and temperature, both influenced significantly by the aspect–the angle of the sun's solar radiation which warms the plants and dries the soil. Classically, south-facing slopes are hotter and drier, while north-facing slopes are wetter and cooler, each with dramatically different plant life.

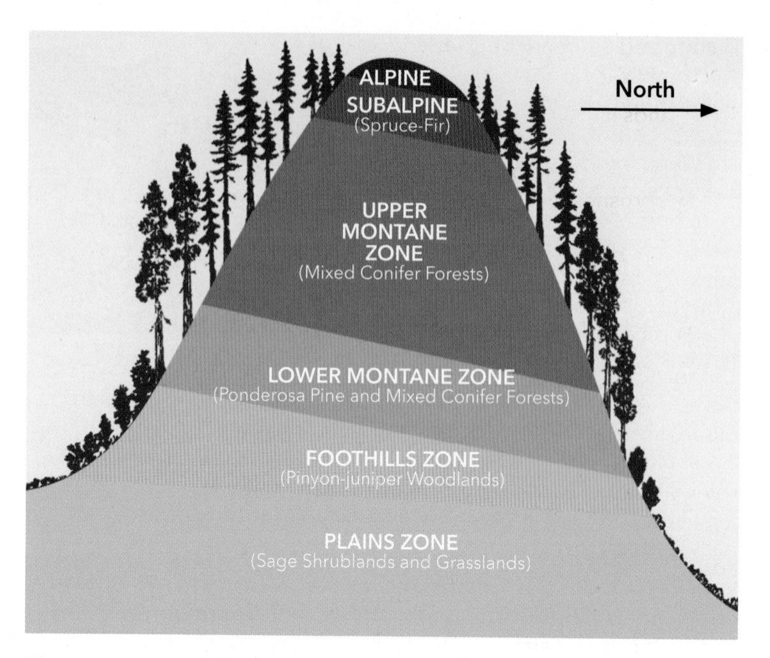

The vegetation of the Rockies can be divided into major life zones, dependent on elevation, latitude, and precipitation, each with dominant or indicator plant species. These can be divided and subdivided arbitrarily. For instance, of the 10 forest zones across the Rockies recognized by the USGS, this book will delineate the most inclusive three: foothills, mixed-conifer montane, and subalpine spruce-fir forests.

Some plants have specialty adaptations that match only a narrow niche within a single life zone (alpine plants, wetland orchids). Many are more generalist and common throughout two or more life zones. In most instances, life zones create vegetation mosaics that gradually transition from one to another, like junipers slowly encroaching on grasslands as foothills gain elevation. Others, like the treeline separating subalpine forests from alpine, can be dramatic and easy to detect.

Lamar Valley, Yellowstone National Park

Grasslands

Mixed-grass and short-grass prairies of the Great Plains parallel the eastern front of the Rockies for 3,000 miles (4,828 km) from New Mexico through Colorado, Wyoming, and Montana into Alberta, Canada. The high plateau, semi-arid grasslands dominate between 5,000–6,000 feet (1,524–1,828 m), often reaching into the pinyon-juniper/mountain mahogany foothills along valleys, rolling hills, riparian woods, and dry slopes.

Grasslands integrate with sage species in the sagebrush steppe ecosystem, and they are prominent components in the intermountain parks, plateaus, and basins. Semi-arid, sun-loving wildflowers, such as paintbrushes, buckwheats, and sunflowers thrive in this zone.

Sagebrush Steppe

Yellowstone National Park

Vast expanses of sagebrush dominate the plateaus and basins of the Intermountain West, primarily west of the Continental Divide, except in the Wyoming Basin where it spreads east into the Great Plains grasslands. It occurs between 5,000–11,000 feet (1,525–3,350 m) on moderately deep, coarse soils. Big Sagebrush, *Artemisia tridentata,* and other *Artemisa* species, create a shrub-dominated overstory with an understory of perennial grasses and wildflowers. Other widespread shrubs include Antelope Bitterbush and rabbitbrush, with Arrowhead Balsamroots, buckwheats, buscuitroots, and lupines among the most common wildflowers.

Foothills

Pinyon-juniper foothills, New Mexico

As the transition zone between low-elevation grasslands and mid-elevation montane forests, the semi-arid woodlands and shrub communities occur on the lower slopes and low hills at the foot mountain ranges. In the Southern Rockies an association of Pinyon Pine, juniper, Scrub Oak, and Mountain Mahogany dominates the slopes from about 5,500–8,000 feet (1,676–2,438 m). Gambel's Oak, spreading by roots, can form dense stands on sunny slopes, especially in fire scars. Cottonwood and box elder follow the streams, and Ponderosa Pine and Douglas-fir begin mixing in at higher elevations. As a transition community, the composition of the Foothills zone varies greatly from south to north. In the Middle Rockies, Mountain Mahogany, Antelope Bitterbush, and rabbitbrush become the dominate species. In the Northern Rockies, the zone becomes shrubbier and often patchy, with Mountain Ninebark, Chokecherry, serviceberries, and Mountain Spray often dominant.

Rocky Mountain National Park

Montane Forests

With open forests, valleys, flowery meadows, park-like savannas, and snow-fed streams, mid-elevation forests stretch between the shrubby foothills and the spruce-fir subalpine forests. Ranging from 7,500–9,500 feet (2,286–2,895 m) in the Southern Rockies, Ponderosa Pine dominates east of the Continental Divide and Douglas-fir to the west. Stands of aspen and Lodgepole Pine pioneer in fire scars, and Blue Spruce (east) and White Fir (west) occur in riparian areas. In the Middle Rockies, Ponderosa Pine mingles with Douglas-fir, and Lodgepole Pine forms dense stands. In the Northern Rockies, Douglas-fir dominates dry forests from 5,500–7,500 feet (1,675–2,285 m), along with Lodgepole Pine (east) and Western Larch (west). In moist forests west of the Continental Divide that receive Pacific maritime moisture, Western Red Cedar, Western Hemlock, and Grand Fir dominate between 2,000–5,000 feet (6,190–1,524 m).

Subalpine Forests

Yellowstone National Park

These conifer forests occur between the upper montane forests and treeline. Dense forests are intermingled with wet and dry meadows, rolling grasslands, and open avalanche chutes. Engelmann Spruce and Subalpine Fir dominate, along with stands of Lodgepole Pine and aspen. The spruce-fir belt extends 9,500–11,500 feet (2,895–3,350 m) in the Southern Rockies, 2,900–6,500 feet (884–1,980 m) in the Middle and Northern Rockies west of the Continental Divide, and 5,200–8,800 feet (1,585–2,682 m) east of the Divide. On high-elevation, dry, exposed slopes, stands of Lodgepole and Whitebark Pine often dominate.

Colorado

Alpine

Above treeline, cold temperatures make the growing season too short for trees to survive. Going south, the elevation of treeline increases steadily at the rate of 330 feet (100 m) per degree of latitude. In the Canadian Rockies, treeline occurs around 6,500 feet (1,980 m) but increases to 12,000 feet (3,658 m) in the Southern Rockies. Trees near their physiological limits become stunted or dwarfed. Despite the harsh environment of the alpine tundra, wildflowers abound in the meadows, fellfields, and scree slopes. Fed by snowmelt, the tundra bursts with color as flowers race to bloom and set seed during the short July–August growing season. Perennial flowers are low growing, often forming dense cushions or mats to protect the buds from freezing, and usually produce showy flowers to attract pollinators. Many flowers have tall stalks to better disperse their seeds into the winds.

PLANT ANATOMY: LEAVES, SEX, FRUIT

Plants are classified in two broad categories. The oldest, dating back 360 million years, are the gymnosperms, including modern pines, firs, spruce, junipers, and other conifers. Gymnosperms produce seeds exposed on the scales of cones. In contrast, angiosperms produce seeds encased in a protected ovule or fruit. This includes all plants that have flowers with an ovary enclosed in a pistil (female) and stamens with anthers that produce grains of pollen (male).

According to the fossil records, angiosperms with seed-producing ovules first appeared about 165–175 million years ago. The reproductive breakthrough enabled flowers to coevolve with pollinators, primarily insects, to ensure targeted cross-pollination. Gymnosperms shed their pollen to the wind, trusting it will reach a receptive female cone. Angiosperms developed showy petals to attract insect pollinators and nectary glands as a reward to manipulate insects to transport pollen to other flowers.

Through the eons, the creative forces of coevolution with pollinators, competition for resources, herbivore predation, and the vicissitudes of climate molded a few common leaf and flower parts into the unimaginable diversity we see today. Every detail, from overt flower color and shape down the microscopic hair structure and intricate chemical defense systems, has been honed to maximize one goal: producing the next generation of the species as efficiently as possible.

Describing the multitude of physical characteristics that make a species unique requires a complex taxonomic language with a lexicon of highly specific terminology. The botanical description of a plant begins belowground with the root system and extends upward to the stem, leaves, flowers, and ultimately to the fruit and seeds. To differentiate one species from another, plant taxonomy uses a language that describes the exact details of each feature down to microscopic levels. This book avoids using these "foreign" terms as much as possible and includes illustrations of the important plant structures, such as types of leaves and flower characteristics.

Leaves

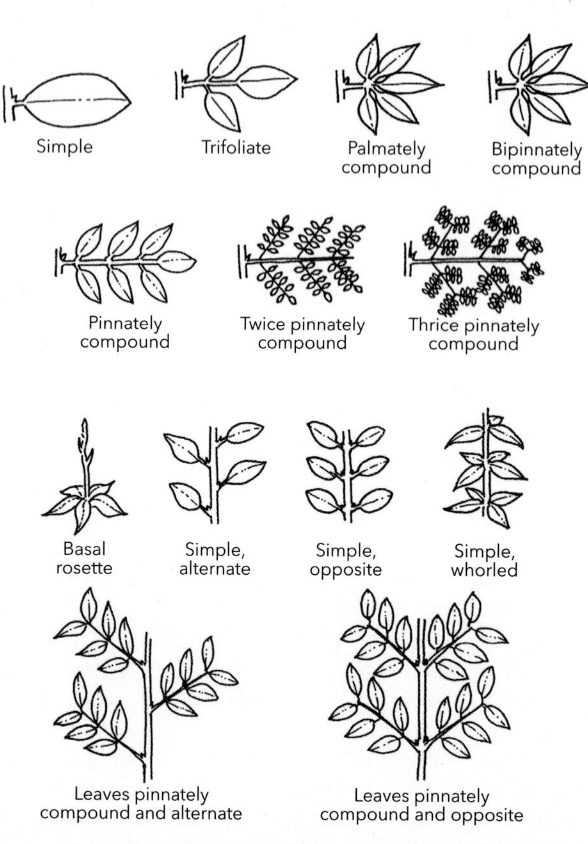

Leaves are the food factories of a plant where photosynthesis occurs. Natural selection has finely tuned leaves to be most efficient in specific habitats. Typically, plants in locations with ample rain have large leaves with pointed tips to channel off excess moisture. Desert plants have tiny leaves with a waxy or hairy surface to minimize water loss. At the extreme, cacti modified their leaves into spines, with photosynthesis occurring in the green stems.

Simple leaves have a single blade attached to the branch with a stalk (petiole) of varying length, or they can be stalkless or clasping the stem. Palmately compound leaves have lobes or leaflets that radiate from a single spot, like fingers on a hand. Pinnately compound leaves have small leaflets spread along the midrib on the leaf. Leaves can form a dense basal rosette, grow in pairs or alternate along the stem, or grow in whorled clusters. The leaf type and arrangement are important factors in plant identification.

The surface of a leaf or leaflet controls how much air is absorbed through pores to power photosynthesis, and how much water is lost by transpiration. Leaves open and close the pores to maintain a sustainable balance between water loss and air intake. The type and amount of hair and glands on a leaf also helps control water loss and maintain the interior heat balance for maximum production, as well as inhibit leaf herbivores.

Parts of a Flower

Flower Cross-section

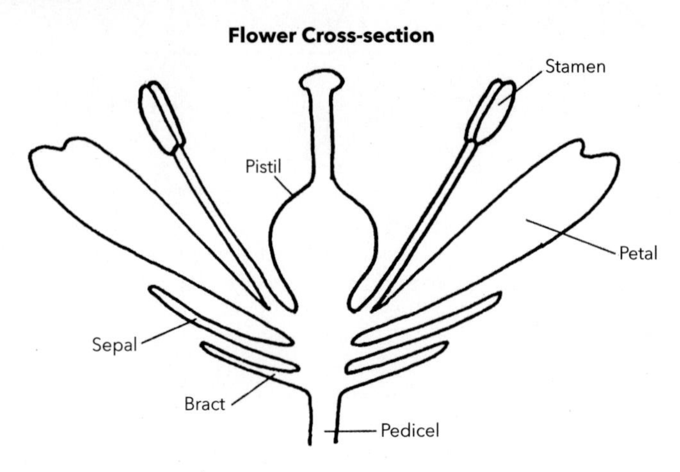

A "simple" flower contains both male and female parts. It consists of a series of four concentric rings of highly modified leaves. Lowermost is a set of sepals, which enclose and protect the bud. Sepals are flexible in both form and function. They are called tepals when they resemble or substitute for petals (cactus, lily species).

The bud opens to reveal one or more rows of petals with various colors and shapes to attract specific pollinators. The pistil contains the ovules that will develop into seeds when pollen grains are deposited on the tip, or stigma, which often has spreading lobes. The stamens have slender filaments tipped with anthers that produce pollen. When pollen is deposited on the stigma, it grows a tube that reaches an ovule and fertilizes it. Separate male and female flowers may be on the same plant, or each plant may have only one sex (junipers, hollies).

Many flowers have bracts beneath the sepals. These are small, leaflike, and in some cases more colorful than the flower (paintbrushes, *Castilleja* species) and assume the role of attracting pollinators. In conifers, they form the woody scales of the cone.

Flower shape

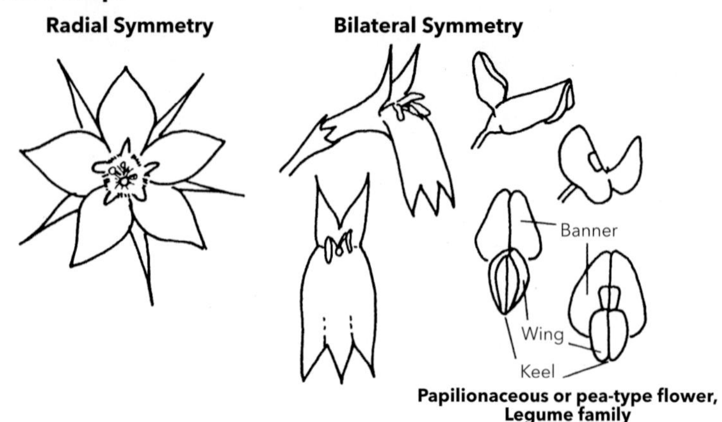

Papilionaceous or pea-type flower, Legume family

The oldest fossil records show round, radially symmetrical flowers. Like a pie, they can be sliced in equal halves in any direction. Later, flowers began to modify their shapes to attract specific pollinators. Bilaterally symmetrical flowers are tubular with spreading petal-like lobes or lips. They can be sliced into equal haves only along one axis. The tube girth is inflated to fit bees of specific sizes, or even hummingbird bills. Some flowers have a totally irregular shape.

Flowers in the Aster family (sunflowers, daisies, etc.) are composed of a head with a disk of dozens of tiny, tubular florets that produce seeds. Showy, petal-like ray florets, often sterile, surrounded the disk and attract pollinators, especially bees. The sepals are called phyllaries and may be stacked in rows beneath the ray flowers.

Flower clusters

To make gathering pollen more energy efficient, many plants produce flowers in clusters to allow one-stop shopping for pollinators. The whole cluster of flowers is called an inflorescence. Flowers may be in narrow spikes along a stem or in branched, elongated, cylindrical clusters. Rounded or flat-topped clusters of tiny flowers (umbels) also offer pollinators dozens of pollen/nectar-rich flowers in one spot. Many trees produce catkins, dense clusters of

Inflorescences (flower clusters)

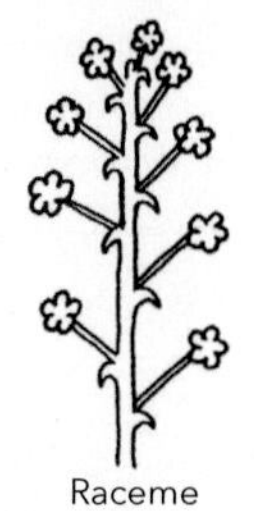

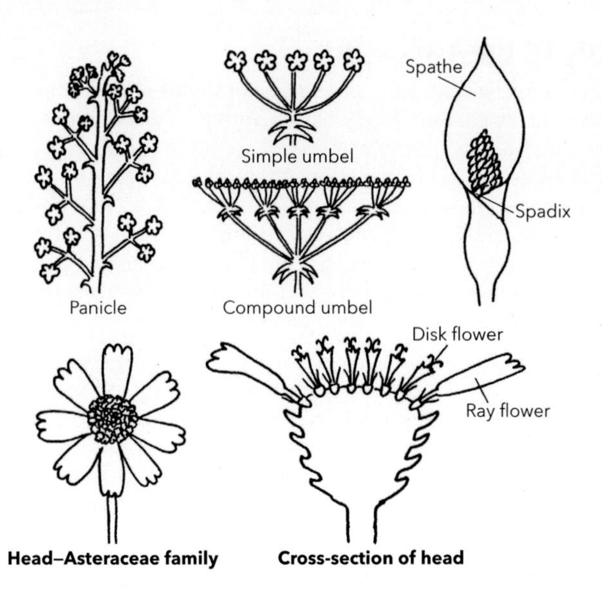

Head–Asteraceae family **Cross-section of head**

unisexual flowers without petals. If they are not wind pollinated, the cluster size and shape are designed to attract specific types of pollinators. Tubular penstemons blooming along one side of a stem enable hummingbirds or bumblebees to efficiently feed moving upward without having to circle around the stem. Flowers in a cluster often bloom over a period of a week or so to extend the period pollinators visit.

Fruit

Flowers expend immense energy-producing roots, stems, branches, leaves, chemical defenses, and flowers, but they still have one energy-intense job to complete. To propagate the next generation, they must produce seeds and devise a method to disperse them. Some plants, especially pioneer, weedy species (mustards), produce thousands of tiny seeds on the odds that some will find favorable habitats. Others produce seeds with feathery tails to waft in the breeze (dandelions). Seed pods may explode and shoot seeds yards away or be covered with clinging hooks to catch a ride on an animal's fur. Or better yet, some plants produce sweet berries, succulent fruit, or nutritious nuts for birds and other animals to eat and distribute. Pinyon pines depend exclusively on birds and small rodents to bury their nuts in winter caches, where some invariably germinate. Fruit or pod features are often essential for species identification (especially milkvetch species).

Toxic, but beautiful, baneberry fruit in the Rockies

HOW TO USE THIS BOOK

In this book, wildflowers and shrubs are lumped together, with trees in a separate section. Herbaceous perennial wildflowers freeze down to the roots every winter and sprout in the spring. Annuals die in the fall and depend on seeds to germinate in the spring. Shrubs have woody stems and branches and reach 3–10 feet tall (1–3 m), sometimes developing into small trees. Trees usually have a single trunk and are greater than 15 feet tall (4.5 m). Herbaceous trees and shrubs lose their leaves in the autumn (aspen, cottonwoods), while evergreen species retain their leaves (pine, spruces, and firs).

The wildflowers and shrubs are organized first by color, then alphabetically by plant family from Alliaceae (onion family) to Zygophyllaceae (caltrop family). This way, related and similar-looking plants will be close together for easy comparison if necessary. Trees are grouped separately and listed alphabetically by family, so the pines, spruce, firs, and other species are respectively grouped together.

Observe each plant carefully. Exact attention even to minor details is often important for plant identification. Each species description provides enough information for a probable, if not positive, identification of the plant. For whatever reason, humans feel a deeper appreciation and greater value once we bestow a name to something, whether a new acquaintance at a party, or a wildflower in a meadow.

The following headings help identify your new "friends":

QUICK ID begins with basic stem, leaf, and flower field characteristics that, taken together, are often sufficient for a positive identification.

RANGE tells the regions of the Rockies where the plant occurs. To expedite things, we've abbreviated the regions. The Southern Rockies (**SR**) encompass ranges in northern New Mexico, all the mountains in Colorado, and three prongs that extend into southern Wyoming. The Middle Rockies (**MR**) span sections of Wyoming, Idaho, Utah, and Montana. The Northern Rockies (**NR**) run through Montana, Idaho, and northeastern Washington into Alberta and British Columbia.

STEM adds information about the height of the plant and other significant features, such as hairiness and branching.

FLOWERS describes the type of cluster; petal number, shape, and size; important features of other flower parts; and the fruit or seeds. Measurements of petals and other features help separate closely related species that look similar. A centimeter ruler and 10x magnifying loupe are helpful if you want to get to this level of exact identification.

LEAVES describes the leaf arrangement, an all-important identifying feature. Note whether the leaves form a basal rosette, or grow alternate, opposite, or whorled around the stem. Size and shape, simple or compound, and surface features add more information helpful for identification, especially when minor characteristics separate related species.

HABITAT lists specific habitats the plant favors, the life zones where it occurs, and the elevation. Note that, in addition to normal altitude variations, the spread in elevation covers the range of the plant from north to south, generally with the higher elevation applying to southern regions and lower to the northern regions.

SIMILAR SPECIES describes unique features that help separate other species that can be easily confused with the plant in question.

The beautiful Subalpine Larkspur *(Delphinium barbeyi)*

Quamash, Common Camas

Camassia quamash, Asparagus Family, Asparagaceae; Perennial herb

QUICK ID: Look for grass-like leaves, tall flower stems with spike-like clusters, and 6 blue to purple petals with the lowest curving down.

RANGE: MR, NR, Canada; widespread, locally common

STEM: Flower stem (scape) 8–20 inches tall (20–50 cm); bulbs are historic food source.

FLOWERS: April–June. Elongated, dense, many-flowered cluster; 6 radiating petals (tepals), pale to light blue or violet, 1½–1⅜ inches long (12–35 mm), oval to linear, tips pointed; anthers showy yellow, blue, or tan.

LEAVES: Basal from bulb. Blades narrow, to 1 foot long (30 cm) by ¼–¾ inch wide (8–20 mm), shorter than flower stalk.

HABITAT: Seasonally moist open areas, meadows; grasslands, montane forests. Elevation 985–8,200 feet (300–2,500 m).

SIMILAR SPECIES: Meadow Death Camas *(Toxicoscordion venenosum)* has creamy flowers and deadly poisonous bulbs.

Largeflower Triteleia

Triteleia grandiflora, Asparagus Family, Asparagaceae; Perennial herb

QUICK ID: Look for 1–2 grass-like leaves and umbrella-like clusters of small flowers with 6 light- to dark-blue petals with dark midveins.

RANGE: NR, MR, Canada; widespread, locally common

STEM: Flower stalk erect, 8–30 inches tall (20–75 cm), smooth.

FLOWERS: April–June. Clusters have 5–20 spreading flowers on stalks up to 2 inches long (5 cm); flowers vase-shaped, ⅜–½ inch long (9–12 mm), with rounded base, tepals fused at base then spread open with 6 rounded lobes; papery bracts at base of cluster.

LEAVES: Basal from bulb, grass-like, 8–28 inches (20–70 cm) by ⅛–⅜ inch wide (4–10 mm), smooth.

HABITAT: Meadows, open areas, woodlands; grasslands to montane forests. Elevation 1,640–6,316 feet (500–1,925 m).

SIMILAR SPECIES: Onions, *Allium* species, don't have blue flowers.

Chicory

Cichorium intybus, Aster Family, Asteraceae; Perennial herb; introduced, invasive

QUICK ID: Look for light-blue flower heads with 5 tiny teeth on each slender, petal-like ray and milky sap.

RANGE: NR, MR, SR, Canada; widespread, common

STEM: Erect, branching stems, 1½–3 feet tall (45–90 cm).

FLOWERS: April–October. Flowers 1–1½ inches wide (25–38 mm) in widely spaced clusters; heads have 10–20+ light- to dark-blue rays (no disk florets); stamens showy blue; styles twin-forked.

LEAVES: Mostly basal; blades variable, oblong to elliptic, 2–13 inches long (5–35 cm); margins entire to irregularly toothed, or coarsely lobed with saw-toothed segments pointing backwards. Stem leaves alternate, much smaller, linear to lance-shaped, clasping the stem, margins toothed to entire.

HABITAT: Roadsides, weedy/unkempt areas, disturbed places. Elevation 5,000–7,300 feet (1,524–2,225 m).

Bull Thistle

Cirsium vulgare, Aster Family, Asteraceae; Biennial herb; introduced noxious weed

QUICK ID: Look for tall stems; spiny wings on the stems; and spiny, woolly flower heads packed with purple, filament-like disk florets.

RANGE: NR, MR, SR; widespread, common

STEM: Erect, branching, to 6 feet tall (2 m).

FLOWERS: June–November. Flower heads rounded to bell-shaped, 1–2 inches long (3–5 cm); phyllaries have loose webby hairs and are densely covered with radiating, tapering, spiny tips.

LEAVES: Basal, alternate on stem. First-year rosettes reach 3 feet in diameter (1 m). Blades oblong to lance-shaped, 6–16 inches long (15–40 cm), margins flat or twisted with spiny lobes along midrib, upper surface with tiny bristle-like spines, lower surface gray-hairy with hairy veins; leaf bases grow down the stem, making it winged.

HABITAT: Sandy, gravelly soils; roadsides, fields, disturbed areas. Elevation 4,500 to 7,500 feet (1,370–2,286 m).

Sticky Aster

Dieteria bigelovii, Aster Family, Asteraceae; Biennial, short-lived perennial herb

QUICK ID: Look for bushy stems with sticky glands, flower heads with blue-to-purple rays, a yellow disk, and clasping mid-stem leaves.

RANGE: SR; widespread, common

STEM: Erect, bushy, 2–4 feet tall (61–122 cm).

FLOWERS: July–September. Heads have 20–60 ray flowers, ⅜–1 inch long (10–25 mm), and orange-yellow disk flowers; phyllaries (below flower) have pointed tips spreading or curled back, upper ½ is green (not just tips as in *D. canescens*), generally with sticky glands.

LEAVES: Alternate. Blades stemless, lance-shaped; mid-stem leaves ¾–3 inches long (20–80 mm) by 3/16–⅝ inch wide (5–15 mm), margins entire or with small teeth tipped with spines.

HABITAT: Openings, roadsides; pinyon-juniper foothills, montane, subalpine forests. Elevation 4,800–12,000 feet (1,463–3,658 m).

SIMILAR SPECIES: Purple Aster, *D. canescens*, favors drier, lower habitats; has phyllaries without sticky glands and mid-stem leaves not clasping.

Purple Aster

Dieteria canescens, Aster Family, Asteraceae; Biennial, short-lived perennial herb

QUICK ID: Look for bushy stems without sticky glands, flower heads with purple rays and yellow disk, non-clasping mid-stem leaves.

RANGE: NR, MR, SR, Canada; widespread, common

STEM: Erect, bushy upper branches, 2–4 feet tall (61–122 cm).

FLOWERS: August–November. Heads have 15–25 purple-to-pink ray flowers, ¼–½ inch long (5–12 mm); orange-yellow disk flowers; phyllary tips green, erect, spreading or curled, lower ¾ white or tan, often with narrow green stripe down the center, no sticky glands.

LEAVES: Alternate. Blade stemless, linear to lance-shaped, mid-stem leaves ⅜–4 inches long (1–10 cm) by 1/16–¼ inch wide (1.5–6 mm), not clasping stem; margins with small teeth tipped with spines.

HABITAT: Grasslands, sagebrush, pinyon-juniper foothills, ponderosa montane forests. Elevation 3,400–9,000 feet (1,036–2,843 m).

Long-leaf Fleabane

Erigeron corymbosus, Aster Family, Asteraceae; Perennial herb

QUICK ID: Look for clumps of slender, hairy basal leaves with multiple branching flower stalks; flower heads packed with narrow, blue-to-whitish rays and yellow disk.

RANGE: NR, MR, Canada; widespread, common

STEM: Erect, branched, 4–20 inches tall (10–50 cm), often purplish, densely short-hairy.

FLOWERS: May–August. Loose clusters with up to 16 flower heads, each with 35–65 slender rays up to ½ inch long (13 mm), light to deep blue to whitish; disk yellow; phyllaries in 2–4 rows, densely hairy.

LEAVES: Mostly basal, ascending; blades linear to narrowly lance-shaped, 2⅜–6¼ inches long (6–16 cm); edges entire, surfaces hairy. Stem leaves alternate, smaller, 3-veined.

HABITAT: Dry soils, open areas; arid grasslands, sagebrush, lower montane forests. Elevation 1,000–8,000 feet (304–2,438 m).

Beautiful Fleabane

Erigeron formosissimus, Aster Family, Asteraceae; Perennial herb

QUICK ID: Look for colonies with leafy basal rosettes, clasping leaves that hug the stems, flowers with lavender-to-white rays, yellow disk.

RANGE: NR: rare; MR, SR: widespread, common

STEM: Erect, branching, 4–16 inches tall (10–40 cm), sparsely to densely hairy.

FLOWERS: July–October. Flower heads have 75–150 rays, each ⅜–⅝ inch long (8–15 mm), 1 mm wide, crowded in layered rows; disk yellow, ⅜–¾ inch (10–20 mm) wide. Phyllaries in 2–3 rows, slender, hairless to densely hairy; tips reddish, tapering, curved.

LEAVES: Basal; blades spatula-shaped, to 6 inches long (15 cm) including stalk, margins entire, surfaces and edges with few hairs. Stem leaves alternate, clasping, narrow, lance-shaped to spatula-shaped, hugging stem, smaller upward; surfaces hairless or with rough, shaggy hairs; margins lined with ciliate hairs.

HABITAT: Meadows, open areas; montane ponderosa pine, subalpine spruce-fir forests. Elevation 7,800–11,000 feet (2,377–3,352 m).

Largeflower Fleabane

Erigeron grandiflorus (E. simplex), Aster Family, Asteraceae; Perennial herb

QUICK ID: Look for mats of basal leaves, stems with one large head, bluish- to pinkish-white rays, yellow disk, and shaggy-hairy phyllaries.

RANGE: NR, MR, SR, Canada; widespread, common

STEM: Erect, 1–10 inches tall (2–25 cm), sparsely to moderately hairy, often with stalked glands.

FLOWERS: June–August. Heads to 2 inches wide (5 cm) with 50–130 narrow ray florets, each ¼–½ inch long (7–11 mm), coiling with age; disks ⅜–¾ inch wide (10-20 mm). Phyllaries in 2–3 equal rows, moderately to densely shaggy with purplish-to-white hairs. High-altitude plants smaller.

LEAVES: Basal, on short stalks, densely clustered; blades spatula- to lance-shaped, ⅜–2⅜ inches long (10–60 mm) by ⅛–⅜ inch wide (3–8 mm); edges entire, surfaces hairless or variously hairy, tips rounded. Stem leaves alternate, abruptly smaller upwards.

HABITAT: Fellfields, tundra; subalpine meadows, alpine. Elevation 9,500–14,000 feet (2,900–4,267 m).

Buff Fleabane

Erigeron ochroleucus, Aster Family, Asteraceae; Perennial herb

QUICK ID: Look for basal clumps of narrow, hairy leaves; short, hairy flower stalks; and flower heads with lavender-to-white rays, yellow disk, and woolly phyllaries.

RANGE: NR, MR; widespread, infrequent

STEM: Erect to spreading, unbranched, 3–10 inches tall (8–25 cm), long white-hairy.

FLOWERS: June–August. Usually solitary flower heads; rays 30–62, white to blue or lavender, narrow, ⁵⁄₁₆–½ inch long (8–12 mm); disk yellow. Phyllaries in 3–4 rows, densely woolly with whitish hairs.

LEAVES: Mostly basal; blades linear to narrowly lance-shaped, 1½–4¾ inches long (4–12 cm) to ³⁄₁₆ inch wide (5 mm); edges entire, surfaces with flat-lying hairs. Stem leaves alternate, smaller, few, hairy or not.

HABITAT: Coarse soils, slopes, talus, meadows; grasslands, sagebrush, foothills, montane, subalpine forests, alpine. Elevation 3,500–9,850 feet (1,066–3,000 m).

Featherleaf Fleabane

Erigeron pinnatisectus, Aster Family, Asteraceae; Perennial herb

QUICK ID: Look for basal rosette of leaves lined with thin, rounded lobes and short stems with large flower heads with light-blue rays.

RANGE: SR; widespread, common

STEM: Erect, stout, 1½–4¾ inches tall (4–12 cm), sparsely to moderately hairy.

FLOWERS: June–August. Single flower head 1 inch wide (3 cm) with 40–60 light blue rays, each ¼–½ inch long (7–12 mm); disk yellow. Phyllaries in 3–5 rows, sparsely to densely hairy.

LEAVES: Mostly basal with long stalks. Blades ¾–1¾ inches long (20–40 mm); surfaces usually hairless, margins lined with finely divided lobes. Stem leaves alternate, linear, smaller, or absent.

HABITAT: Subalpine forest meadows, rocky alpine tundra. Elevation 9,000–13,000 feet (2,743–3,962 m).

Showy Fleabane

Erigeron speciosus, Aster Family, Asteraceae; Perennial herb

QUICK ID: Look for tall, clustered stems with smooth leaves, up to 20 flower heads with pink-to-lavender rays, and a yellow disk.

RANGE: NR, MR, SR, Canada; widespread, common

STEM: Erect, 1–2½ feet tall (30–76 cm), hairless or not.

FLOWERS: June–October. Flower heads up to 2 inches wide (5 cm) with 75–150 rays purple, pink, rarely white, each ⅜–¾ inch long (9–18 mm), 1 mm wide; disk yellow ⅜–¾ inch wide (10–20 mm). Phyllaries in 2–3 rows, linear, pointed, glandular but mostly hairless.

LEAVES: Basal usually withered by blooming; blades spoon-shaped, to 3 inches long (8 cm), surfaces hairless. Stem leaves alternate, blades oval to lance-shaped, evenly sized up the stem, clasping, often 3-nerved; surfaces hairless, edges entire, often with ciliate hairs.

HABITAT: Open woods; montane, subalpine forests, alpine. Elevation 3,000–10,500 feet (912–3,200 m).

Three-nerve Fleabane

Erigeron subtrinervis, Aster Family, Asteraceae; Perennial herb

QUICK ID: Look for stems with even-sized leaves covered with short, stiff hairs and showy flower heads with blue rays, yellow disks.

RANGE: NR, MR, SR, Canada; widespread, common

STEM: Erect, 6–24 inches tall (15–60 cm), hairy.

FLOWERS: June–September. Arrays of 1–13 heads, each 1–2 inches wide (25–50 mm), have 100–150 blue-to-lavender rays ⅜–¾ inch long (9–18 mm), 1 mm wide. Phyllaries hairy, tips tapering, curled.

LEAVES: Basal usually wither by blooming; blades spoon-shaped, 1–3 inches long (3–8 cm), surfaces covered with short, spreading hairs. Stem leaves alternate, clasping, oval to lance-shaped, tips pointed, equal-sized up the stem, 3 nerves from base of leaf; surfaces covered with coarse, stiff hairs; edges entire, lined with ciliate hairs.

HABITAT: Sagebrush, foothill woodlands, montane, subalpine forests, alpine. Elevation 5,900–10,600 feet (1,524–3,230 m).

SIMILAR SPECIES: Showy Fleabane, *E. speciosus*, (same range) has hairless leaf surfaces.

Bear River Fleabane

Erigeron ursinus, Aster Family, Asteraceae; Perennial herb

QUICK ID: Look for dense clumps of narrow basal leaves; flower heads packed with purple-to-white rays; yellow disk; and narrow, purple, woolly-hairy phyllaries with tapering, reflexed tips.

RANGE: NR, MR, SR; widespread, common

STEM: Erect, often mat forming, 2–10 inches tall, (5–25 cm), bases usually purplish, smooth to sparsely hairy, rhizomatous.

FLOWERS: June–September. Flower heads usually singular on stalk; rays 30–100, pinkish purple to white, ¼–⅝ inch long (6–15 mm), not coiling; disk yellow. Phyllaries in 2–4 rows, narrow, points often reflexed, shaggy and glandular-hairy, edges and tips often purple.

LEAVES: Basal; alternate; blades linear to narrowly lance-shaped, ¾–8 inches long (2–20 cm) to ½ inch wide (11 mm); edges entire, ciliate hairy; surfaces smooth to sparsely hairy.

HABITAT: Meadows, open forests; sagebrush, foothills, montane, subalpine, alpine. Elevation 8,000–12,000 feet (2,438–3,656 m).

Elegant Aster

Eucephalus elegans, Aster Family, Asteraceae; Perennial herb

QUICK ID: Look for leafy stems; narrow, sandpapery-rough leaves; and flower heads with 5 or 8 narrow, purple rays; disk yellow.

RANGE: NR, MR; widespread, common

STEM: Erect, clustered, 8–20 inches tall (20–50 cm), rough-hairy.

FLOWERS: July–August. Clusters have 3–8 flower heads with narrow, lavender-to-deep-purple rays, each to ½ inch long (12 mm). Phyllaries in 3–5 rows, oval, pointed; tips and edges often purplish.

LEAVES: Alternate, stalkless. Blades elliptic, ¾–2⅜ inches long (2–6 cm), to ⅗ inch wide (10 mm); edges entire, surfaces moderately rough-hairy and glandular.

HABITAT: Dry meadows, open forests; montane, subalpine forests. Elevation 3,600–10,500 feet (1,100–3,200 m).

SIMILAR SPECIES: The taller Engelmann's Aster, *E. engelmannii*, (all regions) has leaves to 1⅜ inches wide (35 mm) and 8 or 13 white-to-pinkish rays.

Western Showy Aster

Eurybia conspicua, Aster Family, Asteraceae; Perennial herb

QUICK ID: Look for unbranched stems; firm, sandpapery, toothed leaves; flower heads with blue-to-violet rays; and a yellow disk.

RANGE: NR, MR, Canada; widespread, common

STEM: Erect, unbranched, 12–40 inches tall (30–100 cm), hairy or not, densely glandular above.

FLOWERS: June–October. Open, round-topped clusters have 5–50 flower heads, each with 12–35 narrow rays ⅜–⅝ inch long (10–15 mm). Phyllaries in 4–5 overlapping rows, tips spreading, pointed, purplish; edges ciliate hairy.

LEAVES: Alternate. Blades egg-shaped to elliptic, 2⅜–7 inches long (6–18 cm), ¾–3 inches wide (2–8 cm), clasping; edges serrated, tips pointed, surfaces rough with short, stiff hairs.

HABITAT: Dry meadows, open woods; foothills, montane forests. Elevation 2,000–8,200 feet (610–2,500 m).

Thick-stem Aster

Eurybia integrifolia, Aster Family, Asteraceae; Perennial herb

QUICK ID: Look for clumps of reddish, hairy stems with elongated clusters of flower heads with purple rays and yellow-to-reddish disk.

RANGE: MR, NR; widespread, common

STEM: Erect, stout, 6–27 inches tall (15–70 cm), lower hairy or not, upper densely hairy.

FLOWERS: June–September. Up to 40 flower heads on upward-spreading stalks along upper stem. Each head has 8–27 violet-purple rays, ⅜–⅝ inch long (10–15 mm), and a yellow-turning-reddish disk. Phyllaries in 3–4 overlapping rows, inner rows with dark to purple tips, outer somewhat leafy; surfaces densely hairy with stalked glands, tips pointed, curled outward.

LEAVES: Basal on long, winged stalks; blades lance-shaped to narrowly elliptic, to 7 inches long (18 cm); edges entire, surfaces smooth to densely hairy. Stem leaves alternate, clasping, tips pointed.

HABITAT: Grasslands, sagebrush, montane, subalpine forests. Elevation 5,000–10,500 feet (1,600–3,200 m).

Gray Aster

Herrickia glauca, Aster Family, Asteraceae; Perennial herb

QUICK ID: Look for multiple colony-forming stems; blue-green leaves; flower heads with narrow, pale-lavender rays; yellow disks.

RANGE: MR, SR; scattered, common

STEM: Erect, multiple from base, 8–28 inches tall (20–70 cm), hairless, often reddish.

FLOWERS: June–September. Large arrays of light violet-to-whitish flower heads with 10–15 narrow rays, ⅜–⅝ inch long (8–18 mm); disk yellow. Phyllaries in 4–5 rows.

LEAVES: Alternate, lower wither by blooming. Blades blue-green, stalkless, elliptic to lance-shaped, 1½–4¾ inches long (4–12 cm) to 1 inch wide (5–25 mm); edges entire, surfaces hairless with a waxy coating.

HABITAT: Saline seeps, rocky slopes; sagebrush, montane, subalpine forests. Elevation 5,300–9,500 feet (1,615–2,895 m).

Blue Lettuce

Lactuca oblongifolium, Aster Family, Asteraceae; Perennial herb

QUICK ID: Look for tall, smooth stems with narrow clasping leaves; clusters of small, blue heads with ray flowers only; and milky sap.

RANGE: NR, MR, SR, Canada; widespread, common

STEM: Erect, branched above, 1-24 inches tall (20-120 cm), smooth.

FLOWERS: June–September. Open clusters of flower heads, ¾ inch wide (2 cm), with 15-50 blue to purple, narrow rays, tips squared with small teeth; no disk florets.

LEAVES: Alternate. Blades linear to lance-shaped, 3-5 inches long (5-15 cm); surfaces smooth. Lower leaves stalked, mostly pinnate with 3-4 rear-pointing lobes or teeth; upper leaves clasping, mostly entire.

HABITAT: Moist soils, meadows, drainages; grasslands, sagebrush, foothills, montane forests. Elevation 5,200–8,200 feet (1,600–2,500 m).

NOTE: Also referred to as *Lactuca tatairca, L. pulchellum, Mulgedium pulchellum*, and *M. oblongifolium*, but molecular analyses place it with *Lactuca*, and the listed name has historical priority.

Gayfeather, Blazing Star

Liatris punctata, Aster Family, Asteraceae; Perennial herb

QUICK ID: Look for clumps with leafy, erect stems; narrow, hairless leaves; and dense spikes of purple, thread-like flower heads.

RANGE: NR, MR, SR, Canada; widespread, common

STEM: Slender, unbranched, 1–3 feet tall (30-90 cm), hairless.

FLOWERS: August–October. Spikes 3-24 inches long (10–60 cm) on the upper third to half of each stem are crowded with flower heads, each ¼–⅜ inch long (6–9 mm); 3-6 disk flowers have 5 spreading, pointed, petal-like lobes and an extended thread-like style split into 2 branches; ray flowers absent.

LEAVES: Alternate, circling stem. Blades narrow, linear, 2–6 inches long (5-15 cm), 1⁄32–¼ inch wide (1-7 mm), smaller up the stem; margins entire with short, white hairs, surfaces hairless.

HABITAT: Coarse soils, roadsides; grasslands, sagebrush, foothills, montane forests. Elevation 5,200–9,000 feet (1,585–2,743 m).

Western Aster

Symphyotrichum ascendens, Aster Family, Asteraceae; Perennial herb

QUICK ID: Look for stems with short hairs; upper floral branches tipped with several flower heads with 15–40 purple rays; yellow disk.

RANGE: NR, MR, SR, Canada; widespread, common

STEM: Erect, clump forming, 8–24 inches tall (20–60 cm), uniformly short, flat-lying hairy.

FLOWERS: July–September. Loose clusters of 1-inch-wide (25 mm) flower heads, each with violet to light-blue to pink rays in a single row, ¼–½ inch long (6–10 mm); disk yellow, often purple tinted. Phyllaries in 3–5 overlapping rows, densely hairy without glands, base white, tips green, pointed, slightly spreading.

LEAVES: Basal wither by flowering. Stem leaves alternate, stalkless or nearly so; blades linear to narrowly lance-shaped, ¾–4 inches long (2–20 cm); edges entire, lined with ciliate hairs, surfaces nearly smooth to densely rough-hairy, not spine-tipped.

HABITAT: Meadows, open woods, disturbed areas; grasslands to montane forests. Elevation 5,000–10,500 feet (1,524–3,200 m).

Western Meadow Aster

Symphyotrichum campestre, Aster Family, Asteraceae; Perennial herb

QUICK ID: Look for clumps of hairy stems, upper floral branches with flower heads with violet-to-pale-blue rays, and yellow disk.

RANGE: NR, MR, SR, Canada; widespread, common

STEM: Erect, branched from base, 4–16 inches tall (10–40 cm), hairy below, glandular above.

FLOWERS: August–October. Loose clusters along stem have 1–10 flower heads with 15–31 rays, ¼–⅝ inch long (6–15 mm), disk yellow. Phyllaries in 3–4 overlapping rows, glandular-hairy, green, tips pointed to tapering, spreading to reflexed.

LEAVES: Basal, stalkless to clasping, hairless; blades linear to narrowly oblong, ¾–3 inches long (2–8 cm); edges entire; surfaces sparsely short-hairy to glandular. Stem leaves alternate, clasping, smaller towards top.

HABITAT: Dry soils, meadows, disturbed areas; arid grasslands to montane forests. Elevation 5,000–10,000 feet (1,524–3,048 m).

Leafy-bracted Aster

Symphyotrichum foliaceum, Aster Family, Asteraceae; Perennial herb

QUICK ID: Look for stems with loose clusters of 1–12 flower heads with purple-to-white rays; yellow disk; and broad, leaf-like phyllaries.

RANGE: NR, MR, SR, Canada; widespread, common

STEM: Erect, clumped, 4–24 inches tall (10–60 cm), smooth to short-hairy, colony forming.

FLOWERS: July–October. Flower heads single or in loose arrays up to 20 heads, each with 15–60 rays, purple to light blue or white, ⅜–¾ inch long (10–20 mm); disk yellow; phyllaries in 4–6 loose rows, variable within 4 varieties, outer row broad, leaf-like, green to purple-tinted (alpine variety), faces hairless to short-hairy.

LEAVES: Basal often present at flowering. Stem leaves alternate, blades lance-shaped to elliptic, 1⅜–4¾ inches long (3.5–12 cm), upper blades smaller, stemless or clasping, edges entire or serrated, usually hairless, surfaces smooth to soft-hairy, tips pointed.

HABITAT: Moist meadows, open woods; foothills, montane, subalpine forests, alpine. Elevation 4,600–11,600 feet (1,400–3,535 m).

Smooth Blue Aster

Symphyotrichum laeve, Aster Family, Asteraceae; Perennial herb

QUICK ID: Look for multiple stems; smooth, hairless, narrow leaves clasping the upper stem; flat-topped arrays of ½–1-inch-wide (12–25 mm) flower heads with purple rays; yellow disk.

RANGE: NR, MR, SR, Canada; widespread, common

STEM: Erect, branched from base, 8–28 inches tall (20–70 cm), smooth to sparsely short-hairy.

FLOWERS: July–September. Arrays of 15–50 flower heads along upper stem on branches, hairless or with thin lines of hairs; rays 13–23 dark to pale blue, each ¼–½ inch long (7–12 mm); disk yellow turning reddish purple. Phyllaries in 4–6 rows, base white, ends green, pointed.

LEAVES: Basal, usually withered by flowering. Upper leaves clasping stem; oblong, lance-shaped, or linear, to 3–7 inches long (8–18 cm), margins entire to toothed, surfaces smooth.

HABITAT: Moist meadows, open woods, riparian; grasslands, foothills, montane forests. Elevation 6,300–9,600 feet (1,920–2,926 m).

Western Mountain Aster

Symphyotrichum spathulatum var. *spathulatum*, Aster Family, Asteraceae; Perennial herb

QUICK ID: Look for clumped stems, basal leaves, open branches forming round-topped clusters of small flower heads with blue-violet-to magenta rays, yellow disk.

RANGE: NR, MR, SR, Canada; widespread, common

STEM: Erect, 8–32 inches tall (20–80 cm), smooth to sparsely short-hairy, colony forming.

FLOWERS: July–August. Cluster with few branches have 3–10 heads, each with 15–40 rays, ⅜–⅝ inch long (9–15 mm); disk yellow, often becoming reddish. Phyllaries in 3–5 rows, oblong to linear, base white, end green, tips pointed.

LEAVES: Basal, stalked, present at flowering; blades elliptic to oval, 2–6 inches long (5–15 cm); edges entire, ciliate, surfaces mostly smooth, tips pointed. Stem leaves alternate, stalkless but not clasping, linear to elliptic; upper blades smaller.

HABITAT: Meadows, open woods, stream sides; foothills, montane, subalpine forests. Elevation 4,000–10,500 feet (1,200–3,200 m).

Parry's Townsend Daisy

Townsendia parryi, Aster Family, Asteraceae; Perennial herb

QUICK ID: Look for clumps of basal leaves with 1–several stems tipped with large flower heads with lavender rays, yellow disk.

RANGE: NR, MR: widespread, common; Canada: rare

STEM: Erect, unbranched, 2–4¾ inches tall (5–12 cm), short-hairy.

FLOWERS: May–August. Heads on stem tips with 21–67 rays, blue to violet, ½–1 inch long (12–25 mm), yellow disk. Phyllaries in 4–7 rows, surfaces smooth to short-hairy, tips pointed.

LEAVES: Basal, clumped, stalked; alternate on stem. Blades spoon-shaped, ⅜–1⅝ inches long (1–4 cm), base narrow, tip pointed; surfaces smooth to short-hairy; upper leaves smaller.

HABITAT: Meadows, slopes, open ground; arid grasslands to subalpine, rarely alpine. Elevation 4,500–10,500 feet (1,372–3,200 m).

Hound's Tongue

Cynoglossum officinale, Borage Family, Boraginaceae; Biennial herb

QUICK ID: Look for tall, leafy stems densely covered with woolly hairs and clusters of small, cup-shaped, maroon flowers.

RANGE: NR, MR, SR, Canada; widespread, common

STEM: Erect, stout, single, 1–4 feet tall (30 cm–120 m).

FLOWERS: May–July. Leafy, nodding clusters on stems that elongate as mature; 5 petals fused to form tube that flairs open ⅜ inch wide (1 cm); sepals leaf-like, oblong, densely hairy, nearly as long as petal lobes. Seeds ¼ inch long (6 mm), egg-shaped, Velcro-like.

LEAVES: Alternate. Blades narrowly elliptic, 4–12 inches long (10–30 cm) by ¾–2 inches wide (2–5 cm), edges wavy, surfaces soft-hairy, tips pointed; upper leaves smaller, lance-shaped.

HABITAT: Meadows, riparian, disturbed areas; grasslands, sagebrush, montane, subalpine forests. Elevation 5,600–9,800 feet (1,700–3,000 m).

Alpine Forget-Me-Not

Eritrichium nanum, Borage Family, Boraginaceae; Perennial herb

QUICK ID: Look for densely hairy mounding mats of basal leaves, short stems, and blue flowers with yellow-and-white throats.

RANGE: NR, MR, SR, Canada; widespread, locally common

STEM: Erect, ½–4 inches tall (1–10 cm), hairy.

FLOWERS: May–August. Dense clusters have funnel-shaped, blue flowers to ¾ inch wide (20 mm) with 5 rounded, petal-like lobes; throat is ringed with white and yellow.

LEAVES: Basal, alternate on short stalks. Blades oval, to ⅜ inch long (10 mm), thick; surfaces densely loose-hairy, often obscuring the blade and stem; tips pointed to blunt, often with a tuft of hair.

HABITAT: Rocky soils of alpine slopes, scree-covered areas above timberline. Elevation 8,300–13,200 feet (2,530–4,025 m).

SIMILAR SPECIES: Mountain Forget-Me-Not, *Myosotis asiatica* (NR, MR), has lance-shaped leaves 2-5 inches long (5–13 cm). Often grows with Moss Campion, *Silene acaulis* (all).

Many-flowered Stickseed

Hackelia floribunda, Borage Family, Boraginaceae; Perennial, biennial herb

QUICK ID: Look for slender, branching stems; large, hairy leaves; and one-sided, curving clusters of small blue flowers with a yellow center.

RANGE: NR, MR, SR, Canada; widespread, common

STEM: Erect, often single, 1–4 feet tall (30–120 cm), spreading hairs.

FLOWERS: May–September. Elongated, one-sided clusters of pale-blue-to-white flowers from leaf axils and stem tips; flowers ¼ inch wide (4–8 mm) with 5 lobes and a raised, yellow center. Seeds are small, barbed nutlets, ⅛ inch long (4 mm), that snare onto clothes.

LEAVES: Basal wither by flowering. Stem leaves alternate; narrow, linear to elliptic, 2–8 inches long (5–20 cm) to 1 inch wide (25 mm); surfaces with short, flat-lying hairs; upper leaves stalkless, smaller.

HABITAT: Grasslands, sagebrush, foothills, montane, subalpine forests. Elevation 5,570–10,000 feet (1,700–3,048 m).

Jessica's Stickseed

Hackelia micrantha, Borage Family, Boraginaceae; Perennial herb

QUICK ID: Look for multiple branches from stem base, narrow basal and stem leaves, clusters of small blue flowers with a yellow center.

RANGE: NR, MR, SR (absent NM); widespread

STEM: Erect, clump forming, 1–3 feet tall (30–90 cm), hairy.

FLOWERS: May–August. Spreading, elongated clusters on short stalks from leaf axils and stem tips. Flowers pale blue to white, ¼ inch wide (4–8 mm) with 5 lobes and a raised, yellow center. Seeds are small, barbed nutlets, ⅛ inch long (4 mm), on one side of stem.

LEAVES: Basal, stalked; blades lance-shaped to narrowly elliptic, 2–13 inches long (5–35 cm) by 1½ inches wide (4 cm). Stem leaves alternate, 2–8 inches long (5–20 cm) by ¼–¾ inch wide (7–20 mm), stalkless; surfaces hairy.

HABITAT: Meadows, open areas, wetlands; sagebrush, montane, subalpine forests. Elevation 4,000–10,000 feet (1,219–3,048 m).

SIMILAR SPECIES: Many-flowered Stickseed, *H. floribunda*, usually doesn't have basal leaves.

Flat-spine Stickseed

Lappula occidentalis (Lappula redowskii), Borage Family, Boraginaceae; Annual, biennial herb

QUICK ID: Look for slender, hairy stems with narrow, leafy clusters of tiny, pale-blue-to-white flowers with yellow bulges around throat.

RANGE: NR, MR, SR, Canada; widespread, common

STEM: Erect, simple or branched above, 2–20 inches tall (5–50 cm), densely hairy.

FLOWERS: May–July. Slender, arching clusters with leafy bracts throughout. Flowers pale blue to white, ⅛ inch wide (3 mm), tubular with 5 spreading petal lobes and 5 yellow bulges at throat. Fruit 4 nutlets lined with barbed prickles (see inset).

LEAVES: Basal, stalked, often wither by flowering; blades lance-shaped, ¾–2⅜ inches long (2-6 cm) by ⅜ inch wide (1 cm). Stem leaves alternate, stalkless, smaller, linear oblong; edges entire. Surfaces densely soft-hairy.

HABITAT: Disturbed soils; grasslands, sagebrush, foothills, montane forests. Elevation 2,000-9,000 feet (610–2,743 m).

Alpine Bluebells

Mertensia alpina, Borage Family, Boraginaceae; Perennial herb

QUICK ID: Look in alpine tundra for upright to nodding clusters of tubular blue flowers with the anthers inside the throat.

RANGE: NR, MR: locally common; SR: rare

STEM: Erect to prostrate, 2–8 inches tall (5–20 cm).

FLOWERS: June–August. Clusters one-sided on stem, nodding to facing upward. Flowers tubular ¼ inch long (6-9 mm), spreading open with 5 rounded lobes, anthers not extending beyond throat

LEAVES: Basal. Alternate on stem; blades lance-shaped to elliptic, ⅜–2 inches long (1–5 cm); top surface has short, flat-lying hairs above, bottom smooth, veins inconspicuous.

HABITAT: Moist meadows, stony slopes; alpine. Elevation 9,800–14,765 feet (3,000–4,500 m).

SIMILAR SPECIES: Streamside Bluebells, *M. ciliata*, is 16–45 inches tall (40–114 cm) with smooth leaves with prominent veins.

Streamside Bluebells

Mertensia ciliata, Borage Family, Boraginaceae; Perennial herb

QUICK ID: Look in moist areas for masses of stems with waxy, blue-green leaves and one-sided clusters of tubular, blue-to-purple flowers.

RANGE: NR, MR, SR; widespread, common

STEM: Erect, clumped, 16–45 inches tall (40–114 cm).

FLOWERS: May–August. Loose clusters of hanging blue, fragrant flowers ⅜–¾ inch long (10–17 mm); tube expands abruptly into bell shape, throat often fringed with hairs inside; anthers inside throat, style extends beyond throat.

LEAVES: Basal. Alternate on stem. Blades blue-green, elliptic to lance-shaped, pointed, 1–6 inches long (3–15 cm) by ⅜–2 inches wide (1–5 cm); surfaces hairless with prominent network of veins, edges lined with minute, ciliate hairs.

HABITAT: Moist soils, meadows, stream sides; subalpine mountains alpine. Elevation 6,000–12,000 feet (1,830–3,658 m).

SIMILAR SPECIES: Franciscan Bluebells, *M. franciscana*, (SR) has leaves with prominent veins, but stiff hairs cover the top surface.

Franciscan Bluebells

Mertensia franciscana, Borage Family, Boraginaceae; Perennial herb

QUICK ID: Look in moist habitats for leafy clumps of stems, leaves with prominent veins, and showy clusters of tubular, blue flowers.

RANGE: SR; widespread, common

STEM: Erect, arching, 2–3 feet tall (60–90 cm).

FLOWERS: May–August. Loose clusters of hanging, tubular, bell-shaped flowers; floral tube $^{3}/_{16}$–⅜ inch long (5–9 mm), opening with 5 rounded lobes about the same length as the tube; 5 sepal lobes separate nearly to the base, with hairy back and margins, pointed tips.

LEAVES: Basal leaves oblong to elliptic, to 8 inches long (20 cm) by 3½ inches wide (9 cm), with stalks as long as the blades; upper surface with minute stiff, flat-lying hairs, bottom hairless to densely hairy. Stem leaves alternate, similar, with prominent lateral veins.

HABITAT: Moist soils of meadows, stream sides, open forests; mixed conifer forests. Elevation 7,000–11,500 feet (2,134–3,353 m).

Narrowleaf Bluebells

Mertensia lanceolata, Borage Family, Boraginaceae; Perennial herb

QUICK ID: Look for short, arching stems; leaves without a prominent network of veins; clusters of hanging, tubular, blue flowers.

RANGE: NR, MR, SR, Canada; widespread, common

STEM: Erect, few to many, tips arching, 4–16 inches tall (10–40 cm).

FLOWERS: April–June. Loose clusters of drooping flowers; floral tube ⅛–¼ inch long (3-7 mm); 5 spreading, rounded lobes about the same length as the tube; sepals hairy or not but with hairy edges, lobes pointed, separate ½ to ⅔ to the base.

LEAVES: Basal with stalks. Blades lance-shaped to narrowly elliptic, ¾–5½ inch long (2–14 cm) by 3⁄16–1⅜ inch wide (5–35 mm); surfaces smooth or with flat-lying hairs. Stem leaves alternate, similar, without stalks, smaller up the stem.

HABITAT: Coarse soils, stream banks, roadsides; montane, subalpine meadows. Elevation 5,000–13,000 feet (1,524–3,962 m).

SIMILAR SPECIES: Franciscan Bluebells, *M. franciscana*, (SR) are 2-3 feet tall (60–90 cm) with hairy leaves with prominent veins.

Sagebrush Bluebells

Mertensia oblongifolia, Borage Family, Boraginaceae; Perennial herb

QUICK ID: Look for clumps of short stems; broad, oblong leaves; and hanging clusters of tubular blue flowers with bell-shaped lobes ½ as long as tube.

RANGE: NR, MR, SR; widespread, common

STEM: Erect, arching, branching at base, 2–12 inches tall (5–30 cm).

FLOWERS: April–August. Dense, hanging clusters of tubular flowers at branch tips; tube ⅜–¾ inch long (1–2 cm), inside hairless; 5 rounded lobes form bell-shaped opening. Sepals pointed, hairy, ⅛–¼ inch long (4–7 mm), divided nearly to the base.

LEAVES: Basal on short stalks; blades elliptic to lance-shaped, pointed, ¾–6 inches long (2–15 cm) by ¼–2⅜ inches wide (7–60 mm); top surface short-hairy, bottom smooth. Stem leaves, alternate, similar, smaller, stalkless, veins obscure.

HABITAT: Meadows, open forests; grasslands, sagebrush, montane, subalpine forests, alpine. Elevation 5,000–12,500 feet (1,524–3,658 m).

Mountain Forget-Me-Not

Myosotis asiatica, Borage Family, Boraginaceae; Perennial herb

QUICK ID: Look for dense clusters of basal leaves; branching stems; and clusters of small, deep-blue flowers with bulging yellow centers.

RANGE: MR, NR, Canada; widespread, common

STEM: Erect, several from base, unbranched, 2–16 inches tall (5–40 cm), short, spreading, stiff hairs throughout, rhizomatous.

FLOWERS: May–August. Clusters on stem tips have small, tubular flowers that open flat with 5 blue, rounded lobes, each ⅛–⅜ inch wide (4–8 mm), with a yellow bulge at the throat.

LEAVES: Basal on short stalks; blades lance-shaped to elliptic, 2–5 inches long (5–13 cm) to ½ inch wide (12 mm). Stem leaves alternate, smaller upward, stalkless.

HABITAT: Meadows, openings, stream banks; montane, subalpine forests, alpine. Elevation 5,000–11,000 feet (1,524–3,353 m).

True Forget-Me-Not

Myosotis scorpioides, Borage Family, Boraginaceae; Perennial herb; garden escapee

QUICK ID: Look in wet areas for clump-forming stands with coiled clusters of small, pale-blue flowers with yellow bulging throats.

RANGE: MR, NR, SR, Canada; scattered, locally common

STEM: Erect to spreading, generally unbranched, 8–24 inches tall (20–60 cm), stiff, flat-lying hairs sparsely throughout.

FLOWERS: June–August. Stem tips have 2–3 narrow clusters 2–10 inches long (5–25 cm) with tips coiled like a scorpion tail. Flowers tubular, opening flat with 5 rounded, pale-blue lobes with bulging yellow centers.

LEAVES: Alternate; blades lance-shaped to oblong or elliptic, 1–3 inches long (3–8 cm) to ¾ inch wide (2 cm); edges entire, surfaces smooth or with short, flat-lying hairs.

HABITAT: Moist, wet soils, meadows, riparian; wetlands, grasslands, montane forests. Elevation 3,445–8,000 feet (1,050–2,438 m).

Dame's Rocket

Hesperis matronalis, Mustard Family, Brassicaceae; Biennial or perennial herb, introduced, invasive

QUICK ID: Look in disturbed areas for tall, leafy stems topped with showy clusters of purple-to-pink flowers with 4 petals and long, slender seed pods.

RANGE: NR, MR, SR, Canada; scattered, locally common

STEM: Erect, upper branching, 16–32 inches tall (40–80 cm), hairy.

FLOWERS: April–August. Rounded clusters of purple to pink or white flowers, each to ¾–1 inch wide (20–25 mm), with 4 round-tipped petals. Seed pods narrow, wire-like, 2–4 inches long (5–10 cm).

LEAVES: Basal wither by flowering. Stem leaves alternate, lance-shaped to triangular, 1½–6 inches long (4–15 cm) by ⅜–2 inches wide, (1-5 cm); edges entire to toothed, surfaces short-hairy.

HABITAT: Open woods, fields, roadsides, disturbed areas; sagebrush, foothills, montane forests. Elevation sea level to 7,200 feet (2,200 m).

Parry's Bellflower

Campanula parryi, Bellflower Family, Campanulaceae; Perennial herb

QUICK ID: Look for blue to violet, erect to slightly nodding flowers with 5 spreading, pointed petals; usually solitary on stem tips.

RANGE: NR, MR, SR; widespread, uncommon

STEM: Erect, slender, 2–12 inches tall (5–30 cm).

FLOWERS: July–September. Flowers blue to violet, ⅜–⅝ inch long (9–15 mm); petals joined at base forming a cup with 5 pointed lobes about half the length of the flower. Note the 5 narrow sepals under the petals extend beyond the junction of the petal lobes.

LEAVES: Basal leaves elliptic to lance-shaped, ¼–1¼ inches long (7–30 mm). Mid-stem leaves alternate, narrow, ¾–2 inches long (2-5 cm), sometimes with small teeth.

HABITAT: Meadows, streambanks, roadsides; montane, subalpine forests. Elevation 7,600–12,700 feet (2,316–3,870 m).

Harebell

Campanula rotundifolia, Bellflower Family, Campanulaceae; Perennial herb

QUICK ID: Look for clusters of up to 15 purplish-blue, bell-shaped, nodding flowers on delicate, branching stem tips.

RANGE: NR, MR, SR, Canada; widespread, common

STEM: Branched or not, slender, to 2 feet tall (61 cm), colony forming.

FLOWERS: June–September. Blue to violet, bell-shaped, ¾–1¼ inches long (19–31 mm), nodding, multiple flowers per stem. Petals joined at base forming a cup with 5 pointed, petal-like lobes. Note the 5 short sepals beneath the flower do not reach the juncture of the petal lobes.

LEAVES: Basal leaves wither by blooming; blades rounded, 3⁄16–1½ inches long (5–40 mm) with conspicuous stems (petioles). Stem leaves alternate, grass-like reaching 4 inches long (10 cm), ⅛ inch wide (3 mm).

HABITAT: Meadows, streambanks; pinion-juniper foothills, montane, subalpine. Elevation 5,800–12,800 feet (1,768–3,900 m).

Birdbill Dayflower

Commelina dianthifolia, Spiderwort Family, Commelinaceae; Perennial herb

QUICK ID: Look for stems with narrow leaves and bright-blue, 3-petaled flowers that bloom singly from a purse-like sack (spathe).

RANGE: SR (CO and NM); widespread, common

STEM: Erect, usually unbranched, to 10 inches tall (25 cm).

FLOWERS: July-September. Flowers have 3 oval petals, each ½ inch long (12 mm), and 6 stamens. The 3 enlarged upper stamens attract pollinators with showy "dummy anthers" colored bright yellow to mimic large amounts of pollen but produce very little. The 3 lower stamens are blue with small, oval anthers with viable pollen. The spathe, often red tinted and with a long, leaf-like tapered tip, has 2–6 buds. Flowers open in the morning, fade by afternoon.

LEAVES: Alternate. Blade linear, narrow, 1½–6 inches long (4–15 cm), sheathed around stem.

HABITAT: Openings in pinyon-juniper foothills, montane, subalpine forests. Elevation 3,840–10,250 feet (1,200–3,125 m).

Prairie Spiderwort

Tradescantia occidentalis, Spiderwort Family, Commelinaceae; Perennial herb

QUICK ID: Look for clumps of broad, blade-like leaves and clusters of bright-blue to lavender or rose-colored flowers with 3 oval petals; purple, bearded stamens; and yellow anthers.

RANGE: SR; widespread, common

STEM: Erect, branched, fleshy, to 24 inches tall (60 cm), smooth with a waxy, whitish coating.

FLOWERS: April–August. Open clusters at stem tips and nodes have 1–10 flowers on glandular-hairy stalks ¾–1 inch long (1–3 cm); 2 long, slender, leaf-like bracts spread underneath each cluster; 3 petals, ¼–¾ inch long (7–16 mm); hairy sepals enclose the buds.

LEAVES: Alternate, base sheaths the stem. Blades narrow, 2–20 inches long (6–50 cm) to 1 inch wide (3 cm), folded along the mid-vein, veins parallel; surfaces smooth, waxy.

HABITAT: Prairies, disturbed areas; grasslands, foothills, montane forests. Elevation 4,000-8,000 feet (1,220-2,438 m).

Shaggy Dwarf Morning Glory

Evolvulus nuttallianus, Morning Glory Family, Convolvulaceae; Perennial herb

QUICK ID: Look for low stems and foliage densely covered with long, white hairs and small, lavender to white, morning glory–like flowers.

RANGE: NR, MR, SR; widespread, common

STEM: Erect to spreading, branching, 4–8 inches long (5–20 cm).

FLOWERS: May–July. Single in leaf axils along length of stem. Flowers on tiny ⅛-inch long (3 mm) stalks, funnel-shaped, opening to ½ inch wide (12 mm); petals lavender to blue, rarely white, united.

LEAVES: Alternate, spiraling around stem. Blades lance-shaped to elliptic, ⅜–1 inch long (10–25 mm), even-sized along stem; edges entire, tips pointed; both surfaces densely hairy.

HABITAT: Dry, coarse soils; grasslands, sagebrush, pinyon-juniper foothills. Elevation 3,400-8,000 feet (1,036-2,450 m).

Field Milkvetch

Astragalus agrestis, Legume Family, Fabaceae; Perennial herb

QUICK ID: Look for foot-high clumps with rounded clusters of lilac, pea-like flowers, and compound leaves with 13–23 leaflets.

RANGE: NR, MR, SR, Canada; widespread, common

STEM: Erect to spreading, 4–12 inches long (10–30 cm).

FLOWERS: April–August. Clusters have 7–20 erect, purple-white flowers, each about ⅝ inch long (17 mm), with 2 whitish wing petals, 1 narrow upper banner petal, and 2 pointed keel petals in the middle. The sepals (calyx) cupping the flowers have tapering tips and are densely covered with gray to black hairs. Seed pods erect, oval, ⅜ inch long (1 cm), densely hairy.

LEAVES: Alternate, pinnately compound. Leaflets linear to lance-shaped, ⅜–¾ inch long (1–2 cm), surfaces sparsely hairy.

HABITAT: Moist soils; grasslands, sagebrush, foothills, montane, subalpine forests, alpine. Elevation 5,200–9,000 feet (1,585–2,743 m).

Crescent Milkvetch

Astragalus amphioxys, Legume Family, Fabaceae; Perennial herb

QUICK ID: Look for low, spreading stems; 3 purple, pea-like flowers per cluster; and reddish or mottled, inflated, crescent-shaped pods.

RANGE: MR, SR; widespread, common

STEM: Sprawling, clump forming, 1½ feet long (45 cm).

FLOWERS: March–June. Erect clusters of 3–10 tubular flowers at end of leafless stem. Flowers lavender, purple, pink, or white, ⅝–1¼ inches long (16.5–31 mm); 1 banner petal upright with whitish spot at base, 2 side wing petals curved over 2 keel petals. Pods ¾–2 inches long (2–5 cm) by ½ inch thick (12 mm), curved, pointed at both ends, hairy.

LEAVES: Alternate. Blades slivery gray green, ¾–4 inches long (2–10 cm), pinnately compound with 5–21 elliptic leaflets, each ⅛–¾ inch long (3–20 mm), surfaces densely covered with short, silvery, flat-lying hairs.

HABITAT: Grasslands, sagebrush, pinion-juniper foothills. Elevation 5,000–7,000 feet (1,524–2,134 m).

Two-grooved Milkvetch

Astragalus bisulcatus, Legume Family, Fabaceae; Perennial herb

QUICK ID: Look for bushy stems; erect spikes with nodding, magenta or white, tubular flowers; and pods with 2 lengthwise grooves.

RANGE: NR, MR, SR, Canada; widespread, common

STEM: Clump forming, 8–28 inches tall and wide (20–70 cm).

FLOWERS: May–August. Two common varieties with either white or reddish-purple flowers. Elongated, crowded clusters, 4–7 inches tall (10–18 cm); flowers to ¾ inch long (18 mm), 5 petals, 1 banner angled upward, 2 side wing petals arc around 2 central keel petals. Pods dangle, ⅜–⅝ inch long (10–15 mm), hairy, with 2 grooves.

LEAVES: Alternate, pinnately compound. Blade with 7–17 pairs of leaflets to 1¼ inch long (33 mm), elliptic to oval, top surface hairless.

HABITAT: Typically on selenium rich soil; plains, sagebrush, foothills. Elevation 6,350–8,200 feet (1,935–2,500 m).

Groundplum Milkvetch

Astragalus crassicarpus, Legume Family, Fabaceae; Perennial herb

QUICK ID: Look for clumped stems; spikes with either white or magenta, tubular flowers; and plum-like pods.

RANGE: NR, MR, SR, Canada; widespread, common

STEM: Erect to sprawling with erect tip, 4–24 inches long (10–60 cm).

FLOWERS: April–June. Three common western varieties have either white or purple flowers. Dense, elongated clusters have 7–25 pea-like flowers with 5 petals: 1 erect banner petal to 1 inch long (25 mm) with a notched tip, 2 small side wing petals, and 2 fused keel petals to ¾-inch long (20 mm). Pods smooth, fleshy, spherical, ½–1 inch (12–25 mm) long.

LEAVES: Alternate, pinnately compound. Blade with 11–33 oval to linear leaflets ⅛–1 inch long (3–24 mm), hairless above, hairy below.

HABITAT: Grasslands, sagebrush, pinion-juniper foothills. Elevation 4,000–7,600 feet (1,200–2,400 m).

Slender Milkvetch

Astragalus flexuosus, Legume Family, Fabaceae; Perennial herb

QUICK ID: Look for clumps to 3 feet wide (1 m) with loose clusters of pale-purple, tubular flowers on the sprawling, upturned branch tips.

RANGE: NR, MR, SR, Canada; widespread, common

STEM: Flexible, erect to spreading, 8–24 inches tall (20–60 cm).

FLOWERS: May–August. Flower stalks reach 5½ inches tall (14 cm) with elongated clusters of flowers, each with 1 upper banner petal to ½ inch long (12 mm) and bent backward; 2 side petals of similar length; and 2 shorter, fused keel petals in the center. Sepals beneath the petals have gray hairs and short, triangular teeth. Pods hairy, oblong, ½–1 inch long (12–24 mm), not mottled, nearly straight, both ends pointed, spreading or hanging down.

LEAVES: Alternate, pinnately compound, 2–3 inches long (5–8 cm). Leaflets linear to oblong, ⅛–¾ inch long (3–19 mm); surfaces nearly hairless above, bottom flat-hairy.

HABITAT: Prairies, grasslands, sagebrush, pinyon-juniper foothills, montane forests. Elevation 4,000–9,000 feet (1,220–2,750 m).

Freckled Milkvetch

Astragalus lentiginosus, Legume Family, Fabaceae; Perennial herb

QUICK ID: Look for arching, reddish stems; purple and white pea-like flowers; and (usually) red-freckled, inflated pods. Over 50 varieties.

RANGE: NR, MR, SR, Canada; widespread, common

STEM: Sprawling clumps to 3 feet wide (1 m).

FLOWERS: March–July. Clusters of 5–35 purple, flowers on leafless stems about the same length as the leaves. Flowers have 5 petals: 1 upper banner with white base and red lines, 2 small side wings that reach forward around 2 keel petals in the center. Pods oval, ½–1 inch long (15–24 mm), solid pale-green-to-red freckles, tip hooked, indented groove down the middle.

LEAVES: Alternate, pinnately compound, to 6 inches long (15 cm). Leaflets 7–25, oval to elliptic, to 1 inch long (23 mm); hairless to sparsely hairy.

HABITAT: Grasslands, sagebrush, pinyon-juniper foothills. Elevation 4,800–7,600 feet (1,470–2,300 m).

Timber Milkvetch

Astragalus miser, Legume Family, Fabaceae; Perennial herb

QUICK ID: Look for clumps with elongated clusters of white to pinkish-purple, pea-like flowers. Rockies have 6 varieties.

RANGE: NR, MR, SR, Canada; widespread, common

STEM: Erect to prostrate, 2–12 inches tall (5–30 cm), hairless or with shaggy to short, flat-lying hairs.

FLOWERS: May–August. Loose clusters of 5–10 flowers with 5 petals: 1 erect banner petal, ⅜–½ inch long (8–12 mm), pinkish purple to white, often with pink lines from the base; 2 side wings that curve around 2 purple-tipped, keel petals in the center. Pods angle down on stem, tubular, linear to oblong, ½–1 inch long (12–25 mm), hairless or with short hairs.

LEAVES: Alternate, pinnately compound, to 8 inches long (20 cm). Leaflets 7 to 21, linear to oblong, ¼–1 inch long (6–25 mm), top surface nearly hairless, bottom with short hairs, tips rounded to acute.

HABITAT: Grasslands, sagebrush, foothills, montane forests, subalpine meadows. Elevation 2,000 to 11,000 feet (610–3,350 m).

Missouri Milkvetch

Astragalus missouriensis, Legume Family, Fabaceae; Perennial herb

QUICK ID: Look for 1–2-foot wide (30–60 cm) clumps with silvery-hairy leaflets, clusters of 3–15 magenta flowers, and hairy pods with a pointed tip.

RANGE: NR, MR, SR, Canada; widespread, common

STEM: Prostrate, 4–12 inches tall (10–30 cm).

FLOWERS: March–July. Erect, leafless, 6-inch-long (15 cm) stalks have loose clusters of 3–15 flowers with 5 petals: 1 upper banner ⅜–1 inch long (15–28 mm) with a white center; 2 small, purplish-to-white side wings curving around 2 fused keel petals in the middle. Sepal tube beneath petals hairy, purple-tinged, with narrow tips. Pods oblong, ½–1 inch long (14–27 mm).

LEAVES: Alternate, pinnately compound, 1½–5 ½ inches long (4–14 cm). Has 11–21 leaflets, elliptic to oblong, ⅛–½ inch long (3–13 mm), densely covered with silvery, flat-lying hairs.

HABITAT: Grasslands, sagebrush, pinyon-juniper foothills, montane forests. Elevation 4,650–8,200 feet (1,420–2,500 m).

Woolly Locoweed

Astragalus mollissimus var. *thompsoniae*, Legume Family, Fabaceae; Perennial herb

QUICK ID: Look for clumps of spreading, silvery leaves, magenta flower clusters, and densely hairy pods.

RANGE: SR, MR (UT); widespread, common

STEM: Inconspicuous, mostly underground.

FLOWERS: April–June. Elongated clusters have 7–35 flowers on erect to sprawling, hairy, leafless stems; flowers pea-like, ¾–1 inch long (18–25 mm) with 5 petals: 1 upright banner with a white center with red lines, 2 side wings point forward with tips (often white) extending beyond 2 keel petals. Pods oval to elliptic, ⅜–1 inch long (9–25 mm), densely hairy, crowded along stem, bent in the middle.

LEAVES: Basal, pinnately compound, to 8 inches long (20 cm), usually arching upward. Leaflets 15–35, oval, to ¾ inch long (18 mm), densely white-hairy.

HABITAT: Arid grasslands, sagebrush, pinyon-juniper foothills. Elevation 4,400–8,800 feet (1,340–2,685 m).

Woollypod Milkvetch

Astragalus purshii, Legume Family, Fabaceae; Perennial herb

QUICK ID: Look for low clumps with silvery-gray, woolly hairs, clusters of purple, pink, or white flowers, and cotton-ball-like pods.

RANGE: NR, MR, SR (absent NM), Canada; widespread, common

STEM: Mounding, sprawling, to 6 inches tall (14 cm).

FLOWERS: April–September. Erect, leafless stalk to 4 inches long (10 cm) has dense clusters of 3–10 flowers, each with 5 petals: 1 upturned banner, white or often magenta with a white spot; and 2 small side wings arcing around 2 keel petals. Sepal tube (calyx) woolly hairy. Pods oval, ½–1¼ inch long (12–30 mm), densely covered with long, soft hairs; sharp tipped.

LEAVES: Alternate, pinnately compound, to 6 inches long (15 cm). Leaflets 9-13, rounded to elliptic, to ¾ inch long (2 cm), crowded on stalk, woolly hairy, folded along midrib.

HABITAT: Dry soils; grasslands, sagebrush, foothills, montane forests. Elevation 1,000–8,000 feet (305–2,438 m).

Purple Prairie-Clover

Dalea purpurea, Legume Family, Fabaceae; Perennial herb

QUICK ID: Look for clump-forming stems with dense, hairy, cylindric clusters that bloom from the bottom up with tiny, rose-purple flowers.

RANGE: NR, MR, SR, Canada; widespread, common

STEM: Erect, leafy, 8–35 inches tall (20–90 cm), hairless to woolly.

FLOWERS: June–September. Oblong to cylindrical spike ⅝–2½ inches long (15–70 mm) densely packed with short, silky hairs. Flowers tubular, ¼ inch long (6 mm), with 5 petals: 1 upper banner petal, 2 side wing petals, 2 united keel petals; 5 stamens have showy golden-orange anthers.

LEAVES: Alternate. Blades pinnately compound, 1⅛–2 inches long (3–5 cm) with 3–7 leaflets, each linear, ⅜–¾ inch long (8–20 mm). Often smaller leaves grow in the leaf axils.

HABITAT: Drainages, roadsides; grasslands, pinyon-juniper, pine-oak foothills. Elevation 4,200–7,600 feet (1,280–2,316 m).

Bush Peavine

Lathyrus eucosmus, Legume Family, Fabaceae; Perennial herb

QUICK ID: Look for low-growing, bushy stems with compound leaves with tendrils, and showy clusters of rose-purple, pea-like flowers.

RANGE: SR; widespread, common

STEM: Sprawling, climbing, 8–24 inches tall (20–60 cm).

FLOWERS: May–September. Clusters have 2–5 rose to purple or bluish, pea-like flowers, each ⅞–1¼ inches long (20–30 mm); 5 petals: an erect upper banner, 2 forward-pointing side wings (sometimes lighter colored), and 2 fused petals forming the keel. Pods narrow, flat, 1–2¾ inches long (3–7 cm).

LEAVES: Alternate. Blades pinnately compound with 6–10 narrow-elliptic leaflets, 1–2⅜ inches long (3–6 cm) by ¼–⅜ inch wide (5–10 mm), leathery; midrib tendril well-developed on upper leaves, only a bristle on lower leaves.

HABITAT: Drainages, disturbed areas; arid grasslands, sagebrush, montane forests. Elevation 4,500–8,000 feet (1,372–2,438 m).

Longspur Lupine

Lupinus arbustus, Legume Family, Fabaceae; Perennial herb

QUICK ID: Look for bushy plants with palmate leaflets; flower stems with spikes of pea-like flowers that are pale yellow, bluish white, or white with a small, swollen, hairy rear spur.

RANGE: NR, MR, Canada; widespread, common

STEM: Erect, clumping, 8–24 inches tall (20–60 cm), fine-hairy.

FLOWERS: April–July. Loose spikes 2¾–8 inches long (7–20 cm); flowers whorled with 5 petals: 1 upper banner petal bent back, short-hairy on the upper backside; 2 lateral wing petals smooth or minutely hairy near tip; 2 central keel petals hairy on the upper edge; rear spur rounded, ⅛ inch long (3 mm), hairy. Pod ¾–1 inch long (2–3 cm), silky-hairy; 3–6 seeds.

LEAVES: Alternate on long stalks. Blades palmately divided into 7–13 leaflets, each ¾–2¾ inches long (2–7 cm), narrowly oblong, tips pointed or rounded; both surfaces short-hairy or top smooth. Basal leaves occasional, similar.

HABITAT: Open forests, meadows; sagebrush, foothills, montane forests. Elevation 4,900–9,850 feet (1,500–3,000 m).

Silvery Lupine

Lupinus argenteus, Legume Family, Fabaceae; Perennial herb

QUICK ID: Look for erect, densely silver-hairy stems, palmate leaves with narrow, oval leaflets, and spikes of blue, pea-like flowers.

RANGE: NR, MR, SR, Canada; widespread, common

STEM: Erect, clumping, from 4 inches tall (10 cm) to 3 feet tall and wide (1 m). Species is highly variable with many varieties.

FLOWERS: April–May. Slender clusters with 15–90 flowers on short stalks. Flowers light- to dark-blue to violet with 5 petals: 1 banner petal angles upward with a white-to-yellow spot, 2 side wings, and a keel of 2 united petals; rear spur or knob rounded, densely silky-hairy. Fruit is a linear pod ¾–1 inch long (2–3 cm), densely hairy with 3–6 seeds.

LEAVES: Alternate, with stalks ⅝–3⅛ inches long (2–8 cm). Blades palmately divided into 5–10 radiating leaflets, each ¾–2¾ inches long (2–7 cm); both surfaces silver-hairy to hairless.

HABITAT: Coarse soils, open areas; grasslands, sagebrush, foothills, montane, subalpine. Elevation 6,300–10,800 feet (1,920–3,292 m).

Utah (Dwarf) Lupine

Lupinus caespitosus var. *utahensis*, Legume Family, Fabaceae; Short-lived perennial herb

QUICK ID: Look for clumps of basal leaves with hairy, palmate leaflets; flower stalks within the leaves; and blue, pea-like flowers with a white-spotted banner straight to only slightly angled back.

RANGE: NR, MR, SR; widespread, common

STEM: Stemless, flower stalks erect, 4–8 inches tall (10–20 cm).

FLOWERS: May–July. Dense, spike-like clusters with 12–85 flowers, ¼–⅜ inch long (7–10 mm), opening with 5 blue-to-violet petals: 1 upper banner petal straight to slightly bent with a white spot, 2 side wings, 2 keel petals ciliate near tip; sepals with long silky hairs, no rear spur. Pods linear, ⅜–¾ inch long (1–2 cm), hairy.

LEAVES: Basal in dense, arching cluster, on stalks ¾–4 inches long (2–10 cm). Blades palmate with 5–9 narrow, oval, pointed leaflets to 1⅝ inches long (4 cm), densely hairy, folded or not.

HABITAT: Meadows, open woods; grasslands, sagebrush, montane, subalpine forests. Elevation 6,000–8,800 (1,828–2,682 m).

Tailcup Lupine

Lupinus caudatus, Legume Family, Fabaceae; Perennial herb

QUICK ID: Look for leafy clumps of stems with short hairs, palmate leaflets, and spikes of pea-like flowers with light- to dark-blue petals.

RANGE: NR, MR, SR; widespread, common. Sometimes lumped with Silvery Lupine, *L. argenteus*.

STEM: Erect, often branched at base, 8–16 inches tall (20-40 cm), hairy.

FLOWERS: May–August. Loose, spike-like clusters; flowers light- to deep-blue or purple or whitish with 5 petals: 1 banner petal bent upward at midpoint with short hairs on back, 2 wings with ciliate hairs near base, 2 keel petals with ciliate hairs near base; rear spur or knob silky-hairy. Pods 1 inch long (3 cm), silky, with 4–6 seeds.

LEAVES: Alternate. Blades palmately divided into 5-9 narrow, elliptic leaflets ¾–2 inches long (2–5 cm), often partially folded; both surfaces have fine, silvery hairs.

HABITAT: Coarse soils, open areas; grasslands, sagebrush, foothills, montane forests. Elevation 3,000–10,400 feet (916–3,150 m).

Velvet Lupine

Lupinus leucophyllus, Legume Family, Fabaceae; Perennial herb

QUICK ID: Look for bushy, hairy stems; basal leaves with silky-hairy palmate leaflets; and many tall spikes of pale-blue-to-purple flowers.

RANGE: NR, MR, Canada; widespread, common

STEM: Erect, branched from base, 15–36 inches tall, (40–90 cm), with woolly and long-stiff hairs.

FLOWERS: May–September. Dense, whorled, spike-like clusters 3–12 inches long (8–30 cm) with pale-lavender to whitish or purple, pea-like flowers; 5 petals: 1 upper banner petal angled upward with a yellow-to-white spot and densely hairy back; 2 side wings; 2 keel petals with ciliate upper edges; sepals shaggy-woolly, not spurred. Pods linear, ¾–1 inch long (2–3 cm), woolly hairs, seeds 4–6.

LEAVES: Alternate on stalks 1–4 inches long (3–10 cm). Blades palmate with 7–11 narrowly oval, pointed leaflets, 1–3 inches long (3–8 cm); both surfaces dense with tangled, woolly hairs

HABITAT: Dry meadows, open forests; grasslands, sagebrush, foothills, montane forests. Elevation 1,640–8,500 feet (500–2,590 m).

Rusty Lupine

Lupinus pusillus, Legume Family, Fabaceae; Annual herb

QUICK ID: Look in sandy habitats for short stems with long hairs; blue, pea-like flowers; and densely hairy pods.

RANGE: NR, MR, SR: widespread, common; Canada: rare

STEM: Erect, branching from base, 2–8 inches tall (5–20 cm), long-hairy.

FLOWERS: April–July. Clusters on stalks to 6½ inches long (17 cm) with 4–38 flowers, dark- to pale-blue, pinkish, or white, with 5 petals: 1 upper banner petal angled upward with a central white-yellow spot, 2 wing petals, central keel with 2 fused petals. Fruit is a linear, hairy pod ⅝ inch long (15 mm).

LEAVES: Alternate on stalks 1–2⅜ inches long (3–6 cm). Blades palmate with 3–8 radiating leaflets ½–2 inches long (11–48 mm); upper surface mostly hairless, bottom and margins with long hairs.

HABITAT: Sand, soils; arid scrub, grasslands, sagebrush, foothills. Elevation 5,000–8,300 feet (1,524–2,530 m).

Silky Lupine

Lupinus sericeus, Legume Family, Fabaceae; Perennial herb

QUICK ID: Look for robust plants with leafy stems, palmate leaves with silky-hairy leaflets, and spikes of blue (or white) pea-like flowers.

RANGE: NR, MR, SR, Canada; widespread, common

STEM: Erect, branching from base, 16–47 inches tall (40–120 cm), silky-hairy.

FLOWERS: June–September. Loose spikes 5–8 inches long (12–20 cm), mostly blue to purple, sometimes cream to white, ½ inch long (12 mm) with 5 petals: 1 banner angled upward, usually with white patch, silky on back; 2 wings, hairless; 2 fused keel petals edged with hairs; sepals densely silky-hairy, no rear spur. Fruit a pod, linear, ¾–1 inch long (2–3 cm), densely hairy.

LEAVES: Alternate. Blades palmate with 5–9 oval, pointed leaflets 1–3 inches long (3–8 cm); tips pointed, both sides hairy, upper leaves smaller. Basal leaves few, similar.

HABITAT: Dry openings; grasslands, sagebrush, foothills, montane, subalpine forests, alpine. Elevation 7,000–9,500 feet (2,100–2,600 m).

Nodding Locoweed

Oxytropis deflexa, Legume Family, Fabaceae; Perennial herb

QUICK ID: Look for silky-hairy basal leaves and stems; spikes of bluish-purple to whitish, pea-like flowers; and grooved, nodding pods.

RANGE: NR, MR, SR, Canada; widespread common

STEM: Absent or short. Flower stalks erect to sprawling, clustered, leafless, 3–18 inches tall (7–45 cm), hairy, often reddish.

FLOWERS: April–August. Rounded to elongated clusters have 3–30 flowers, each ⅜ inch (10 mm) long with 5 petals: 1 erect banner with lines; 2 wings cupping a keel of 2 petals, tips pointed; calyx beneath petals has long white and short black hairs. Pods drooping, oblong, ⅜–¾ inch long (8–20 mm), short-hairy, top grooved.

LEAVES: Basal, 1–3 alternate on stem (if present), pinnately compound with 15 to 41 leaflets, oval to lance-shaped, ⅛–1 inch long (3–25 mm); surfaces soft-hairy to smooth on top.

HABITAT: Coarse soils, meadows, open woods; montane, subalpine forests, alpine. Elevation 6,000–13,000 feet (1,828–3,962 m).

Purple Locoweed

Oxytropis lambertii, Legume Family, Fabaceae; Perennial herb

QUICK ID: Look for densely hairy basal leaves; leafless stalks with spikes of magenta, pea-like flowers; and silky-hairy foliage.

RANGE: NR, MR, SR, Canada; widespread, common

STEM: Erect, clumped, 6–20 inches tall (14–50 cm), hairy.

FLOWERS: May–July. Rounded to elongated spikes with 8–45 magenta-to-bluish flowers, ½–1 inch long (13–25 mm) with 5 petals: 1 erect banner with white patch, pink lines; 2 wing petals cover a beak-shaped keel of 2 fused petals; vase-like calyx beneath petals densely hairy. Pods cylindrical, ½ inch long (12 mm), silky hairy, tip hooked.

LEAVES: Basal, pinnately compound with 7–19 leaflets, lance-shaped to oblong, ¼–1½ inches long (6–38 mm), ¼ inch wide (6 mm); surfaces densely covered with silvery-white hairs.

HABITAT: Coarse soils, open areas; arid grasslands to subalpine forests. Elevation 2,000–10,700 feet (610–3,262 m).

SIMILAR SPECIES: Crosses with White Locoweed, *O. sericea*, to produce lavender-tinted flowers.

American Vetch

Vicia americana, Pea Family, Fabaceae; Perennial herbaceous vine

QUICK ID: Look for low-climbing vines with pinnate leaves tipped with a coiling tendril, and one-sided clusters of purple, tubular flowers.

RANGE: NR, MR, SR, Canada; widespread, common

STEM: Clambering, twining vine, to 3 feet long (1 m), smooth to sparsely hairy.

FLOWERS: May–September. Loose clusters in leaf axils have 2-9, purple-to-pink flowers, ½–1 inch long (12–25 mm); 5 petals, 1 upper notched banner, 2 side wings, 2 united into a keel; calyx tube holding petals hairless. Pods straight, 1–1¾ inches long (25–45 mm).

LEAVES: Alternate. Blade pinnately compound with 8–18 leaflets, elliptic to oval or lance-shaped, each ⅝–1⅜ inches long (15–35 mm) by ¼–9/16 inch wide (6–14 mm), generally hairless.

HABITAT: Meadows, open woods, disturbed areas; foothills, montane forests. Elevation 5,000–11,000 feet (1,524–3,352 m).

SIMILAR SPECIES: The exotic Hairy Vetch, *V. villosa*, (all regions) has stems with soft, long hairs and clusters of 10–40 flowers.

Pleated Gentian

Gentiana affinis, Gentian Family, Gentianaceae; Perennial herb

QUICK ID: Look for low clumps of leafy stems with clusters of erect, tubular, blue-lined flowers which never open widely.

RANGE: NR, MR, SR, Canada; widespread, locally common

STEM: Erect, 6–15 inches tall (15–40 cm).

FLOWERS: August–October. Flowers bloom from the leaf axils along the stem; tube-shaped, 1–1½ inches long (3–4 cm), often smaller at top than middle, 5 petals united with pleat-like membranes that spread at the top of the floral tube with small, pointed tips; throat white, lined with blue, 5 white stamens.

LEAVES: Opposite, stalkless, numerous. Blades linear to lance-shaped, 1–1½ inches long (3–4 cm), ¼–¾ inch wide (7–20 mm), smaller upward.

HABITAT: Moist soils; montane, sub-alpine forests and meadows. Elevation 5,700–11,300 feet (1,524–3,444 m).

SIMILAR SPECIES: Parry's Mountain Gentian, *G. parryi* (SR), has spreading blue-tipped petals with dots; blooms from stem tips.

Mountain Bog Gentian

Gentiana calycosa, Gentian Family, Gentianaceae; Perennial herb

QUICK ID: Look for clustered, leafy stems with dark-blue, funnel-shaped flowers with blue tips and a spotted white throat.

RANGE: NR, MR, Canada; widespread, infrequent, locally common

STEM: Erect, unbranched, 4–12 inches tall (10–30 cm).

FLOWERS: June–September. Usually in clusters of 3 at stem tips; erect, funnel-shaped, 1–1¾ inches long (3–5 cm) with 5 erect to spreading, petal lobes separated by fringed plaits; tips usually deep blue, throat whitish green with lines and spots.

LEAVES: Opposite 7–9 pairs. Blades oval to broadly lance-shaped, ⅜–1 inch long (10–25 mm) by ⅜–⅝ inch wide (9–14 mm); surfaces hairless; lower leaves smallest.

HABITAT: Moist meadows, stream banks; subalpine forests, alpine meadows. Elevation 4,000–11,000 feet (1,220–3,353 m).

SIMILAR SPECIES: Pleated Gentian, *G. affinis,* has tubular flowers in upper leaf nodes.

Parry's Mountain Gentian

Gentiana parryi, Gentian Family, Gentianaceae; Perennial herb

QUICK ID: Look for leafy stems tipped with erect, tubular flowers with spreading blue tips and a white throat with lines and spots.

RANGE: Erect, 3–16 inches tall (8–40 cm), hairy in rows

STEM: SR; widespread, locally common

FLOWERS: July–September. Singled or 3–5 clustered on stem tips. Flowers 1¼–1⅝ inches long (3–4 cm) with 5 spreading petal lobes separated by fused, pointed sepals; tips blue, pointed to rounded; throat white with greenish-purple spots and lines often extending onto the tips. Closed flowers open fully in sun.

LEAVES: Opposite. Blades lance-shaped to oval, pointed, ⅝–¾ inch long (15–20 mm), often angling toward the stem.

HABITAT: Moist meadows, stream banks; montane, subalpine forests, alpine. Elevation 8,450–12,050 feet (2,560–3,672 m).

SIMILAR SPECIES: Pleated Gentian, *G. affinis*, (all regions) has tubular flowers in upper leaf nodes that never spread fully open.

Autumn Dwarf Gentian

Gentianella amarella, Gentian Family, Gentianaceae; Annual herb

QUICK ID: Look for erect, branching stems; clusters in the upper leaf nodes; and small flowers with 5 blue-violet, triangular petals.

RANGE: NR, MR, SR, Canada; widespread, common

STEM: Erect, branching, 1–30 inches tall (3–76 cm), hairless.

FLOWERS: June–September. Clusters in upper 2–5 leaf nodes. Tubular flowers have 5 spreading, triangular petal lobes, each ⅛–¼ inch long (3–5 mm), blue-violet, occasionally creamy; a fringe of protruding white hairs circles the throat at the base of the lobes.

LEAVES: Basal, soon withering; blades on short stalks, lance- to egg-shaped, ⅝–1¾ inches long (15–45 mm), edges entire to minutely serrated, surfaces hairless. Stem blades opposite, 5–8 pairs, clasping,⅜–2⅜ inches long (1–6 cm) by ⅛–¾ inch wide (3–20 mm).

HABITAT: Meadows, open woods; sagebrush, foothills, montane, subalpine forests, alpine. Elevation 4,700–11,500 feet (1,450–3,505 m).

Rocky Mountain Fringed Gentian

Gentianopsis thermalis, Gentian Family, Gentianaceae; Annual herb

QUICK ID: Look for long stalks from leaf axils with a single, tubular flower with 4 blue, fringed petals that fold in a pinwheel spiral.

RANGE: MR, SR; widespread, locally common

STEM: Erect, single to multiple, 7–24 inches tall (18–60 cm), hairless.

FLOWERS: June–September. Funnel-shaped, solitary flowers 1⅜–2 inches long (4–5 cm) bloom on a 1–4 inch long (3–10 cm) stalk from mid-stem leaf axils, with no leaves or leaf-like bracts directly beneath the flower; 4 petals have pointed, finely toothed, fringe-like edges; throat white striped.

LEAVES: Basal, opposite on stem. Stem leaves numerous, lance- to spatula-shaped, ¾–2¾ inches long (2–7 cm), smaller up the stem.

HABITAT: Moist areas; montane, subalpine forests and meadows. Elevation 6,000–12,300 feet (1,829–3,750 m).

SIMILAR SPECIES: Perennial Fringed Gentian, *G. barbellata*, (MR, SR) solid blue flowers.

Star Gentian

Swertia perennis, Gentian Family, Gentianaceae; Perennial herb

QUICK ID: Look in wet mountain meadows for clumps of large basal leaves and stems lined with purple, star-like flowers.

RANGE: NR, MR, SR; widespread, common

STEM: Erect, unbranched, 4–18 inches tall (10–45 cm), smooth.

FLOWERS: July–September. Purple flowers, 1 inch wide (3 cm), have 4 or 5 narrow, petal-like lobes separated from the base (not tubular), and streaked with dark veins; 2 dark nectar pits at the base of each petal often fringed with short hairs; slender, green sepals show between the petals; stamens purple; pistil swollen, tipped with a pointed style.

LEAVES: Basal, long stalked; blade elliptic to oval, 2¾–4 inches long (7–10 cm). Stem leaves smaller, opposite, stalkless, lance-shaped, well-separated along the stem.

HABITAT: Wet soils, stream sides, meadows; montane, subalpine forests, alpine. Elevation 8,000–11,800 feet (2,438–3,600 m).

Ballhead Waterleaf

Hydrophyllum capitatum, Waterleaf Family, Hydrophyllaceae; Perennial herb

QUICK ID: Look for long-stalked basal leaves that overtop compact, rounded clusters of lavender-to-white, bell-shaped flowers.

RANGE: NR, MR, SR (absent NM), Canada; widespread, common

STEM: Erect to spreading, 4–16 inches tall (10–40 cm), hairy.

FLOWERS: March–July. Rounded clusters near ground level or below leaves. Flowers have 5 spreading petals, lavender to purple or whitish; stamens extend well beyond petals. Buds densely bristly hairy.

LEAVES: Mostly basal, alternate on stem; on 1–6-inch long (3–15 cm) stalks. Blades 4–6 inches long (10–15 cm), pinnately compound with 7-11 leaflets along midrib, each deeply divided into uneven, rounded to pointed lobes.

HABITAT: Moist open areas; sagebrush, foothills, montane, subalpine forests. Elevation 1,000–10,000 feet (305–1,048 m).

Franklin's Phacelia

Phacelia franklinii, Waterleaf Family, Hydrophyllaceae; Annual herb

QUICK ID: Look for deeply pinnately dissected leaves; coiled clusters of small blue-to-purple flowers with stamens longer than petals.

RANGE: NR, MR: widespread, common; Canada: infrequent

STEM: Erect; 1–few, 4–36 inches tall (10–90 cm), hairy, glandular.

FLOWERS: May–August. Compact, short-stalked arrays have loose, coiled clusters of small, bell-shaped flowers with a white throat and blue to purple petal lobes, ¼–⅜ inch long (6–10 mm), externally hairy, internally hairless; sepals hairy, stamens equal or slightly longer than throat; style forked less than half its length.

LEAVES: Basal, stalked, pinnately compound; blade ½–4 inches long (1–10 cm), deeply cut into narrow, lance-shaped lobes along midrib, surfaces coarsely spreading-hairy. Stem leaves alternate, gradually smaller upwards.

HABITAT: Dry coarse soils, open woods, disturbed areas; sagebrush, foothills, montane forests. Elevation 5,500–9,500 feet (1,676–2,895 m).

Threadleaf Phacelia

Phacelia linearis, Waterleaf Family, Hydrophyllaceae; Annual herb

QUICK ID: Look for hairy stems with narrow leaves and clusters of small, showy lavender flowers with a white throat and 5 oval petals.

RANGE: NR, MR, Canada; widespread, common

STEM: Erect, branched or not, 4–20 inches tall (10–50 cm), densely short-hairy.

FLOWERS: April–July. Hairy clusters have bell-shaped flowers 5⁄16–¾ inch wide (8–18 mm) with 5 spreading petal-lobes; stamens and style extend slightly beyond throat.

LEAVES: Basal few, soon withering. Stem leaves alternate, linear to narrowly lance-shaped, ⅝–4 inches long (1.5–10 cm); edges entire or with 1–2 pairs of narrow lobes near base, surfaces stiff-hairy.

HABITAT: Dry meadows, open woods; grasslands, sagebrush, foothills, montane forests. Elevation 1,000–7,000 feet (304–2,133 m).

Silky Phacelia

Phacelia sericea, Waterleaf Family, Hydrophyllaceae; Perennial herb

QUICK ID: Look for silky stems and leaves with elongated clusters packed with showy blue flowers with long stamens.

RANGE: NR, MR, SR, Canada; widespread, common

STEM: Erect, 1–few, 4–16 inches tall (10–40 cm), silky-hairy.

FLOWERS: May–August. Dense, spike-like clusters one-sided, coiled; flowers bell-shaped, hairy inside and out, ¼ inch (6 mm) long, spreading open with 5 blue-to-purple petal-lobes; stamens 2–3 times longer than flower, pollen yellow; style split half its length.

LEAVES: Mostly basal, stalked; blades oblong in outline, deeply pinnately cut along midrib with linear-oblong lobes, each ¾–2½ inches long (2–6 cm), entire to toothed, silky-hairy to stiff-hairy. Stem leaves similar, alternate, smaller up the stem.

HABITAT: Rocky slopes, meadows, open woods; montane, subalpine forests, alpine. Elevation 5,000–13,000 feet (1,524–3,962 m).

Wild Iris

Iris missouriensis, Iris Family, Iridaceae; Perennial herb

QUICK ID: Look in moist habitats for erect flower stems from basal leaves with "classic" iris-type blue flowers; colony forming.

RANGE: NR, MR, SR, Canada; widespread, common

STEM: Erect, simple or 1–2 branched, 8–24 inches tall (20–60 cm).

FLOWERS: May–July. Clusters of 1–3 flowers with showy sepals and petals, 1½–2 inches long (4–5 cm); 3 erect petals blue to purple, rarely white; 3 reflexed sepals variegated with dark-purple veins, yellow towards base.

LEAVES: Mostly basal; blades erect, linear, flat, sword-like, 18–24 inches long (45–60 cm), surfaces smooth. Alternate on stem, 2–3.

HABITAT: Seasonally wet grasslands, sagebrush, foothills, montane, subalpine forests. Elevation 4,000–12,000 feet (1,220–3,658 m).

Mountain Blue-eyed Grass

Sisyrinchium montanum, Iris Family, Iridaceae; Perennial herb

QUICK ID: Look for dense, grass-like clumps with stems tipped with a purse-like bundle holding buds that emerge as small, star-shaped violet flowers; oblong petals, bristle tip, yellow base.

RANGE: NR, MR, SR, Canada; widespread, common

STEM: Erect, unbranched, winged, 6–18 inches tall (15–45 cm).

FLOWERS: May–June. Each ½–¾-inch wide (1–2 cm) flower has 6 dark blue to purple, oblong petals (tepals), ⅜–⅝ inch long (9–15 mm), tipped with a tiny bristle; throat yellow, stamens yellow. Two bracts form a purse-like spathe enclosing 2–4 flower buds; the outer bract is about twice as long as inner bract, extends far above flower.

LEAVES: Basal, grass-like. Blades narrow, 5–10 inches long (12–25 cm).

HABITAT: Moist soils, meadows, open woods; grasslands to montane forests. Elevation 6,500–10,000 feet (1,980–3,048 m).

Drummond's Pennyroyal

Hedeoma drummondii, Mint Family, Lamiaceae; Perennial herb

QUICK ID: Look for branching, square stems with tiny, purplish flowers with 2 lips, and narrow, hairy leaves with a minty aroma.

RANGE: NR: infrequent; MR, SR: widespread, common

STEM: Erect, branching, 4–12 inches tall (10-30 cm), hairy.

FLOWERS: April–September. Flowers bloom along stem from leaf axils; Flowers lavender to magenta, tubular, narrow, ¼–½ inch long (5–12 mm); lower lip has 3 tiny lobes, the middle largest; upper lip entire or 2-lobed, and flat to hood-like; sepal tube beneath flower hairy, swollen, narrow at top with 5 slender teeth.

LEAVES: Opposite, stemless. Blades linear to elliptic, ⅜–¾ inch long (1–2 cm); margins entire, surfaces with pitted glands, hairy.

HABITAT: Dry, rocky soils; grasslands, sagebrush, pinyon-juniper, montane forests. Elevation 3,500–8,000 feet (1,066–2,438 m).

Hooded Skullcap

Scutellaria galericulata, Mint Family, Lamiaceae; Perennial herb

QUICK ID: Look for square stems; narrow, opposite leaves; tubular blue flowers with 2 lips: upper hood-like, lower with 2 white ridges.

RANGE: NR, MR, SR, Canada; widespread, common, circumboreal

STEM: Erect, weak, branched or not, 8–30 inches tall (20–80 cm), stiff-hairy, rhizomatous.

FLOWERS: July–October. Elongated cluster has 1-2 flowers per leaf node; flowers light to dark blue, hairy, ⅝–1 inch long (15–25 mm); upper lip hooded, lower lip has 2 white ridges, blue dots.

LEAVES: Opposite, barely stalked; blades lance-shaped to oblong; ¾–2 inches long (2–5 cm); edges blunt-toothed, tips pointed; surfaces flat, net-veined, top hairless, bottom minutely hairy.

HABITAT: Wet soils, meadows, drainages, riparian; foothills, montane, subalpine forests. Elevation 6,100–9,500 feet (1,000–3,050 m).

SIMILAR SPECIES: Britton's Skullcap, *S. brittonii*, (SR) has leaves with no teeth and curled edges.

Self-heal

Prunella vulgaris, Mint Family, Lamiaceae; Perennial herb

QUICK ID: Look for groundcover with square stems and leafy spikes with small, purple-to-pink flowers with a fringed lower lip.

RANGE: NR, MR, SR, Canada; widespread, common

STEM: Erect, leafy, 4–20 inches tall (8–50 cm), hairy or not.

FLOWERS: April–September. Spikes have flowers ¾ inch long (20 mm) with 2 unequal lips: upper lip purple, hood-like, unlobed; lower lip has 3 lobes, center lobe largest, whitish, drooping, with fine fringe on the edge. Small leaf-like bracts beneath each flower are purple-tinged with hairy margins.

LEAVES: Opposite, stalked. Blades elliptic to lance-shaped to oblong, to ¾–3 inches long (2–8 cm) to 1½ inches wide (4 cm); edges mostly entire, tip pointed.

HABITAT: Moist soils, steam sides, meadows; foothills, montane, subalpine forests. Elevation 5,000–10,000 feet (1,524–3,048 m).

Marsh Hedgenettle

Stachys pilosa var. *pilosa,* Mint Family, Lamiaceae; Perennial herb

QUICK ID: Look for square, leafy stems with long hairs; serrated leaves; whorls of pale-pink flowers with dark lines and spots; and an upper hood petal and lower, declining lip.

RANGE: SR: widespread, common; NR, MR, Canada: scattered, infrequent

STEM: Erect, branched, 1–3 feet tall (30–90 cm), long, soft-hairy.

FLOWERS: July–September. Spikes with hairy, whorled clusters with 2–6 tubular flowers, each ⅜–⅝ inch long (8–15 mm); 2 lips: upper hooded over stamens, lower angled down, 3-lobed, the middle the largest.

LEAVES: Opposite, stalkless or nearly so. Blades oblong to triangular or elliptic, 1¼–3½ inches long (3–9 cm); edges coarsely toothed, surfaces strongly veined, bottom long-hairy.

HABITAT: Moist soils, stream banks, meadows, wetlands; sagebrush, foothills, montane forests. Elevation 6,000–9,000 feet (1,828–2,743 m).

Blue Flax

Linum lewisii, Flax Family, Linaceae; Perennial herb

QUICK ID: Look for slender stems with narrow leaves, delicate blue flowers with yellow throats, and nodding buds.

RANGE: NR, MR, SR, Canada; widespread, common

STEM: Erect to ascending, branching from base, 8–28 inches tall (20–70 cm), hairless.

FLOWERS: May–September. Loose clusters of flowers bloom on one side of the stem with the upper buds drooping. Flowers ½–1 inch (12–25 mm) wide; 5 petals, light to dark blue, occasionally white, with dark lines radiating from a yellow center. Flowers bloom only one day.

LEAVES: Alternate. Blades narrow, linear to lance-shaped, 3⁄16–1 3⁄16 inches long (4–30 mm) to 3⁄16 inch wide (4 mm), often hugging the stem.

HABITAT: Meadows, grasslands, sagebrush, foothills, montane, subalpine forests. Elevation 5,000–11,000 feet (1,525–3,353 m).

Dwarf Lousewort

Pedicularis centranthera, Broomrape Family, Orobanchaceae; Perennial herb, hemiparasitic

QUICK ID: Look for dense clusters of fern-like leaves and a short flower stalk with crowded clusters of tubular, white-to-yellowish flowers with pinkish-purple tips.

RANGE: MR, SR; widespread, common

STEM: Erect, unbranched, to 6 inches tall (15 cm), hairless.

FLOWERS: March–June. Short spikes to 3 inches tall (7 cm) from ground level have a dense cluster of tubular flowers 1 3⁄8 inches long (35 mm); upper lip a curved hood enclosing stamen, lower lip has 3 rounded lobes. Calyx cupping the petals is pinkish purple.

LEAVES: Basal, 6–8, long stalked; lowest blades undivided, linear, 2 3⁄8–6 inches long (6–15 cm), upper blades with deeply cut fern-like segments with crinkly teeth along a purplish midrib. Stem leaves 0–4, alternate.

HABITAT: Coarse soils, open to shaded areas; pinyon-juniper foothills, sagebrush, montane forests. Elevation 6,200–10,000 feet (1,890–3,048 m).

Fernleaf Lousewort

Pedicularis cystopteridifolia, Broomrape Family, Orobanchaceae; Perennial herb, hemiparasitic

QUICK ID: Look for fern-like leaves and spikes with purplish tubular flowers with a hooded upper lip arching over a spreading lower lip.

RANGE: MR (MT, WY); endemic, locally common

STEM: Erect, solitary, unbranched, 4–16 inches tall (10–40 cm).

FLOWERS: May–August. Elongated, clusters lined with hairy, leaf-like bracts and 10–40 purple to pink tubular flowers; upper lip hooded, beakless, with tip arching over 3 spreading lobes of the lower lip.

LEAVES: Mostly basal, 2–10; blade elliptic to lance-shaped, ¾–4 inches long (2–10 cm), pinnately divided into fern-like lobes that often overlap; surfaces hairless. Stem leaves 2–8, similar, alternate.

HABITAT: Meadows, open slopes; sagebrush, montane, subalpine, alpine. Elevation 6,890–10,170 feet (2,100–3,100 m).

Sudeten Lousewort

Pedicularis sudetica ssp. *scopulorum*, Broomrape Family, Orobanchaceae; Perennial herb, hemiparasitic

QUICK ID: Look in high elevations for deeply cut, fern-like leaves and densely white-woolly spikes of magenta tubular flowers with an arching, hooded upper lip and spreading lower lip.

RANGE: SR; scattered, infrequent

STEM: Erect, ¾–18 inches tall (2–45 cm).

FLOWERS: July–August. Spike-like clusters have 10–50 tubular, magenta to purple flowers with 2 lips: upper hooded arching over the 3 spreading lobes of lower lip. Bracts and the calyx beneath the petals densely white woolly.

LEAVES: Basal, 1–20; blades elliptic to lance-shaped, ⅜–4 inches long (1–10 cm), pinnate with lobes deeply cut 1–2 times into fern-like segments; edges serrate, surfaces hairless. Stem blades 0–5, alternate, similar.

HABITAT: Moist meadows, open forests, tundra; subalpine forests, alpine. Elevation 10,170–12,140 feet (3,100–3,700 m).

Purple Monkeyflower

Erythranthe lewisii (Mimulus lewisii), Lopseed Family, Phrymaceae; Perennial herb

QUICK ID: Look in wet places for leafy plants with clusters of showy, purple flowers with spreading upper and lower lobes.

RANGE: NR, MR, SR (absent NM), Canada; widespread, common

STEM: Erect, unbranched, 10–24 inches tall (25–60 cm), sticky-glandular hairy, rhizomatous.

FLOWERS: June–September. Clusters from leaf nodes have 2–6 flowers on stalks 1–4 inches long (3–10 cm); flowers tubular, 1–2 inches long (3–5 cm); upper lip has 2 spreading, rounded lobes, lower lip has 3 with yellow, hairy ridges on middle lobe.

LEAVES: Opposite, clasping. Blade elliptic to oval, 1–3 inches long (3–8 cm); edges entire to irregularly toothed, tips pointed; surfaces 3–5 veined, sticky-glandular hairy.

HABITAT: Wet soils, meadows; montane forests to lower alpine zones. Elevation 1,970–10,170 feet (600–3,100 m).

Dwarf Purple Monkeyflower

Erythranthe nana (Mimulus nanus), Lopseed Family, Phrymaceae; Annual herb

QUICK ID: Look for dwarf plants with magenta flowers with showy, spreading lobes and yellow markings from bottom lip into throat.

RANGE: NR, MR; uncommon

STEM: Erect to branching, 1–5 inches tall, (3–12 cm), finely hairy.

FLOWERS: May–August. Paired (or single) on short stalks from leaf axils, tubular ⅜–¾ inch long (10–20 mm), with 2 rounded upper lobes, 3 bottom lobes; the middle has 2 hairy, yellow ridges with red spots. Dark patches run from middle of each lobe into the throat.

LEAVES: Basal; opposite on stem. Blades even-sized, narrowly elliptic to lance-shaped, to 1⅜ inches long (4 cm); edges entire, flat; surfaces with very fine, glandular hairs.

HABITAT: Seasonally moist areas; sagebrush, foothills, montane, subalpine forests. Elevation 3,000–8,000 feet (915–2,438 m).

Alberta Penstemon

Penstemon albertinus, Plantain Family, Plantaginaceae; Perennial herbaceous

QUICK ID: Look for leafy stems; elongated clusters of inflated tubular blue flowers with 5 spreading, equal, petal-like lobes; and a golden-hairy beardtongue.

RANGE: NR, Canada; widespread, common

STEM: Erect to sprawling, clustered, 4–16 inches tall (10–40 cm), smooth near bottom, slightly hairy near flowers.

FLOWERS: May–August. Cylindrical clusters with 4–8 whorls, continuous or spaced along stem, with 2–6 flowers per whorl; flowers blue to violet, glandular-hairy outside, sparsely white-hairy inside; beardtongue golden-hairy.

LEAVES: Basal, stalked, firm; blades oval to lance-shaped, 1½–4 inches long (4–10 cm); edges smooth to irregularly toothed, surfaces smooth. Stem leaves opposite, 2–6 pairs, smaller.

HABITAT: Gravelly slopes, open woods, roadsides; foothills, montane, subalpine. Elevation 2,500–8,000 feet (762–2,438 m).

Narrow-leaf Penstemon

Penstemon angustifolius, Plantain Family, Plantaginaceae Perennial herb

QUICK ID: Look in sandy soils for stems with fleshy, tapering leaves; clusters of blue tubular flowers; and a golden-hairy beardtongue.

RANGE: MR, SR; widespread, common

STEM: Erect, 1 to several, 8–20 inches tall (20–50 cm).

FLOWERS: April–June. Dense cylindrical whorls in leaf axils have blue to lavender, funnel-shaped flowers ⅝–1 inch long (17–23 mm) with 2 protruding upper lobes and 3 spreading lower lobes; exterior hairless, inside sparsely white-hairy; beardtongue tip dilated, curved, densely golden-hairy. Leaf-like bracts have slender, tapering tips.

LEAVES: Basal absent at flowering. Stem leaves opposite, stalkless, fleshy; blades lance-shaped, ¾–3½ inches long (2–9 cm) to 1 inch wide (25 mm); edges entire, surfaces hairless, gray green with waxy covering, tip tapering.

HABITAT: Deep sand, gravelly soils, roadsides; grasslands, sagebrush, foothills. Elevation 2,000–8,530 feet (610–2,600 m).

Taper-leaf Penstemon

Penstemon attenuatus, Plantain Family, Plantaginaceae; Perennial herb

QUICK ID: Look for stems with both basal and stem leaves; whorls of blue, tubular flowers with spreading lobes; a whitish throat; and a golden-hairy beardtongue.

RANGE: NR, MR; widespread, common

STEM: Erect to sprawling, 2–28 inches tall (5–70 cm), smooth or with short hairs.

FLOWERS: May–August. Cylindrical whorls separated along the stem have 2–8 flowers, each to ¾ inch long (2 cm), glandular-hairy, pale blue to violet or bluish purple; the slightly inflated tube spreads open with 2 erect upper lobes, 3 drooping lower lobes; throat hairy, whitish with red nectar guidelines, beardtongue densely golden-hairy.

LEAVES: Basal, short-stalked, well developed; blades elliptic to lance-shaped, 2–3½ inches long (55–90 mm); base tapered, edges entire. Stem leaves 2–5 pairs, opposite, similar, upper leaves clasping.

HABITAT: Moist hillsides, rocky slopes, meadows; montane, subalpine forests, alpine. Elevation: 5,250–10,500 feet (1,600–3,200 m).

Mat Penstemon

Penstemon caespitosus, Plantain Family, Plantaginaceae; Perennial herb

QUICK ID: Look for spreading, leafy mats; short flower stems with clusters of bluish-purple, tubular flowers with rounded lobes; and a golden-hairy beardtongue.

RANGE: MR, SR; widespread, common

STEM: Prostrate, rooting; flower stalks ¾–3 inches tall (2–8 cm), short hairs point downward.

FLOWERS: May–August. Clusters cylindric to one-sided continuous along stem, 1–3 flowers each; ⅜–¾ inch long (10–17 mm) with 5 spreading petal-like lobes; outer floral tube blue to lavender-purple, short hairy to glandular; inside whitish with 2 ridges, yellow hairs, dark nectar guidelines.

LEAVES: Stem leaves opposite, 3–20 pairs, short-stalked; blades linear to elliptic, ⅛–⅜ inch long (4–10 mm) to ⅛ inch wide (3 mm); edges entire, surfaces short-hairy.

HABITAT: Coarse soils, meadows, openings; sagebrush, foothills, montane forests. Elevation 6,000–9,000 feet (1,828–2,743 m).

Crandall's Penstemon

Penstemon crandallii, Plantain Family, Plantaginaceae; Perennial herb

QUICK ID: Look for densely leafy stems with narrow, pointed leaves and light-blue to purple, tubular flowers on one side of the stem with a whitish throat and a beardtongue with golden hairs along its length.

RANGE: SR; widespread, common

STEM: Erect, prostrate to mat forming, rooting, 10 inches tall (25 cm), hairy throughout.

FLOWERS: May–August. One-sided clusters have flowers ⅝–¾ inch long (14–20 mm), blue, purple, or lavender; 2 rounded petal-like lobes curve upward, 3 lower lobes point forward. Flower tube densely glandular-hairy externally, 2 ridges internally, beardtongue densely golden-hairy.

LEAVES: Opposite, evergreen. Blades narrow, linear to elliptic, ⅜–1⅜ inches long (10–35 mm); base tapering, tip pointed, upper surfaces with fine hair or hairless, depending on variety.

HABITAT: Slopes, meadows; arid grasslands, sagebrush, foothills, montane forests. Elevation 6,300–10,000 feet (1,920–3,048 m).

Wasatch Penstemon

Penstemon cyananthus, Plantain Family, Plantaginaceae; Perennial herb

QUICK ID: Look for clumped stems with cylindrical to almost one-sided clusters of hairless blue flowers with 5 petal-like lobes and a golden-tipped beardtongue.

RANGE: MR; locally common

STEM: Erect to sprawling, clustered, 8–28 inches tall (20–70 cm), smooth to densely short-hairy.

FLOWERS: May–August. Flowers ½–1 inch long (12–25 mm), blue to violet; 2 rounded lobes curve upward, 3 lower lobes bend down. Flower tube gradually inflated, hairless externally and internally, beardtongue tip moderately golden-hairy.

LEAVES: Basal, blades oval to lance-shaped, ¾–6¼ inches long (2–16 cm); edges entire, surfaces smooth to short-hairy, base tapered, tip pointed. Stem leaves similar, smaller, opposite, 1–6 pairs, base heart-shaped to clasping.

HABITAT: Dry, coarse, clay soils; arid grasslands, sagebrush, foothills, montane forests, alpine. Elevation 5,000–10,000 feet (1,524–3,048 m).

Blue Penstemon

Penstemon cyaneus, Plantain Family, Plantaginaceae; Perennial herb

QUICK ID: Look for hairless stem and leaves, and continuous to separated, one-sided clusters of tubular, blue-to-violet flowers with 5 rounded, petal-like lobes.

RANGE: NR, MR; widespread, common

STEM: Erect, 12–32 inches tall (30–80 cm), smooth.

FLOWERS: June–August. Flowers average 1¼ inch long (3 cm), blue to violet or purple; 2 rounded lobes curve upward, 3 lower lobes bend downward. Flower tube gradually inflated, hairless externally and internally, beardtongue tip sparsely golden hairy.

LEAVES: Basal; blades elliptic to oblong 20–70 inches tall (50–177 cm); edge entire, surfaces hairless, base tapered, tip pointed. Stem leaves similar, smaller, opposite, 3–7 pairs, unstalked.

HABITAT: Coarse soils, slopes, disturbed areas; arid grasslands, sagebrush, foothills, montane forests. Elevation 5,000–9,000 feet (1,524–2,793 m).

Fuzzy-tongue Penstemon

Penstemon eriantherus, Plantain Family, Plantaginaceae; Perennial herb

QUICK ID: Look for clumps of leafy stems with hairy whorls of lavender to purple or pink, tubular flowers; the bottom lip has a densely fuzzy, yellow beardtongue.

RANGE: NR, MR, SR; widespread, common

STEM: Erect, clump-forming, 2⅜–24 inches tall (6–60 cm), short-hairy to glandular.

FLOWERS: May–July. Cylindrical whorls have glandular-hairy, tubular flowers ¾–1⅜ inches long (18–35 mm); 2 protruding lips have 2 upper lobes, 3 lower lobes with red stripes, throat densely white-hairy, beardtongue tip fuzzy with yellow and white hairs.

LEAVES: Basal, stalked; blades elliptic, linear or lance- to egg-shaped, ½–5 inches long (1–13 cm); edges entire to toothed, base tapered; top short- to glandular-hairy, bottom smooth to sparsely short-hairy. Stem leaves similar, opposite, 2–6 pairs.

HABITAT: Coarse soils, slopes, open woods; grasslands, sagebrush, foothills, montane forests. Elevation 1,640–8,860 feet (500–2,700 m).

Bush Penstemon

Penstemon fruticosus, Plantain Family, Plantaginaceae; Perennial subshrub

QUICK ID: Look for low-growing, leafy, bushy plants with one-sided clusters of lavender to purple, tubular flowers with 5 petal-like lobes.

RANGE: NR, MR, Canada; widespread, common

STEM: Woody, upright, branching, 5–16 inches tall (13–40 cm), smooth to short-hairy.

FLOWERS: April–August. Few-flowered clusters have flowers 1–2 inches long (3–5 cm), 2 forward-facing lips with 5 lobes, bluish-lavender to purplish; floral tube externally smooth, internally the lower lip has 2 ridges with white hairs; flower stalk and calyx cupping the petals glandular-hairy; beardtongue tip sparsely to densely yellow-hairy.

LEAVES: Opposite, evergreen, 2–6 pairs, short stalked; blades lance-shaped to elliptic, ⅝–2 inches long (15–50 mm); base tapered to clasping, edges toothed to entire; surfaces hairless.

HABITAT: Rocky outcrops, open woods; sagebrush to alpine zones. Elevation 985–9,842 feet (300–3,000 m).

Western Smooth Penstemon

Penstemon glaber, Plantain Family, Plantaginaceae; Perennial herb

QUICK ID: Look for stout, leafy stems with dense, one-sided clusters with smooth, bluish-purple, tubular flowers with 5 spreading lobes.

RANGE: MR, SR; widespread, common

STEM: Erect, clumped, 20–26 inches tall (50–65 cm), smooth below to short-hairy above.

FLOWERS: June–August. Elongated clusters have tubular flowers, usually hairless, with 2 lips: upper with 2 erect lobes, lower with 3 pointing down; throat white-hairy, with reddish nectar guidelines, beardtongue tip smooth to sparsely yellow-hairy.

LEAVES: Basal often present; blades lance-shaped to oblong-pointed, ¾–3 inches long (2–8 cm) to ¾ inch wide (20 mm); margins entire, usually wavy, surfaces usually smooth, base tapered. Stem leaves similar, opposite, 3–6 pairs, smooth, base clasping.

HABITAT: Coarse soils, plains, open areas; grasslands, foothills, montane forests. Elevation 4,920–9,515 feet (1,500–2,900 m).

Low Penstemon

Penstemon humilis var. *humulis*, Plantain Family, Plantaginaceae; Perennial herb

QUICK ID: Look for cylindrical to one-sided, glandular-hairy clusters with blue to purple, tubular flowers with spreading, rounded lobes and a red-striped throat.

RANGE: MR, NR, SR; widespread, common

STEM: Erect, multiple stems, 2–14 inches tall (5–35 cm), short-hairy.

FLOWERS: May–July. Loose to crowded clusters spaced along stem have flowers ½–¾ inch long (12–19 mm) with 2 lips: 2 spreading upper lobes, 3 lower; tube glandular-hairy externally, internally 2 ridged, sparsely white- to yellow-hairy; features highly variable; beardtongue tip sparsely to densely yellow-hairy.

LEAVES: Basal, long stalked; blades elliptic, pointed, ½–4 inches long (1–10 cm) to ½ inch wide (13 mm); edges entire, base tapering, surfaces smooth to short-hairy. Stem leaves similar, opposite, 2–4 pairs.

HABITAT: Dry, rocky plains, slopes; sagebrush, foothills, montane, subalpine forests. Elevation 3,280–10,500 feet (1,000–3,200 m).

Lyall's Penstemon

Penstemon lyallii, Plantain Family, Plantaginaceae; Perennial herb

QUICK ID: Look for stems with one-sided clusters of lavender to purple, tubular, glandular-hairy flowers with 5 petal-like lobes.

RANGE: NR, Canada; widespread, common

STEM: Erect to sprawling, clumped, 12–32 inches tall (30–80 cm), short- to glandular-hairy.

FLOWERS: June–August. Long-stalked clusters separated along stem, stalks and the calyx holding the petals densely glandular-hairy; flowers 1⅜–1¾ inches long (35–46 mm) with 2 lips: upper slightly pleated with 2 lobes pointing forward, lower lip with 3; tube hairless externally, moderately woolly internally, beardtongue tip hairless.

LEAVES: Basal absent. Stem leaves opposite, 8–13 pairs, lance-shaped, 1–5 inches long (3–13 cm); edges entire to irregularly toothed, base tapered, tip pointed, surfaces smooth to short-hairy.

HABITAT: Coarse soils, rocky outcrops, road cuts; foothills, montane, subalpine forests. Elevation 2,000–7,875 feet (609–2,400 m).

Cordroot Penstemon

Penstemon montanus, Plantain Family, Plantaginaceae; Perennial herb

QUICK ID: Look for multiple, sometimes mat-forming stems with few-flowered clusters of pale lavender, tubular flowers.

RANGE: NR, MR; widespread, common

STEM: Erect, branched from base, 2–12 inches tall (5–30 cm), hairy.

FLOWERS: June–August. Clusters loose, rounded, stalk and calyx holding petals glandular-hairy; flowers 1–1⅛ inches long (25–33 mm), 2 lips with 2 upper lobes, 3 lower; floral tube hairless externally, white-wooly internally; beardtongue tip hairless or with white hairs.

LEAVES: Opposite, 4–7 pairs, blades elliptic to lance-shaped, ¾–2 inches long (1–5 cm); var. *montana*: edges toothed, surfaces glandular-hairy; var. *idahoensis*: edges entire to slightly toothed, surfaces short-hairy or not, glaucous (gray-waxy).

HABITAT: Open rocky areas, talus slopes; foothills, montane, subalpine forests. Elevation 6,000–11,483 feet (1,829–3,500 m).

Wax-leaf Penstemon

Penstemon nitidus, Plantain Family, Plantaginaceae; Perennial herb

QUICK ID: Look for hairless stem and leaves; showy cylindrical clusters of blue to violet, tubular flowers with red nectar guidelines; and a beardtongue with a yellow-hairy tip.

RANGE: NR, MR, Canada; widespread, common

STEM: Erect, clump forming, 4–16 inches tall (10–40 cm), hairless.

FLOWERS: May–July. Elongated clusters have whorls of tubular flowers with 2 lips: upper with 2 lobes bent up, lower with 3 lobes spreading down; tube hairless externally, hairless to sparsely white-hairy internally; throat whitish, beardtongue yellow-woolly.

LEAVES: Basal, long-stalked; blades, thick, lance-shaped to elliptic, ½–5½ inches long (15–140 mm); edges entire, surfaces hairless, glaucous (gray-waxy), base tapered. Stem leaves similar, opposite, 2–4 pairs, elliptic, base clasping, tip pointed.

HABITAT: Plains, hills, roadsides; grasslands, sagebrush, foothills, montane forests. Elevation 1,500–7,000 feet (460–2,133 m).

Small-flowered Penstemon

Penstemon procerus var. *procerus*, Plantain Family, Plantaginaceae; Perennial herb

QUICK ID: Look for stems topped with dense, rounded clusters of blue-purple, tubular flowers, beardtongue tip yellow-woolly.

RANGE: NR, MR, SR (absent NM), Canada; widespread, common

STEM: Erect, 6–20 inches tall (15–50 cm), smooth to short-hairy.

FLOWERS: June–August. Whorled clusters well separated along upper stem; flowers ⅜–½ inch long (8–11 mm) with 2 lips: upper with 2 rounded lobes angled up, lower 3 lobes slanted down; floral tube externally hairless, internally white-woolly; throat white with red nectar guidelines, beardtongue tip densely yellow-hairy.

LEAVES: Basal, stalked; blades lance-shaped to elliptic, 1–3½ inches long (3–9 cm); edges entire, tip rounded to pointed. Stem leaves similar, opposite, 2–6 pairs, base tapered to clasping.

HABITAT: Dry meadows, slopes, open woods; grasslands to alpine meadows. Elevation 1,968–12,140 feet (600–3,700 m).

Matroot Penstemon

Penstemon radicosus, Plantain Family, Plantaginaceae, Perennial herb

QUICK ID: Look for leafy stems with no basal leaves; clusters of tubular, blue, glandular-hairy flowers; and a yellow-hairy beardtongue.

RANGE: NR, MR; widespread, common; SR, rare.

STEM: Erect, clumped, 8–17 inches tall (20–42 cm), short-hairy.

FLOWERS: May–July. Loose, cylindrical clusters have glandular-hairy stalks and calyx cupping the petals; flowers pale to dark blue, purple or violet, ⅝–1 inch long (16–24 mm) with 2 lips: upper has 2 lobes angled up; lower lip is longer, 3 lips slant down; floral tube glandular-hairy externally, moderately yellow-woolly hairy internally with 2 ridges; throat white, beardtongue yellow-hairy.

LEAVES: Basal absent at blooming. Stem leaves stalkless, opposite, 5–8 pairs, oval-pointed to lance-shaped, 1–2½ inches long (30–65 mm); margins entire, surfaces short-hairy.

HABITAT: Dry open areas; arid grasslands, sagebrush, foothills, montane forests. Elevation 5,000–7,875 feet (1,524–2,400 m).

Rydberg's Penstemon

Penstemon rydbergii, Plantain Family, Plantaginaceae, Perennial herb

QUICK ID: Look for dense whorls of blue, purple, or violet; tubular flowers with no nectar guides; beardtongue with a yellow-hairy tip.

RANGE: NR, MR, SR; widespread, common

STEM: Erect, 8–28 inches tall (20–70 cm), smooth to short-hairy.

FLOWERS: June–August. Dense, cylindrical clusters are separated along stem; flowers ⅜–¾ inch long (10–20 mm) with 2 lips: 2 petal-like lobes angled up, 3 lobes slanted down; floral tube hairless externally, yellow-to-white hairs internally, white throat, reddish nectar guidelines absent, beardtongue tip densely yellow-hairy.

LEAVES: Basal rosette, stalked; blades oblong to elliptic, 1⅛–4¾ inches long (3–12 cm) to ¾ inch wide (20 mm); edges entire, surfaces hairless. Stem leaves similar, opposite, clasping to tapered.

HABITAT: Moist soils, meadows, open woods; sagebrush to subalpine forests. Elevation 5,900–11,500 feet (1,800–3,500 m).

Sidebells Penstemon

Penstemon secundiflorus, Plantain Family, Plantaginaceae, Perennial herb

QUICK ID: Look for hairless stems, one-sided arrays of lavender-to-violet flowers with 5 petal-like lobes, and a yellow-hairy beardtongue.

RANGE: SR; widespread, common

STEM: Erect, unbranched, 6–20 inches tall (15–50 cm), hairless.

FLOWERS: May–July. Clusters along one side of stem, flowers ⅝–1 inch long (17–25 mm) with 2 lips: upper with 2 lobes bent upward; lower with 3 lobes angled down; floral tube hairless externally, hairless to sparsely white-hairy internally, with reddish nectar guidelines, beardtongue densely yellow-hairy.

LEAVES: Basal, stalked, thick; blades lance-shaped to oval-pointed, ¾–3 inches long (2–8 cm); edges entire, surfaces hairless, base tapering. Stem leaves similar, opposite, 4–6 pairs, base clasping.

HABITAT: Sandy, gravelly soils; grasslands, sagebrush, foothills, montane forests. Elevation 5,000–9,515 feet (1,524–2,900 m).

Rocky Mountain Penstemon

Penstemon strictus, Plantain Family, Plantaginaceae; Perennial herb

QUICK ID: Look for hairless stems and leaves, one-sided clusters of blue-to-purple tubular flowers, and a beardtongue with few to no hairs.

RANGE: MR, SR; widespread, common

STEM: Erect, single to multiple, 12–32 inches tall (30–81 cm), hairless

FLOWERS: May–August. Elongated, one-sided clusters have flowers. ¾–1¼ inches long (18–32 mm) with 2 lips; upper has 2 lobes pointed forward; lower has 3 lobes bent downward; floral tube hairless outside and inside, anthers long-hairy.

LEAVES: Basal, short stalked; blades linear to lance-shaped, 2–6 inches long (5–15 cm) to ⅝ inch wide (16 mm); smooth, edges entire. Stem leaves similar, 4–8 pairs, opposite, stalkless, base tapered, tip pointed, often folded along midrib.

HABITAT: Coarse soils, open areas; sagebrush, foothills, montane, subalpine forests. Elevation 5,500–11,500 feet (1,700–11,483 m).

Front Range Penstemon

Penstemon virens, Plantain Family, Plantaginaceae; Perennial herb

QUICK ID: Look for dense clusters of tubular, blue to violet, glandular-hairy flowers and a beardtongue with yellow hairs.

RANGE: SR; widespread, locally common

STEM: Erect, clumped, 4–16 inches tall (10–40 cm), short-hairy.

FLOWERS: May–August. Elongated, cylindrical clusters circle the stem, stalks glandular-hairy; flowers ⅜–¾ inch long (10–18 mm) with 2 lips: upper lip has 2 rounded lobes angled up, bottom lip has 3 lobes spreading down; throat white with 2 ridges and dark nectar guidelines; floral tube glandular-hairy externally, beardtongue tip yellow-hairy.

LEAVES: Basal; blades lance- to spatula-shaped, ¾–4 inches long (2–10 cm) to ⅝ inch wide (15 mm); edges toothed, surfaces hairless, base tapered, tip blunt to pointed. Stem leaves similar, opposite, 3–5 pairs.

HABITAT: Coarse soils; grasslands, sagebrush, foothills, montane forests. Elevation 5,250–9,000 feet (1,600–2,743 m).

Wand-bloom Penstemon

Penstemon virgatus, Plantain Family, Plantaginaceae; Perennial herb

QUICK ID: Look for stems with hairless white, pink, lavender, purple, or violet flowers along one side; red guidelines; hairless beardtongue.

RANGE: SR; widespread, common

STEM: Erect, 1–7 from base, 8–25 inches tall (20–65 cm), smooth to short-hairy.

FLOWERS: June–September. Dense, elongated clusters along one side of the stem have flowers ⅝–1 inch long (15–28 mm) with 2 lips: upper 2 lobes slanted up; lower 3 lobes angled downward; floral tube exterior hairless; throat interior smooth to sparsely white-hairy with red nectar guidelines; beardtongue hairless.

LEAVES: Basal often absent. Stem leaves opposite, 5–11 pairs; blades linear to narrowly lance-shaped, 2⅜–4¾ inches long (6–12 cm), ½–¾ inch wide (12–20 mm), margins entire, surface smooth to short-hairy, tip pointed to blunt.

HABITAT: Coarse soils, open forests, roadsides; foothills, montane, subalpine forests. Elevation 6,100–9,500 feet (1,825–2,895 m).

Whipple's Penstemon

Penstemon whippleanus, Plantain Family, Plantaginaceae; Perennial herb

QUICK ID: Look for widely separated, one-sided clusters with purple to violet, densely glandular-hairy flowers; lower lip white-hairy.

RANGE: MR, SR; widespread, common

STEM: Erect, 8–25 inches tall (20–65 cm), lower smooth, top hairy.

FLOWERS: June–September. Flower stalks and calyx glandular-hairy; flowers dark violet to pink lavender, ¾–1⅛ inches long (2–3 cm) with 2 forward-pointing lips: 2 upper lobes, 3 longer lower lobes with white hairs; floral tube inflated, glandular-hairy externally, interior with white nectar guidelines, beardtongue tip smooth to yellow-hairy.

LEAVES: Basal, stalked; blades lance-shaped, elliptic or oval, 1½–5 inches long (4–13 cm); edges entire to toothed, surfaces hairless, tip sharp to blunt. Stem leaves opposite, 2–5 pairs, clasping.

HABITAT: Coarse soils; meadows, openings; foothills, montane, subalpine forests. Elevation 7,500–13,000 feet (2,286–3,962 m).

Wilcox's Penstemon

Penstemon wilcoxii, Plantain Family, Plantaginaceae; Perennial herb

QUICK ID: Look for leaves with fine teeth, whorls of blue, glandular-hairy flowers separated along the stem, yellow-hairy beardtongue.

RANGE: NR; widespread, common

STEM: Erect, 12–40 inches tall (30–100 cm), smooth to short-hairy.

FLOWERS: May–August. Flower stalks and the calyx cupping the petals glandular-hairy; flowers light blue to violet, ½–1 inch long (13–23 mm) with 2 lips: upper 2 lobes curl up; lower 3 point forward; floral tube exterior densely glandular-hairy; throat interior pale, sparsely hairy with 2 ridges and dark nectar guide-lines; beardtongue tip densely yellow-hairy.

LEAVES: Basal, long-stalked; blades triangular to elliptic, 1–3½ inches long (3–9 cm) to 2 inches wide (5 cm); edges with spaced teeth, surfaces smooth to short-hairy, tip pointed. Stem leaves similar, opposite, 2–5 pairs, base tapered to clasping, tip sharp to blunt.

HABITAT: Dry, rocky soils; slopes; openings; sagebrush, foothills, montane forests. Elevation 984–7,545 feet (300–2,300 m).

Wyoming Kittentails

Synthyris wyomingensis, Plantain Family, Plantaginaceae; Perennial herb

QUICK ID: Look for sharp-toothed basal leaves; short woolly stalks with dense cluster of flowers with showy purple stamens but no petals.

RANGE: NR, MR, Canada; scattered, rare to locally common

STEM: Erect to lax, 1 to few, 4–16 inches tall (10–40 cm), soft, white-hairy.

FLOWERS: April–August. Dense, cylindrical, woolly spikes on stem ends are packed with tiny flowers with no petals; 2 stamens have red to purple filaments, 3⁄16–½ inch long (5–12 mm).

LEAVES: Basal, long stalked, blades oblong to lance-shaped, ¾–2¾ inches long (2–7 cm); edges strongly toothed, surfaces soft woolly-hairy. Stem leaves alternate, smaller, unstalked.

HABITAT: Meadows, open woods, fellfields; grasslands to alpine. Elevation 3,000–12,000 feet (915–3,658 m).

Pale Trumpets

Ipomopsis longiflora, Phlox Family, Polemoniaceae; Annual or biennial herb

QUICK ID: Look in arid habitats for slender stems with clusters of light blue to white, trumpet-shaped flowers with long floral tubes.

RANGE: MR, SR; widespread, common

STEM: Erect to branching, 4–24 inches tall (10–60 cm), smooth to sparsely hairy.

FLOWERS: May–September. Open clusters of 1–3 trumpet-shaped, flowers on branch tips; floral tube, white to pale blue or pale purple, 1–2 inches long (25–50 mm), spreading open with 5 lobes, tips pointed; stamens inside or extending slightly beyond the throat.

LEAVES: Alternate. Blades ¾–2 inches long (2–5 cm) with 5–7 thread-like, linear segments along the midrib; surfaces smooth to sparsely hairy.

HABITAT: Coarse soils; arid plains, sagebrush, pinyon-juniper, ponderosa woodlands. Elevation: 3,800–7,400 feet (1,158–2,255 m).

SIMILAR SPECIES: Iron skyrocket, *I. laxiflora*, (prairies of eastern Colo., NM) has flowers only reaching 1 inch long (25 mm).

Dwarf Skyrocket

Ipomopsis pumila, Phlox Family, Polemoniaceae; Annual herb

QUICK ID: Look in arid habitats for short plants with hairy stems and clusters of small, lavender funnel flowers with spreading petal lobes.

RANGE: MR, SR; widespread, locally common

STEM: Erect, branching, 1–7 inches tall (3–18 cm), short-glandular to short-woolly hairy.

FLOWERS: March–September. Dense rounded clusters on branch tips. Flowers tubular, ⅛–⅜ inch long (4–8 mm), with 5 spreading petal lobes, lavender to pink or purplish, tips rounded to pointed; anthers blue, protruding.

LEAVES: Basal deeply lobed, usually wither by flowering. Stem leaves alternate, ⅜–1½ inches long (1–4 cm), lobed to entire, surfaces nearly hairless to short-woolly, bristle tipped.

HABITAT: Sandy, rocky soils; arid shrub lands, sagebrush, pinyon-juniper foothills. Elevation 4,000–7,000 feet (1,220–2,134 m).

Tall Jacob's Ladder

Polemonium foliosissimum, Phlox Family, Polemoniaceae; Perennial herb

QUICK ID: Look for tall stems, pinnately compound leaves, rounded clusters of bell-shaped, blue flowers, and 5 spreading petals.

RANGE: MR, SR: widespread, common; NR: isolated

STEM: Erect, clumping, branching, 1–3 feet tall (30–100 cm), smooth to long-hairy.

FLOWERS: June–August. Glandular-hairy clusters have 2-3 symmetrical flowers with 5 oval petal lobes ¼–¾ inch long (6–20 mm), blue to purple or pink, occasionally white or cream, with dark lines and a whitish-green throat.

LEAVES: Alternate. Blades pinnately compound, 1⅛–4 inches long (3–10 cm) with 11–27 leaflets, oval to elliptic, 3⁄16–1 inch long (5–25 mm); surfaces smooth to glandular-hairy; smelly when crushed.

HABITAT: Coarse soils, riparian, disturbed areas; montane, subalpine forests, alpine. Elevation 6,800–10,600 feet.

SIMILAR SPECIES: Showy Jacob's Ladder, *P. pulcherrimum*, (all regions) is 4–10 inches tall (10–25 cm), flower throat white or yellow.

Showy Jacob's Ladder

Polemonium pulcherrimum, Phlox Family, Polemoniaceae; Perennial herb

QUICK ID: Look for clustered stems with pinnate leaves; bell-shaped, showy flowers with blue-to-violet petals; and usually a yellow throat.

RANGE: NR, MR, SR, Canada; widespread, common

STEM: Erect, branched from base, 4–10 inches tall (10–25 cm), smooth to sparsely glandular-hairy.

FLOWERS: May–August. Congested to loose clusters with flowers ¼–½ inch long and wide (7–14 mm); 5 petal lobes, light blue to violet, rarely white, strongly lined, equal to twice as long as the tube.

LEAVES: Mostly basal, pinnately compound, 3–4 inches long (8–10 cm) with 11–25 oval leaflets, surfaces long-hairy to glandular. Stem leaves alternate, smaller.

HABITAT: Moist, open woods, meadows; montane, subalpine forests. Elevation 6,000–12,500 feet, (1,828–3,510 m).

Sky Pilot

Polemonium viscosum, Phlox Family, Polemoniaceae; Perennial herb

QUICK ID: Look for low-growing, dense clumps of glandular-smelly, compound leaves with small leaflets, and clusters of blue flowers.

RANGE: NR, MR, SR: widespread, common; Canada: rare

STEM: Dwarfed, branched from base, 4–12 inches tall (10–30 cm), densely glandular-hairy.

FLOWERS: June–August. Clusters spherical to fan-shaped, flowers funnel-shaped, ¾–1 inch long (17-25 mm), longer than wide, 5 petal lobes shorter than the tube; anthers yellow to orange.

LEAVES: Mostly basal; blade to 8 inches long (20 cm), pinnately compound with 17–21 crowded leaflets, each deeply cut into 2-5 lobes appearing whorled; surfaces densely glandular-hairy, skunky smelling.

HABITAT: Rocky ridges, slopes, fellfields, tundra: subalpine, alpine, Elevation 9,600–13,200 feet (2,926–4,010 m).

SIMILAR SPECIES: Rocky Mountain Jacob's Ladder, *P. confertum*, (CO; often lumped with *P. viscosum*) has spherical clusters.

Alpine Primrose

Primula angustifolia, Primrose Family, Primulaceae; Perennial herb

QUICK ID: Look in alpine habitats for low-growing plants covered with small flowers with magenta petals and a yellow throat.

RANGE: SR; widespread, locally common

STEM: Mat forming, ⅜–3 inches tall (1–8 cm), hairless.

FLOWERS: June–August. Flowers ¾ inch wide (19 mm) on stalks 1–4 inches tall (3–10 cm); 5 oblong, notched petals, occasionally white.

LEAVES: Basal, clump forming. Blade linear to narrowly lance-shaped, to ¾ inch long (17 mm); margins entire or with a few teeth, surfaces hairless. Leaves tend to fold lengthwise.

HABITAT: Moist gravelly soils, scree slopes, ridges; subalpine meadows, alpine tundra. Elevation 11,000–14,000 feet (3,352–4,267 m).

SIMILAR SPECIES: Alpine Forget-me-not, *Eritrichium nanum*, is blue with a yellow throat. Pink-colored phlox do not have a yellow center.

Parry's Primrose

Primula parryi, Primrose Family, Primulaceae; Perennial herb

QUICK ID: Look near timberline for clumps of erect basal leaves and clusters of magenta flowers with 5 petals and a yellow throat.

RANGE: NR, MR, SR; widespread, common

STEM: Flower stalk erect, leafless, 6–20 inches tall (15–50 cm), smooth to glandular-hairy.

FLOWERS: June–August. Rounded to elongated clusters at stem tips have 5–25 flowers ⅜–1 inch wide (10–25 mm); 5 petals, oval.

LEAVES: Basal rosette; blades erect, broadly lance-shaped to elliptic or oblong, 1½–12 inches long (4–30 cm) by ⅝–2 inches wide (15–50 mm); edges entire or with tiny teeth, surfaces smooth to glandular-hairy; fetid smelling.

HABITAT: Wet meadows, bogs, stream sides; upper subalpine, alpine tundra. Elevation 8,860–13,780 feet (2,700–4,200 m).

Shooting Star

Primula pauciflora (Dodecatheon pulchellum), Primrose Family, Primulaceae; Perennial herb

QUICK ID: Look in damp soils for basal rosettes with broad oval leaves and flower stalks with clusters of nodding flowers with magenta petals folded backward and stamens pointed forward.

RANGE: NR, MR, SR, Canada; widespread, common

STEM: Erect, leafless, 4–18 inches tall (10–45 cm), smooth.

FLOWERS: April–August. Loose clusters have 2–15 flowers; buds and flowers nod downward; 5 magenta petal lobes ¼–⅝ inch long (7–15 mm) pointed upwards, with a wavy red line around the white throat; stamen pollen sacs maroon, point downward like a dart point.

LEAVES: Basal; blade 1½–4 inches long (4–20 cm), 1 inch wide (3 cm) in middle tapering to a point, margins entire, surfaces hairless.

HABITAT: Damp woods, wet meadows, seeps; montane forests. Elevation: 7,900–12,200 feet (2,408–3,718 m).

Monkshood

Aconitum columbianum, Buttercup Family, Ranunculaceae; Perennial herb

QUICK ID: Look for flowers with a hood-like, petal-like upper sepal and large leaves with deeply cut lobes; all parts are toxic.

RANGE: NR, MR, SR, Canada; widespread, common

STEM: Erect leafy, hairy, 1-6 feet tall (30-180 cm).

FLOWERS: June–September. Spikes have blue, rarely whitish flowers, each ¾-2 inches long (18–50 mm), with 5 hairy, petal-like sepals: 1 forms the upper hood, 2 the rounded side sepals, and 2 the narrow lower sepals. The hood contains the 2 small, spurred petals with the nectaries that attract long-tongued bumblebees for pollination.

LEAVES: Basal, alternate on stem becoming stemless (sessile) upward. Blade 1-6¾ inches long (3-17 cm), 2-5½ inches wide (5-14 cm), palmately divided (palm/finger-shaped) into 3-5 lobes with variable-size teeth.

HABITAT: Moist slopes, meadows, stream sides; montane, subalpine forests. Elevation 5,900-12,000 feet (1,800-3,650 m).

Pasqueflower

Anemone patens (Pulsatilla patens), Buttercup Family, Ranunculaceae; Perennial herb

QUICK ID: Look for dainty, pale-blue-to-whitish flowers with densely hairy stems. Early blooming in mountains, often in melting snow.

RANGE: NR, MR, SR, Canada; widespread, common

STEM: Erect, unbranched, 6-15 inches tall (15-38 cm), long-hairy.

FLOWERS: April–August. Solitary, cup-shaped, 1½-3 inches wide (4-8 cm) with 5-8 oblong, petal-like sepals and 150+ yellow stamens; 3 densely long-hairy, leaf-like bracts whorl at mid-stem. Seed cluster has slender, hairy plumes.

LEAVES: Basal, 5-8 leaves on stalks 2-4 inches long (5-10 cm). Blades oval, hairy, palmately divided into 3 leaflets, each deeply segmented into narrow lobes.

HABITAT: Dry, open woodlands, moist meadows; montane transition to subalpine forests. Elevation 6,500-10,000 feet (1,980-3,050 m).

SIMILAR SPECIES: Western Pasqueflower, *A. occidentalis,* (NR, Canada) typically has white flowers.

Colorado Blue Columbine

Aquilegia coerulea (Aquilegia caerulea), Buttercup Family, Ranunculaceae; Perennial herb

QUICK ID: Look for dramatic blue-and-white flowers, long spurs on the base, and small, fan-shaped leaflets.

RANGE: SR, MR: widespread; NR: uncommon

STEM: Erect, multiple 1–3 feet tall (30–90 cm).

FLOWERS: June–August. Pale- to dark-blue-and-white flowers are 2–3 inches long (5–8 cm) with 5 showy, lance-shaped sepals 1–2 inches long (28–51 mm) spread perpendicular; 5 white petals have rounded tips and backward-pointing blue spurs 1⅛–2 inches long (3–5 cm).

LEAVES: Basal; alternate, smaller on stem. Blade compound, divided twice in sets of 3, leaflets fan-shaped, each with 2–3 lobes. Basal leaves 3½–14½ inches long (9–37 mm).

HABITAT: Moist soils of shady woodlands, stream banks, meadows, slopes; sagebrush, pinyon-juniper foothills, montane, subalpine forests, tundra. Elevation 6,000–13,000 feet (1,828–3,962 m).

SIMILAR SPECIES: Utah Columbine, *A. scopulorum*, occurs in the Wasatch Mt., Utah.

Columbia Rock Clematis

Clematis columbiana, Buttercup Family, Ranunculaceae; Perennial vine

QUICK ID: Look for trailing, slender vines; nodding, bell-shaped, blue-to-pinkish-purple flowers; and compound leaves with lobed leaflets.

RANGE: NR, MR, SR; widespread, common

STEM: Low climbing, sprawling to 5 feet long (15 m).

FLOWERS: May–July. Blue, purple, or pink (rarely white), bell-shaped with 4 tissue-like petals (sepals), 1–2 inches (3–5 cm) long, not united, slightly hairy, solitary and nodding on the stems. Seed head a bushy bundle of long, silky tails, like a small feather duster.

LEAVES: Opposite. Blade palmately compound with 2–3 lance-shaped leaflets, ⅝–2 inches wide (15–48 mm), each deeply divided 2–3 times into lobes with pointed teeth on margins.

HABITAT: Pinyon-juniper-oak foothills, montane, subalpine forests. Elevation 5,600–10,500 feet (1,700–3,200 m).

SIMILAR SPECIES: Purple Clematis, *C. occidentalis*, (in much the same range) blooms in the spring and has 3 unlobed leaflets.

Hairy Leatherflower

Clematis hirsutissima, Buttercup Family, Ranunculaceae; Perennial herb

QUICK ID: Look for nodding, urn-shaped, hairy, violet-blue flowers, and compound leaves with leaflets deeply cut into 2 or more lobes.

RANGE: NR, MR, SR; widespread, common

STEM: Erect (not vining), hairy stems to 2 feet tall (60 cm).

FLOWERS: May–June. Nodding, bell- to urn-shaped, 1–1¾ inches long (3–5 cm); petal-like sepals thick, dark violet blue, densely hairy, with pointed tips curled back exposing whitish-yellow stamens; seed head a spherical cluster with silky tails.

LEAVES: Opposite. Blades compound with linear to lance-shaped lobed leaflets, each ¾–2⅜ inches long (2–6 cm), less than ⅜ inch wide (1 cm), deeply cut with 2 or more lobes, surfaces hairy.

HABITAT: Slopes, meadows, thickets; pinyon-juniper foothills, montane, subalpine forests. Elevation 2,300–10,825 feet (700–3,300 m).

Subalpine Larkspur

Delphinium barbeyi, Buttercup Family, Ranunculaceae; Perennial herb

QUICK ID: Look for tall, leafy stems; leaves with radiating lobes; and spikes of showy blue-to-purple flowers with rear spurs. Poisonous.

RANGE: SR; widespread, common

STEM: Erect, unbranched 4–6 feet tall (122–182 cm), sticky-hairy.

FLOWERS: June–September. Elongated clusters have 10–50 hairy flowers with 5 blue, petal-like sepals: 1 forms a spur ⅜–¾ inch long (10–18 mm), rear pointing, tip curved, often hooked; 2 small, white upper petals unite to form a small tube that guides insects to the nectar glands at the tip of the spur; 2 blue, hairy, lower petals cover the stamens.

LEAVES: Alternate; leaf stems (petioles) to 5½ inches long (14 cm). Blades rounded, to 5 inches long (13 cm), with 5–9 radiating lobes, each divided again and lined with pointed teeth.

HABITAT: Moist soils; montane, subalpine forests, alpine meadows. Elevation 8,000–12,600 feet (2,438–3,840 m).

Little Larkspur

Delphinium bicolor, Buttercup Family, Ranunculaceae; Perennial herb

QUICK ID: Look for short stems, round leaves with narrow lobes, and dark-blue flowers with spreading side sepals and a rear spur. Toxic.

RANGE: NR, MR, Canada; widespread, locally common

STEM: Erect, unbranched, 4–16 inches tall (10–40 cm), hairy.

FLOWERS: May–July. Elongated clusters have 3-12 dark-blue-to-purple flowers with 5, petal-like sepals: 2 spread sideways, and 1 forms the rear spur, ½–1 inch long (13–23 mm), tip straight to curved; 2 white upper petals, blue-lined, united to form a small tube that guides insects to the nectar glands at the tip of the spur; 2 blue, hairy lower petals cover the stamens. Fruit capsules erect.

LEAVES: Basal, 2-7 at flowering. Alternate, 3–6, mostly on bottom ⅓ of stem. Blades round, ¾–4 inches wide (2–10 cm), divided into 3–19 narrow lobes.

HABITAT: Grasslands, sagebrush, foothills, montane, subalpine forests, alpine. Elevation 3,000–11,600 feet (900–3,500 m).

Dwarf Larkspur

Delphinium nuttallianum, Buttercup Family, Ranunculaceae; Perennial herb

QUICK ID: Look for stems lined with blue-to-purple flowers with spreading petal-like sepals, a rear spur, and spreading fruit capsules.

RANGE: NR, MR, SR, Canada; widespread, common

STEM: Unbranched 4–16 inches tall (10–40 cm).

FLOWERS: May-September. Elongated clusters have 3–18 blue to purple flowers with 5 showy, petal-like, hairy sepals: 2 spread sideways or slightly forward, 1 upper forms a rear spur to ¾ inch long (20 mm), straight or down-curved, 2 lower spread downward; 2 small, white upper petals have blue lines; 2 lower petals are blue with white hairs, cleft ¼–½ way to base, and elevated to expose the stamens.

LEAVES: Basal, alternate on stem; leaf stalks to 4¾ inches long (12 cm). Blades circular in outline, ⅜–2⅜ inches long (1–6 cm), palmately divided into 5-21 narrow lobes, to ¼ inch wide (6 mm).

HABITAT: Grasslands, sagebrush, pinyon-juniper foothills, montane, subalpine forests. Elevation 885–9,540 feet (270–2,900 m).

Tall Mountain Larkspur

Delphinium x occidentale, Buttercup Family, Ranunculaceae; Perennial herb

QUICK ID: Look for tall, robust, leafy stems with dense spikes of deep-blue-to-whitish flowers with rear spurs.

RANGE: NR, MR, SR; widespread, locally common

STEM: Erect, numerous, 24–80 inches tall (60–200 cm), hairless.

FLOWERS: June–August. Cylindric clusters to 14 inches long (35 cm) with more than 25 flowers: 5 hairy, petal-like sepals; 1 upper forms the spur ⅜–⅝ inch long (10–15 mm) angled upward, 2 spread sideways, 2 spread down; 2 upper petals white to pale-blue; 2 lower pale- to dark-blue, oval, barely cleft. Seed capsules erect, narrow.

LEAVES: Basal wither by blooming; stem leaves alternate. Blades palmately compound, 2-6 inches wide (5–15 cm); 3-5 main lobes each divided again into segments.

HABITAT: Moist soils of sagebrush, grasslands, montane, subalpine forests. Elevation 5,200–10,000 feet (1,575–3,030 m).

NOTE: Considered a cross between *Delphiunium barbeyi* × *Delphinium glaucum*.

Mountain Larkspur

Delphinium ramosum, Buttercup Family, Ranunculaceae; Perennial herb

QUICK ID: Look for tall, leafy stems with dense clusters of blue flowers with rear spurs and seed capsules in a tight, erect bundle.

RANGE: SR; widespread, common

STEM: Erect, 28–40 inches tall (70–100 cm), finely hairy.

FLOWERS: June–September. Elongated clusters have 15–40 flowers with 5 bright-blue, hairy, petal-like sepals: 1 upper forms the spur ½ inch long (13 mm), straight; 2 spread sideways, 2 lower spread down; 2 upper petals blue and white; 2 lower petals covered with curly, white hairs; stamens exposed.

LEAVES: Basal absent. Alternate stem leaves present on full length of stem at flowering. Blades rounded in outline reaching 3 inches wide (8 cm) by 5½ inches long (14 cm), with 5-21 narrow, deeply cut lobes.

HABITAT: Sagebrush, montane, subalpine forests, alpine meadows. Elevation 6,500–11,200 feet (1,980-3,114 m).

Purple Mountain Saxifrage

Saxifraga oppositifolia, Saxifrage Family, Saxifragaceae; Perennial herb

QUICK ID: Look in the alpine zone for dense cushions of short stems, overlapping leaves, and small, magenta flowers that can cover plant.

RANGE: NR, MR, Canada; widespread, locally common

STEM: Trailing, leafy, forming mats to 8 inches wide (20 cm) by ¾–3 inches high (2–7 cm), generally smooth.

FLOWERS: May–August. Solitary flower on branch tips, 5 purple to pink petals, spatula-shaped, ¼–⅜ inch long (6–9 mm), veined.

LEAVES: Basal absent. Stem leaves opposite, stalkless; blades oblong to egg-shaped, 3/16 inch long (1–5 mm), edges bristly-hairy, bottom surface hairy or smooth depending on variety.

HABITAT: Meadows, slopes, rocky outcrops; upper subalpine forest, alpine. Elevation near treeline to 13,000 feet (4,000 m).

SIMILAR SPECIES: In the alpine, look for Whiplash Saxifrage, *S. flagellaris*, (SR, MR) with yellow flowers and red runners that root.

Dakota Mock Vervain

Glandularia bipinnatifida, Verbena Family, Verbenaceae; Perennial herb

QUICK ID: Look for low, clump-forming, square stems; hairy, lobed leaves; and rounded clusters of small, purple-to-pink flowers. Flower color, leaf division, and hairiness are highly variable.

RANGE: MR: infrequent; SR: widespread, common

STEM: Erect to sprawling, branching from base, 4–24 inches tall (10–61 cm), hairy.

FLOWERS: March–October. Rounded clusters dense with ½ inch long (12 mm) by ⅜ inch wide (10 mm) tubular flowers, each with 5 purple, pink, or lavender petals with deep, rounded notches, especially the bottom-middle one; the floral tube extends beyond the sepals.

LEAVES: Opposite. Blade shape 1–2½ inches long and wide (3–6 cm), divided into narrow lobes that are divided again into narrow, pointed lobes; surfaces hairy.

HABITAT: Dry, sandy, gravelly soils; prairie, scrublands, foothills, montane forests. Elevation 3,650–8,500 feet (1,066–2,490 m).

Big-bract Verbena

Verbena bracteata, Verbena Family, Verbenaceae; Annual herb, weedy

QUICK ID: Look for leafy, hairy, 4-sided stems; lobed leaves; and spikes of tiny, blue or purple flowers with long, leaf-like bracts.

RANGE: MR, SR: widespread, common; NR, Canada: infrequent

STEM: Sprawling, branched from base, to 1 foot tall (30 cm) by 2 feet long (60 cm), long white hairs throughout.

FLOWERS: April–October. Terminal spike to 6 inches long (15 cm) with leaf-like bracts beneath each flower; flowers funnel-shaped, ⅛ inch wide (3 mm) with 5 rounded petal-lobes that are blue, lavender, or purple; bracts long-hairy, narrow, pointed, 5/16–⅝ inch long (8–15 mm).

LEAVES: Opposite with a winged or flattened stalk to ¾ inch long (2 cm). Blades ⅜–2⅜ inches long (1–6 cm), usually 3-lobed with the central lobe largest, lobes coarsely toothed; surfaces long-hairy.

HABITAT: Coarse soils, disturbed areas; grasslands, sagebrush, foothills, montane forests. Elevation 3,000–9,000 feet (915–2,743 m).

Spike Verbena

Verbena macdougalii, Verbena Family, Verbenaceae; Perennial herb

QUICK ID: Look in mountain openings for clumps of tall, hairy, 4-sided stems; hairy, toothed leaves; and elongating spikes tipped with a ring of small, purple flowers.

RANGE: SR; widespread, common

STEM: Erect, branched, 1–3 feet tall (30–90 cm), densely long-hairy.

FLOWERS: June–October. Dense spikes bloom in a ring from the bottom up with tube-shaped flowers; 5 petal-lobes, each ¼ inch wide (6 mm), purple to dark blue.

LEAVES: Opposite, short stalked. Blades narrowly elliptic to oval, 1⅝–4 inches long (4–10 cm); edges have coarse, irregular teeth; surfaces densely hairy, veins prominent, tips pointed.

HABITAT: Meadows, open woods, disturbed areas; foothills, montane forests. Elevation 5,900–9,000 feet (1,800–2,743 m).

SIMILAR SPECIES: Also tall, Blue Verbena, *V. hastata*, (scattered, all regions) favors moist soils and has short, flat-lying hairs throughout.

Hooked-spur Blue Violet

Viola adunca, Violet Family, Violaceae; Perennial herb

QUICK ID: Look for dense basal clumps of egg-shaped leaves, branching stems, and blue flowers; the lowest petal has a rear spur.

RANGE: NR, MR, SR, Canada; most common blue violet in the Rockies

STEM: Erect, ¾–12 inches tall (2–30 cm), smooth to short-hairy.

FLOWERS: April–August. Leafless stalks to 4 inches long (10 cm), have a single flower ¼–⅝ inch long (5–15 mm) with 5 pale-blue-to-violet petals: upper 2 dark-lined; side 2 often whitish, dark-lined with white beard at base, often curled back; bottom petal dark-lined with rear spur, straight, curved, or hooked at tip.

LEAVES: Basal, long stalked; blades egg-shaped, ¼–1¾ inches long (5–47 mm) to 1¾ inches wide (45 mm); edges with rounded teeth, surfaces smooth to short-hairy. Stem leaves alternate, smaller.

HABITAT: Meadows, riparian, damp wood; montane, subalpine forests. Elevation 7,100–11,700 feet (2,164–3,566 m).

Northern Bog Violet

Viola nephrophylla, Violet Family, Violaceae; Perennial herb

QUICK ID: Look in damp soils for leafy clumps with heart- to kidney-shaped leaves and blue flowers on stalks directly from the roots.

RANGE: NR, MR, SR, Canada; widespread, common

STEM: No stem; leaves and flower on stalks directly from roots.

FLOWERS: June–August. Leafless stalk 2–6 inches long (5–15 cm) directly from rhizomes; 5 petals, light to dark blue or white, ¾ inch long and wide (20 mm), throat white with dark-blue lines; 2 lateral petals bearded with tiny hairs; nubby rear spur, ⅛ inch long (3 mm).

LEAVES: Basal. Clumps of 20–30 leaves from roots on stalks 1–6 inches long (3–15 cm). Blades 1–4 inches long and wide (3–10 cm); edges entire or lined with small, uniform, rounded teeth; surfaces usually smooth, tips rounded to pointed.

HABITAT: Wet soils, meadows, riparian; foothills, montane, subalpine forests, alpine. Elevation 5,600–10,400 feet (1,707–3,170 m).

Gray's Angelica

Angelica grayi, Parsley Family, Apiaceae; Perennial herb

QUICK ID: Look in moist, high-elevation habitats for stout stems with pinnately compound, sheathing leaves tipped with umbrella-like clusters of tiny, brownish-white flowers.

RANGE: SR; scattered, locally common

STEM: Erect, unbranched, 1-2 feet tall (30-60 cm), hollow.

FLOWERS: July–September. Umbrella-shaped clusters have 10-25 radiating stalks (rays) 1-2 inches long (3-5 cm); each ray tipped with a small, dense, spherical cluster of tiny brownish-white flowers; conspicuous, narrow, lance-shaped bractlets, ¼–¾ inch wide (6-20 mm), with tapering tips beneath each small cluster.

LEAVES: Alternate, sheathed around stem; blades 1-2 pinnate with leaflets along midrib; leaflets lance-shaped to oval, pointed, ¾-2 inches long (2-5 cm); edges toothed, sometimes lobed.

HABITAT: Moist meadows, scree slopes; montane, subalpine forests, alpine. Elevation 9,800-13,420 feet (2,987-4,090 m).

Western Coneflower

Rudbeckia occidentalis, Aster Family, Asteraceae; Perennial herb

QUICK ID: Look for tall, stout stems; broad, smooth leaves; and flower heads with leaf-like phyllaries, no rays, and brown columnar disk.

RANGE: NR, MR; widespread, common

STEM: Erect, little branched, 20–78 inches tall (50-200 cm), smooth to hairy near top, colony forming.

FLOWERS: June–September. Long stalks have solitary flower heads with no petal-like rays, disk a dark brown column to 2 inches long (5 cm); phyllaries spread beneath disk in 2-3 rows, narrow, pointed, to 1 inch long (3 cm), sparsely hairy.

LEAVES: Basal; blades elliptic to broadly oval, 4¾-12 inches long (12-30 cm), edges entire to coarsely toothed, surfaces smooth to short-hairy, tips pointed. Stem leaves alternate, broadly lance-shaped, upper stem leaves stalkless.

HABITAT: Moist meadows, seeps, open woods; foothills, montane forests. Elevation 3,280-9,500 feet (1,000-2,895 m).

Cocklebur

Xanthium strumarium, Aster Family, Asteraceae; Annual herb

QUICK ID: Look in damp soils for robust stems with large, triangular, rough leaves; tiny flowers; and clusters of ovular, hooked burs.

RANGE: NR, MR, SR: widespread, common; Canada: infrequent

STEM: Erect, branched, 1-3 feet tall (30-90 cm), smooth to stiff-hairy.

FLOWERS: April-October. Separate male and female flower heads have inconspicuous brownish to greenish flowers; spherical male flower clusters have 20-60 tiny disk florets at the top on the stem; female flowers in the leaf axils have 2 exposed stigma lobes. Seed pods oval, ¾-1½ inches long (2-4 cm), green turning brown; covered with stout, hooked prickles.

LEAVES: Alternate, long stalked. Blades 1½-7 inches long (4-18 cm), triangular to oval with shallow lobes; edges coarsely toothed, surfaces rough-hairy.

HABITAT: Drainages, disturbed areas; arid grasslands, sagebrush, foothills, montane forests. Elevation 3,600-8,000 feet (2,000-2,438 m).

Canada Buffaloberry

Shepherdia canadensis, Oleaster family, Elaeagnaceae; Deciduous shrub

QUICK ID: Look for a thornless shrub with elliptic leaves with bottoms dotted with silver hairs and brown scales, and small red berries.

RANGE: NR, MR, SR, Canada; widespread, common

STEM: Upright, rounded, branched, 3-7 feet tall and wide (1-2 m).

FLOWERS: April-July. Flowers inconspicuous, male and female separate on same plant; sepals 4-lobed, brownish yellow, to ⅛ inch long (3 mm). Berries, red, oval, fleshy, ¼-⅜ inch long (6-9 mm).

LEAVES: Opposite, stalked; blade elliptic to oval, 1-3 inches long (3-7 cm), base rounded; edges entire, flat; top surface green, sparsely dotted with hair; bottom dotted with silver, star-shaped hairs and brown scales.

HABITAT: Open woods, slopes, stream sides; montane, subalpine forests. Elevation 7,500-10,800 feet (2,300-3,270 m).

SIMILAR SPECIES: Silver Buffaloberry, *S. argentea*, (all regions) is thorny with narrow, oblong leaves with silvery hairs on both sides.

Clustered Lady's Slipper Orchid

Cypripedium fasciculatum, Orchid Family, Orchidaceae; Perennial herb

QUICK ID: Look for stems with 2 large, oval leaves and clusters of small, reddish-brown, nodding flowers with a slipper-like lower petal.

RANGE: NR, MR, SR; scattered, rare

STEM: Erect, clustered, 2–14 inches tall (6–35 cm).

FLOWERS: April–August. Clusters of 2–4; petals and sepals mottled dark reddish brown: 2 twisted petals, each ⅝–1 inch long (15–25 mm), spread sideways; one upper sepal arcs above the flower and two fused into one curl below. The small, pouch-like lip has a greenish bottom and brown-tinted around the opening. Using "deceit pollination," the plant emits a fetid scent to attract tiny wasps or flies for pollination but provides no nectar reward.

LEAVES: Opposite, 2 near mid-stem, blades elliptic to oval, 1½–4¾ inches long (4–12 cm) by 1–3 inches wide (3–8 cm).

HABITAT: Dry to moist, shady forests; montane, subalpine forests. Elevation 1,000–10,500 feet (330–3,200 m).

Stream Orchid

Epipactis gigantea, Orchid Family, Orchidaceae; Perennial herb

QUICK ID: Look for tall, leafy stems lined with brownish-yellow orchid flowers, often forming colonial stands in streams or wetlands.

RANGE: NR, MR, SR, Canada; scattered, infrequent

STEM: Erect, leafy, branching, 1–4 feet tall (30–120 cm). Colonies can reach 1,000 plants.

FLOWERS: April–July. Upper stem has 18–32 small, showy flowers 1½ inches wide (4 cm) with 3 lance-shaped sepals to ¾ inch long (2 cm) lined with dark veins; 2 upper petals similar to sepals, ⅝ inch long (15 mm) by ¼ inch wide (7 mm). Lower petal (lip) is hinged and movable, with 2 rounded side lobes with red to purple veins, and a central lobe, rose-colored, triangular, flattened.

LEAVES: Alternate. Blades elliptic to lance-shaped, 2¾–10 inches long (7–25 cm), ⅜–2¾ inches wide (1–7 cm), with parallel veins and clasping the stem, smaller towards top.

HABITAT: Wet soils, meadows, streams, lakes; pinyon-juniper foothills, montane forests. Elevation 3,000–8,000 ft (914–2,438 m).

Purple (Water) Avens

Geum rivale, Rose Family, Rosaceae; Perennial herb

QUICK ID: Look for reddish stems; long, basal leaves lined with large and small leaflets; and clusters of 3-7 nodding, brownish-red flowers.

RANGE: NR, MR, SR, Canada; widespread, common

STEM: Erect, branching, 1-2 feet tall (30-60 cm), hairy.

FLOWERS: May–August. Clusters of 3-7 flowers, each to 1 inch wide (25 mm) with 5 dull red to yellowish petals exposed between 5 brownish-purple sepals; many stamens with yellow anthers. Seeds have hairy, hooked tails for animal dispersal.

LEAVES: Basal; blades 4–16 inches long (10–40 cm), pinnately compound with 5-7 large oval to rounded leaflets and 7-14 small ones, terminal leaflet much larger than others; surfaces sparsely hairy, edges serrated. Stem leaves 3-5, smaller, alternate with 3 leaflets.

HABITAT: Stream sides, wet meadows; montane, subalpine forests. Elevation sea level to 6,374 feet (1,943 m).

SIMILAR SPECIES: Prairie Smoke, *G. triflorum*, has opposite stem leaves and 3 flowers.

Lanceleaf Figwort

Scrophularia lanceolata, Figwort Family, Scrophulariaceae; Perennial herb

QUICK ID: Look for tall stems; large, sharp-toothed leaves; and branching, terminal clusters of small, tubular, maroon-tinted flowers.

RANGE: NR, MR, SR, Canada; widespread, common

STEM: Erect, clustered, 3–5 feet tall (80–150 cm), 4 angled, smooth to sparsely glandular-hairy.

FLOWERS: May–July. Much-elongated, open-branching clusters have urn-shaped flowers ⅜–⅝ inch long (9-14 mm), brownish red to yellowish green, with 2 lips: upper lip 2-lobed, flat, pointing forward; lower lip shorter with 3 lobes, the middle folded down.

LEAVES: Opposite, long-stalked; blades lance-shaped to triangular, 4–6 inches long (9-15 cm); edges coarsely toothed, tips pointed, surfaces smooth to glandular-hairy.

HABITAT: Moist meadows, woods, stream sides; sagebrush to subalpine forests. Elevation 4,600–10,800 feet (1,400-2,800 m).

SIMILAR SPECIES: Mountain Figwort, *S. montana*, (NM endemic) has yellowish-green, occasionally maroon-tinted, flowers.

Broad-leaf Cattail

Typha latifolia, Cattail Family, Typhaceae; Perennial herb

QUICK ID: Look in shallow water for erect, long, narrow, flat leaves and long, cylindrical, brown flower clusters on the stem ends.

RANGE: NR, MR, SR, Canada; widespread, common

STEM: Erect, pithy 5–10 feet tall (1.5–3 m), colony forming.

FLOWERS: May–September. Separate male and female spikes packed with tiny flowers without petals or sepals. Brown male spike narrow, to 2⅜ inches long (12 cm); female spike thick, 4–7 inches long (10–18 cm), begins immediately below the male spike with no exposed stem between them. The spike matures as a reddish-brown, cigar-like cluster with fluffy seeds dispersed by wind.

LEAVES: Alternate, 12–16 per stem. Blades light-green, spongy, ⅜–1 inch wide (10–23 mm), about as long as stem.

HABITAT: Wet soils, stream sides, marshes; grasslands to montane forests. Elevation 3,750–9,200 feet (1,143–2,804 m).

Green Milkweed

Asclepias viridiflora, Dogbane Family, Apocynaceae; Perennial herb

QUICK ID: Look for dense, spherical clusters of pale-green flowers that don't open; stout narrow to oval leaves; and milky sap.

RANGE: NR, MR, SR, Canada; widespread, locally common

STEM: Erect, unbranched, 6–15 inches tall (15–38 cm).

FLOWERS: May–September. Rounded clusters in upper leaf axils; 5 green, petal-like lobes that bend back tightly against the stem, 5 erect, green- to purplish-tinged hoods without horns held tightly against, and nearly equal in length, to the anther column. Seed pods 4 inches long (10 cm), pointed, surface smooth.

LEAVES: Opposite to irregularly spaced, on short stems (petioles). Blades highly variable, lance-shaped to oblong, 1½–5⅛ inches long (4–13 cm) by ⅜–2½ inches wide (1–6 cm), margins wavy, surfaces minutely hairy or not.

HABITAT: Prairies, sagebrush, pinyon-juniper-oak foothills. Elevation 4,000–7,300 feet (1,220–2,225 m).

Common Hops

Humulus lupulus var. *neomexicanus*, Hemp Family, Cannabaceae; Perennial, deciduous vine

QUICK ID: Look for sprawling vines with large, deeply lobed leaves and clusters of dangling, cone-like, greenish-yellow flowers.

RANGE: NR, MR, SR, Canada (introduced); scattered, infrequent

STEM: Clambering, climbing, 3–20 feet long (1–6 m), rhizomatous.

FLOWERS: June–October. Female flowers in cone-like clusters with greenish-yellow bracts; clusters ⅜–2⅜ inches long (1–6 cm). Tiny male flowers on separate plants are whitish yellow in spike-like catkins 2¾–6 inches long (7–15 cm). Female flowers are used in brewing beer.

LEAVES: Opposite, on 1–5-inch (3–12 cm) stalks. Blades 1–6 inches long (3–15 cm), deeply cut into 3-7 palmate lobes; edges with sharp teeth, surfaces strongly veined, midrib hairy, tips pointed.

HABITAT: Moist areas, meadows, canyons; foothills, montane, subalpine forests. Elevation: 6,000–9,000 feet (1,830–2,745 m).

Sidebells Wintergreen

Orthilia secunda (Pyrola secunda), Heath Family, Ericaceae; Perennial herb

QUICK ID: Look for small, bell-shaped, whitish-green flowers along one side of a slender stem, and leaves at the base and lower stem.

RANGE: NR, MR, SR, Canada; widespread common

STEM: Erect to nodding, 4–10 inches tall (10–25 cm), smooth.

FLOWERS: June–August. 3–25 bell-shaped, partially opened flowers face downward along one side of stem; 5 oval petals greenish to creamy white; style extends beyond petals.

LEAVES: Basal and alternate in whorls of 3 crowded along lower stem. Blade oval to elliptic ¾–2 inches long (20–50 mm); margins entire to finely toothed; base and tip rounded to pointed.

HABITAT: Forest understory; foothills, montane, subalpine forests, alpine. Elevation 8,200–11,150 feet (2,500–3,505 m).

SIMILAR SPECIES: Green-flowered Wintergreen, *Pyrola chlorantha*, has nodding flowers that spiral around the stem.

Green-flowered Wintergreen

Pyrola chlorantha, Heath Family, Ericaceae; Perennial herb

QUICK ID: Look for rosettes of solid green, rounded leaves and leafless flower stalks with cylindrical clusters of small, nodding, greenish-white flowers with long, extended styles.

RANGE: NR, MR, SR, Canada; widespread, common

STEM: Flower stalk erect, unbranched, 4–10 inches tall (10–25 cm).

FLOWERS: June–August. Cylindrical clusters have 3–9 nodding, greenish-white-to-creamy flowers; style curved, longer than petals.

LEAVES: Basal, long-stalked, sometimes absent. Blades solid green, smooth, leathery, oval to broadly elliptic or rounded, ¾–1 inch long (2–3 cm); edges entire to finely toothed.

HABITAT: Dry to moist leafy forest soils; foothills, montane, subalpine forests. Elevation 6,500–11,000 feet (1,980–3,352 m).

SIMILAR SPECIES: White-vein Wintergreen, *P. picta*, has basal leaves mottled with white veins. Sidebells Wintergreen, *Orthilia secunda*, has clusters of bell-shaped flowers along one side of the stem.

Monument Plant, Elkweed

Frasera speciosa, Gentian Family, Gentianaceae; Perennial herb

QUICK ID: Look for dense basal rosettes with 18-inch (45 cm) leaves and a foot-tall bloom stalk with whorls of greenish-white flowers.

RANGE: NR, MR, SR; widespread, common

STEM: Erect, unbranched, 2–6 feet tall (60–182 cm). The plant adds leaves to the basal rosette for years, then blooms once and dies.

FLOWERS: May–September. Dense to open, elongated clusters in whorls from axils of leafy bracts; 4 petals, each ⅝–¾ inch long (15–20 mm), elliptic, pointed, white to greenish with purplish spots, 2 nectar pits outlined with hair, and a fringed crown around the base.

LEAVES: Basal leaves 6–18 inches long (15–45 cm), 1–6 inches wide (3–15) cm; stem leaves (bracts) in whorls of 3–5, reduced upward.

HABITAT: Meadows, open forests; sagebrush, foothills, montane, subalpine, alpine. Elevation 6,200–10,500 feet (1,890–3,200 m).

SIMILAR SPECIES: Clustered Green Gentian, *F. fastigiata*, (NR) has dense clusters of blue to purple flowers on the stem tip.

Tall Green Bog Orchid

Platanthera huronensis, Orchid Family, Orchidaceae; Perennial herb

QUICK ID: Look for spikes of small, fragrant, whitish-green flowers with short, curved, cylindrical to club-shaped rear spurs.

RANGE: NR, MR, SR, Canada; widespread, common

STEM: Erect, slender, 8–40 inches tall (20–100 cm).

FLOWERS: June–August. Spines dense to loose with 50-100 flowers ⅜–⅝ inch long (10–15 mm); 2 side sepals usually spread to the side; 1 upper sepal and 2 upper petals form a hood over the stamen column; lip petal ½ inch long (12 mm), points downward, tapered, base slightly wider than rounded, swollen tip; rear spur about as long as the lip. In newly opened flowers, the lip curves up, covering the column.

LEAVES: Alternate, few, erect, well-spaced. Blades oblong to lance-shaped, 2–12 inches long (5–30 cm), smaller up the stem.

HABITAT: Wet soils, bogs, meadows, drainages; montane, subalpine forests, alpine. Elevation 7,000–12,000 feet (2,133–3,656 m).

SIMILAR SPECIES: Northern Green Orchid, *P. aquilonis*, has yellow-green flowers.

Slender Bog Orchid

Platanthera stricta, Orchid Family, Orchidaceae; Perennial herb

QUICK ID: Look in wet soils for spikes of small, fragrant, yellowish-green flowers with short rear spurs with pouch-like tips.

RANGE: NR, Canada: widespread, common; MR, SR: infrequent

STEM: Erect, slender, 8–40 inches tall (20–100 cm).

FLOWERS: June–August. Spines dense to loose, flowers ⅜–⅝ inch long (1–1.5 cm); 2 side sepals spread or angle back; 1 upper sepal and 2 upper petals form a hood over the stamen column; lip petal linear to lance-shaped, to ⅜ inch long (9 mm), points forward or down; rear spur shorter than lip, has pouch-like tip.

LEAVES: Alternate, few, well-spaced, often spreading to 90 degrees from stem; blades linear lance-shaped to oblong-pointed, 1–12 inches long (3–32 cm), smaller up the stem.

HABITAT: Wet soils, bogs, drainages; foothills, montane, subalpine forests. Elevation 3,000–8,000 feet (914–2,438 m).

SIMILAR SPECIES: Round-leaved Bog Orchid, *P. orbiculata*, has paired basal leaves.

Curly Dock

Rumex crispus, Buckwheat Family, Polygonaceae; Perennial herb, introduced, noxious

QUICK ID: Look for a basal rosette and robust stems; long leaves with crinkly edges; and dense clusters of tiny, greenish flowers and red, wafer-like seed capsules.

RANGE: NR, MR, SR, Canada; widespread, common, naturalized

STEM: Erect, upper branching 15–40 inches tall (40–100 cm), smooth to sparsely hairy.

FLOWERS: March–October. Dense elongated whorls, each have 10–25 small flowers ¼ inch wide (6 mm); 6 rounded to oval tepals, 3 fuse to form a showy, reddish-brown, paper-like disk with 3 wings around 1 embedded seed. Each wing has a rice-like tubercle called a grain.

LEAVES: Basal rosette, alternate on stem. Blades long stalked, narrowly elliptic to lance-shaped, 6–12 inches long (15–30 cm) by ¾–2⅜ inches wide (2–6 cm); edges entire, strongly wavy, crinkly.

HABITAT: Moist soils. pastures, disturbed areas; naturalized through all regions. Elevation 3,000–10,000 feet (914–3,050 m).

White Willow Dock

Rumex triangulivalvis, Buckwheat Family, Polygonaceae; Perennial herb

QUICK ID: Look for smooth stems and narrow leaves (no basal leaves); flat, showy clusters of small, greenish-white flowers; and seeds with triangular wings.

RANGE: NR, MR, SR, Canada; widespread, common

STEM: Erect, branched, 12–40 inches tall (30–100 cm), smooth.

FLOWERS: June–September. Branching clusters have whorls of 10–25 flowers, each ⅛ inch long (3 mm), white to yellowish green or pinkish; 6 triangular tepals, 3 fuse to form a rusty-brown, 3-sided winged capsule holding the seed. Each wing has a rice-like tubercle called a grain.

LEAVES: Basal absent. Stem leaves alternate, narrowly lance-elliptic, 2¾–6¼ inches long (7–16 cm) by ¾–2 inches wide (2–5 cm), usually widest in the middle; edges entire, flat; surfaces hairless, faintly veined.

HABITAT: Stream banks, drainages, disturbed areas; sagebrush to montane forests. Elevation 4,000–8,200 feet (1,220–2,500 m).

Fendler's Meadowrue

Thalictrum fendleri, Buttercup Family, Ranunculaceae; Perennial herb

QUICK ID: Look for leafy stems, leaflets with 3 lobes, male flowers with tassel-like dangling red filaments and yellow anthers, and female flowers with short, white stigmas.

RANGE: NR, MR, SR; widespread, common

STEM: Erect, branched, 2–3 feet tall (60–90 cm), smooth, colonial.

FLOWERS: June–August. Open-branching clusters have small flowers with 4 greenish-white sepals, no petals. Male and female flowers on separate plants: males have dangling stamens, filaments reddish, anthers yellow; females more erect with white-to-purplish stigmas.

LEAVES: Alternate, compound. The main leaf stem divides into 3–4 sets with three leaflets; leaflets rounded to triangular, ⅜–¾ inch long (1–2 cm), 3 lobes near tip.

HABITAT: Moist forests, riparian areas, drainages; foothills, montane, subalpine forests. Elevation 5,300–10,000 feet (1,615–3,048 m).

SIMILAR SPECIES: Purple (Tall) Meadowrue, *T. dasycarpum*, (all regions) has male flowers with white filaments.

Five-stamen Miterwort

Mitella pentandra, Saxifrage Family, Saxifragaceae; Perennial herb

QUICK ID: Look for beds of rounded leaves and slender, leafless stalks lined with tiny, odd-looking, green flowers with 5 minuscule petals cut onto rows of hair-like lobes.

RANGE: NR, MR, SR, Canada; widespread, common

STEM: Flower stalks 1–3, erect, 3–19 inches tall (8–48 cm), smooth to glandular-hairy, rhizomatous, colony forming.

FLOWERS: June–August. Spike-like clusters on all sides of stalk with 6–25 flowers. Tiny, saucer-shaped flowers with 5 greenish petals, each dissected into 5–11 linear, thread-like lobes spreading opposite each other.

LEAVES: Basal on long stalks; blades heart-shaped, 1–3⅜ inches long and wide (23–85 mm); edges shallowly lobed, blunt toothed; surfaces hairless to sparsely hairy. Stem leaves 0 or 1.

HABITAT: Moist woods, meadows, slopes; montane, subalpine forests, alpine. Elevation 4,000–11,500 feet (1,220–3,500 m).

Stinging Nettle

Urtica dioica, Nettle Family, Urticaceae; Perennial herb

QUICK ID: Look for prickly stems, leaves with coarse teeth, and dense clusters of small greenish-creamy flowers along the stem in the leaf axils. Contact causes intense itching and burning pain; for relief, immediately wash with soap and water.

RANGE: NR, MR, SR, Canada; widespread, common

STEM: Erect, branching, 2–6 feet tall (60–182 cm); bristly, hollow hairs filled with formic acid cover the stem and leaves.

FLOWERS: May–September. Elongated, densely packed clusters of knobby flowers grow in arching, dangling strands from the leaf axils along most of the stem; male and female flowers on same plant.

LEAVES: Opposite, stalked; blade elliptic to lance-shaped, 2⅜–8 inches long (6–20 cm); edges coarsely toothed, tip pointed, base tapered to rounded; upper surface hairless, bottom with stinging hairs.

HABITAT: Meadows, open woods, stream sides; foothills, montane, subalpine forests. Elevation 5,000–10,800 feet (1,524–3,292 m).

Taper-tip Onion

Allium acuminatum, Onion Family, Alliaceae; Perennial herb

QUICK ID: Look for clusters of grass-like leaves and pink, urn-shaped flowers with spreading, pointed tips; basal leaves wither by flowering. Favors dry soils.

RANGE: SR, MR, NR, Canada (BC); widespread, locally common

STEM: Erect, solitary, round, solid, 4–14 inches tall (10–35 cm).

FLOWERS: April–July. Loose clusters have 10–40 erect small flowers with pink to magenta or white petals (tepals) with tapering, spreading to recurved tips.

LEAVES: Basal from bulb, wither by flowering. Blades 2–3, grass-like, solid, flat, 2¾–12 inches long (7–30 cm) to ⅛ inch wide (3 mm), flat to channeled. Onion scented.

HABITAT: Dry soils of plains, slopes, openings woods; foothills, montane forests. Elevation 2,000–7,000 feet (610–2,134 m).

Short-style Onion

Allium brevistylum, Onion Family, Alliaceae; Perennial herb

QUICK ID: Look for grass-like leaves, flat stems with clusters of erect pink, urn-shaped flowers with the stamens and style deep inside. Favors moist soils.

RANGE: NR, MR, SR; widespread, common

STEM: Flower stem (scape) solitary, flattened, solid, 8–24 inches tall (20–60 cm).

FLOWERS: June–August. Erect, loose-flowered clusters (umbels) have 7–20 small flowers with 6 pink to magenta petals (tepals) with sharp-pointed, spreading tips. The stamens and style inside the flowers are only ½ as long as the petals.

LEAVES: Basal from bulb. Blades 2–5, linear, flat, 4–16 inches long (10–40 cm) to ⅜ inch wide (9 mm). Onion scented.

HABITAT: Moist soils of bogs, meadows, stream banks; montane, subalpine forests. Elevation 7,000–11,600 feet (2,130–3,500 m).

Nodding Onion

Allium cernuum, Onion Family, Alliaceae; Perennial herb

QUICK ID: Look for onion-scented, grass-like leaves and stalks with umbrella-like cluster of nodding, urn-shaped, pink-to-white flowers.

RANGE: NR, MR, SR, Canada; widespread, common

STEM: Flowering stem (scape) round, solid, 4–20 inches tall (10–50 cm), abruptly hooked near tip.

FLOWERS: June–October. Nodding cluster of 8–35 small flowers, each with 6 petals (tepals), tips erect (not spreading) and not sharp pointed; stamens and style extend beyond petal tips.

LEAVES: Basal from bulb. Blades 3–5, linear, 4–10 inches long (10–25 cm) to ¼ inch wide (6 mm), flat to channeled, shorter than flower stalk.

HABITAT: Moist, gravelly soils; grasslands, foothills, montane, subalpine forests. Elevation 5,900–10,100 feet (1,800–3,000 m).

Geyer's Onion

Allium geyeri, Onion Family, Alliaceae; Perennial herb

QUICK ID: Look for dense clusters of erect, pinkish, urn-shaped flowers on leafless stalks taller than the grass-like basal leaves.

RANGE: NR, MR, SR, Canada; widespread, common

STEM: Solitary, round to ridged, solid, 4–20 inches tall (10–50 cm).

FLOWERS: June–September. Compact clusters have 10–25 small, pinkish-white flowers (var. *geyeri*), or 0–5 flowers and a cluster of small bulblets (var. *tererus*). Both varieties are widespread from Canada to NM. Bracts under flower usually have 1 vein.

LEAVES: Basal, usually 3 per bulb. Blades linear, 4¾–12 inches long (12–30 cm) to 3/16 inch wide (5 mm); flat to channeled. Onion scented.

HABITAT: Moist mountain meadows, stream sides; foothills montane, subalpine forests, alpine. Elevation 5,300–12,500 feet (1,600–3,810 m).

Wild Chives

Allium schoenoprasum, Onion Family, Alliaceae; Perennial herb

QUICK ID: Look for dense clumps of grass-like, onion-scented leaves and stalks with spherical clusters packed with small, pink flowers.

RANGE: NR, MR: common; SR, Canada: widespread, infrequent

STEM: Flower stalks 8–24 inches tall (20–60 cm), leafless.

FLOWERS: June–September. Stalks 2–12, topped with spherical clusters 1–1½ inches wide (25–37 mm) with 20–50 densely packed flowers; 6 petal-like tepals erect, pink to lavender or white, often with a dark midrib, becoming papery; anthers purple, pollen white; 2 bracts under flower are papery with 5–11 veins.

LEAVES: Basal; typically 2 per bulb; bulbs often clustered. Blade cylindrical, hollow, 8–24 inches long (20–60 cm) to ¼ inch wide (7 mm).

HABITAT: Wet meadows, riparian, disturbed areas; montane, alpine. Elevation 6,000–9,000 feet (1,830–2,473 m).

Tumbleweed, Prickly Russian Thistle

Salsola tragus, Amaranth Family, Amaranthaceae; Annual herb; introduced, invasive

QUICK ID: Look for the rounded shape; dense, interlocking branches; reddish stripes on fresh stems; and tiny, dish-like, pinkish flowers in the leaf axils.

RANGE: NR, MR, SR, Canada; widespread, common, naturalized

STEM: Rounded, many-branched, to 40 inches tall (10 cm), prickly, detaches at base when dies in winter.

FLOWERS: July–October. Solitary in upper leaf axils, 3 spiny green bracts spread beneath 5 pinkish petal-like sepals, each oval, ⅛ inch long (3 mm); no petals.

LEAVES: Alternate. Blades threadlike, ⅜–2 inches long (1–5 cm), becoming rigid, spine-tipped.

HABITAT: Dry sandy, disturbed soils, degraded farms, overgrazed range lands. Elevation 3,500–8,000 feet (1,066–2,438 m).

SIMILAR SPECIES: Slender Russian Thistle, *S. collina*, (throughout) has flowers in a dense spike and a more slender, upright form.

Showy Milkweed

Asclepias speciosa, Dogbane Family, Apocynaceae; Perennial herb

QUICK ID: Look for rounded clusters of showy rose-to-pink flowers; broad, oval leaves with white-woolly bottoms; and milky sap.

RANGE: NR, MR, SR, Canada; widespread, common

STEM: Erect to cluster-forming, 2–4 feet tall (60–120 cm).

FLOWERS: June–August. 5 petal-like lobes bend back against the stem, tips spread outward; 5 radiating, lance-shaped hoods ⅜–⅝ inch long (10–15 mm); narrow, thin horns arch over the central anther column. Seed pods 2¾–4⅜ inches long (7–11 cm), covered with warty prickles; seeds have silky tufts of hair.

LEAVES: Opposite. Blades oval, 2⅜–7¾ inches long (6–20 cm); woolly hairs on bottom, less hair on top, strong parallel veins spread from midrib. Host plant for Monarch butterfly caterpillars.

HABITAT: Grasslands, sagebrush, foothills, montane forests. Elevation 4,500–8,400 feet (1,370–2,560 m).

Rosy Pussytoes

Antennaria rosea, Aster Family, Asteraceae; Perennial herb

QUICK ID: Look for hairy stems 4–12 inches tall (10–30 cm) with dense clusters of 3–20 small, red, bristly flower heads.

RANGE: NR, MR, SR, Canada; widespread, common

STEM: Erect, densely white-woolly hairy, with spreading stolons.

FLOWERS: May–August. Tight clusters of 3–20 heads, each ⅜ inch long (10 mm); tiny florets obscured by thick tufts of erect, white bristles; reddish phyllaries (white or brown) tightly clasp the heads.

LEAVES: Basal, often mat forming. Blades 1-nerved, oval to spatula-shaped, reaching 1⅜ inches long (4 cm), gray-hairy, tips pointed. Stem leaves smaller, linear, alternate.

HABITAT: Pinyon-juniper foothills, montane, subalpine forests, alpine tundra, and fellfields. Elevation 6,000–13,000 feet (1,828–4,000 m).

Lesser (Common) Burdock

Arctium minus, Aster Family, Asteraceae; Biennial herb; introduced, naturalized, invasive

QUICK ID: Look for clusters of purplish-pink, thistle-like flower heads; broad, oval leaves; and bur-like seed capsules.

RANGE: NR, MR, SR, Canada; widespread, common

STEM: Erect, to 5 feet tall (1.5 m), colony forming.

FLOWERS: April–September. Flower heads dome-shaped, ¾–1 inch wide (20–25 mm) and packed with purplish-to-pink disk florets; extended filament-like white styles are sheathed with dark-purple anthers; phyllaries beneath flower are spiny with hooked tips.

LEAVES: Basal with long stalks (petioles) for first year; alternate on stem second year. Leaves 1–2 feet long (30–60 cm) by 6–12 inches wide (15–30 cm); blades oval, tips pointed, margins unlobed; upper surface smooth to sparsely hairy, lower surface sparsely gray-hairy.

HABITAT: Disturbed soils, riparian areas; sage-brush, foothills, montane forests. Elevation 5,000–9,400 feet (1,524–2,865 m).

SIMILAR SPECIES: Thistles, *Cirsium* species, generally have lobed leaves and feathery seed heads.

Musk Thistle, Nodding Thistle

Carduus nutans, Aster Family, Asteraceae; Annual or biennial herb; introduced, invasive

QUICK ID: Look for nodding flower heads with dense clusters of pink, tassel-like disk flowers above rows of broad, spiny, purple phyllaries.

RANGE: NR, MR, SR, Canada; widespread, common

STEM: Branching or not, 1–7 feet tall (30–213 cm), spiny wings below leaves.

FLOWERS: June–September. Flower head 2–3 inches wide (5–8 cm), with up to 1,000 disk florets, no ray florets; similar to thistles *(Cirsium)*.

LEAVES: Basal rosette up to 2 feet wide (61 cm). Stem leaves alternate, 3–6 inches long (8–15 cm), deeply lobed, hairless, and lined with silvery, thorn-like spines up to ½ inch long (12 mm).

HABITAT: Invades pastures, roadsides, disturbed areas; scrublands, pinyon-juniper foothills, montane forests. Elevation 4,500–10,000 feet (1,370–3,040 m). Considered one of the most serious noxious weeds in North America.

Spotted Knapweed

Centaurea stoebe, Aster Family, Asteraceae; Perennial or biennial herb; introduced, invasive

QUICK ID: Look in disturbed areas for tall, branching stems with small, pink to purple, thistle-like heads with thread-like florets.

RANGE: NR, MR, SR, Canada; widespread, common; introduced from Europe

STEM: Erect, branching, 1–5 feet tall (30–150 cm), sparsely hairy.

FLOWERS: June–October. Flower heads ¾ inch wide (20 mm) with only disk florets, outer ones longest with several pitchfork-like lobes; middle bracts pointed with dark tips and comb-like lobes.

LEAVES: Basal; blades stalked, pinnately compound, to 3½ inches long (9 cm), lined with narrow lobes, surfaces short-hairy. Stem leaves few, alternate, smaller, unlobed near flower head.

HABITAT: Roadsides, fields, disturbed areas; grasslands to subalpine forests. Elevation 100–10,000 feet (30–3,040 m).

Canada Thistle

Cirsium arvense, Aster Family, Asteraceae; Perennial herb; introduced, invasive

QUICK ID: Look for small flower heads with pink, thread-like flowers and purple-tinged phyllaries tipped with tiny spines.

RANGE: NR, MR, SR, Canada; widespread, common

STEM: Branching, to 6 feet tall (2 m) with spreading, budding roots forming colonies 115 feet wide (35 m) with roots 22 feet deep (7 m).

FLOWERS: June–October. Small, egg-shaped flower heads ⅜–1 inch long (1–3 cm), with pink to purple, filament-like disk flowers (no ray flowers); flower heads either male or female.

LEAVES: Basal leaves absent at flowering, stem leaves alternate; blades highly variable, oblong to elliptic, 1¼–12 inches long (3–30 cm); margins spiny, lobed or unlobed, flat or wavy; upper surface hairless to thinly hairy, bottom hairless to densely gray-woolly.

HABITAT: Roadsides, pastures, riparian, disturbed areas; wetlands, grasslands, sagebrush, pinyon-juniper foothills, montane, subalpine forests. Elevation 4,200–9,600 feet (1,229–2,926 m).

Mountain Thistle

Cirsium eatonii, Aster Family, Asteraceae; Perennial herb

QUICK ID: Look for stout stems; spiny leaves; heads with woolly hairs; and pink, purple, white, or yellow filament-like florets.

RANGE: NR, MR, SR with 4 varieties; widespread, common

STEM: Erect, single or branched, 1–5 feet tall (30–150 cm).

FLOWERS: July–September. Erect to nodding heads, thinly hairy to obscured with woolly hairs, disk flowers only. Flower head features highly variable depending on variety.

LEAVES: Basal, alternate on stem. Blades oblong, 4–12 inches long (10–30 cm) to 2 inches wide (5 cm); margins wavy with 10–20 deep lobes closely spaced, spine tipped; top surface hairless or thinly hairy, bottom thinly to densely covered with cobwebby hairs.

HABITAT: Slopes, meadows; montane forests to alpine. Elevation 7,200–12,800 feet (2,200–3,900 m).

Yellow-spined Thistle

Cirsium ochrocentrum, Aster Family, Asteraceae; Perennial herb

QUICK ID: Look for leaves and flower heads with long, yellow spines and heads with pink, purple, red, or white filament-like florets.

RANGE: MR, SR; widespread, common

STEM: Erect, 1–3 feet tall (30–91 cm), densely gray-hairy.

FLOWERS: April–July. Flower heads rounded to oval; phyllaries with a whitish mid-stripe and often with hairy margins, tipped with spines to ½ inch long (12 mm).

LEAVES: Basal; alternate, smaller up the stem. Blades elliptic to lance-shaped, 4–12 inches long (10–30 cm) by ¾–3 inches wide (2–8 cm), gray-hairy above, white-woolly below; blade with 8–15 pairs of lobes with yellow spines ⅛–¾ inch long (3–20 mm); margins strongly wavy.

HABITAT: Dry soils; arid grasslands, pinyon-juniper foothills, montane forests. Elevation 3,275–10,000 feet (1,000–3,048 m).

SIMILAR SPECIES: Wavy-leaf Thistle, *C. undulatum*, has phyllaries with white mid-stripes and tiny spines 3/16 inch long (5 mm).

Meadow (Elk) Thistle

Cirsium scariosum, Aster Family, Asteraceae; Perennial herb

QUICK ID: Look for stems with long, slender, spiny leaves that overtop clusters of flower heads with pink, purple, or white disk florets.

RANGE: NR, MR, SR, Canada; widespread, common

STEM: Stemless or erect, branched or not, 1–3 feet tall (30–100 cm).

FLOWERS: June–September. Heads single along stem or 5–20 crowded on stem top. Phyllaries may be tipped with spreading spines, blunt-toothed, or obscured by woolly hairs depending on variety.

LEAVES: Basal, alternate on stem. Blades linear to oblong, shallow to deeply lobed, spiny; top surface hairless to woolly, bottom hairless or with short hairs; upper leaves narrow, unpigmented to purple tinted, spiny, often overtopping the flower heads.

HABITAT: Moist meadows, grasslands, forest openings; sagebrush zone to subalpine forests. Elevation 1,968–12,467 feet (600–3,800 m).

Wavy-leaf Thistle

Cirsium undulatum, Aster Family, Asteraceae; Perennial herb

QUICK ID: Look for stems with spiny leaves; heads with pink, rosy, lavender, or white flowers; and phyllaries with short, yellow spines.

RANGE: NR, MR, SR, Canada; widespread, scattered

STEM: Erect, often branching, 1–3 feet tall (30–90 cm), white-woolly.

FLOWERS: May–September. Flower heads egg-shaped, 1–2 inches tall and wide (3–5 cm), with a dense cluster of tubular, thread-like disk flowers; phyllaries have a whitish mid-ridge and stubby spines less than 3⁄16 inch long (5 mm), spreading to bent back or hooked.

LEAVES: Alternate and smaller up the stem. Blades oblong to lance-shaped, 4–16 inches long (10–40 cm), with shallow leaf lobes tipped with yellow spines to ½ inch long (12 mm); margins wavy, surfaces thinly gray-woolly above, densely white-woolly below.

HABITAT: Prairies, sagebrush, pinyon-juniper foothills, montane forests. Elevation 5,000–9,800 feet (1,524–2,900 m).

Southwestern Cosmos

Cosmos parviflorus, Aster Family, Asteraceae; Annual herb

QUICK ID: Look for slender, leafy stems with opposite leaves and daisy-like flowers with pink rays and a yellow disk.

RANGE: SR; widespread, infrequent

STEM: Slender, branching, 1–3 feet tall (30–90 cm).

FLOWERS: June–August. Single 1-inch-wide (25 mm) flower head on branch tip; 8 petal-like rays; pink, violet to white, each ¼–⅜ inch long (6–9 mm), with 3 coarse teeth; beneath the flower, 8 spreading outer phyllaries with tapering tips are slightly separated from the short inner phyllaries that tightly clasp the head.

LEAVES: Opposite. Blades 1–2½ inches long (25–65 mm) divided into numerous thread-like segments.

HABITAT: Open woodlands; pinyon-juniper foothills, lower montane forests. Elevation 4,500–8,800 feet.

SIMILAR SPECIES: Escaped Garden Cosmos, *C. bipinnatus*, has white to red flowers with rays to 1½ inches long (38 mm).

Subalpine Fleabane

Erigerion glacialis, Aster Family, Asteraceae; Perennial herb

QUICK ID: Look for stems with long basal leaves and clasping stem leaves; pink-to-magenta rays; yellow disk; and tapering, curling phyllaries covered with stalked glands.

RANGE: NR, MR, SR, Canada; widespread, common

STEM: Erect, upper branching, 3–18 inches tall (8–45 cm), hairy.

FLOWERS: June–September. Heads with 30–80 rays, pink, blue, or magenta (rarely white), each ⅜–1 inch long (8–25 mm) by ⅛ inch wide (3 mm); disk yellow. Phyllaries in 2–3 rows, narrow with tapering tips that curl back, densely covered with glands on hair-like stalks.

LEAVES: Basal; blades spatula- to lance-shaped, 1–6 inches long (3–16 mm); edges entire, surfaces smooth to long-hairy. Stem leaves alternate, gradually smaller upward, clasping.

HABITAT: Moist meadows, open forest; upper montane, subalpine forests, alpine. Elevation 4,500–12,500 feet (1,370–3,810 m).

SIMILAR SPECIES: This species now includes several varieties once considered part of *E. peregrinus*.

Largefower Skeletonweed

Lygodesmia grandiflora, Aster Family, Asteraceae; Perennial herb

QUICK ID: Look for narrow, linear lower leaves; flower heads with linear, pink rays square-tipped with tiny teeth; and long styles.

RANGE: MR, SR; widespread, common

STEM: Branching, 2–15 inches tall (5–40 cm), smooth.

FLOWERS: May–June. Flower heads single on branch tips; 5 or 8–12 rays, each ⅝–1 inch long (15–25 mm), pink to lavender; long styles have divided, curled tips; phyllaries 8–12 in 1 row, smooth.

LEAVES: Lower blades linear 2–4 inches long (5–10 cm) by ⅛ inch wide (3 mm); upper leaves much smaller, scale-like in some varieties.

HABITAT: Sandy, gravelly soils; grasslands, sagebrush, pinyon-juniper foothills. Elevation 4,920–9,200 feet (1,300–2,800 m).

SIMILAR SPECIES: 5 varieties (or species): only var. *grandiflora* has more than 5 rays; var. *dianthopsis* has 5 rays and erect, leafy stems; var. *arizonica* is common in AZ, NM, UT.

Rush Skeletonweed

Lygodesmia juncea, Aster Family, Asteraceae; Perennial herb

QUICK ID: Look for bushy clumps; small, linear lower leaves; no upper leaves; and flower heads with 5 pink rays with toothed tips.

RANGE: NR, MR, SR, Canada; widespread, common

STEM: Stiff, branching, 4–10 inches tall (10–35 cm), smooth, rhizomatous; often with galls ⅜ inch (10 mm) in diameter.

FLOWERS: June–September. Flower heads 1–50, singly on branch tips; 5 narrow rays, pink to lavender, ½ inch long (12 mm), tipped with tiny teeth; long styles have divided, arching tips; 5 phyllaries in 1 row, linear, smooth, without tiny appendages.

LEAVES: Basal absent at flowering. Stem leaves alternate, stiff, linear, ¼–1½ inches long (5–40 mm) surfaces smooth, upper leaves scale-like.

HABITAT: Dry, sandy soils, open woods; grasslands, sagebrush. Elevation 1,000–8,000 feet (305–2,438 m).

Brownplume Wirelettuce

Stephanomeria pauciflora, Aster Family, Asteraceae; Perennial herb

QUICK ID: Look in arid habits for bushy, wiry, greenish, nearly leafless stems; flower heads with 5–6 small, pale-pink-to-lavender rays tipped with tiny teeth; and milky sap.

RANGE: SR; widespread, common

STEM: Erect, intricately branched, usually rounded, 7–20 inches tall (18–50 cm), smooth.

FLOWERS: May–September. Flower heads ½ inch wide (12 mm); stamens purple; seeds tufted with tan to dirty-white feathery bristles.

LEAVES: Basal, wither by blooming. Blades linear ¾–2⅜ inches (2–6 cm), margins entire or toothed. Stem leaves alternate, small, linear, scale-like; the green stems photosynthesize.

HABITAT: Dry soils, mesas, washes; arid grasslands, sagebrush, foothills. Elevation 3,400–7,500 feet (1,036–2,286 m).

SIMILAR SPECIES: Slender Wirelettuce, *S. tenuifolia*, (all regions) has enough common features to make a separate field identification problematic.

Spinystar Cactus

Coryphantha vivipara (Escobaria vivipara), Cactus Family, Cactaceae; Perennial cactus

QUICK ID: Look for short, cylindrical stems with thorn-tipped nipples and showy, reddish-pink flowers that crowd the stem apex.

RANGE: NR, MR, SR, Canada; widespread, locally common

STEM: Cylindrical, single or clumping, 1-8 inches tall (3-20 cm) by 4 inches diameter (10 cm); covered with nipples tipped with dark central spines and shorter white radial spines.

FLOWERS: May–June. Flowers 1⅛–2½ inches wide (3-6 cm) with many narrow petals (tepals) with pointed tips, the outer ones lined with hair-like fringe, stigma white. Fruits green to dull red or brownish, oval, ⅝–1⅝ inches long (15-41 mm).

HABITAT: Open areas; sagebrush, grasslands, foothills, lower montane forests. Elevation 3,700–8,000 feet (1,160–2,438 m).

Kingcup Cactus

Echinocereus triglochidiatus, Cactus Family, Cactaceae; Perennial succulent cactus

QUICK ID: Look for a small cactus with cylindrical stems with 5-8 ribs, widely spaced areoles with angular spines, and bright-red flowers.

RANGE: SR; widespread, locally common

STEM: Single or clumps, 2-12 inches tall (5-30 cm) by 2-6 inches diameter (5-15 cm). Areoles have short, white felt, 1-10 radial spines, and 0-1 central spine, all flat to angular in cross section.

FLOWERS: April–June. Funnel-shaped, 1-2½ inches wide (3-7 cm), on sides of stem; petals stiff, rounded, brilliant red with pale to white bases; stigma green, filaments have pinkish-purple anthers. Fruit egg-shaped, ¾-1½ inches long (20-38 mm), fleshy, green maturing red.

HABITAT: Arid grasslands and scrub, sagebrush, pinyon-juniper foothills, montane forests. Elevation 4,500-9,500 feet (1,229-2,895 m).

NOTE: The red petals are rigid to support hummingbirds, and the flowers sized to fit their heads. Bees are also pollinators.

Common Snowberry

Symphoricarpos albus, Honeysuckle Family, Caprifoliaceae; Deciduous shrub

QUICK ID: Look for dense shrubs with oval leaves; clusters on branch tips with small, bell-shaped, pink flowers; and snow-white berries.

RANGE: NR, MR, SR, Canada; widespread, common

STEM: Upright, multi-branching, spreading, 2–6 feet tall (60–180 cm).

FLOWERS: May–July. Clusters on branch tips and leaf axils have 2–10 wide, bell-shaped flowers with 5 round-tipped petal-lobes shorter or equal to the floral tube; note the stamens are shorter than lobes. Fruit is white, round drupe 3⁄16–9⁄16 inch wide (5–15 mm).

LEAVES: Opposite; blades elliptic to round, 3⁄8–1 inch long (1–3 cm); edges entire, occasionally with few teeth; upper surface hairless, dark green to blue green, lower paler, hairless to sparsely hairy.

HABITAT: Moist to dry forests, open slopes; grasslands, sagebrush, foothills, montane forests. Elevation 2,000–10,000 feet (610–3,048 m).

SIMILAR SPECIES: Western Snowberry, *S. occidentalis*, (all regions) has leaves twice as big and stamens noticeably longer than petals.

Mountain Snowberry

Symphoricarpos oreophilus, Honeysuckle Family, Caprifoliaceae; Deciduous shrub

QUICK ID: Look for leafy bushes with clusters of drooping pink to white, funnel-shaped flowers and white, egg-shaped berries.

RANGE: NR, MR, SR: widespread common; Canada: locally common

STEM: Upright, 20–60 inches tall (50–150 cm), twigs smooth to hairy.

FLOWERS: May–September. Flowers nodding, solitary or several; funnel-shaped, 3⁄8–5⁄8 inch long (9–15 mm) with 5 round-tipped petal-lobes. Fruit a white, elliptic drupe 1⁄4–3⁄8 inch wide (7–10 mm).

LEAVES: Opposite, short-stalked; blades; oval to elliptic, 3⁄8–1 inch long (1–3 cm); edges entire to irregularly toothed, surfaces smooth to bottom hairy, prominently veined, tips pointed.

HABITAT: Dry meadows, open woods; grasslands to subalpine forests. Elevation 6,000–10,000 feet (1,828–3,048 m).

SIMILAR SPECIES: Some sources consider this species a phase of Roundleaf Snowberry, *S. rotundifolius*.

Moss Campion

Silene acaulis, Pink Family, Caryophyllaceae; Perennial herb

QUICK ID: Look in tundra for densely matted cushion plants covered with small leaves and small flowers with 5 bright-pink petals.

RANGE: NR, MR, SR, Canada; widespread, common

STEM: Mounding, branching, ⅜–1 inch tall (1–3 cm) spreading to 6–20 inches wide (15–500 cm).

FLOWERS: June–August. Solitary flowers ½ inch wide (12 mm) with 5 pink to lavender (rarely white), oval petals; tips entire or notched.

LEAVES: Mostly basal. Opposite to overlapping, densely crowded on stems. Blades linear to lance-shaped, 3⁄16–⅜ inch long (4–10 mm) by 1⁄16 inch wide (2 mm), tips pointed. The ground-hugging stems and crowded leaves protect the buds from frigid temperatures and harsh winds.

HABITAT: Rocky outcrops, disturbed areas; upper subalpine ridges, alpine tundra. Elevation 11,500–14,000 feet (3,500–4,270 m).

Scouler's Catchfly

Silene scouleri ssp. *hallii*, Pink Family, Caryophyllaceae; Perennial herb

QUICK ID: Look for slender stems; opposite leaves; pairs of erect flowers with white to pink, deeply forked petals; and a bell-shaped calyx with 10 dark ribs.

RANGE: NR, SR: widespread, common; Canada: infrequent

STEM: Erect, branched from base, 4–15 inches tall (10–40 cm), glandular-hairy.

FLOWERS: May–September. Spikes have 3–8 nodes with paired flowers with 5 petals, each deeply cut into 2 narrow lobes, a fringe of tiny petal-like appendages surrounds the throat; calyx bell-shaped, ⅜–½ inch long (8–13 mm), glandular-hairy, 10 dark ribs.

LEAVES: Basal, stalked; blades elliptic, 2¾–6 inches long (7–15 cm), both ends pointed; margins entire, surfaces short-hairy. Stem leaves stalkless, opposite, narrow, 2–3 pairs.

HABITAT: Coarse soils, thickets, open woods; grasslands to alpine meadows. Elevation 6,000–12,470 feet (1,800–3,800 m).

Mountain Lover

Paxistima myrsinites, Bittersweet Family, Celastraceae; Evergreen shrub

QUICK ID: Look for a low-growing groundcover with small, glossy, evergreen leaves with few small teeth, and tiny maroon flowers.

RANGE: NR, MR, SR, Canada; widespread, common

STEM: Spreading, leafy, densely branched, 2-3 feet tall (50-100 cm).

FLOWERS: April-October. Solitary or clusters of 1-3 flowers in leaf axils; 4 triangular petals ⅛ inch wide (3 mm). Fruit a dry capsule ⅛ inch long (3 mm).

LEAVES: Opposite, glossy green, leathery. Blades oval to elliptic, ⅜-1⅜ inches long (8-34 mm); edges minutely toothed, surfaces smooth.

HABITAT: Rocky soils, shaded forests; sagebrush, foothills, montane, subalpine forests. Elevation 2,000-11,000 feet (610-3,353 m).

Rocky Mountain Beeplant

Peritoma serrulata (Cleome serrulata), Beeplant Family, Cleomaceae: Annual herb

QUICK ID: Look for tall, leafy stems (often in stands) covered with clusters of pink flowers with 4 petals and long, drooping seed pods.

RANGE: NR, MR, SR, Canada; widespread, common

STEM: Erect, branched, 2-5 feet tall (60-150 cm), hairless.

FLOWERS: June-September. Dense, elongated clusters have pink-to-purple flowers with 4 oval petals, ¼-½ inch (7-12 mm) long, stamens extend well beyond petals. Seed pods narrow, 1-3 inches long (3-8 cm), drooping downward.

LEAVES: Alternate, palmately compound with 3 leaflets, elliptic, 1-2⅜ inches (3-6 cm) long, both ends pointed; edges entire or with minute teeth.

HABITAT: Moist soils, open woods, disturbed areas; grasslands, sagebrush, foothills, montane forests. Elevation 3,600-9,600 feet (1,100-2,926 m).

King's Crown

Rhodiola integrifoia, Stonecrop Family, Crassulaceae; Perennial succulent

QUICK ID: Look for clumps of tall stems, succulent leaves, and dense, crown-like clusters of dark-red flowers with pointed petals.

RANGE: NR, MR, SR, Canada; widespread, common

STEM: Erect, 2–20 inches tall (5–50 cm), smooth, rhizomatous.

FLOWERS: May–September. Dense, flat-topped, terminal clusters have many reddish-purple flowers with 5 tiny, pointed petals to ¼ inch long (6 mm); 5 stamens longer than petals.

LEAVES: Alternate, densely crowded, circling the stem. Blades elliptic to oval, to 2 inches long (5 cm), tips pointed, margins entire to irregularly toothed.

HABITAT: Coarse soils, rocky slopes; subalpine forests, alpine meadows. Elevation 8,000-13,200 feet (2,438–4,023 m).

SIMILAR SPECIES: Queen's Crown, *R. rhodantha*, (MR, SR) has a rounded cluster of pink flowers and narrow leaves.

Queen's Crown

Rhodiola rhodantha, Stonecrop Family, Crassulaceae; Perennial succulent

QUICK ID: Look for clumped stems, narrow succulent leaves, and rounded to spike-like clusters of small, pink to rosy flowers with whitish tips.

RANGE: MR, SR; widespread, common

STEM: Erect, clustered, 2–12 inches tall (5–30 cm), smooth.

FLOWERS: June–September. Crowded, terminal clusters have up to 50 flowers with 5 narrow petals, erect, pointed 5⁄16–½ inch long (8–13 mm); stamens shorter than petals.

LEAVES: Alternate, succulent; blades narrowly elliptic to linear-oblong, ⅜–1¾ inch long (1–5 cm) to ¼ inch wide (7 mm); edges entire or few-toothed

HABITAT: Wet meadows, stream banks; montane, subalpine forests, alpine tundra. Elevation 9,000–13,000 (2,743–3,962 m).

Pipsissewa, Prince's Pine

Chimaphila umbellata, Heath Family, Ericaceae; Perennial herb

QUICK ID: Look for small rosettes of evergreen leaves and a short stem with an umbrella-like cluster of small, pink, nodding flowers.

RANGE: NR, MR, SR, Canada; widespread, common

STEM: Flower stems (scapes), 4–12 inches tall (10–30 cm); slender, branches from root to form a spreading groundcover.

FLOWERS: June–August. Clusters of 3–7 flowers hang upside down on radiating stalks; flowers ½–¾ inch wide (12–20 mm) with 5 oval petals, rose to whitish pink, bent abruptly backwards around a plump pistil and a circle of 10 swollen, reddish anthers.

LEAVES: Basal; 3–8 whorled stem leaves. Blades lance-shaped to oval, 1¼–2¾ inches long (3–7 cm), base tapered, tip pointed; upper surface dark green, shiny; edges serrated.

HABITAT: Dry mixed coniferous forests in the montane zone. Elevation 6,000–9,500 feet (1,800–2,900 m).

Pinesap

Hypopitys monotropa, Heath Family, Ericaceae; Perennial herb; parasitic

QUICK ID: Look in mixed conifer forests for delicate, near-leafless stems, reddish to white or yellowish; nodding flower; erect fruit.

RANGE: NR, MR, SR, Canada; widespread, common

STEM: Often clustered, 4–12 inches tall (10–32 cm), parasitic.

FLOWERS: July–October. Spike-like clusters of small, bell-shaped flowers the same color as the stem, red to orange (common SR) or white to yellowish; 4–5 oblong, scale-like petals reach ½ inch long (12 mm). The stem turns erect when the fruit capsules form.

LEAVES: Alternate; scale-like, overlapping, ⅝ inches long (15 mm), not photosynthetic. The plant lacks chlorophyll and grows in leaf litter in dense mixed-conifer forests. Its roots are parasitic on mycorrhizal fungus, not tree roots.

HABITAT: Moist, shady forest soils; mixed montane forests. Elevation 6,800–9,200 feet (2,072–2,804 m).

Alpine Laurel

Kalmia microphylla, Heath Family, Ericaceae; Evergreen subshrub

QUICK ID: Look for low, densely branched shrubs with evergreen leaves and clusters of small, rose-pink, cup-shaped flowers.

RANGE: NR, MR, SR (absent NM), Canada; widespread, common

STEM: Erect to prostrate, 8–20 inches tall (20–50 cm), rhizomatous.

FLOWERS: April–June. Loose clusters on stem tips have 1–12 rose-pink flowers, each ½–¾ inch wide (12–18 mm); with petals fused with 5 lobes. The 10 anthers initially are locked in tiny pockets in the petals, which spring loads the arching filaments. Bees landing in flower release the anthers, which pop up and forcefully dust it with pollen.

LEAVES: Opposite. Blades leathery, oval to broadly elliptic, ¾–1½ inches long (2–4 cm); edges flat to rolled under, top surface smooth, shiny-green, bottom densely gray-hairy and glandular.

HABITAT: Bogs, wet meadows, stream banks; subalpine forests to alpine. Elevation 3,000–11,500 feet (900–3,505 m).

Fool's Huckleberry

Menziesia ferruginea, Heath Family, Ericaceae; Deciduous shrub

QUICK ID: Look for large, mounding shrubs with dull, bluish-green leaves; drooping clusters of reddish-salmon, urn-shaped flowers; fruit an erect brown capsule; thicket forming.

RANGE: NR, MR, Canada; widespread, common

STEM: Erect, branching, 2–8 feet tall (60–244 cm).

FLOWERS: May–July. Clusters in leaf axils of new growth have 5–10 glandular-hairy, drooping stalks with red-tinged, urn-shaped flowers to ⅜ inch long (10 mm). Though flowers resemble huckleberries, the clusters are glandular-hairy, and fruit is an erect, brown capsule.

LEAVES: Alternate, short stalked, clustered at branch tips; blades oblong to elliptic, 1–2 inches long (3–6 cm); edges glandular-ciliate, surfaces hairy to glandular, tip with tiny bristle; stinky when crushed.

HABITAT: Moist forest understory, stream banks; foothills, montane, subalpine forests. Elevation 3,000–12,000 feet (915–3,600 m).

Pink Mountain Heather

Phyllodoce empertriformis, Heath Family, Ericaceae; Evergreen shrub

QUICK ID: Look in moist mountain meadows for low, matted plants with short, linear leaves and clusters of nodding, pink, bell-shaped flowers with the stamens inside, stigma protruding.

RANGE: NR, MR, Canada; widespread, common

STEM: Erect to prostrate, branching 2–20 inches tall (5–50 cm).

FLOWERS: July–August. Erect, clusters have 1–14 nodding flowers, each on 1-inch-long (25 mm), glandular-hairy stalks on branch tips. Flowers ¼–⅜ inch long (5–9 mm), 5 lobes curled back; sepals triangular, reddish, hairless.

LEAVES: Alternate, ascending, overlapping; blades narrow, linear, ⅛–⅝ inch long (4–15 mm); edges entire to tiny-toothed, surfaces hairless, bottom deeply grooved.

HABITAT: Moist slopes, meadows; subalpine forests, alpine. Elevation 4,595–11,485 feet (1,400–3,500 m).

Woodland Pinedrops

Pterospora andromedea, Heath Family, Ericaceae; Perennial herb; parasitic

QUICK ID: Look in pine forest leaf litter for pencil-thin, leafless stems lined with small, nodding, bell-shaped, red-to-cream flowers.

RANGE: NR, MR, SR, Canada; widespread, common

STEM: Flower stalk erect, clustered, 6–36 inches tall (15–90 cm), reddish-brown, densely hairy.

FLOWERS: June–August. Flower stems emerge directly from ground with an elongated cluster of nodding, stalked, reddish to creamy flowers ¼–⅜ inch long (6–9 mm).

LEAVES: None. The plant links with mycorrhizal soil fungi to parasitize pine tree roots for nutrients.

HABITAT: Pine humus; foothills, montane forests. Elevation 3,000–9,700 feet (915–2,960 m).

SIMILAR SPECIES: A smaller parasitic plant, Pinesap, *Hypopitys monotropa*, (similar habitats) has red stems with nodding flowers on one side.

Pink Wintergreen

Pyrola asarifolia, Heath Family, Ericaceae; Perennial herb

QUICK ID: Look for rosettes of heart-shaped leaves, slender stems lined with small pinkish, nodding flowers with a protruding style.

RANGE: NR, MR, SR, Canada; widespread, common

STEM: Flower stalk erect, unbranched, 6–17 inches tall (15–43 cm).

FLOWERS: June–August. Flower stalk lined with 8–25 cup-shaped, nodding flowers, each ½–¾ inch wide (12–20 mm); 5 petals, whitish-pink, edges curve down around a curved style much longer than the petals.

LEAVES: Basal, long-stalked, evergreen, leathery; blade heart-shaped to rounded, 1–3 inches long (3–8 cm) nearly as wide; edges entire to toothed, surfaces hairless, top bright green.

HABITAT: Bogs, moist woods, stream banks; foothills, montane, subalpine forests. Elevation 5,500–10,500 feet (1,675–3,200 m).

SIMILAR SPECIES: Lesser Wintergreen, *P. minor,* reaches 8 inches tall (20 cm) and has a straight style shorter than the petals.

Thinleaf Huckleberry

Vaccinium membranaceum (V. globulare), Heath Family, Ericaceae; Deciduous shrub

QUICK ID: Look for tall, leafy shrubs with large, thin leaves; single urn-shaped flowers in leaf axils; and juicy black berries.

RANGE: NR, MR, Canada; widespread, common

STEM: Erect, stiff branches, 16–47 inches tall (40–120 cm), smooth.

FLOWERS: Solitary in leaf axis on smooth stalks ¼–⅝ inch long (5–16 mm); urn-shaped to cylindrical, pink to whitish. Berries black, ¼–½ inch diameter (6–12 mm); edible, commercially harvested.

LEAVES: Alternate, stalked, thin; blades elliptic to oval, ¾–5 inches long (2–13 cm) by ⅝–1⅜ inches wide (15–35 mm), base rounded, tip pointed; edges finely serrated, surfaces with scattered hairs.

HABITAT: Meadows, slopes, open woods; montane, subalpine forests. Elevation 5,250–11,500 feet (1,600–3,500 m).

Grouse Whortleberry

Vaccinium scoparium, Heath Family, Ericaceae; Deciduous shrub

QUICK ID: Look for low shrubs with erect, stiff, broom-like stems; single, small, pink, urn-shaped flowers in leaf axils; and red berries.

RANGE: NR, MR, SR, Canada; widespread, common

STEM: Erect, compact, 3–10 inches tall (7–25 cm), hairless throughout.

FLOWERS: May–August. Flowers on short (2 mm) stalks, single, 3⁄16 inch long (4 mm), pinkish. Berries, bright red, ¼ inch diameter (6 mm).

LEAVES: Alternate, stalked; blades elliptic to lance-shaped, ¼–½ inch long (7–12 mm) by ⅛–¼ inch wide (3–7 mm); edges finely toothed, surfaces hairless, shiny above, dull below, tips pointed.

HABITAT: Open, dry forests; montane, subalpine forests, alpine. Elevation 2,300–11,500 feet (700–3,500 m).

Boreal Sweetvetch

Hedysarum boreale, Legume Family, Fabaceae; Perennial herb

QUICK ID: Look for mounding plants; long clusters of pink to purple, pea-like flowers; and flat, oval pods in chain-like strings.

RANGE: NR, MR, SR, Canada; widespread, locally common

STEM: Erect to spreading, 6–24 inches tall (15–60 cm), hairy or not.

FLOWERS: May–August. Dense, spike-like clusters, erect to arching to 6 inches long (15 cm) with 5–50 flowers, each ⅜–¾ inch long (1–2 cm) with 5 petals: 1 erect, lobed banner; 2 side petals pointed forward; 2 longer, fused keel petals bent upward. Sepal tips long, tapering. Fruit a chain of 2–5 oval, disk-like pods.

LEAVES: Alternate. Blade pinnately compound, 2–4 inches long (5–11 cm), with 7–15 linear-oblong to elliptic leaflets, each ⅜–¾ inch long (1–2 cm); edges entire; tips rounded; top surface, sparsely hairy or not, bottom with short hairs.

HABITAT: Dry, open sites; montane, subalpine forests, alpine. Elevation 3,000–9,000 feet (918–2,743 m).

Western Chainpod

Hedysarum occidentale, Legume Family, Fabaceae; Perennial herb

QUICK ID: Look for mounding plants with dangling spikes of deep pink to purple, pea-like flowers and chains of flat, oval pods.

RANGE: NR, MR, SR (absent NM), Canada (rare); locally common

STEM: Branching, 8–32 inches tall and wide (20–80 cm), sparsely hairy or not.

FLOWERS: June–September. Erect to arching, spike-like clusters have 20–75 drooping, deep pink to purplish, pea-like flowers with 5 petals: a lobed banner curved upward, 2 side petals, and 2 longer fused keel petals that point forward. Note the sepals have short, pointed tips. Fruit a chain of 2–5 oval, disk-like pods.

LEAVES: Alternate. Blades pinnately compound, 3–6 inches long (8–15 cm), with 9–21 oval to elliptic leaflets, each ⅜–1½ inch long (1–4 cm); edges entire; tips pointed; surfaces hairless or bottom thinly hairy.

HABITAT: Meadows, open areas; montane, subalpine forests, alpine. Elevation 4,000–11,000 feet (1,220–3,353 m).

Sainfoin

Onobrychis viciifolia, Legume Family, Fabaceae; Perennial herb; exotic, naturalized

QUICK ID: Look for tall stems with pinnate leaflets and dense spikes of ½-inch long (12 mm), pink, pea-like flowers with red stripes.

RANGE: NR, MR, SR, Canada; scattered, infrequent

STEM: Erect, sparingly branched, 8–28 inches tall (20–70 cm).

FLOWERS: June–August. Spikes from leaf axils with 10–50 pink-to-lavender flowers, each with 5 petals: 2 tiny side wings, 1 larger erect banner, 2 joined to form a central keel. Pod oval, flat, ¼ inch long (6 mm), hairy, 1-seeded.

LEAVES: Alternate. Blades odd-pinnately compound with 15–21 linear-oblong to elliptic leaflets, each ½–1 inch long (1–3 cm); upper surface finely red dotted, bottom slightly hairy.

HABITAT: Roadsides, disturbed areas; grasslands, foothills, montane forests. Elevation 2,000–8,500 feet (610–2,590 m).

Bessey's Locoweed

Oxytropis besseyi, Legume Family, Fabaceae; Perennial herb

QUICK ID: Look for basal clusters with silvery-hairy leaves; rounded clusters of magenta, pea-like flowers; and hairy, inflated pods.

RANGE: NR, MR, SR (rare), Canada; widespread, common

STEM: Flower stalk, 1-several, leafless, to 8 inches tall (20 cm).

FLOWERS: May–July. Dense, rounded clusters on erect stalks have 5–30 flowers, each ¾–1 inch long (18–24 mm) with 5 petals: 1 upright banner whitish with dark lines, 2 shallowly lobed side wings, 2 petals fused form a distinctively pointed keel; calyx beneath the petals hairy. Pods upright, woolly, inflated, ⅝–¼ inch long (15–20 mm), pointed.

LEAVES: Basal, densely clustered; pinnately compound with 7–21 lance-shaped leaflets, ¼–¾ inches long (5–20 mm), woolly-hairy.

HABITAT: Coarse soils; arid grasslands, sagebrush, foothills, montane, subalpine forests. Elevation 3,500–8,000 feet (1,066–2,438 m).

SIMILAR SPECIES: Missouri Milkvetch, *Astragalus missouriensis*, has a rounded keel.

Sticky Oxytrope, Boreal Locoweed

Oxytropis borealis var. *viscida*, Legume Family, Fabaceae; Perennial herb

QUICK ID: Look for clumps of pinnate basal leaves; spikes of magenta, pea-like flowers; sticky glands, long hairs throughout.

RANGE: NR, MR, SR, Canada; widespread but discontinuous, common

STEM: Flower stalk leafless, 3–12 inches tall (1–30 cm), hairy.

FLOWERS: June–August. Rounded to elongated clusters have 7–30 flowers, each ⅜–¾ inch long (1–2 cm) with 5 petals: 1 upturned banner with a dark-lined white patch, 2 wings folded over a beak-like keel of 2 petals. Calyx beneath petals long-hairy, sticky glandular. Pods erect, oval, inflated, ½ inch long (12 mm), sticky, tip pointed.

LEAVES: Basal, pinnately compound with 15–45 leaflets, narrowly oblong to lance-shaped, each to ⅛–1 inch long (3–25 mm), hairy.

HABITAT: Meadows, scree fields; subalpine forests, alpine. Elevation 4,000–13,000 feet (1,220–3,962 m).

Haresfoot Locoweed

Oxytropis lagopus, Legume Family, Fabaceae; Perennial herb

QUICK ID: Look for mats of basal leaves and flower stalks with long, silvery hairs; magenta, pea-like flowers; oval, densely hairy, pods.

RANGE: NR, MR, SR, Canada (rare); scattered, locally common

STEM: Flower stalks erect, leafless, 2-6 inches tall (5-15 cm).

FLOWERS: May–August. Rounded to elongated clusters have 5–20 magenta, fading purple, flowers, each with 5 petals: 1 erect banner with a lined white patch; 2 spreading wing petals; a beak-like keel of 2 fused petals; calyx densely long white-hairy mixed with short, black hairs. Pods oval, erect to spreading, ⅜–¾ inch long (1–2 cm), densely white-hairy, inflated, tip pointed.

LEAVES: Basal, pinnately compound with 7–15 lance-shaped leaflets, ¼–⅝ inch long (5–15 mm); surfaces densely long, silvery-hairy.

HABITAT: Coarse soils, open areas; grasslands, sagebrush, foothills, montane, subalpine forests, alpine. Elevation 4,000–10,500 feet (1,220–3,200 m).

Showy Locoweed

Oxytropis splendens, Legume Family, Fabaceae; Perennial herb

QUICK ID: Look for clustered stems and foliage densely covered with silky-white hairs, and spikes of small, pink to blue, pea-like flowers.

RANGE: SR, NR, Canada; widespread, common

STEM: Erect, branched from base, leafless, 4–16 inches tall (10–40 cm), densely long, silvery-hairy.

FLOWERS: June–August. Elongated to rounded spikes with 9–35 small flowers, pink to magenta, fading to blue, ½ inch long (12 mm) with 5 petals: 1 erect, banner with a lined white patch, 2 wing petals cupping a beak-like keel of 2 fused petals. Calyx beneath petals densely long-hairy. Pods elliptic, ⅜–¾ inch long (1–2 cm), hairy.

LEAVES: Basal, pinnately compound, 4–10 inches long (10–25 cm), with whorled clusters with 2–5 elliptic to lance-shaped leaflets, each ¼–1 inch long (7–25 mm), long soft-hairy throughout.

HABITAT: Dry meadows, openings; grasslands, foothills, montane, subalpine forests, alpine. Elevation sea level to 11,000 feet (3,352 m).

Alpine Clover

Trifolium dasyphyllum, Legume Family, Fabaceae; Perennial herb

QUICK ID: Look for loose mats; leaves with 3 leaflets; and flower stalks with heads packed with tubular, red to purple, pea-like flowers.

RANGE: NR, MR, SR; widespread, common

STEM: Mat forming, ¾–6 inches tall (2–14 cm), short-hairy.

FLOWERS: June–August. Spherical heads have 6–16 tubular flowers erect to ascending, never drooping; flowers ½–⅝ inch long (12–16 mm), pea-like with 1 pale upper banner petal, 2 darker-colored side petals, 2 keel-shaped center petals around the stamens, all compacted together forming a narrow tube; sepals smooth to sparsely hairy.

LEAVES: Basal, stalks to 1⅝ inches long (4 cm); palmately compound with 3 elliptic leaflets, each ⅛–1⅛ inches long (3–28 mm) to 3⁄16 inch wide (5 mm).

HABITAT: Meadows, rocky slopes; subalpine forests, alpine. Elevation 11,000–12,800 feet (3,350–3,900 m).

SIMILAR SPECIES: Rocky Mountain Clover, *T. attenuatum*, (SR) has drooping flowers.

Dwarf Clover

Trifolium nanum, Legume Family, Fabaceae; Perennial herb

QUICK ID: Look in alpine tundra for dense, low mats; leaves with 3 hairless leaflets; flowers nestled in the leaves with erect, pale pink, pea-like petals.

RANGE: MR, SR; widespread, common

STEM: Mat forming, ¾–3 1/8 inches tall (2–8 cm), hairless.

FLOWERS: June–August. Heads on short stalks with 2 erect, narrow, tubular, whitish-pink-to-reddish flowers, each ⅝–½ inch long (15–23 mm) with 1 banner, 2 side wings, 2 keel-shaped petals.

LEAVES: Basal, short-stalked; blades palmately compound with 3 egg-shaped leaflets, each ⅛–½ inch long (3–11 mm) by ⅛–¼ inch wide (2–5 mm); edges entire or with tiny teeth, folded or flat, tips pointed.

HABITAT: Tundra meadows, rocky slopes; alpine. Elevation 11,000–13,000 feet (3,350–3,962 m).

Parry's Clover

Trifolium parryi, Legume Family, Fabaceae; Perennial herb

QUICK ID: Look at high elevations for long-stalked leaves with 3 leaflets; flower stalks taller than the leaves; tight clusters of erect, pale pink to magenta, pea-like flowers.

RANGE: NR (rare), MR, SR; widespread, common

STEM: Flower stalk erect, ⅜–4 inches tall (1–10 cm), hairless.

FLOWERS: June–August. Leafless stalk topped with single head above leaves with 15–20 erect (never drooping) flowers, pale pink to reddish purplish, ½–⅞ inch long (12–22 mm), with 1 banner, 2 side wings, 2 darker-colored, keel-shaped petals.

LEAVES: Basal with erect stalks to 5 inches tall (13 cm). Blades palmate with 3 elliptic to oblong leaflets, ⅜–1⅝ inches long (10–40 mm); edges entire to toothed; surfaces smooth, flat.

HABITAT: Moist meadows, open woods, tundra; subalpine forests, alpine. Elevation 10,000–13,200 feet (3,048–4,025 m).

SIMILAR SPECIES: Brandegee's Clover, *T. brandegeei*, (SR) has heads with magenta, drooping flowers.

Red Clover

Trifolium pratense, Legume Family, Fabaceae; Perennial herb; introduced

QUICK ID: Look for compound leaves with 3 leaflets each with a light-green crescent, and spherical clusters on stem tips with erect to spreading, deep-red, pea-like flowers.

RANGE: NR, MR, SR, Canada; widespread, common, naturalized

STEM: Erect, 8–28 inches tall (20–70 cm), long-hairy.

FLOWERS: April–October. Leafless stalk topped with 1–3 leaves beneath a single head with numerous tubular flowers, each ½–¾ inch long (13–20 mm), with 1 banner, 2 side wings, 2 keel-shaped petals.

LEAVES: Alternate, stalked; blades palmate with 3 leaflets, elliptic to egg-shaped, ¾–2⅛ inches long (2-6 cm); edges entire to tiny-toothed, lined with ciliate hairs; surfaces soft-hairy, tip pointed to blunt.

HABITAT: Open disturbed areas, roadsides; grasslands to montane forests. Elevation 2,854–8,910 feet (870–2,715 m).

Purple Geranium

Geranium caespitosum, Geranium Family, Geraniaceae; Perennial herb

QUICK ID: Look for delicate, branching stems, showy flowers with 5 pinkish-purple petals, and arching stamens around an erect style.

RANGE: SR; widespread, common

STEM: Erect to sprawling, 4–20 inches (20–50 cm), hairy.

FLOWERS: June–September. Loose clusters of flowers with 5 dark-pink-to-magenta petals, usually bent backwards over 5 green, bristle-tipped sepals; petals rounded, ⅜–⅝ inch long (10–15 mm), often marked with darker lines, lower half sparsely hairy. Fruit is a slender capsule, ¾–1⅛ inches (20–30 mm) long, pointed like a crane's bill.

LEAVES: Basal rosette on stalks to 7½ inches long (19 cm); blades rounded, ⅝–3 inches wide (15–76 mm), deeply cut into 3–5 palmate segments, each cut again into 3–5 lobes, usually rounded, surfaces glandular- to short-hairy or not. Stem leaves opposite, smaller.

HABITAT: Foothills; montane, subalpine forests and meadows. Elevation 6,000–11,200 feet (1,829–3,414 m).

Sticky Geranium

Geranium viscosissimum, Geranium Family, Geraniaceae; Perennial herb

QUICK ID: Look for stems with sticky hairs, leaves with deeply cut lobes, and flowers with 5 light- to dark-pink petals with dark lines.

RANGE: NR, MR, SR, Canada; widespread, common

STEM: Erect, clumped, ½–3 feet tall (15–90 cm), sticky-hairy.

FLOWERS: April–September. Open clusters of flowers 1 inch wide (25 mm) with 5 dark-lined, pink (rarely white) petals, each ½–¾ inch long (12–20 mm), lower half with soft hairs; 10 arching stamens, sepals to ½ inch long (12 mm), bristle tipped. Fruit is a slender capsule, 1–1½ inches long (3–4 cm), pointed like a crane's bill.

LEAVES: Basal on long stalks, blades ¼–⅝ inch wide (5–14 mm), deeply cut palmately into 5–7 sharp-toothed lobes; surfaces covered with sticky, glandular hairs. Stem leaves few, opposite or alternate.

HABITAT: Grasslands, sagebrush, foothills; montane and subalpine forests and meadows. Elevation 3,000–9,850 feet (915–3,000 m).

Gooseberry Currant

Ribes montigenum, Currant Family, Grossulariaceae; Deciduous shrub

QUICK ID: Look for spiny, prickly branches, 1-5 lobed, glandular-hairy leaves, clusters of cup-shaped, pinkish-red flowers, red berries.

RANGE: NR, MR, SR, Canada; widespread, common

STEM: Upright to spreading, 2-6 feet tall (0.6-2 m), 1-5 nodal spines, abundant bristles, young stems smooth.

FLOWERS: May-July. Clusters have 3-8 cup-shaped flowers with long glandular hairs; 5 spreading petal-like sepals, red to orange, greenish, or yellowish, and 5 smaller, erect red petals. Fruit a round, red-orange berry to ⅜ inch diameter (10 mm) with short, black, glandular hairs.

LEAVES: Alternate or crowded whorl-like on short branchlets, long stalked. Blades ⅝-1⅜ inches wide (15-35 mm), deeply cut into 3-5 irregular lobes, margins with teeth, surfaces sticky glandular-hairy.

HABITAT: Stream sides, forests openings, meadows; montane, subalpine, alpine. Elevation 8,000-12,500 feet (2,438-3,657 m).

SIMILAR SPECIES: Black Gooseberry, *R. lacustre*, (all regions) has prickly branches, black berries.

Nettleleaf Giant Hyssop

Agastache urticifolia, Mint Family, Lamiaceae; Perennial herb

QUICK ID: Look for multiple, leafy stems with mint-scented leaves and tipped with spikes of rosy, tubular flowers.

RANGE: NR, MR, SR (absent NM): widespread, common; Canada: rare

STEM: Erect, 2-6 feet (0.6-2 m) tall, hollow, square.

FLOWERS: May-August. Clusters 1-6 inches long (3-15 cm) with whorled flowers, each ⅜-⅝ inch long (10-14 mm), white, rose, or purple; upper lip erect, 2-lobed, lower lip spreading, 3-lobed. The tube (calyx) holding the flower is showy with pointed, purple tips.

LEAVES: Opposite. Blades triangular to oval, 1½-4 inches long (4-10 cm) by ¾-3¼ inches wide (2-8 cm), edges toothed, surfaces smooth to finely hairy; highly aromatic.

HABITAT: Grasslands, sagebrush, foothills; montane, subalpine forests, alpine. Elevation: 5,400-10,800 feet (1,650-3,330 m).

Wild Bergamot

Monarda fistulosa, Mint Family, Lamiaceae; Perennial herb

QUICK ID: Look for stands of leafy stems each with 1 pom-pom-like cluster of pink to purple or whitish, tubular flowers.

RANGE: NR, MR, SR, Canada; widespread, common

STEM: Erect, usually unbranched, square, 1–3 feet tall (30–90 cm).

FLOWERS: May–September. Terminal head-like clusters have up to 75 small flowers surrounded by one row of green, leaf-like bracts with pink markings; flowers ¾–1⅛ inches long (20–28 cm) with 2 lips: 1 hairy, arching upper lip folds around the stamens and style; 1 lower lip has 3 tiny lobes.

LEAVES: Opposite with short stalks, aromatic. Blades lance-shaped to triangular, 1–2½ inches (25–65 mm) long, to 1½ inches (4 cm) wide; edges toothed, tips pointed.

HABITAT: Coarse soils, meadows, streams; grasslands, sagebrush, pinyon-juniper foothills, montane, subalpine forests. Elevation 5,000–9,000 feet (1,524–2,743 m).

Twinflower

Linnaea borealis, Twinflower Family, Linnaeaceae; Perennial evergreen

QUICK ID: Look for beds of small, evergreen leaves with delicate, forked flower stems with 2 dangling, funnel-shaped, pink flowers.

RANGE: NR, MR, SR, Canada; widespread, common

STEM: Erect, creeping, branching, 6–8 inches long (15–20 cm), thinly hairy, semi-woody.

FLOWERS: April–October. Paired, nodding flowers on forked stalks, 4 inches long (10 cm); flowers pink to whitish, tubular, ⅜–½ inch long (10–13 mm) with 5 flaring, petal-like lobes.

LEAVES: Opposite. Blades dark green, egg-shaped to circular, ½–1 inch long (12–25 mm), leathery; edges with few shallow teeth.

HABITAT: Moist, shady forests; montane, subalpine forests, alpine. Elevation sea level to 8,200 feet (2,500 m).

New Mexico Checkerbloom

Sidalcea neomexicana, Mallow Family, Malvaceae; Perennial herb

QUICK ID: Look for tall stems with palmate leaves with narrow lobes, and spikes of showy pink flowers blooming from the bottom up.

RANGE: MR, SR; widespread, common

STEM: Erect, single or several, 20-36 inches tall (20-90 cm), bottom short-hairy, colony forming.

FLOWERS: April–September. Clusters have many flowers, each 1½ inch wide (4 cm) with 5 rose-pink petals with whitish veins. The central stamen column stands about ¼ inch tall (5 cm) topped with a cluster of white stamens, like a miniature garden hibiscus.

LEAVES: Basal, long-stalked; blades rounded, 1-2 inches wide (3-5 cm), unlobed to 5-7 shallow lobes; surfaces sparsely hairy. Stem leaves alternate with 5 narrow lobes shallowly to deeply cut.

HABITAT: Wet meadows, seeps, stream banks, ditches; montane, subalpine forests. Elevation 5,000-9,500 feet (1,524-2,895 m).

Pygmy (Alpine) Bitterroot

Lewisia pygmaea, Miner's Lettuce Family, Montiaceae; Perennial herb

QUICK ID: Look in moist meadows for this dwarf plant with narrow basal leaves, short flower stems, and showy, usually pink flowers.

RANGE: NR, MR, SR, Canada; widespread, locally common

STEM: Stem, 1-2 inches tall (3-8 cm), tap rooted.

FLOWERS: May–August. Flowers ⅝-¾ inch wide (15-20 mm), with 5-9 oblong to elliptic petals, ½ inch long (12 mm), deep pink (rarely white), tips pointed; 2 opposite, linear bracts at mid-stem; 2 sepals oval, to ¼ inch long (6 mm), margins usually have minute glandular teeth along top, a defining but difficult-to-see feature (use lens).

LEAVES: Basal. Blades fleshy, narrowly linear to lance-shaped, 1-3½ inches long (3-9 cm), margins entire.

HABITAT: Meadows, open woods; montane, sub-alpine meadows, alpine tundra. Elevation 7,300-13,800 feet (2,225-4,200 m).

Bitterroot

Lewisia rediviva, Miner's Lettuce Family, Montiaceae; Perennial herb

QUICK ID: Look for dwarf plants with short stems and large rosy flowers in a dense bed of long, narrow leaves that soon wither.

RANGE: NR, MR, SR (rare), Canada; widespread, locally common

STEM: Erect, sprawling, few to many, ¾–2⅜ inches long (2–6 cm).

FLOWERS: May–July. Single on stem 2 inches wide (5 cm); 18–25 petals, each ¾–1⅜ inches long (18–35 mm), rose to pink (rarely white), narrowly oblong; 5–6 small, linear bracts whorled mid-stem.

LEAVES: Basal, withering to reddish by flowering; blade linear, ⅝–2 inches long (15–50 mm), edges entire, round in cross section.

HABITAT: Dry, gravelly, open areas; grasslands, sagebrush, foothills, montane slopes. Elevation 3,000–6,233 feet (915–1,900 m).

Narrowleaf Four-O'Clock

Mirabilis linearis, Four-O'Clock Family, Nyctaginaceae; Perennial herb

QUICK ID: Look for narrow, linear leaves and slender stems tipped with clusters of 3 purplish-red to pink or white flowers.

RANGE: MR, SR: widespread, common; NR, Canada: infrequent

STEM: Erect, open branching, 8–40 inches tall (20–100 cm).

FLOWERS: June–September. Flowers funnel-shaped, ½ inch wide (12 mm), less than ⅜ inch long (1 cm); 5 notched sepal lobes, pink, purple, or white; stamens long, showy, tipped with yellow anthers. Seed in the center of a tan, flat, star-shaped, papery disk.

LEAVES: Opposite, spreading or angling upward, stalkless or on short stalks. Blades linear to narrowly lance-shaped, 1½–4¾ inches long (4–12 cm), less than ⅜ inch wide (1 cm); edges entire, surfaces with or without hair.

HABITAT: Coarse soils, valleys, hills, roadsides; plains, sagebrush to subalpine forests. Elevation 3,500–9,000 feet (1,066–2,743 m).

Giant Four-O'Clock

Mirabilis multiflora, Four-O'Clock Family, Nyctaginaceae; Perennial herb

QUICK ID: Look for mounding, sprawling leafy stems with clusters of trumpet-shaped, deep-pink-to-magenta flowers that open near disk.

RANGE: SR; widespread, common

STEM: Multi-branched, tangled, to 6 feet across (2 m), smooth to hairy.

FLOWERS: May–October. Rounded clusters have 6 flowers that bloom one per day; floral tube 1–2⅜ inches long (3–6 cm); 5 notched, petal-like lobes open 1½ inches wide (38 mm); 3–5 stamens have showy, yellow anthers extending beyond the throat.

LEAVES: Opposite on stalks. Blades fleshy, oval to heart-shaped, 2–4 inches long (5–10 cm) by 1½–3⅛ inches wide (4–8 cm); surfaces hairless to sparsely hairy.

HABITAT: Coarse soils, shaded understory; arid grasslands, sagebrush, pinyon-juniper woodlands, montane ponderosa forests. Elevation 3,500–8,500 feet (1,066–2,590 m).

Spreading Four-O'Clock

Mirabilis oxybaphoides, Four-O'Clock Family, Nyctaginaceae; Perennial herb

QUICK ID: Look for clump-forming, tangled stems with heart-shaped leaves; flowers with glandular-sticky buds and bracts; and clusters of 3 small, pink flowers that usually bloom once per day.

RANGE: SR; widespread, common

STEM: Sprawling, mounding, 8–48 inches long (20–120 cm); smooth, short-hairy, or glandular-hairy.

FLOWERS: May–October. Clusters from leaf axils; funnel-shaped with a ⅜-inch-long (9 mm) tube that spreads open with 5 notched, pink-to-magenta petal lobes; 3 stamens have yellow anthers. Bracts beneath the floral tube densely glandular-hairy with triangular lobes.

LEAVES: Opposite, on stalks to 1⅜ inches long (35 mm). Blades fleshy, broadly triangular to heart-shaped, ⅜–3 inches long (1–8 cm).

HABITAT: Moist, coarse soils; hillsides, roadsides, disturbed areas, arid grasslands, pinyon-juniper woodlands, montane forests. Elevation 4,500–8,500 feet (1,372–2,590 m).

Fireweed

Chamerion angustifolium, Evening Primrose Family, Onagraceae; Perennial herb

QUICK ID: Look for tall, leafy stems with spikes of showy pink flowers with 4 petals that bloom from the bottom up; often in dense stands.

RANGE: NR, MR, SR, Canada; widespread, common

STEM: Erect, unbranched, 1½–10 feet tall (0.5–3 m), colony forming.

FLOWERS: July–September. Petals spatula-shaped, pink to magenta, ⅜–1 inch long (1–3 cm), separated by 4 lance-shaped, spreading sepals; 8 stamens have bluish pollen. Seed capsules are slender, 1–3 inches long (3–8 cm), ascending, with numerous fluffy seeds.

LEAVES: Alternate, crowded on stem. Blade narrow to lance-shaped, 2–8 inches long (5–20 cm), margins entire; turns red in fall.

HABITAT: Slopes, meadows, disturbed areas (especially after fires); montane, subalpine forests. Elevation 5,500–11,000 feet (1,675–3,353 m).

SIMILAR SPECIES: Dwarf Fireweed, *C. latifoliun*, (all regions) reaches 2 feet tall (60 cm), has short spikes with 2–12 flowers, and grows from montane forests to alpine.

Fringed Willowherb

Epilobium ciliatum, Evening Primrose Family, Onagraceae; Perennial herb

QUICK ID: Look for tiny flowers with 4 white to rose-pink, deeply notched petals on upper half of slender stems; favors moist soils.

RANGE: NR, MR, SR, Canada; widespread, common

STEM: Erect, upper branched, often glandular-hairy, 1–3 feet tall (30–100 cm).

FLOWERS: May–November. Loose, erect clusters of tiny flowers, each about ⅜ inch wide (9 mm), petals white, pink, or magenta; sepals pointed, densely glandular-hairy. Seed capsules long, slender, angled upward, 1–4 inches long (3–10 cm).

LEAVES: Basal rosette; opposite on stem. Blades lance-shaped to elliptic, 1–3 inches long (3–7 cm), tips pointed; edges spaced with tiny teeth, surfaces hairy or not, veins conspicuous.

HABITAT: Riparian areas, wetlands; montane, subalpine forests. Elevation 5,000–11,200 feet (1,500–3,400 m).

Velvetweed

Oenothera curtiflora (Gaura mollis), Evening Primrose Family, Onagraceae; Annual herb

QUICK ID: Look for tall, robust stems covered with velvety hairs and topped with whip-like, arching spikes with tiny, white-to-pink flowers.

RANGE: NR, MR, SR; widespread, common

STEM: Erect, generally unbranched or upper branched, 2-7 feet tall (60–215 cm), soft, glandular-hairy.

FLOWERS: April–September. Spikes 7-12 inches long (18–30 cm) dense with tiny flowers; stamens and style equal length, extending beyond the 4 white (aging to pink) petals, each ⅛ inch long (3 mm); 4 sepals bend back against the stem. The small stigma is disk-shaped.

LEAVES: Basal rosette usually withered by flowering. Stem leaves alternate, narrow, oval to elliptic, pointed, 2-5 inches long (5–13 cm) by ¼–1 inch wide (6–25 mm); edges with shallow teeth, surfaces densely glandular-hairy.

HABITAT: Roadsides, disturbed areas, riparian; grasslands, sage, pinyon-juniper foothills. Elevation 4,300-9,100 feet (1,310–2,800 m).

Fairy Slipper Orchid

Calypso bulbosa, Orchid Family, Orchidaceae; Perennial herb

QUICK ID: Look in shady forest leaf litter for a short stem with one oval basal leaf and one small, slipper-shaped, pink flower.

RANGE: NR, MR, SR, Canada; widespread, uncommon

STEM: Erect, slender, leafless, 5 inches tall (13 cm).

FLOWERS: May–June. Purple to pink, ¾–1⅜ inch (2–4 cm) wide; purple lines and spots on pouch, bright-yellow markings and hairs at opening of white lip; 5 lance-shaped sepals and petals ½-¾ inch long (1-2 cm) spread above pouch.

LEAVES: Basal, oval, 1⅜ long (4 cm) by 1 inch wide (3 cm), dark green, margin entire; appears in fall, withers after blooming.

HABITAT: Deep humus soil in partial to deep shade; subalpine forests. Elevation 8,000-11,300 feet (2,438–3,444 m).

NOTE: Fairy Slipper Orchids have aroma but no nectar, so they deceive pollinating bees.

Spotted Coralroot Orchid

Corallorhiza maculata, Orchid Family, Orchidaceae; Perennial herb

QUICK ID: Look in forest leaf litter for clusters of red to yellowish-brown, leafless, pencil-like stems; small flowers have a red-spotted lip.

RANGE: NR, MR, SR, Canada; widespread, infrequent

STEM: Erect, single or clustered, thin, 4–25 inches tall (10–64 cm).

FLOWERS: May–August. Loose spikes of 5–35 flowers, ½ inch long (12 mm), cover upper half of the stem. Sepals petal-like, reddish, tan, or yellowish, about ½ inch long (12 mm): 2 spread forward, 1 forms the arching hood with 2 upper petals; 1 white lower petal (lip) has red dots, tip slightly curved down, and 2 pointed, ear-like basal lobes.

LEAVES: None. Lacking chlorophyll, coralroots depend on root fungi to absorb nutrients from decomposing organic material.

HABITAT: Dry, forest leaf litter; montane, subalpine forests. Elevation 7,000–10,000 feet (2,134–3,048 m).

Western Coralroot Orchid

Corallorhiza mertensiana, Orchid Family, Orchidaceae; Perennial herb

QUICK ID: Look in forest leaf litter for leafless, pencil-size, reddish stems with small flowers with red-and-white-marked lips.

RANGE: NR, Canada; widespread, common

STEM: Erect, slender, single or in clumps, 6–18 inches tall (15–45 cm).

FLOWERS: May–August. Spikes of 8–35 small flowers cover upper half of the stem. Sepals petal-like, narrow, reddish, ¼–½ inch long (7–12 mm): 2 spread sideways, 1 forms an arching hood with the 2 upper petals; 1 white to red lower petal (lip) has red marks and a tiny tooth on each side near base, tip curves down. Colors vary with yellow and lavender forms occurring.

LEAVES: None. Lacking chlorophyll, coralroots depend on root fungi to absorb nutrients from decomposing organic material.

HABITAT: Moist forest leaf litter, montane forests. Elevation sea level to 7,000 feet (2,134 m).

Striped Coralroot Orchid

Corallorhiza striata, Orchid Family, Orchidaceae; Perennial herb

QUICK ID: Look in forest leaf litter for slender, pale-yellow to reddish-purple stems; small flowers have red-striped petals and sepals.

RANGE: NR, MR, SR, Canada; widespread, infrequent.

STEM: Erect, single or clustered, 3-6 inches tall (8–15 cm).

FLOWERS: April–July. Spike-like cluster of 5–35 flowers on stem (scape). Sepals petal-like, 5⁄16–3⁄4 inch long (8–18 mm), reddish or yellowish with red-purple stripes: 2 curve forward, 1 forms the hood with 2 upper petals; 1 lower petal (lip) has 3-5 reddish-purple stripes. Note the lower lip is unlobed, pointed, edges cupped and upturned.

LEAVES: None. Lacking chlorophyll, coralroots depend on root fungi to absorb nutrients from decomposing organic material.

HABITAT: Dry, forest leaf litter; montane, subalpine forests. Elevation 7,000–10,600 feet (2,134–3,230 m).

Desert Paintbrush

Castilleja chromosa (Castilleja angustifolia var. *dubia),* Broomrape Family, Orobanchaceae; Perennial herb, hemiparasitic

QUICK ID: Look for often purplish stems and leaves; clusters of flowers with showy, scarlet, forked bracts; and forked leaves densely covered with short and long hairs.

RANGE: NR, MR, SR; widespread, common

STEM: Single or clustered, erect, 6–8 inches tall (15-20 cm).

FLOWERS: March–June. Spikes have colorful bracts with bright-red to red-orange ends, most with 3-7 slender lobes. The small, yellowish-green, beak-like flower protrudes beyond the red sepal tube.

LEAVES: Alternate. Mid-stem leaves 1–2¾ inches long (3–7 cm), dull green to a striking purplish red, deeply divided into 3–5 narrow, spreading lobes; margins often folded along the midrib. Though the leaves photosynthesize, the roots are parasitic on grass roots.

HABITAT: Dry soils; sagebrush scrub, pinyon-juniper foothills, montane forests. Elevation 3,700–8,800 feet (1,127–2,682 m).

Harsh Paintbrush

Castilleja hispida, Broomrape Family, Orobanchaceae; Perennial herb, hemiparasitic

QUICK ID: Look for densely hairy clumps with spikes of flowers with red, orange, or yellow, petal-like bracts with finger-like lobes.

RANGE: NR, Canada; widespread, locally common

STEM: Erect, unbranched, 5–20 inches tall (13–50 cm), hairy.

FLOWERS: April–September. Spikes have long hairs and broad, deeply lobed bracts with prominent veins; lobes 3–5, scarlet to red-orange or yellow with sharp to rounded tips. The small, greenish, beak-like flower protrudes beyond the red-tipped sepal tube (calyx).

LEAVES: Alternate. Blades green, often purple-tinged, linear to lance-shaped, ⅜–3⅜ inches long (1–9 cm); surfaces hairy, tip pointed; lower leaves entire; upper with 3–5 short, narrow lobes.

HABITAT: Dry open woods, slopes; grasslands, sagebrush, foothills, montane forests. Elevation 1,640–7,220 feet (500–2,200 m).

SIMILAR SPECIES: To the southeast, Desert Paintbrush, *C. chromosa*, replaces this species.

Wholeleaf Paintbrush

Castilleja integra, Broomrape Family, Orobanchaceae; Perennial herb, hemiparasitic

QUICK ID: Look for clumps of stems covered with fine, woolly-white hair; narrow, unlobed leaves; and spikes with showy, red bracts.

RANGE: SR; widespread, common

STEM: Erect, green to reddish, 4–20 inches tall (10–50 cm), hairy.

FLOWERS: March–September. A dense, hairy, 1–4-inch-long (2–10 cm) spike of showy, entire to 3-lobed, red bracts surround small, green, beak-like pointed flowers that extend beyond the red sepal tube (calyx); all parts covered with fine hair.

LEAVES: Alternate. Blades green to reddish, to 2¾ inches long (7 cm), narrow, linear, often rolled inward along midrib; upper surface mostly hairless, bottom woolly; margins without teeth or lobes.

HABITAT: Dry soils; arid grasslands, sagebrush, foothills, montane, subalpine forests. Elevation 4,200–10,700 feet (1,280–3,260 m).

Wyoming Paintbrush

Castilleja linariifolia, Broomrape Family, Orobanchaceae; Perennial herb, hemiparasitic

QUICK ID: Look for slender, chest-high stems with showy spikes of flowers with red to orangish bracts.

RANGE: NR: rare; MR, SR: widespread, common

STEM: Erect, multiple stems, 3½ feet tall (1 m), hairless or with short hairs, gray-green aging to purplish red.

FLOWERS: April–October. A loose spike 2–8 inches long (5–20 cm) with short, woolly hairs; bracts red or red-tipped, ⅝–1¼ inches long (15–30 mm), lance-shaped, and with 3 narrow lobes; the green, beak-like flower has a red margin and extends ⅜–1 inch (10–24 mm) beyond the red sepal tube (calyx) and bracts.

LEAVES: Alternate. Linear, narrow, ¾–3 inches long (2–8 cm), unlobed or upper ones with 2–3 narrow lobes; margins often curl inward, surfaces mostly hairless. Though the leaves photosynthesize, the roots are parasitic, usually on grass or sagebrush.

HABITAT: Grasslands, sagebrush; pinyon-juniper foothills, montane, subalpine forests. Elevation 4,300–10,450 feet (1,319–3,165 m).

Scarlet Paintbrush

Castilleja miniata, Broomrape Family, Orobanchaceae; Perennial herb, hemiparasitic

QUICK ID: Look for stems with spikes of red to orange bracts with 1–5 pitchfork-like lobes and narrow, unlobed, 3-veined leaves.

RANGE: NR, MR, SR, Canada; widespread, common

STEM: Erect, branched, 4–28 inches tall (10–71 cm), from green to dark reddish purple.

FLOWERS: June–October. Spikes 1–6 inches long (3–15 cm) and densely woolly with bright-red bracts surrounding small, yellowish-green, beak-like, tubular flowers. The lance-shaped, ¾–1⅜-inch-long (20–35 mm) bracts are red to orange on the outer half and have 1–5 lobes with the central lobe the longest. The beak-like flower extends slightly to fully beyond the red sepal tube (calyx).

LEAVES: Alternate. Blade 1–4 inches long (3–10 cm), lance-shaped to linear, usually mostly hairless; margins entire at mid-stem, occasionally 3-lobed on the upper stem.

HABITAT: Rocky slopes, meadows; grasslands, foothills, montane, subalpine forests, alpine. Elevation 6,000–12,150 feet (1,828–3,700 m).

Rosy Paintbrush

Castilleja rhexiifolia, Broomrape Family, Orobanchaceae; Perennial herb, hemiparasitic

QUICK ID: Look for compact spikes of hairy flowers, rose-to-scarlet bracts, and linear to lance-shaped leaves with 3 main veins.

RANGE: NR, MR, SR, Canada; widespread, common

STEM: Erect, 6–24 inches tall (15–61 cm), hairy or not.

FLOWERS: June–September. Bracts are hairy, pink, crimson, or lilac, often with greenish bases, oval with 1–2 pairs of short side lobes. Small, beak-like, green flowers with a red margin extend beyond the sepal tube (calyx).

LEAVES: Alternate. Blades often reddish, linear to lance-shaped, ¾–2⅜ inches long (2–6 cm); lower leaves usually without lobes, upper leaves sometimes have deeply cut lobes.

HABITAT: Subalpine forests, alpine meadows. Elevation 7,000–12,300 feet (2,133–3,750 m).

SIMILAR SPECIES: Where ranges overlap, this species hybridizes with Yellow Paintbrush, *C. septentrionalis*, and Western Paintbrush, *C. occidentalis*, creating a dazzling variety of flower colors.

Clustered Broomrape

Orobanche fasciculata, Broomrape Family, Orobanchaceae; Annual/Perennial herb, root parasite

QUICK ID: Look for clusters of 5–20 slender, leafless, reddish-to-yellow stalks, each bearing 1 similarly colored tubular flower.

RANGE: NR, MR, SR, Canada; widespread

STEM: Primary stem underground, flower stalks clustered, 2–6 inches tall (5–15 cm), glandular-hairy.

FLOWERS: April–July. Flowers tubular, ⅝–1⅛ inches long (15–30 mm), with 5 hairy lobes with dark lines, yellow spot on lower lobe. Calyx tube holding the petals ¼–½ inch long (7–11 mm), hairy. Note the slender, pointed tips are shorter or equal to the calyx tube.

LEAVES: Alternate, scale-like; parasitic plant, no chlorophyll.

HABITAT: Coarse soils, bare areas, often with Artemisia and Eriogonum species; grasslands, sagebrush, foothills, montane forests. Elevation 2,000–8,000 ft (610–2,438 m).

SIMILAR SPECIES: Oneflower Broomrape, *O. uniflora*, has 1–3 flower stalks.

Thinleaf Owl's-clover

Orthocarpus tenuifolius, Broomrape Family, Orobanchaceae; Annual herb, hemiparasitic

QUICK ID: Look for leafy stems with spikes with showy, leaf-like, pink-tipped bracts and small, tubular yellow flowers; colony forming.

RANGE: NR, MR, Canada; widespread, common

STEM: Erect, 3–14 inches tall (8–35 cm), with soft, short hairs.

FLOWERS: May–August. Spikes densely short-hairy; bracts showy, petal-like, oval to lobed, ⅜–2 inches long (1–5 cm), tips pinkish purple; flowers yellow, tubular, ⅝–⅞ inch long (14–20 mm), almost hidden by bracts, 2-lipped: upper lip beak-like; lower lip broader, moderately pouched, tipped with 3 tiny teeth.

LEAVES: Alternate. Blades ⅜–2 inches long (1–5 cm), lower linear, entire; others with 1–2 pairs of narrow lobes; surfaces short-hairy.

HABITAT: Open sites, meadows, slopes; grasslands, sagebrush, foothills, montane forests. Elevation 2,000–7,000 feet (610–2,133 m).

Elephant Head

Pedicularis groenlandica, Broomrape Family, Orobanchaceae; Perennial herb, hemiparasitic

QUICK ID: Look for fern-like leaves and a spike of tubular pink-purple-to-reddish flowers with lobes that resemble tiny elephant heads.

RANGE: NR, MR, SR, Canada; widespread, common

STEM: Erect, stout, unbranched, single or clustered, 4–28 inches tall (10–70 cm), hairless.

FLOWERS: June–September. Elongated clusters have 20–75 flowers with 2 lips: a small rounded, hooded upper lip that narrows into a slender beak that curves upward like an elephant trunk, and a lower lip with two side lobes resembling elephant ears.

LEAVES: Basal rosette; blades 2–10 inches long (5–25 cm), lance-shaped, fern-like, midrib lined with oblong to tooth-like lobes. Stem leaves alternate, similar, smaller upwards. Early leaves are reddish.

HABITAT: Moist meadows, riparian, seeps; montane, subalpine forests, alpine. Elevation 5,000–11,800 feet (1,524–3,600 m).

Scarlet Penstemon

Penstemon barbatus var. *torreyi*, Plantain Family, Plantaginaceae; Perennial herb

QUICK ID: Look for tall stems with one-sided rows of red tubular flowers; note upper lobes point forward, lower lobes bend backward.

RANGE: SR; widespread, common

STEM: Erect, 1–3 from base, 1–3 feet tall (30–100 cm), green to dark red, hairless to short-hairy.

FLOWERS: May–September. Loose, one-sided rows have scarlet flowers, 1–1½ inches long (25–38 mm); 2 upper lobes form a protruding hood over 4 stamens; 3 bottom lobes, often white-striped, curl sharply backwards, a distinguishing feature; petals hairless to sparsely white-hairy internally, beardtongue hairless. Designed for hummingbird pollination.

LEAVES: Basal rosette, stalked; blades narrow, linear to lance-shaped, 1–4 inches long (3–10 cm); edge entire. Stem blades similar, 3–7 pairs, opposite, clasping, base tapered, tips pointed.

HABITAT: Coarse soils, meadows, roadsides; pinyon-juniper foothills, montane, subalpine forests. Elevation 4,500–10,700 feet (1,372–3,261 m).

Larch-leaf Penstemon

Penstemon laricifolius, Plantain Family, Plantaginaceae; Perennial herb

QUICK ID: Look for densely clumped, grass-like basal leaves; loose clusters of pink or white, tubular flowers with 5 equal lobes; and a beardtongue tipped with yellow hairs.

RANGE: NR (WY), barely into MT, CO; widespread

STEM: Erect, branched, 4–12 inches tall (10–30 cm), hairy or not.

FLOWERS: June–August. Elongated, cylindrical arrays have whorls of flowers ½–¾ inch long (11–20 mm); 2 lips equal with 5 spreading lobes; tube hairless externally, internally moderately yellow-woolly; throat without nectar guidelines, beardtongue tip yellow-hairy. Two varieties within range: var. *lacicifolius* with pink flowers (MT, WY); var. *exilifolius* with white flowers (CO, WY).

LEAVES: Basal clumps; blades linear, grass-like, ⅝–¾ inch long (15–20 mm), hairless. Stem leaves similar, opposite, 3–7 pairs.

HABITAT: Coarse soils, plains, open woods; grasslands, sagebrush, foothills, montane forests. Elevation 5,000–9,515 feet (1,525–2,900 m).

Kittentails

Synthyris plantaginea (Besseya plantaginea)
Plantain Family, Plantaginaceae
Perennial herb

QUICK ID: Look for clusters of erect, oval basal leaves and long, densely woolly spikes packed with tiny pink-to-white flowers.

RANGE: SR; widespread, common

STEM: Erect, 7-18 inches tall (18-45 cm), long-hairy.

FLOWERS: June-August. Densely woolly spikes 2-5 inches long (5-13 cm); tiny flowers pinkish purple to white with 2 lips that extend only slightly beyond woolly calyx lobes; stamens have pale filaments that protrude well beyond the petals.

LEAVES: Basal, long stalked; blades oval to oblong, 2-8 inches long (5-20 cm); edges serrated, surfaces hairy. Stem leaves alternate, much smaller.

HABITAT: Moist meadows, streams, open woods; foothills, montane, subalpine forests, alpine. Elevation 6,500-12,500 feet (1,981-3,810 m).

SIMILAR SPECIES: Alpine Kittentails, *S. alpina*, (SR) is less than 6 inches tall (15 cm), has 2-inch (5 cm) basal leaves, and reddish-to-purplish flowers.

Tiny Trumpet

Collomia linearis, Phlox family, Polemoniaceae; Annual herb

QUICK ID: Look for tall, single or clumped stems lined with narrow, pointed leaves, and heads of small, trumpet-shaped, pink flowers

RANGE: NR, MR, SR, Canada; widespread, common

STEM: Erect, unbranched or branched above, 4-24 inches tall (10-60 cm), finely hairy below, long-hairy and glandular above.

FLOWERS: May-August. Head-like clusters have 7-20 tubular flowers, each ⅜-⅝ inch long (8-15 mm), flaring open ¼ inch wide (6 mm) with 5 rounded lobes, pink, bluish, or white.

LEAVES: Basal; lance-shaped, edges toothed or not. Alternate on stem, unstalked, lance-shaped to linear, even-sized, ⅜-2 inches long (1-5 cm) by ⅛-⅜ inch wide (3-10 mm); edges entire, top surfaces smooth, bottoms minutely hairy; leaves below flower head widest.

HABITAT: Open woods, disturbed sites; grasslands, sagebrush, foothills, montane forests. Elevation 2,000-10,000 feet (610-3,048 m).

Skyrocket, Scarlet Gilia

Ipomopsis aggregata, Phlox Family, Polemoniaceae; Short-lived perennial herb

QUICK ID: Look for tall, slender stems; leaves with thread-like segments; and one-sided clusters of red, trumpet-shaped flowers.

RANGE: NR, MR, SR, Canada; widespread, common

STEM: One to several from base, erect, branching; 8–40 inches tall (20–100 cm), short glandular hairs.

FLOWERS: May–September. Scarlet to red orange, occasionally pink magenta, tubular ⅝–1⅛ inches long (15–30 mm), flaring open with 5 long, spreading, pointed lobes, usually with red and white splotches; sepals have pointed tips curved back.

LEAVES: Basal rosette. Blades ¾–3 inches long (2–8 cm) with thin, linear segments along the midrib, surfaces hairy or not. Stem leaves alternate, smaller up the stem.

HABITAT: Meadows, open woods; grasslands, sagebrush, foothills, montane forests. Elevation 6,000–11,000 feet (1,830–3,353 m).

Slendertube Skyrocket

Ipomopsis tenuituba, Phlox Family, Polemoniaceae; Biennial, short-lived perennial herb

QUICK ID: Look for slender stems with narrow, lobed leaves and clusters of tubular flowers pink to pale violet, often purple speckled.

RANGE: SR; widespread, common

STEM: Erect, branching, 14–40 inches tall (35–100 cm), woolly hairs.

FLOWERS: June–September. Clusters one-sided with 3–7 flowers along stem and at top; floral tube slender, 1–1½ inches long (25–45 mm), spreading open with 5 petal lobes, pink, lavender, or white, often speckled, tips pointed. The colors attract moths for pollination.

LEAVES: Basal, often wither by flowering; blades 1–2⅜ inches long (3–6 cm), deeply divided into narrow, linear lobes along midrib; surfaces smooth to woolly-hairy. Stem leaves alternate, smaller.

HABITAT: Meadows, open areas; grasslands, sagebrush, foothills, montane, subalpine. Elevation 7,000–10,500 feet (2,100–3,200 m).

SIMILAR SPECIES: Skyrocket, *I. aggregata*, (all regions) has red flowers for hummingbird pollination.

Spreading Phlox

Phlox diffusa, Phlox Family, Polemoniaceae; Perennial herb

QUICK ID: Look for mats or loose mounds; short, linear leaves with bristle tips; and small, pink-to-white flowers with 5 spreading petals.

RANGE: NR, MR, SR, Canada; widespread, common

STEM: Mounding to mat forming, 2–4 inches tall (5–10 cm), hairless to white-hairy.

FLOWERS: May–August. Solitary tubular flowers ⅜–⅝ inch long (9–17 mm) with 5 spreading petal lobes, each to ⅜ inch long (9 mm), white, pink, or lavender; sepals (calyx) cupping petals long-hairy. Flowers often obscure leaves.

LEAVES: Opposite, fused at base in pairs; blades narrow, linear, ¼–⅝ inch long (5–15 mm); edges lined with short hairs, surfaces hairless except white-woolly base, tip prickly.

HABITAT: Rocky areas, forest openings; upper montane forest, alpine. Elevation 4,000–9,000 feet (1,220–2,743 m).

Cushion Buckwheat

Eriogonum ovalifolium, Buckwheat Family, Polygonaceae; Perennial herb

QUICK ID: Look for dense mats of hairy basal leaves, leafless stems, and tight, spherical clusters of pinkish-white-to-purplish flowers.

RANGE: NR, MR, SR, Canada; widespread, common, 11 varieties

STEM: Erect, unbranched, 1–16 inches tall (3–40 cm), hairy.

FLOWERS: April–August. Ball-like clusters on stem tips packed with small, pink-tinged, cream, purple, or yellow flowers (depending on variety), each ⅛ inch wide (3–7 mm), hairless; stamens inside flower tube.

LEAVES: Basal mats can reach 16 inches diameter (40 cm). Leaves erect with slender stalks ⅜–4 inches long (1–10 cm); blades elliptic, spoon-shaped to rounded, ¼–¾ inch long (5–20 mm); edges entire, flat; both surfaces hairy to densely woolly.

HABITAT: Arid grasslands, sagebrush, foothills, montane, subalpine forests, alpine. Elevation 4,000–13,450 feet (1,220–4,100 m).

Alpine Mountain Sorrel

Oxyria digyna, Buckwheat Family, Polygonaceae; Perennial herb

QUICK ID: Look for long-stalked, round basal leaves and stems with whorls of tiny, greenish flowers and showy, reddish seed disks.

RANGE: NR, MR, SR, Canada; widespread, locally common

STEM: 1-4, erect, branched or not, 2-20 inches tall (5-50 cm), often red, hairless.

FLOWERS: June-September, fruiting July-October. Whorled clusters have miniscule, reddish-green flowers 1⁄16 inch long (1-2 mm), followed by dense clusters of seeds in showy reddish, oval disks ¼ inch wide (4-6 mm).

LEAVES: Mostly basal, on stalks 1½-3 inches long (4-8 cm). Blades rounded, ⅜-2 inches wide (1-5 cm); edge and surfaces smooth. If present, stem leaves similar, alternate.

HABITAT: Moist, rocky outcrops; talus slopes; upper montane, subalpine forests, alpine. Elevation 1,300-13,780 feet (300-4,200 m).

Water Smartweed

Persicaria amphibia, Buckwheat Family, Polygonaceae; Perennial herb

QUICK ID: Look in shallow water or moist soil for floating or rooting stems with elliptical leaves and spikes packed with tiny, pink flowers.

RANGE: NR, MR, SR, Canada; widespread, common

STEM: Submerged to 10 feet long (3 m); occasionally terrestrial, prostrate to erect to 40 inches long (1 m), colony forming.

FLOWERS: June-September. Single or paired spikes have reddish-to-pinkish-white flowers ¼ inch long (4-6 mm) with 5 petal-like tepals, reddish anthers extend beyond the petals. Water plants produce short spikes ⅜-1½ inches long (1-4 cm); spikes of terrestrial plants in moist soil reach 1½-4⅝ inches long (4-11 cm).

LEAVES: Alternate, on stalks to 1¼ inches long (3 cm). Blades elliptic to lance-shaped, ¾-6 inches long (2-15 cm); margins entire, surfaces hairy or smooth, no dark blotches.

HABITAT: Wetlands, moist soils; grasslands to subalpine forests. Elevation 3,000-9,600 feet (915-2,926 m).

Sheep Sorrel

Rumex acetosella, Buckwheat Family, Polygonaceae; Perennial herb, introduced, noxious

QUICK ID: Look for clumps of slender stems, arrowhead-shaped leaves, spaced whorls of tiny red flowers, and rusty seed capsules.

RANGE: NR, MR, SR, Canada; widespread, common, naturalized

STEM: Erect, upper branching, 4–16 inches tall (10–40 cm), hairless.

FLOWERS: April–September. Long, narrow clusters of separated whorls of 5-8 tiny, reddish-to-yellowish flowers, each about 1⁄16 inch wide (2 mm); 6 sepals green turning reddish. Male and female plants separate: male flowers have 6 stamens; females a fringed, white style; capsules not winged.

LEAVES: Mostly basal; long stalked; blades lance-elliptic ¾-2⅜ inches long (2–6 cm) with 3 lobes, middle longest, side lobes small, pointed, pointing outward; edges entire, surfaces hairless. Stem leaves smaller.

HABITAT: Coarse soils, pastures, disturbed areas; throughout region. Elevation 5,500–10,860 feet (1,676–3,310 m).

Red Windflower, Cutleaf Anemone

Anemone multifida, Buttercup Family, Ranunculaceae; Perennial herb

QUICK ID: Look for long-stemmed clusters of 1-7 flowers, red (or blue, purple, yellow, white, green) petals (sepals), and 3-5 leaf-like bracts midway up the stem.

RANGE: NR, MR, SR, Canada; widespread, locally common

STEM: Often clustered, erect, hairy, 4–27 inches tall (10–70 cm).

FLOWERS: April–September. Flowers ½ inch wide (12 mm) with 5–9 colorful sepals on stems (peduncles) rising from 3-5 leaf-like bracts about mid-stem. Sepals have hairy bottoms, smooth tops; may be different colors. Seed heads egg-shaped with fluffy hairs.

LEAVES: Basal, 3–10 blades on stalks (petioles) to 5½ inches long (14 cm). Palmate blades deeply cut into narrow, pointed lobes; surfaces nearly hairless to short-haired to silky.

HABITAT: Moist to dry soils of open forests, meadows prairies, shrub lands, forests. Elevation 6,400–14,000 feet (1,959–4,267 m).

Western Red Columbine

Aquilegia elegantula, Buttercup Family, Ranunculaceae; Perennial herb

QUICK ID: Look for dangling flowers with yellow petal-like sepals that hug the body and red spurs that point upward; leaflets fan-shaped.

RANGE: SR; widespread, common

STEM: Slender, 4–24 inches tall (10–60 cm).

FLOWERS: May–July. Cylindrical 1-1½ inch long (25-38 mm) flowers nod on slender stems; 5 yellow petal-like sepals are parallel to the flower (not spreading outward); 5 yellow petal blades have rounded tips barely shorter than the sepals; red spurs straight, about 1 inch long. Note the stamens barely extend beyond the petals.

LEAVES: Basal, alternate on stem. Leaves compound, divided twice in sets of 3 with fan-shaped leaflets, each with 2-3 lobes. Basal leaves 2¾–12 inches long (7–30 cm), stem leaves smaller.

HABITAT: Moist soils; sagebrush, pinyon-juniper foothills, montane, subalpine forests. Elevation 5,000–13,000 feet (1,524–3,962 m).

Western Columbine

Aquilegia formosa, Buttercup Family, Ranunculaceae; Perennial herb

QUICK ID: Look for nodding red-and-yellow flowers with red, petal-like sepals extending outward from the flower body like little bird wings; leaflets fan-shaped.

RANGE: NR, MR, Canada; widespread, uncommon

STEM: Clump forming, 6–30 inches tall (15–76 cm).

FLOWERS: April–August. Flowers to 2 inches wide (5 cm); 5 red sepals extend at right angles to the flower body; 5 yellow petal blades with rounded tips point downward; 5 straight red spurs ⅜–¾ inch long (9–19 mm) point upward and contain nectar glands in the tips.

LEAVES: Basal, alternate on stem. Leaves compound, divided twice in sets of 3 with fan-shaped leaflets, each with 2–3 lobes. Basal leaves 4–16 inches long (10–40 cm), stem leaves smaller.

HABITAT: Moist soils of foothill, open montane, subalpine forests, subalpine meadows. Elevation 2,500–9,500 feet (762–2,900 m).

Prairie Smoke, Old Man's Whiskers

Geum triflorum, Rose Family, Rosaceae; Perennial herb

QUICK ID: Look for fern-like basal leaves, hairy red stems, and clusters of 3 nodding red, urn-shaped flowers.

RANGE: NR, MR, SR, Canada; widespread, common

STEM: Erect, clumping, 8–20 inches tall (20–50 cm), densely hairy.

FLOWERS: May–July. Clusters have 1–3 (or 5) nodding flowers, each with 5 showy, reddish, densely hairy sepals with 5 small petals hidden inside; 5 narrow bractlets spread from base. Fruit is an erect cluster of feathery plumes for wind dispersal.

LEAVES: Basal; blades 2–8 inches long (5–20 cm), fern-like with 7–17 pairs of wedge-shaped leaflets cut about ½ way to midrib. Note the one opposite pair of small leaves about mid-stem.

HABITAT: Sagebrush, foothills, montane, subalpine forests, alpine. Elevation 6,000–10,500 feet (1,800–3,200 m).

Woods' Rose

Rosa woodsii, Rose Family, Rosaceae; Deciduous subshrub

QUICK ID: Look for thorny stems, pinnate leaves with serrated leaflets, clusters of flowers with 5 pink-to-red petals, and red fruit.

RANGE: NR, MR, SR, Canada; widespread, common

STEM: Upright, 1–10 feet tall/wide (1–3 m), paired thorns to ¼ inch long (6 mm) at nodes, smaller prickles along stem, thicket forming.

FLOWERS: May–August. Flowers to 1⅜ inches wide (35 mm), usually 2–3 in a cluster at branch tips; 5 oval petals ⅝–¾ inch long (15–20 mm), many stamens with showy yellow anthers. Fruit a red, rounded to elliptical hip ¼–½ inch diameter (7–12 mm), not prickly.

LEAVES: Alternate. Blade pinnately compound with 5-7 elliptic-to-oval leaflets, to 2 inches long (5 cm), 1 inch wide (25 mm), edges serrated.

HABITAT: Moist soils, open woods; foothills, montane, subalpine forests. Elevation 5,500–11,000 feet (1,676-3,352 m).

SIMILAR SPECIES: Nootka Rose, *R. nutkana*, has flowers twice as big, to 2 ¾ inches wide (7 cm), usually solitary on stem.

Rose Spirea

Spiraea douglasii, Rose Family, Rosaceae; Deciduous shrub

QUICK ID: Look in moist areas for low-to-medium shrubs with dense, elongated terminal clusters of small pink flowers.

RANGE: NR, Canada; widespread, common

STEM: Upright, branching, 3–10 feet tall (1–3 m).

FLOWERS: May–August. Clusters conical to cone-shaped with short floral stalks along upper stem; flowers ⅛ inch diameter (2–4 mm), 5 oval petals; stamens pink, twice petal length.

LEAVES: Alternate, stalked; blades elliptic to oval, 1–4 inches long (3–10 cm); edges serrated above middle, top surface smooth, green, bottom smooth to short-hairy, pale.

HABITAT: Moist soils, stream sides, wet meadows, slopes; sea level to subalpine forests. Elevation below 8,200 feet (2,500 m).

Pink Spirea

Spiraea splendens, Rose Family, Rosaceae; Deciduous shrub

QUICK ID: Look for dense, leafy shrubs; oval leaves with toothed ends; rounded-to-flat clusters packed with showy, small, pink flowers.

RANGE: NR, MR, Canada; widespread, common

STEM: Upright, spreading, branching, 20–40 inches tall (50–100 cm).

FLOWERS: June–August. Terminal clusters rounded to flat-topped, flowers ⅛ inch diameter (2–4 mm), 5 oval petals rosy pink; stamens pink, twice petal length.

LEAVES: Alternate, short-stalked; blades oval, ¾–2⅛ inches long (2–6 cm); edges serrated above middle, top surface smooth, green, bottom smooth to short-hairy, pale.

HABITAT: Moist meadows, open woods, slopes; montane, subalpine forests. Elevation 3,000–11,500 feet (915–3,500 m).

Wild White Onion

Allium textile, Onion Family, Alliaceae; Perennial herb

QUICK ID: Look for 2 grass-like leaves from bulb and leafless stalks with rounded clusters of small white flowers, usually red striped.

RANGE: NR, MR, SR, Canada; widespread, common

STEM: Leafless flower stalk 2–12 inches tall (5–30 cm).

FLOWERS: May–July. Rounded, umbrella-like clusters have 15–30 small flowers; 6 petal-like tepals, erect with spreading tips, white (sometimes pinkish) with red or brownish midrib stripes; anthers and pollen creamy yellow; 3 bracts under flower are papery with 1 vein.

LEAVES: Basal, 2 per stalk from bulb; bulbs often clustered. Blades grass-like, 4–16 inches long (10–40 cm) by 1/16 inch wide (1–2 mm), solid, channeled (folded).

HABITAT: Dry sandy, rocky plains, hills; arid grasslands, sagebrush, foothills, montane. Elevation 2,000–8,000 feet (610–2,438 m).

SIMILAR SPECIES: Large-flower Onion, *A. macropetalum*, (arid lands, SR) has bracts with 3–5 veins.

Arumleaf Arrowhead

Sagittaria cuneata, Arrowhead Family, Alismataceae; Perennial aquatic herb

QUICK ID: Look in shallow water for plants with floating or exposed, arrowhead-like leaves, and flowers with 3 white petals and a center of either yellow stamens or green pistils.

RANGE: NR, MR, SR, Canada; widespread, common

STEM: Submerged with long leaf stalks.

FLOWERS: July–August. Exposed stalks have whorls of three flowers, each 1 inch wide (25 mm) with 3 rounded petals. Male flowers have yellow stamens in the center, females a green dome of pistils.

LEAVES: Exposed leaves have stalks to 20 inches long (50 cm), blades 7 inches long (17 cm), linear to arrowhead-shaped with pointed rear lobes. Floating leaves have a triangular stalk to 40 inches long (1 m), blades arrowhead- to heart-shaped, to 3½ inches long (9 cm). Submerged leaves have a ribbon-like stalk to 18 inches long (45 cm).

HABITAT: Shallow, stagnant water, bogs, ditches, muddy shores; throughout. Elevation 5,350–7,050 feet (1,630–2,150 m).

Western Poison Ivy

Toxicodendron rydbergii, Sumac Family, Anacardiaceae: Perennial subshrub/shrub

QUICK ID: Look for leaves with three shiny, green leaflets; tiny, creamy flowers; and small, round fruit spread by birds. Can cause severe dermatitis if touched.

RANGE: NR, MR, SR, Canada; widespread, common

STEM: Upright, single or branching, 1-3 feet tall (30-90 cm), colony-forming; all parts contain the toxic compound urushiol.

FLOWERS: May–August. Dense, elongated clusters from leaf axils; flowers ⅛ inch long (3 mm), white to creamy. Fruit small, 3⁄16 inch (5 mm), round drupes in clusters.

LEAVES: Alternate. Three leaflets on the end of a ⅝-10-inch-long (1.5–25 cm) stalk. Blades oval, 1-4 inches long (3-10 cm), tip pointed, surfaces usually hairless, margins unevenly toothed. Leaves turn yellow, orange, and red in autumn.

HABITAT: Riparian areas, canyons, open areas; grasslands to montane forests. Elevation 5,300–9,200 feet (1,585–2,805 m).

Sharp-tooth Angelica

Angelica arguta, Parsley Family, Apiaceae; Perennial herb

QUICK ID: Look for showy, flat-topped arrays with spherical clusters of small white flowers. Large, twice-compound leaves sheath the stems.

RANGE: MR, NR, Canada; widespread, common

STEM: Robust, erect, hollow stems reach 3–6 feet tall (1–2 m).

FLOWERS: June–August. Flowering stem (peduncle), 1⅜–5½-inches long (3.2–14 cm), divides like an open umbrella with 18–45 radiating rays, each up to 3 inches long (7.6 cm). Rays tipped with spherical clusters of 20–60 small, white-to-creamy flowers with 5 petals; no small, leaf-like bracts or bractlets on the stem beneath the flower clusters.

LEAVES: Alternate, base swollen, clasping and often sheathing the stem. Blade compound divided into 3 midribs, each lined with opposite, elliptic leaflets up to 3½ inches long (9 cm) and sharply toothed.

HABITAT: Moist meadows, riparian areas; foothills to montane forests. Elevation 200–7,500 feet (60–2,285 m).

Small-leaf Angelica

Angelica pinnata, Parsley Family, Apiaceae; Perennial herb

QUICK ID: Look for showy arrays with rounded clusters of small white flowers. Large, once-compound leaves sheath the stems.

RANGE: NR, MR, SR; scattered, locally common

STEM: Single, slim, smooth, branching, 18–40 inches tall (45–100 cm).

FLOWERS: June–August. Flowering stem (peduncle) 1⅜–5½ inches long (4–14 cm) divides like an open umbrella, topped with 6–25 radiating rays, each up to 2¾ inches long (7 cm). Rays tipped with a cluster of small flowers with 5 white, notched petals; no small, leaf-like bracts or bractlets on the stem beneath the flower clusters.

LEAVES: Alternate with swollen, often maroon, sheaths around the stem. Blades once-pinnately compound with 5-7 oval, serrated leaflets along the midrib; bottom of the leaf often has compound leaflets with 2-3 segments.

HABITAT: Moist soils; montane oak-maple, Douglas-fir, subalpine forests. Elevation 7,000–12,000 feet (2,134–3,658 m).

Spotted Water Hemlock

Cicuta maculata (incl. *Cicuta douglasii*), Parsley Family, Apiaceae; Perennial herb

QUICK ID: Look in wet areas for tall, robust, purple-spotted stems; rounded clusters of tiny, white flowers. All parts deadly poisonous.

RANGE: NR, MR, SR, Canada; widespread, common

STEM: Erect, smooth, leafy, hollow, 2-9 feet tall (0.6–3 m).

FLOWERS: June–September. Flower stalks, ¾–7 inches long (2–18 cm), radiate from a single point to form a rounded array with numerous umbrella-shaped clusters (umbels) of tiny white flowers, each with 5 petals.

LEAVES: Alternate. Blade pinnately compound, 6–18 inches (15–45 cm) long, divided into opposite-spaced leaflets along midrib. Leaflets divided again 2-3 times, lance-shaped, ¾–4 inches long (2–10 cm), serrated margins.

HABITAT: Wet meadows, stream banks; grasslands, foothills, montane zones. Elevation 5,300–8,800 feet (1,615–2,682 m).

SIMILAR SPECIES: Poison Hemlock, *Conium maculatum*, has parsley-like leaves.

Hemlock Parsley

Conioselinum scopulorum, Parsley Family, Apiaceae; Perennial herb

QUICK ID: Look in wet habitats for tall stems with dense, umbrella-like clusters of tiny white flowers, and compound parsley-like leaflets.

RANGE: SR; widespread, locally common

STEM: Erect, unbranched 1–4 feet tall (30–120 cm).

FLOWERS: June–September. Stems are tipped with 15–25 radiating stalks, each up to 2⅜ inches long (6 cm). Each stalk is tipped with a small, umbrella-like cluster of tiny, white, ¼-inch-wide (6 mm) flowers. Note 3–6 slender, leaf-like bractlets grow at the base of each small cluster. No (or only minute) bracts grow on the main stem at the base of the radiating stalks of the compound umbel.

LEAVES: Basal and alternate on stem. Blades 2–7⅞ inches long (5–20 cm), once- to twice-pinnately compound with 2–5 pairs of lobed, parsley-like leaflets, each leaflet ⅜–1⅜ inches long (1–4 cm). Stem leaves have an expanded base that sheathes the stem.

HABITAT: Moist soils; montane, subalpine forests. Elevation 7,400–10,900 feet (2,255–3,322 m).

Poison Hemlock

Conium maculatum, Parsley Family, Apiaceae; Biennial herb, introduced, naturalized

QUICK ID: Look in wet places for tall, purple-spotted stems; parsley-like leaflets; and rounded clusters of tiny white flowers. All parts deadly poisonous; even touching can cause dizziness and nausea.

RANGE: NR, MR, SR, Canada; widespread, locally common

STEM: Erect, branched, to 10 feet tall (3 m).

FLOWERS: May–August. Umbrella-shaped clusters (umbels) have radiating stalks, each tipped with a smaller, round umbel of tiny white flowers with 5 petals. Note the smaller flower umbels have several tiny, lance-shaped, leaf-like braclets at the base of the rays.

LEAVES: Alternate. Blades 8–16 inches long (20–40 cm), pinnately compound, usually divided 2–4 times; leaflets glossy green, oval, divided parsley-like, deeply toothed, ¼–⅜ inch long (4–10 mm).

HABITAT: Streams, ditches, disturbed areas; wetlands, grasslands, foothills, montane forests. Elevation 4,000–9,000 feet (1,200–2,745 m).

Cow Parsnip

Heracleum maximum, Parsley Family, Apiaceae; Perennial herb

QUICK ID: Look for tall, robust stems; huge 3-lobed leaves; and umbrella-shaped clusters of small white flowers; sap caustic.

RANGE: NR, MR, SR, Canada; widespread, common

STEM: Erect, upper branching, 3-9 feet tall (1-3 m), hairy.

FLOWERS: June–August. Round to flat-topped clusters, 4–12 inches wide (10–30 cm), umbrella-shaped with 12–30 hairy rays, 5 inches long (12 cm); 5 petals to ⅜ inch long (9 mm), notched; petals on outer edge of umbel often noticeably larger and deeply notched.

LEAVES: Alternate on hollow, hairy stalks 4–16 inches long (10–40 cm) sheathing the stem. Blade palmate with 3 large leaflets 4–12 inches long and wide (10–30 cm); edges toothed, lower surface thinly woolly, lobes pointed.

HABITAT: Mountain streams, wet meadows, shady areas; subalpine forests. Elevation 7,100-10,400 feet (2,165–3,170 m).

SIMILAR SPECIES: Spotted Water Hemlock, *Cicuta maculata*, has pinnately compound leaves with narrow leaflets along midrib.

Fernleaf Licorice-root

Ligusticum filicinum, Parsley Family, Apiaceae; Perennial herb

QUICK ID: Look for tall, hairless, branching stems with large, parsley-like leaves and umbrella-like clusters with small white flowers.

RANGE: NR, MR, SR; widespread, common

STEM: Erect, branched, 16–40 inches tall (40–100 cm), hairless.

FLOWERS: June–August. Double-compound clusters with 12-20 radiating, umbrella-like stalks, each tipped with small, dense, spherical clusters with short stalks with tiny white flowers; 5 petal-lobes, 5 stamens.

LEAVES: Basal, triple-compound; blades ½-1 inch long (12-25 mm). Leaflets linear to deeply lobed, ⅜–1⅝ inches long (1–4 cm), less that ⅛ inch wide (3 mm), pointed; surfaces hairless. Stem leaves alternate, smaller, with fewer leaflets.

HABITAT: Moist meadows, forest openings; foothills, montane, subalpine forests. Elevation 6,000-11,000 feet (1,828–3,352 m).

SIMILAR SPECIES: Oshá, *L. poretri*, (MR, SR) has lobed leaflets wider than ⅛ inch (3 mm).

Oshá

Ligusticum porteri, Parsley Family, Apiaceae; Perennial herb

QUICK ID: Look for tall, robust, branching stems with large, parsley-like leaves and umbrella-like clusters of small white flowers.

RANGE: MR, SR; widespread, common

STEM: Erect, 2-5 feet tall (0.5-1.5 m), smooth to short-hairy.

FLOWERS: June-August. Clusters have 12-30 umbrella-like stalks, each tipped with a small terminal umbellet with 13-25 short stalks and small, white flowers 3⁄16 inch wide (5 mm) with 5 petals. The primary umbel has leaf-like bracts at the base, but the small flowering umbellets do not. Fruit oblong, ribbed capsules 3⁄16-3⁄8 inch long (5-8 mm), reddish.

LEAVES: Basal, arching on stalks 3-12½ inches long (8-32 cm). Blades triple-compound, 3½-12 inches long (9-30 cm), oval. Leaflets deeply cut into oblong, pointed segments to 5⁄16 inch wide (8 mm). Stem leaves alternate, forming sheaths around stem.

HABITAT: Meadows, open forests; montane, subalpine forests, alpine. Elevation 7,000-11,500 feet (2,132-3,505 m).

Bigseed Biscuitroot

Lomatium macrocarpum, Parsley Family, Apiaceae; Perennial herb

QUICK ID: Look for clumps of basal leaves, woolly flower stems, and spreading, spoke-like arrays with clusters of whitish flowers.

RANGE: NR, MR, SR (absent NM), Canada; widespread, common

STEM: Stemless, flower stalks branching from taproot, erect to spreading, 4-12 inches tall (10-30 cm), hairy to woolly.

FLOWERS: March-July. Flower stems have flat-topped arrays of 5-25, spoke-like stalks tipped with clusters of tiny, whitish-to-purplish flowers; pointed, leaf-like bracts below the small clusters are as long as the flowers.

LEAVES: Basal on stalks 5⁄8-2¾ inches long (15-70 mm). Blades oval in outline, 1-6 inches long (3-15 cm), pinnately compound, deeply divided 3 times, ultimate segments 3⁄8 inch long (9 mm) by 1⁄8 inch wide (2 mm); surfaces gray-green with woolly hairs.

HABITAT: Dry rocky areas, woodlands; grasslands, sagebrush, foothills, montane forests. Elevation sea level to 8,000 feet (2,438 m).

Salt and Pepper Biscuitroot

Lomatium orientale, Parsley Family, Apiaceae; Perennial herb

QUICK ID: Look for fern-like basal leaves, hairy stalks, and umbrella-shaped clusters of tiny white flowers with protruding pinkish stamens.

RANGE: MR, SR; widespread, common

STEM: Absent or short; flower stalk erect, 4–8 inches tall (10–20 cm).

FLOWERS: April–June. Flower stems topped with rounded-to-flat-topped arrays with 6–16 radiating, hairy, spoke-like stalks, each tipped with smaller clusters densely packed with up to 30 tiny flowers with 5 white-to-pinkish petals; stamens have pinkish anthers; short, leaf-like bracts below the small clusters.

LEAVES: Mostly basal on stalks ¾–4¾ long (2–12 cm) that sheath the stem; blades pinnately compound, triangular to lance-shaped in outline, 1–4 inches long (3–10 cm), divided 2–3 times into crowded, feathery segments to 3⁄16 inch long (5 mm); surfaces soft-hairy, bluish green. Stem leaves alternate, similar.

HABITAT: Dry open areas, rocky outcrops; grasslands, sagebrush, foothills, montane forests. Elevation 4,000–9,000 feet (1,219–2,743 m).

Sweet-Cicely

Osmorhiza depauperata, Parsley Family, Apiaceae; Perennial herb

QUICK ID: Look for delicate stems; clusters of tiny white flowers on radiating stalks; tiny, club-shaped fruit distinctively licorice flavored.

RANGE: NR, MR, SR, Canada; widespread, common

STEM: Erect, upper branching, 6–31 inches tall (18–80 cm), stiff-hairy.

FLOWERS: May–July. Loose clusters have 3–8 short radiating stalks; flowers tiny with 5 white petals. Fruit stalks lengthen to 4–6 inches long (10–15 cm); capsules narrow, club-shaped ⅜–⅝ inch long (10–15 mm), tip blunt, rounded (not pointed) tip.

LEAVES: Basal, alternate on stem. Blades compound, divided 3 times, each segment with 3 elliptic-to-oval leaflets ⅜–1¼ inches long (1–3 cm); edges toothed or lobed.

HABITAT: Shady forests; montane, subalpine forests. Elevation 6,500–10,500 feet (1,980–3,200 m).

SIMILAR SPECIES: Mountain Sweet-cicely, *O. berteroi*, has tiny white flowers and pointed fruit capsules. Western Sweet-cicely, *O. occidentalis*, has tiny yellow flowers and pointed fruit capsules.

Fendler's Cowbane

Oxypolis fendleri, Parsley Family, Apiaceae; Perennial herb

QUICK ID: Look for solitary, slender stems with pinnately compound leaves and 3-6 umbrella-shaped clusters of small white flowers.

RANGE: SR; widespread, common

STEM: Erect, branching, 1-3 feet tall (30-90 cm).

FLOWERS: June–September. Compound umbels have 5-15 small umbellets on short rays or spokes, each with 10-20 individual flowers, each with 5 white, notched petals. They do not have slender bractlets beneath each cluster.

LEAVES: Basal, alternate on stem. Blade 2¾-6⅝ inches long (7-17 cm), pinnately compound with 5-13 oval-to-lance-shaped leaflets aligned opposite along the midrib; each leaflet is ¾-2¾ inches long (2-7 cm); margins vary from entire to toothed; blades are largest near the base, upper blades smaller with a sheath around the stem.

HABITAT: Moist coarse soils, riparian sites; montane, subalpine forests. Elevation 7,600-12,000 feet (2,316-3,656 m).

SIMILAR SPECIES: Hemlock Parsley, *Conioselinum scopulorum*, (SR) has deeply cut leaflets.

Spreading Dogbane

Apocynum androsaemifolium, Dogbane Family, Apocynaceae; Perennial herb

QUICK ID: Look for drooping leaves; small, pinkish-white, bell-shaped flowers; petals with red stripes on the inside and backward-curling tips; and milky sap (toxic).

RANGE: NR, MR, SR, Canada; widespread, common

STEM: Erect, stout, 8-40 inches tall (20-100 cm).

FLOWERS: June–August. Rounded clusters of slightly nodding bell-shaped flowers ¼-⅜ inch long (6-10 mm) have 5 petal-like lobes that curl backwards (reflexed).

LEAVES: Opposite, drooping (not ascending). Blades tree-like, bright green, oval, 1⅛-2⅜ inches long (3-6 cm) by ¾-1⅜ inches wide (2-3.5 cm), pointed at both ends, with prominent veins.

HABITAT: Moist soils; pinyon-Gambel oak foothills, montane, subalpine forests. Elevation 6,000-9,200 feet (1,828-2,808 m).

SIMILAR SPECIES: Indian Hemp, *A. cannabinum*, has erect leaves.

Indian Hemp

Apocynum cannabinum, Dogbane Family, Apocynaceae; Perennial herb

QUICK ID: Look for shiny, oval, light-green leaves; clusters of small white, bell-shaped flowers with spreading petals; and milky sap (toxic).

RANGE: NR, MR, SR, Canada; widespread, common

STEM: Erect, branching, 1–5 feet tall (30–150 cm), tough-fibrous, reddish-brown.

FLOWERS: May–September. Loose clusters grow from branch tips and leaf axils; white-to-greenish flowers have 5 erect-to-slightly spreading petals, each ⅛ inch long (3 mm). Fruit is a 4–8-inch long (1–40 cm) slender, cylindrical pod.

LEAVES: Opposite, spreading to erect. Blades oval to elliptic, 2–4½ inches long (5–11 cm), top surface smooth, edges smooth, tip with a spiny point, veins prominent.

HABITAT: Cottonwood-willow riparian, pinyon-juniper foothills. Elevation 3,500–7,500 feet (1,067–2,286 m).

SIMILAR SPECIES: Spreading Dogbane, *A. androsaemifolium*, has drooping leaves.

Antelope Horns Milkweed

Asclepias asperula, Dogbane Family, Apocynaceae; Perennial herb

QUICK ID: Look for low, mounding clumps with narrow leaves, round clusters of creamy-greenish flowers, and milky sap.

RANGE: SR, MR (UT); widespread, locally common

STEM: Rounded to spreading clumps, 8–24 inches tall (20–61 cm).

FLOWERS: March–October. Round clusters (umbels) 2–3 inches in diameter (5–8 cm); 5 erect-to-spreading, petal-like lobes cup around 5 arching reddish-to-greenish hoods that surround the anther column. Seed pods slender, smooth, horn-shaped, 2–5 inches long (5–13 cm), with S-shaped stems; dry pods split open to release a mass of flat seeds attached to fluffy hairs.

LEAVES: Alternate, irregularly spaced, clustered. Blades narrow, lance-shaped, 2–7½ inches long (5–19 cm) by ¼–1 inch wide (6–27 mm), often folded lengthwise along midrib.

HABITAT: Arid scrub, sagebrush, foothills, montane. Elevation 4,000–9,000 feet (1,219–2,745 m).

Broadleaf Milkweed

Asclepias latifolia, Dogbane Family, Apocynaceae; Perennial herb

QUICK ID: Look for broad leaves closely stacked up the stem, clusters of creamy flowers nestled within the leaves, and milky sap.

RANGE: SR; locally common

STEM: Erect, leafy, unbranched, 2–3 feet tall (60–90 cm).

FLOWERS: June–October. Clusters 2–3 inches wide (5–8 cm). 5 petal-like lobes bend back against the stem, horns extend slightly beyond the hoods toward the central anther column. Seed pods, 2¾–3½ inch long (7–9 cm), smooth with a tapering tip, stem bends back against the pod (not S-shaped).

LEAVES: Opposite to loosely whorled around the stem, stalkless (sessile) or on short stalks. Blades thick, shiny, stiff, 3–6 inches long (8–15 cm) and half as wide, elliptic to egg-shaped with prominent parallel veins radiating from the midvein.

HABITAT: Dry prairies, mesas, roadsides; arid grasslands, sagebrush, foothills. Elevation 2,500–7,000 feet (762–2,134 m).

Plains Milkweed

Asclepias pumila, Dogbane Family, Apocynaceae; Perennial herb

QUICK ID: Look for dense foliage of needle-like leaves, tight clusters of whitish-green-to-rose-tinted flowers, and milky sap.

RANGE: SR; common

STEM: Erect, 4–12 inches tall (10–30 cm), usually unbranched.

FLOWERS: April–September. Dense clusters form just below the branch tips. 5 erect, tubular hoods with small, pointed horns surround the central anther column, and 5 white, petal-like lobes fold back against the stem with the tips spreading wide beneath the flower. Seed pods upright, 1½–2½ inches long (4–6 cm).

LEAVES: Alternate in irregular spirals, densely crowded on the stems. Blades ½–2 inches long (1–5 cm) by 1 mm wide, resembling miniature pine needles.

HABITAT: Shortgrass prairies, mesquite grasslands, foothills. Elevation 4,000–7,200 feet (1,220–2,200 m).

Horsetail Milkweed

Asclepias subverticillata, Dogbane Family, Apocynaceae; Perennial herb

QUICK ID: Look for whorls of narrow, linear leaves, clusters of white flowers, and milky sap.

RANGE: SR; widespread, common

STEM: Erect, 8–48 inches tall (20–120 cm), colony forming.

FLOWERS: May–September. Flat-topped clusters ¾–1½ inches wide (2–4 cm) in the upper leaf nodes have creamy-white-to-greenish flowers with 5 tiny petal-like lobes bending back along the stem, 5 tiny hoods about as tall as the central anther column, and horns arching over the column. Fruit is a slender, smooth pod.

LEAVES: Whorls of 3–4 leaves per node. Blades ¾–4¾ inches long (2–12 cm) by 3⁄16-inch (1–4 mm) wide, hairless. Note the shoots of dwarf leaves in some of the axils.

HABITAT: Drainages, pastures, roadsides; grasslands, pinyon-juniper-oak foothills. Elevation 3,100–7,800 feet (945–2,375 m).

False Solomon's-Seal

Maianthemum racemosum, Asparagus Family, Asparagaceae; Perennial herb

QUICK ID: Look for multiple slender stems lined with broad leaves with parallel veins, and branched clusters of tiny white flowers.

RANGE: NR, MR, SR, Canada; widespread, common

STEM: Erect, unbranched, 8–24 inches tall (20–60 cm)

FLOWERS: May–July. Terminal clusters 2–5 inches (5–12 cm) long, numerous side branches densely covered with small white flowers; 6 tiny tepals, 6 longer stamens. Fruit a red berry, ¼ inch wide (6 mm).

LEAVES: Alternate. Blades stalkless, clasping, elliptic, 4–7 inches long (10–17 cm) by 2–3 inches wide (5–8 cm), base rounded, tip pointed.

HABITAT: Stream sides, shady slopes, moist woods; montane, subalpine forests. Elevation 6,000–10,400 feet (1,828–3,170 m).

SIMILAR SPECIES: Starry Solomon's-Seal, *M. stellatum*, (similar habitats) has flower stalks with a single flower on each side branch.

Starry Solomon's-Seal

Maianthemum stellatum, Asparagus Family, Asparagaceae; Perennial herb

QUICK ID: Look for stout stems, sword-like leaves with parallel veins, and clusters with one star-shaped, white flower per branch.

RANGE: NR, MR, SR, Canada; widespread, common

STEM: Erect, unbranched, 6-20 inches tall (15-50 cm), colony forming.

FLOWERS: May–July. Terminal clusters 1–4 inches long (3–10 cm) with 6–18 flowers borne singly on short side branches; 6 petal-like tepals ¼ inch long (8 mm). Note the 6 stamens are shorter than the tepals. Fruit a round, red berry about ⅜ inch in diameter (8 mm).

LEAVES: Alternate on opposite sides of stem. Blades broad, lance-shaped, 2–6 inches long (5–15 cm), base rounded, tips pointed, margins entire.

HABITAT: Stream banks, shady slopes moist woods; montane, subalpine forests. Elevation 6,500–12,100 feet (1,980–3,638 m).

SIMILAR SPECIES: False Solomon's-Seal, *M. racemosum*, (similar habitats) has flower clusters with multiple flowers on each branch.

Soapweed Yucca

Yucca glauca, Asparagus Family, Asparagaceae; Perennial shrub

QUICK ID: Look in arid, sandy soils for mounding clusters of rigid, sword-like leaves and a bloom stalk with a dense, spike-like, unbranched cluster of white flowers.

RANGE: NR, MR, SR, Canada; widespread, common

STEM: Flower stalk erect, 18–36 inches long (50–100 cm).

FLOWERS: May–June. Flowers bell-shaped, 2 inches long (5 cm) with 6 white-to-greenish-white tepals, outer 3 sometimes red-tinted. Note the flowers begin within or close to the top of the leaves, and the stigma is dark green. Fruit an erect, egg-shaped capsule.

LEAVES: Basal rosette; blades linear, 15–24 inches long (40–60 cm) and ⅜–½ inch wide (8–12 mm); edges have a narrow, white edge and few to many thread-like fibers.

HABITAT: Plains, hills, disturbed areas; grasslands, foothills, montane forests. Elevation 4,750–8,700 feet (1,450–2,650 m).

NOTE: Each species of yucca is pollinated only by a single moth species in the genus *Tegeticula*.

Common Yarrow

Achillea millefolium, Aster Family, Asteraceae; Perennial herb

QUICK ID: Look for a flat-to-rounded array with dozens of tiny white flower heads, and aromatic, fern-like leaves.

RANGE: NR, MR, SR, Canada; widespread, common

STEM: Erect, 1–3 feet tall (30–90 cm).

FLOWERS: Spring–summer. Clusters densely packed with 20–35 tiny white, sometimes pinkish flower heads. The ¼ inch (6 mm) wide heads have 3–8 petal-like rays each with three notches; disk flowers white, stamens yellow. Yellow and red varieties occur, popular in gardens.

LEAVES: Basal, alternate on stem. Blades 1¼–14 inches long (3.5–35 cm), smaller towards top of plant; fern-like, divided 1–3 times, with a lance-shaped outline; surfaces covered with soft, woolly hairs.

HABITAT: Meadows, grasslands; pinyon-juniper, ponderosa, spruce-fir forests. Elevation 4,000–12,500 feet (1,220–3,800 m).

Trail Plant

Adenocaulon bicolor, Aster Family, Asteraceae; Perennial herb

QUICK ID: Look on shaded forest floors for low-growing plants with large, oak-like leaves and slender flower stems with tiny white heads.

RANGE: NR, Canada; widespread, common

STEM: Erect, branching, 1–3 feet tall (30–90 cm); colony forming.

FLOWERS: March–October. Stems have spreading branches tipped with small, compact flower heads with tiny disk flowers.

LEAVES: Mostly basal on long stalks; blades broadly triangular, 4–12 inches long (10–30 cm) by 1–6 inches wide (3–15 cm); edges smooth to coarsely lobed, surfaces smooth on top, white-woolly on bottom.

HABITAT: Shady, rich forest understory; montane forests. Elevation sea level to 6,000 feet (1,828 m).

Pearly Everlasting

Anaphalis margaritacea, Aster Family, Asteraceae; Perennial herb

QUICK ID: Look for the snow-white phyllaries that look like pearls scattered on the forest floor and the narrow, two-toned leaves.

RANGE: NR, MR, SR, Canada; widespread, common

STEM: Erect woolly-white, densely hairy stems 8–36 inches tall (20–90 cm), spread by rhizomes to form dense colonies.

FLOWERS: July–October. Clusters of pearl-shaped flower heads ⅜ inch wide (5 mm) have white, papery, petal-like bracts tightly surrounding yellow disk florets. Male and female flowers grow in separate flower heads on the same plant.

LEAVES: Basal. Alternate on stem. Blades narrow, 1–4 inches long (3–10 cm) by ¾ inch wide (2 cm); surfaces bicolored, green above, white-woolly below; margins often slightly roll under.

HABITAT: Stream banks, slopes, meadows; pinyon-juniper, pine, spruce-fir, aspen forests. Elevation 5,200–12,520 feet (1,585–3,816 m).

Tall Pussytoes

Antennaria anaphaloides, Aster Family, Asteraceae; Perennial herb

QUICK ID: Look for clusters of densely packed flowers with papery, pure-white bracts and narrow leaves with woolly-white surfaces.

RANGE: NR, MR, SR (absent NM), Canada; widespread, common

STEM: Erect, slender, hairy, 6–14 inches tall (15–36 cm).

FLOWERS: June–August. Clusters on the branch tips have 8–30 flower heads, each about ¼ inch wide (6 mm); yellow disk florets are surrounded by many white bracts with a dark spot at the base; male and female flowers separate.

LEAVES: Basal, not mat forming. Blades narrow, 1–6 inches long (3–15 cm), tip pointed. Stem leaves alternate, ½–3 inches long (1–8 cm), linear with a prominent central vein.

HABITAT: Dry meadows, open forest; foothills, montane, subalpine forests, alpine meadows. Elevation 3,000–11,000 feet (914–3,353 m).

Flat-topped Pussytoes

Antennaria corymbosa, Aster Family, Asteraceae; Perennial herb

QUICK ID: Look for a thick, mat-forming groundcover with all parts densely gray-hairy, flower stems to 6 inches tall (15 cm), and tight clusters of small brownish-white flowers.

RANGE: NR, MR, SR: widespread, locally common; Canada: rare

STEM: Erect, slender, 2⅜–6 inches tall (6–15 cm), with short-woolly hairs.

FLOWERS: June–August. Dense clusters with 3–12 small brownish-white flower heads, each to ¼ inch long (6 mm). Phyllaries beneath the flower overlapping, thin, papery, white-tipped above a dark spot.

LEAVES: Basal rosette up to 9 feet (3 m) wide. Blades spatula-shaped, to 1 inch long (22 mm), gray-woolly on both sides. Stem leaves few, alternate, linear.

HABITAT: Moist meadows, willow thickets, fell-fields; subalpine forests, alpine meadows. Elevation 9,860–12,075 feet (3,240–3,680 m).

Littleleaf Pussytoes

Antennaria microphylla, Aster Family, Asteraceae; Perennial herb

QUICK ID: Look for mat-forming stems with woolly-hairy leaves and flower stalks; flower cluster crowded with bristle-like flower heads with white paper-like bracts.

RANGE: NR, MR, SR: widespread, common; Canada: infrequent

STEM: Erect, branching, 3–16 inches tall (8–40 cm), woolly-hairy, also glandular hairs on upper stem, stoloniferous.

FLOWERS: June–September. Clusters dense, flat-topped to rounded with 6–13 heads packed with bristly white disk flowers. Phyllaries bright white to pale-yellow. Male and female plants separate.

LEAVES: Basal; blades spoon-shaped, ¼–⅝ inch long (6–16 mm), 1-veined; surfaces silvery-hairy, tips sharp-pointed. Stem leaves linear, ¼–1 inch long (5–25 mm), silvery-hairy, tips pointed.

HABITAT: Wet meadows, floodplains; sagebrush, foothills, montane, subalpine forests. Elevation 5,000–10,500 feet (1,524–3,200 m).

Small-leaf Pussytoes

Antennaria parvifolia, Aster Family, Asteraceae; Perennial herb

QUICK ID: Look for the dense mat of hairy leaves with 2-4-inch (5-10 cm) stems and an array of 2-7 bristly heads with white-to-pinkish flowers.

RANGE: NR, MR, SR, Canada; widespread, common

STEM: Erect, ¾-3 inches (2-8 cm), slender, with matted white-woolly hairs.

FLOWERS: May-July. Tight clusters with hairy flower heads, each ¼-⅜ inch long (7-10 mm); flowers obscured by thick tufts of erect, white bristles; male and female flowers separate; phyllaries thin, papery, with white, green, brown, or pink tips.

LEAVES: Basal, mat forming. Blades spatula-shaped to oblong, ⅜-1⅜ inches long (8-35 mm), with 1 nerve. Alternate stem leaves linear to lance-shaped, to ¾ inch long (20 mm); both surfaces densely hairy.

HABITAT: Sagebrush, pinyon-juniper, mixed conifer, Douglas fir-aspen, spruce-fir forests. Elevation 3,000-11,300 feet (914-3,444 m).

Douglas' Dustymaiden

Chaenactis douglassii, Aster Family, Asteraceae; Perennial, biennial herb

QUICK ID: Look for clumps with matted-hairy foliage, clusters of white-to-pinkish flowers, and deeply cut leaves with narrow lobes.

RANGE: NR, MR, SR, Canada; widespread, common

STEM: Erect to spreading, 2-20 inches tall (5-50 cm), densely hairy.

FLOWERS: May-September. Flower heads 1-25 per stem; disk flowers only, each with 5 small, star-shaped, whitish petals.

LEAVES: Basal, alternate on stem. Blades ¾-5 inches long (2-12 cm), pinnately compound with 5-9 crowded pairs of narrow lobes along midrib; surfaces cobwebby-hairy; tips twisted or curled.

HABITAT: Open, disturbed areas; foothills to alpine. Elevation 3,500-11,500 feet (1,067-3,500 m). Two intergrading varieties have overlapping features: var. *douglassii* is tall from shrublands to montane forests; var. *alpina*, is short stemmed in alpine zones.

Tufted Fleabane

Erigeron caespitosus, Aster Family, Asteraceae; Perennial herb

QUICK ID: Look for matted clusters with hairy foliage and numerous flower heads with white-to-bluish rays and a yellow disk.

RANGE: NR, MR, SR, Canada; widespread, common

STEM: Erect, branching, 2–10 inches tall (5–25 cm), densely hairy.

FLOWERS: June–August. Solitary flower heads with 30–100 ray florets, each to ⅝ inch long (15mm), coiling as age; disk yellow. Phyllaries (beneath flower) densely hairy, in 3–4 rows. Higher elevation plants tend to have short stems and bluer rays.

LEAVES: basal; alternate on stem. Blades narrow, ¾–3½ inches long (2–9 cm) by ⅛–⅝ inch wide (3–15 mm), 3 nerved; surfaces densely hairy, edges entire; upper leaves smaller.

HABITAT: Grasslands, sagebrush, foothills, montane, subalpine forests, alpine. Elevation 3,000–10,000 feet (915–3,048 m).

Cutleaf Fleabane

Erigeron compositus, Aster Family, Asteraceae; Perennial herb

QUICK ID: Look for mats of hairy leaves with fan-shaped tips cut into shallow lobes, and leafless flower stems with white, daisy-like flowers.

RANGE: NR, MR, SR, Canada: widespread, common

STEM: Erect, unbranched, 1–10 inches (3–25 cm), hairy.

FLOWERS: May–August; Single flower heads up to 1¾ inches wide (44 mm) with 20–60 slender, white-to-pinkish ray florets, each ¼–½ inch long (6–12 mm) by 1⁄16 inch (2 mm) wide; disk yellow; phyllaries beneath flower densely hairy, in 2–3 rows, purple tipped.

LEAVES: Basal; blade spoon-shaped, ⅜–2 inches long (1–5 cm), with end cut into small, rounded lobes; densely hairy. Stem leaves absent or small.

HABITAT: Sagebrush to subalpine forests, alpine. Elevation 5,000–12,000 feet (1,524–3,658 m).

Navajo Fleabane

Erigeron concinnus, Aster Family, Asteraceae; Perennial herb

QUICK ID: Look for leafy clusters of multiple stems covered with long hairs; flower heads have narrow, white rays and a yellow disk.

RANGE: NR, MR, SR; widespread, common

STEM: Erect, mat-like, branching, 2–10 inches tall (5–25 cm).

FLOWERS: April–September. Flower heads have 50–100 narrow ray florets ¼–⅝ inch long (6–15 mm), white to pink or bluish; buds nodding; phyllaries in 2–4 rows, hairy.

LEAVES: Mostly basal; blades erect, narrow, ⅜–2 inches long (10–50 mm) by ⅛ inch wide (4 mm); edges entire, lined with ciliate hairs; surfaces dense with long hairs. Stem leaves similar, alternate.

HABITAT: Sagebrush, pinyon-juniper foothills, montane forests. Elevation 4,000–8,040 feet (1,220–2,450 m).

Coulter's Daisy

Erigeron coulteri, Aster Family, Asteraceae; Perennial herb

QUICK ID: Look for stems with upper clasping leaves and white, daisy-like flowers with shaggy dark hairs around the phyllaries.

RANGE: NR, SR; widespread, locally common

STEM: Erect, 0–4 upper branches, 8–28 inches tall (20–70 cm).

FLOWERS: July–September. Solitary on branch tips; flower heads with 45–140 narrow, white rays to 1 inch long (25 mm), coiling with age; disk yellow; phyllaries in 2 rows covered with shaggy black-and-white hairs, tips tapering.

LEAVES: Basal; alternate on stem. Blades lance-shaped, 2–5 inches long (5–12 cm); edges entire or with 1–5 pairs of shallow teeth, surfaces hairless to sparsely or long-hairy; upper leaves clasping, little reduced.

HABITAT: Moist forests, meadows; montane, subalpine forests, alpine. Elevation 6,000 to 11,100 feet (1,828–3,350 m).

Spreading Fleabane

Erigeron divergens, Aster Family, Asteraceae; Annual, short-lived perennial herb

QUICK ID: Look for branching stems densely covered with spreading hairs, nodding buds, and ½ inch wide (1 cm), daisy-like flowers with white-to-lavender rays around a yellow disk.

RANGE: NR, MR, SR, Canada; widespread, common

STEM: Branching from base, 10–18 inches tall (25–45 cm).

FLOWERS: April–August. Flower head has 75-150 ray florets, white, pinkish tinged, or lavender; disk flat, yellow. Phyllaries densely hairy, in 3-4 layered rows, pointed.

LEAVES: Basal; blades vary from linear to oval or spatula-shaped, ¾–2⅜ inches long (2–6 cm) by ⅛–½ inch wide (3–12 mm); margins entire or lobed. Stem leaves alternate, linear, narrow, ⅛–¼ inch wide (3–6 mm); surfaces with erect, spreading hairs, margins hairy and entire or with 2–3 lobes; upper leaves smaller.

HABITAT: Grasslands, sagebrush, pinyon-juniper foothills, montane, subalpine forests. Elevation 3,500–10,300 feet (1,066–3,140 m).

Eaton's Fleabane

Erigeron eatonii, Aster Family, Asteraceae; Perennial herb

QUICK ID: Look for 3-nerved basal leaves; reddish-purple, leafy, hairy flower stalks; and white, pink, or bluish rays and a yellow disk.

RANGE: NR, MR, SR; widespread, common

STEM: Erect, branched or not, 2–12 inches tall (5–30 cm), hairy.

FLOWERS: May–July. Clusters of 1–4 flower heads on leafy stalks; rays 16–42, white, pink to bluish purple, to 5⁄16 inch long (8mm), not coiling with age; disk yellow; phyllaries equally long, in 2–3 overlapping rows, densely hairy, pointed.

LEAVES: Basal; blades linear to lance-shaped, 2–4¾ inches long (5–12 cm), up to ½ inch wide (12 mm), with 3 parallel nerves; edges entire, surfaces hairy. Stem leaves alternate, much smaller.

HABITAT: Sagebrush, pinyon-juniper foothills, montane, subalpine forests. Elevation 5,000–10,000 feet (1,524–3,058 m).

Tall Fleabane

Erigeron elatior, Aster Family, Asteraceae; Perennial herb

QUICK ID: Look for tall, leafy stems; flower heads with white, pink, or lavender rays; a yellow disk; phyllaries with tangles of purple hairs.

RANGE: SR; widespread, locally common.

STEM: Erect, 8–24 inches tall (20–60 cm), hairy, rhizomatous.

FLOWERS: July–September. Flower heads have 75–150 pink-to-lavender ray florets, each ⅜–¾ inch long (1–2 cm), coiling with age; disk yellow; phyllaries in 2–4 rows, densely tangled with woolly, purple hairs; tips spreading and pointed.

LEAVES: Basal wither by flowering. Stem leaves alternate, lance-shaped, 1–3½ inches long (3–9 cm) by ¼–1 inch wide (5–25 mm); bases clasping, edges entire, surfaces sparsely to moderately hairy, tips tapering; blades nearly equally sized and evenly spaced up stem.

HABITAT: Forest openings, meadows; montane, subalpine forests, alpine. Elevation 7,900–12,500 feet (2,400–3,800 m).

Spruce-fir Fleabane

Erigeron eximius, Aster Family, Asteraceae; Perennial herb

QUICK ID: Look for stems with long-stalked basal and clasping stem leaves, and large flower heads with white-to-pink rays and yellow disk.

RANGE: MR, SR; widespread, common

STEM: Erect, upper branching, 4–24 inches tall (10–60 cm), hairless to short-hairy at base of flower heads.

FLOWERS: July–October. Have 1–5 flower heads with 40–80 narrow ray florets (white, pink, or lavender) each ½–¾ inch long (12–20 mm), coiling with age; buds nodding; phyllaries in 3–4 rows, hairless to sparsely hairy at base, tips taper, reflexed, often purplish.

LEAVES: Basal with long stalk. Blades spatula-shaped to elliptic, 1–6 inches long (3–15 cm) by ⅜–1⅜ inches wide (9–35 mm). Stem leaves alternate, gradually smaller and well-spaced upwards, clasping, hairless, 1-nerved, edges entire or with few tiny teeth.

HABITAT: Slopes, meadows; montane, subalpine spruce-fir forests. Elevation 7,550–11,485 feet (2,300–3,500 m).

Trailing Fleabane

Erigeron flagellaris, Aster Family, Asteraceae; Biennial, short-lived perennial herb

QUICK ID: Look for a mat-forming rosette with leafy rooting runners; a single flower stem; and a head with white rays and yellow disk.

RANGE: MR, SR: widespread, common; NR, Canada: rare

STEM: Erect, unbranched, 1–6 inches tall (3–15 cm), hairy, late-season runners usually have terminal plantlets.

FLOWERS: May–September. Buds single, nodding, pink-tinged; flower head 1 inch wide (25 mm) with 40–125 rays, white, often lavender tinted or a stripe on the backside; disk yellow; phyllaries in 2 rows, covered with loose to flat-lying hairs.

LEAVES: Basal rosette, blades elliptic to lance-shaped, ¾–2 inches long (2–5 cm) by ⅛–⅜ inch wide (3–9 mm); surfaces covered with flat-lying hairs. Stem leaves alternate, much smaller, often with only one leaf on the stem; margins entire to toothed.

HABITAT: Grasslands, sagebrush, foothills, montane, subalpine forest and meadows. Elevation 4,265–11,000 feet (1,300–3,350).

Blackhead Fleabane

Erigeron melanocephalus, Aster Family, Asteraceae; Perennial herb

QUICK ID: Look for mats of spoon-shaped basal leaves, stems with one head with white rays, and phyllaries densely covered with blackish hairs.

RANGE: SR; widespread, common

STEM: Erect, 1–5 inches tall (3–12 cm), dark hairs near tip.

FLOWERS: June–September. Flower head about 1 inch wide (25 mm) with 45–75 white, occasionally lavender, ray florets, each ¼–½ inch long (7–11 mm); disk yellow. Phyllaries in 2 equal rows, linear with tapering tips, densely covered with purplish-black hairs.

LEAVES: Mostly basal; blades spoon-shaped, ¾–2 inches long (20–50 mm) by ⅛–⅜ inch wide (4–8 mm); edges entire, surfaces hairless to sparsely hairy. Stem leaves few, alternate, smaller, linear, often twisting.

HABITAT: Subalpine forests and meadows, alpine. Elevation 10,170–13,125 feet (3,100–4,000 m).

Philadelphia Fleabane

Erigeron philadelphicus, Aster Family, Asteraceae; Perennial herb

QUICK ID: Look for leafy, hairy, branching stems; upper clasping leaves; heads with 150 white, threadlike rays; and a yellow disk.

RANGE: SR, NR, Canada; widespread, locally common

STEM: Erect, upper branching, 8–30 inches tall (20–76 cm), sparsely to densely hairy.

FLOWERS: February–June. Numerous ½–1-inch wide (12–25 mm) flower heads densely packed with 150–200 white, sometimes pinkish, rays, each 3⁄16–⅜ inch long (5–10 mm); disk yellow. Phyllaries in 2–3 rows, hairy or not. Flowers close at night.

LEAVES: Basal usually withered by blooming; blades spoon-shaped, 3–6 inches long (8–15 cm) by 1 inch wide (3 cm); edges toothed. Stem leaves alternate, oblong to lance-shaped, clasping, surfaces hairy, tips pointed, edges entire to widely spaced teeth.

HABITAT: Open woodlands, riparian; grasslands, sagebrush, foothill, montane forests. Elevation 4,700–9,500 feet (1,433–2,896 m).

Shaggy Fleabane

Erigeron pumilus, Aster Family, Asteraceae; Perennial herb

QUICK ID: Look for clustered stems, narrow leaves dense with shaggy, spreading hairs; heads packed with white rays, disk yellow.

RANGE: NR, MR, SR, Canada; widespread, common

STEM: Erect, clustered from base, branched or not, 2–12 inches tall (5–30 cm), densely hairy.

FLOWERS: May–July. Stem clusters have 1–15 heads to 1½ inches wide (38 mm) with 50–100 rays, each ¼–⅝ inch long (6–15 mm) by 1⁄16 inch wide (2 mm), white to pinkish, occasionally pale blue; buds nod. Phyllaries in 2–3 rows, dense with long, white hairs, tips taper to a point.

LEAVES: Basal; blades clustered, erect, linear to narrowly lance-shaped, ¾–8 inches long (2–8 cm) to ⅜ inch wide (8 mm). Stem leaves alternate, similar, smaller, few.

HABITAT: Grasslands, sagebrush, foothills, montane forests. Elevation 1,050–8,500 feet (320–2,590 m).

Prairie Fleabane

Erigeron strigosus, Aster Family, Asteraceae; Annual, biennial herb

QUICK ID: Look for stems with spreading upper branches; small upper leaves; 5–50 heads with short, narrow, white rays; yellow disk.

RANGE: NR, MR, SR, Canada; scattered, uncommon

STEM: Erect, branching, 12–28 inches tall (30–70 cm), hairs stiff.

FLOWERS: May–October. Clusters have 5–50 heads, each ½–¾ inch wide (12–20 mm), with 80–125 narrow, white rays about ¼ inch long (6 mm), densely stacked in layers; disk to ½ inch wide (12 mm). Phyllaries in 2–4 rows, light green, narrow, sparsely hairy.

LEAVES: Basal, may wither by blooming; blades elliptic narrowing to a slender base (spatula-shaped), 1–6 inches long (3–15 cm), to 1 inch wide (25 mm); edges mostly entire, surfaces hairy. Stem leaves alternate, smaller and becoming linear up the stem, stalkless.

HABITAT: Open, disturbed areas; grasslands, sagebrush to montane forests. Elevation 250 to 3,400 feet (75–1,038 m).

Early Blue-top Fleabane

Erigeron vetensis, Aster Family, Asteraceae; Perennial herb

QUICK ID: Look for dense clumps with long, narrow basal leaves, short stems, and single, showy heads with white rays and yellow disk.

RANGE: SR; widespread, common

STEM: Erect, 2–10 inches tall (5–25 cm), scattered long or short-stiff hairs and gland-tipped hairs.

FLOWERS: April–June. Single flower heads have 30–90 white-to-pale-blue rays, each ¼–⅝ inch long (6–16 mm); disk yellow. Phyllaries sparsely to moderately hairy with coarse, stiff hairs, with or without glands.

LEAVES: Basal rosette dense; blades long, narrow, linear, ¾–3½ inches long (2–9 cm); edges entire, usually folded over, lined with rough hairs, surfaces hairy or not. Stem leaves 1–2, alternate, smaller, narrow; surfaces sparsely hairy.

HABITAT: Rocky, exposed slopes, ridges; foothills, montane, subalpine forests. Elevation 7,000–11,600 feet (2,133–3,535 m).

Engelmann's Aster

Eucephalus engelmannii, Aster Family, Asteraceae; Perennial herb

QUICK ID: Look for tall, leafy, branching stems with clusters of flower heads with 8-13 white-to-pinkish-purple rays and yellow disks.

RANGE: NR, MR, SR (absent NM), Canada; widespread, common

STEM: Erect, upper branched, 20–60 inches tall (50–152 cm), hairy or not.

FLOWERS: July–September. Clusters have 5-15 flower heads to 2 inches wide (5 cm) with 8 or 13 narrow, white-to-pinkish-purple rays, each ⅜–1 inch long (15–25 mm). Phyllaries in 4–6 unequal rows, tips pointed or tapering and often reddish, surface and edges hairy.

LEAVES: Alternate, stalkless, mostly equal-sized. Blades elliptic to lance-shaped, 2–4 inches long (5–10 cm) by ⅝–1 inch wide (15–25 mm); edges entire, bottom surface smooth, top smooth to hairy.

HABITAT: Open forests, meadows; montane, subalpine forests. Elevation 1,640–10,500 feet (500–3,200 m).

White Hawkweed

Hieracium albiflorum, Aster Family, Asteraceae; Perennial herb

QUICK ID: Look for hairy basal leaves, slender stalks with spreading branches, and small flowers with white rays with tiny teeth; sap milky.

RANGE: NR, MR, SR (absent NM), Canada; widespread, common

STEM: Erect, upper branching, 6–16 inches tall (15–40 cm), hairy.

FLOWERS: May–September. Slender, spreading branches have 12–50 compact heads, each with 12–25 linear rays, ⅛–¼ inch long (3-5 mm), tipped with tiny teeth; no disk florets. Phyllaries linear, equal length, pointed, with few black hairs.

LEAVES: Basal, 3–8, short stalked, oval with narrow base, 1½–6¾ inches long (4–17 cm); edges entire to shallow to wavy toothed, surfaces hairy. Middle and upper leaves alternate, stalkless, smaller.

HABITAT: Open woods, meadows, roadsides; grasslands, sagebrush, foothills, montane forests. Elevation 2,000–9,500 feet (610–2,895 m).

Wild Cosmos

Hymenopappus newberryi, Aster Family, Asteraceae; Perennial herb

QUICK ID: Look for basal rosettes with compound leaves with small, narrow leaflets and flower heads with 8 white rays and a yellow disk.

RANGE: SR; widespread, common

STEM: Erect, branching, 8–24 inches tall (20–60 cm).

FLOWERS: May–September. Open clusters of 3–8 flower heads per stem, 1–1½ inches wide (25–38 mm); rays white, ⅝–¾ inch long (14–20 mm); disk yellow.

LEAVES: Basal from root crown, 5–10 inches long (12–25 cm), twice divided into narrow lobes along midrib, lobes 1⁄16 inch wide (1 mm). Stem leaves alternate, 1–3, smaller.

HABITAT: Meadows, forest openings; plains, foothills, montane, subalpine forests. Elevation 7,000–10,225 feet (2,133–3,116 m).

Oxeye Daisy

Leucanthemum vulgare, Aster Family, Asteraceae; Perennial herb; introduced, invasive

QUICK ID: Look for clumps with leafy stems, large flower heads, white rays, and yellow disks; introduced from Eurasia as a garden plant and spread throughout North America.

RANGE: NR, MR, SR, Canada; widespread, common

STEM: Erect to mounding, 1–2 feet tall (30–60 cm), rhizomatous.

FLOWERS: June–August. Flowers solitary on branch ends; 1–2 inches wide (3–5 cm) with 15–35 white rays with notched tips; disk yellow.

LEAVES: Basal, alternate on stem. Blades spatula to lance-shaped, or linear, 1–6 inches long (3–15 cm) with small, irregular teeth.

HABITAT: Meadows, forest openings, roadsides, riparian; prairies, foothills, montane forests. Elevation sea level to 9,500 feet (2,895 m)

SIMILAR SPECIES: Native fleabanes and asters with white, daisy-like flowers are much smaller in diameter.

Macoun's Cudweed

Pseudognaphalium macounii, Aster Family, Asteraceae; Annual to biennial herb

QUICK ID: Look for leafy stems, leaves with green tops, white-woolly bottoms, yellow disk florets, no rays, and rows of pearly-white bracts.

RANGE: NR, MR, SR, Canada; scattered, common

STEM: Erect, upper branched, 16–36 inches tall (40–90 cm), gland-tipped hairs.

FLOWERS: July–October. Dense, flat-topped, woolly-hairy clusters on branch ends have small flower heads with 4–5 rows of shiny, white-to-creamy, overlapping bracts; disk flowers evenly yellow, tightly packed.

LEAVES: Alternate. Blades linear to lance-shaped, 1–4 inches long (3–10 cm) by ¼–½ inch wide (3–13 mm); bicolored with the top surface green, covered with tiny gland-tipped hairs, bottom side whitish, lightly covered with woolly hairs; edges entire, often wavy; tiny wings grow down the stem from the leaf base.

HABITAT: Dry, open areas, disturbed sites; grasslands to subalpine forests. Elevation 5,200–10,400 feet (1,584–3,170 m).

White Heath Aster

Symphyotrichum ericoides, Aster Family, Asteraceae; Perennial herb

QUICK ID: Look for stems with tiny, spine-tipped leaves, solitary flowers on branchlets along stem with small, flower heads ½–1 inch wide (12–25 mm) with white rays and yellow disk.

RANGE: NR, MR, SR, Canada; widespread, common

STEM: Erect, single or branched from base, 1–3 feet tall (30–90 cm), hairs short, flat-lying, colony-forming.

FLOWERS: July–October. Cylindrical arrays have up to 200 flower heads; rays 10–18, narrow, ⅛–½ inch long (4–12 mm). Phyllaries spine-tipped, reflexed to spreading.

LEAVES: Basal, lower stem leaves wither by flowering. Upper leaves alternate, linear, ⅜–1 ½ inches long (1–4 cm) by ⅛ inch wide (3 mm), crowded on flowering branchlets; spine tipped, hairy.

HABITAT: Wet meadows, ditches, riparian woodlands; grasslands to montane forests. Elevation 3,800–8,000 feet (1,158–2,438 m).

SIMILAR SPECIES: White Prairie Aster, *S. falcatum*, (all regions) has 20–35 longer, white rays.

White Prairie Aster

Symphyotrichum falcatum, Aster Family, Asteraceae; Perennial herb

QUICK ID: Look for short-hairy stems; many floral branchlets along stem with hundreds of flower heads with white rays and yellow disk.

RANGE: NR, MR, SR, Canada; widespread, common

STEM: Erect, 1-5 branched from base, 4-32 inches tall (10-80 cm), colony forming, moderately to dense with short, flat-lying hairs.

FLOWERS: July–October. Solitary to clustered on branchlets along stem with up to 200 flower heads, each with 20–35 rays, ¾–1¼ inch long (18–30 mm). Phyllaries hairy, spine-tipped, in 3–4 rows, base whitish, upper with a diamond-shaped green zone, tips spreading to reflexed.

LEAVES: Basal often wither by flowering. Stem leaves alternate, stalkless, linear to lance-shaped, ⅜-1½ inches long (1–4 cm), small leaves often in axils; edges entire, surfaces gray-green, smooth to stiff-hairy, often tipped with tiny spine; smaller upward.

HABITAT: Dry sites. open woods, disturbed areas; grasslands to montane forests. Elevation 3,500–8,000 feet (1,100–2,400 m).

Stemless Townsend Daisy

Townsendia exscapa, Aster Family, Asteraceae; Perennial herb

QUICK ID: Look for flower heads nestled in mats of dense rosettes; flowers have long white rays and a densely hairy yellow disk.

RANGE: SR: widespread, common; NR, MR, Canada: infrequent

STEM: Flower stalk to 1 inch tall (3 cm) directly from root crown.

FLOWERS: March–June. Flower heads 1–1½ inches wide (25–38 mm) with 20–40 white-to-pinkish rays, each ½–⅞ inch long (12–22 mm); disk flowers densely surrounded by pappus hairs. Phyllaries in 4–6 rows, narrow, 6x longer than wide, edges ciliate, tips pointed.

LEAVES: Basal rosette. Blades linear to slightly spatula-shaped, ½–2 inches long (12–50 mm), to ¼ inch wide (2–6 mm), tips pointed; top and bottom surfaces covered with tiny, white, flat-lying hairs.

HABITAT: Coarse soils; pinyon-juniper foothills, montane pine forests. Elevation 4,000–9,000 feet (1,220–2,743 m).

White-head Mule's Ears

Wyethia helianthoides, Aster Family, Asteraceae; Perennial herb

QUICK ID: Look for clumps of large, elliptic basal leaves and leafy stems with a large, showy flower head with white rays and yellow disk.

RANGE: NR, MR; widespread, locally common

STEM: Erect to sprawling, 10–16 inches tall (25–40 cm), soft-hairy.

FLOWERS: May–July. Stems have a single head 3–4 inches wide (8–10 cm), with 11–25 rays, each 1–1¾ inches long (25–45 mm), disk yellow. Phyllaries in loose rows, linear, leaf-like, edges densely hairy.

LEAVES: Basal, stalked; blades elliptic to lance-shaped, 8–12 inches long (20–30 cm); edges entire, smooth or lined with ciliate hairs; surfaces sparsely soft-hairy. Stem leaves alternate, smaller, stalked.

HABITAT: Wet meadows, damp woods; grasslands, sagebrush, montane, subalpine forests. Elevation 3,000–8,530 feet (915–2,600 m).

Thicksepal Cryptantha

Cryptantha crassisepala, Borage Family, Boraginacaea; Annual herb

QUICK ID: Look for foliage covered with bristly hairs, and ¼-inch-wide (6 mm), white flowers on a one-sided, curving spike with a hooked end.

RANGE: SR; widespread, common

STEM: Erect to spreading, base branching, 2–6 inches long (5–15 cm).

FLOWERS: March–July. Funnel-shaped with 5 petal-like lobes, each 1⁄32–¼ inch wide (1–6 mm), white with yellow throat scales. The flowering stem curves at the tip as it develops with pairs of bristly seed pods, to ¼ inch long (6 mm), pointing upward.

LEAVES: Basal cluster, alternate on stem. Blades linear to lance-shaped, ¾–2½ inches long (2–6 cm), ⅛–¼ inch wide (3–6 mm), smaller up the stem; margins entire, densely covered with long and short, bristly hairs.

HABITAT: Dry soils of disturbed areas, grasslands, sagebrush, pinyon-juniper foothills. Elevation 3,300–7,200 feet (975–2,200 m).

Miner's Candle

Oreocarya celosiodes (Cryptantha celosiodes), Borage Family, Boraginaceae; Biennial, perennial herb

QUICK ID: Look for silky-hairy stems and leaves, and bristly-hairy spikes of tiny white flowers with 5 lobes and yellow bulges in throat.

RANGE: NR, MR: widespread, common; SR, Canada: scattered, infrequent

STEM: Erect, often branched from base, 4–20 inches tall (10–50 cm), silky-hairy, bristly throughout.

FLOWERS: May–August. Spikes densely hairy, bristly; flowers funnel-shaped, opening to ½ inch wide (12 mm) with 5 oval lobes; yellow bulges prominent in throat.

LEAVES: Basal on stalks; blades spoon-shaped, tips rounded, ¾–3 inches long (2–8 cm). Stem leaves alternate, similar, smaller.

HABITAT: Dry, coarse soils; arid grasslands, sagebrush, foothills, montane forests. Elevation 2,000–8,000 feet (610–2,438 m).

Bow-nut Cryptantha

Oreocarya suffruticosa (Cryptantha cinerea), Borage Family, Boraginacaea; Perennial herb

QUICK ID: Look for foliage densely covered with long and short slivery hairs, and one-sided, hooked spikes with ⅜-inch-wide (10 mm), white flowers with yellow throats.

RANGE: MR, SR; widespread, common

STEM: Erect to spreading, single or branching base, 2–8 inches tall (5–20 cm).

FLOWERS: April–October. Clusters narrow to broad, elongating with a hooked tip at maturity. Flowers funnel-shaped with 5 white, petal-like lobes, each $^{3}/_{16}$–⅜ inch wide (5–9 mm), usually with yellow scales around the throat; the floral tube does not extend above the tips of the sepals; sepals densely covered with loose to bristly hairs.

LEAVES: Basal rosette blades to 3½ inches long (9 cm), ascending, silver-hairy, spatula- to lance-shaped, pointed. Alternate stem blades similar, smaller, narrow.

HABITAT: Disturbed areas; sagebrush, pinyon-juniper foothills, montane forests. Elevation 3,500–8,500 feet (1,065–2,590 m).

Hoary Alyssum

Berteroa incana, Mustard Family, Brassicaceae; Annual to perennial herb; introduced, invasive

QUICK ID: Look for stems covered with flat-laying hairs and topped with dense clusters of small white flowers with 4 deeply notched petals. Classified as a noxious weed in some states.

RANGE: NR, MR, SR, Canada; widespread, common

STEM: Single to multiple, branching, 1–3 feet tall (30–91 cm).

FLOWERS: May–September. Rounded clusters, 1–2 inches wide (3–5 cm) on branch tips; 4 petals so deeply notched they look like 8. Hairy pods, ¼ inch long (6 mm), slightly flattened, line the flower stalk.

LEAVES: Basal wither by flowering. Stem leaves alternate, stemless; blades linear to elliptic, ¾–3 inches long, (2–8 cm) by ½ inch wide (12 mm); surfaces covered with short, grayish hairs; tips blunt to pointed.

HABITAT: Disturbed, sandy soils; grasslands, sagebrush, foothills, montane forests. Elevation 2,000–9,200 feet (610–2,800 m).

Drummond's Rockcress

Boechera stricta (Arabis drummondii), Mustard Family, Brassicaceae; Biennial, short-lived perennial herb

QUICK ID: Look for a single stem per rosette; small white flowers with 4 petals; and the thin, cylindrical, upward-pointing fruit capsules.

RANGE: NR, MR, SR, Canada; widespread, common

STEM: Slender, unbranching, nearly hairless, 6–30 inches tall (15–76 cm).

FLOWERS: May–July. Erect, tight clusters at stem tips have 8–35 flowers, each ⅜ inch wide (10 mm), with 4 narrow petals in a cross pattern, white aging to lavender; sepals erect, pale green, hairless. Seed capsules erect, wire-like, 2–4 inches long (5–10 cm).

LEAVES: Basal rosette, often several bunched together; blades oblong with stalks, tips pointed. Alternate stem leaves clasp and conceal stem near base, more spaced upward; blades to 3 inches long (8 cm), narrowly lance-shaped with 2 small lobes at base.

HABITAT: Montane, subalpine forests, alpine meadows. Elevation 7,700–12,800 feet (2,350–3,900 m).

Heartleaf Bittercress

Cardamine cordifolia, Mustard Family, Brassiaceae; Perennial herb

QUICK ID: Look for dense clusters on stem tips; flowers with 4 white petals; heart-shaped leaves; and erect, linear seed pods.

RANGE: SR, NR, Canada; widespread, common

STEM: Erect, leafy, 7-32 inches tall (18-81 cm), colony forming.

FLOWERS: June–September. Flowers ⅝ inch wide (15 mm) with 4 oval petals, each ¼-½ inch long (7-12 mm). Seed pod is a slender capsule (silique), erect, linear, ¾-1½ inches long (2-4 cm).

LEAVES: Alternate. Blades variable, oval to heart- or kidney-shaped, ¾-2¾ inches long (2-7 cm); margins wavy to lined with coarse, shallow, rounded teeth or pointed lobes; surfaces hairless to hairy.

HABITAT: Moist soils, stream sides, meadows; montane, subalpine forests, alpine tundra. Elevation 7,872-10,075 feet (2,400-3,070 m).

Mesa Pepperwort

Lepidium alyssoides, Mustard Family, Brassicaceae; Perennial herb

QUICK ID: Look for rounded clumps covered with dense, spherical arrays of small white flowers, 6 stamens, and egg-shaped seed pods.

RANGE: SR; widespread, common

STEM: Erect, branching from woody base, 4-19 inches tall (10-48 cm).

FLOWERS: March–July. Dense clusters on branch tips; flowers tiny, 4 white, egg-shaped petals; 6 stamens, 4 long, 2 short. Seed pods on ¾-inch-long (20 mm) pedicels, flat to cupped, egg-shaped, tip is shallowly notched with a protruding mature style.

LEAVES: Basal, often in a rosette; blades ½-8 inches long (1-20 cm), deeply lobed along midrib. Stem leaves alternate; upper blades without stalks, narrow, linear, ½-2¾ inches long (12-38 mm) ; edges entire.

HABITAT: Coarse soils, disturbed areas; arid grasslands, sagebrush, foothills, montane forests. Elevation 2,500-9,500 feet (765-2,895 m).

SIMILAR SPECIES: Common Pepperweed, *L. densiflorum* (all regions), has petals tiny to absent.

Whitetop, Hoary Cress

Lepidium draba, Mustard Family, Brassicaceae; Perennial herb; introduced, invasive

QUICK ID: Look for colonies up to 5 feet wide (1.5 m), tall stems with clasping leaves, and dense clusters of small white flowers with 4 petals.

RANGE: NR, MR, SR, Canada; scattered, locally common

STEM: Erect, branching, 2 feet tall (60 cm), rhizomatous.

FLOWERS: April–August. Dense, flat-topped clusters on branch ends; 4 oval petals, ⅛–3/16 inch long (3–4 mm); fruit pods on short stalks, heart-shaped with notched to rounded tip. Considered a noxious weed, each plant can produce up to 5,000 seeds.

LEAVES: Basal leaves usually wither by flowering. Stem leaves alternate; blade elliptic to lance-shaped, ¾–4 inches long (2–10 cm), stalkless; surfaces hairy or not, margins entire, toothed, or wavy.

HABITAT: Disturbed areas, riparian, agricultural fields, roadsides. Elevation sea level to 7,800 feet (2,377 m).

Virginia Pepperweed

Lepidium virginicum, Mustard Family, Brassicaceae; Annual, biennial herb

QUICK ID: Look for bushy plants with compact, elongated clusters of small white flowers with 4 petals, 2 stamens, and round pods.

RANGE: NR, MR, SR, Canada; widespread, common

STEM: Erect, upper branching, 6–28 inches tall (15–70 cm), with short, white hairs.

FLOWERS: February–November. Flowers have 4 white petals ⅛ inch long (3 mm), longer than the 4 sepals separating them; 2 stamens. Clusters elongate in fruit; pods flat, notched, round, ⅛ inch wide (3 mm), on short stalks lining an elongated stem.

LEAVES: Basil, egg-shaped, pinnately lobed, wither by flowering. Stem leaves alternate, smaller up the stem; blades linear to oval, ⅜–2⅜ inches long (1–6 cm) by ⅛–⅜ inch wide (3–10 mm), base tapered, tip pointed, edges entire or serrated, surfaces sparsely hairy.

HABITAT: Dry disturbed areas, waste places, meadows; sagebrush, foothills, montane forests. Elevation 2,300–9,125 feet (700–2,775 m).

Watercress

Nasturtium officinale, Mustard Family, Brassicaceae; Perennial herb; introduced, naturalized

QUICK ID: Look in shallow water for floating mats of leafy stems with rounded clusters of small white flowers with 4 petals. Stems and leaves have a peppery flavor popular in salads.

RANGE: NR, MR, SR, Canada; widespread, common

STEM: Floating, creeping, rooting at nodes, highly branching, 1–3¼ feet long (30–100 cm).

FLOWERS: April–September. Rounded clusters above water have 4 oval petals, ¼ inch long (5 mm). Fruit a slender pod, ½–1¼ inches long (12–30 mm).

LEAVES: Alternate. Blade pinnate with 3–9 leaflets along midrib, each lance-shaped to oblong, ⅜–1½ inches long (1–4 cm), terminal leaflet largest, rounded; edges entire to wavy, surfaces smooth.

HABITAT: Wet soils, shallow water, streams, ponds, wetlands. Elevation 1,500–8,300 feet (460–2,525 m).

Wild Candytuft

Noccaea fendleri, Mustard Family, Brassicaceae; Perennial herb

QUICK ID: Look for leafy stems with rounded clusters of small white-to-pinkish flowers with 4 oval petals, and disk-like pods circling stem.

RANGE: NR, MR, SR; widespread, common

STEM: Erect, 1 to many from base, single or upper branched, to 10 inches tall (25 cm).

FLOWERS: May–August. Rounded to elongated clusters of flowers with 4 white-to-pinkish, oblong petals, $^{3}/_{16}$–½ inch long (5–13 mm), buds purplish; stamens and style extend outside flower throat; fruit a flat, oval disk on short, horizontal-to-descending stalks.

LEAVES: Basal rosette; blades to 3 inches long (8 cm). Stem leaves alternate, clasping; blades oval, to 1¼ inches long (3 cm) by ¾ inch wide (19 mm); edges entire to toothed, tips rounded to pointed.

HABITAT: Coarse soils, open woods, meadows; foothills, montane, subalpine forests, alpine. Elevation 6,000–13,000 feet (1,829–3,962 m).

SIMILAR SPECIES: Heartleaf Bittercress, *Cardamine cordifolia*, has heart-shaped leaves.

American False Candytuft

Smelowskia americana, Mustard Family, Brassicaceae; Perennial herb

QUICK ID: Look in the alpine zone for soft-hairy basal leaves, several stems topped with dense clusters of small flowers with 4 white petals.

RANGE: NR, MR, SR: widespread, common; Canada: infrequent

STEM: Erect, branched or not, ¾–8 inches tall (2–20 cm), hairy.

FLOWERS: June–August. Clusters rounded, hairy; flowers have 4 petals, white, rarely pinkish or lavender, each ¼ inch long (5–7 mm long); pods erect, oblong, ¼–½ inch long (5–12 mm), smooth.

LEAVES: Basal, long stalked, mat forming; blades pinnate, lobes oblong to fan-shaped, ⅜–1⅜ inches long (10–35 mm); surfaces sparsely to densely hairy. Stem leaves similar, few, alternate.

HABITAT: Tundra, scree, talus slopes, crevices; alpine. Elevation 6,500–13,125 feet (2,080–4,000 m).

Utah Honeysuckle

Lonicera utahensis, Honeysuckle Family, Caprifoliaceae; Deciduous woody shrub

QUICK ID: Look for spreading, leafy shrubs with twin, funnel-shaped, white-to-creamy flowers, and pairs of small, round, red berries.

RANGE: NR, MR, Canada; widespread, common

STEM: Erect, 1 ½–7 feet tall (0.5–2 m), branches slender, hairless.

FLOWERS: June–July. Paired flowers from leaf axils, tubular, ⅜–¾ inch long (1–2 cm), with 5 lobes flaring open, tube hairy within; bracts are minute. Fruit is paired red berries, united at the base.

LEAVES: Opposite; blades oblong to elliptic, ¾–3 inches long (2–8 cm) by ⅜–1½ inches wide (1–4 cm); edges entire, surfaces smooth to sparsely hairy beneath, tips rounded.

HABITAT: Moist woods, openings; grasslands, sagebrush, foothills, montane, subalpine. Elevation 2,000–10,000 feet (610–3,048 m).

Sharpleaf Valerian

Valeriana acutiloba, Honeysuckle Family, Caprifoliaceae; Perennial herb

QUICK ID: Look for 1-3 pairs of widely spaced, opposite stem leaves with slender, pointed lobes, and dense clusters of small white flowers.

RANGE: NR, MR, SR; widespread, common

STEM: Erect, may be upper branched, 8–30 inches tall (20–76 cm), hairless throughout.

FLOWERS: May–July. Dense clusters of small pinkish-white flowers on short, radiating branches at the stem apex; floral tube funnel-shaped, 3⁄16–1⁄4 inch long (4–6 mm) with 5 spreading oval lobes; stamens and style extend beyond the throat.

LEAVES: Mostly basal; blades oblong to spatula-shaped 1¼–5½ inches long (3–14 cm), edges usually entire. Stem leaves opposite, 1–3 pairs widely spaced, blade lance-shaped; upper leaves smaller, pinnate with long, narrow, pointed lobes.

HABITAT: Moist meadows, slopes; foothills, montane, subalpine forests. Elevation 5,700–11,000 feet (1,738–3,353 m).

Tobacco Root

Valeriana edulis, Honeysuckle Family, Caprifoliaceae; Perennial herb

QUICK ID: Look for tall stems with long basal leaves lined with tiny white hairs, and broad, airy clusters of tiny white flowers.

RANGE: NR, MR, SR, Canada; widespread, common

STEM: Erect, upper branching, 1–4 feet tall (30–120 cm), smooth to short-hairy.

FLOWERS: May–September. Flower cluster freely branched; tiny flowers are male, female, or combined, with 5 white-to-creamy petal-lobes that curl backwards.

LEAVES: Basal with winged stalk; blades linear to egg-shaped, 4–12 inches long (10–30 cm); edges lobed or not, lined with short, white hairs; surfaces hairless, veined. Stem leaves smaller, opposite, 2–6 pairs, pinnate with narrow lobes.

HABITAT: Moist meadows, open woods, slopes; sagebrush, foothills, montane, subalpine forests. Elevation 6,578–12,850 feet (2,000–3,917 m).

Spreading Sandwort

Arenaria lanuginosa var. *saxosa*, Pink Family, Caryophyllaceae; Perennial herb

QUICK ID: Look for loose clumps (not mats) with up to 80 stems covered with small white flowers.

RANGE: SR; widespread, common

STEM: 2–24 inches tall (5–60 cm), clump forming.

FLOWERS: June–October. Flat-topped clusters of flowers with 5 green, pointed sepals and 5 white, oval petals, each about ¼ inch long (6 cm); 10 stamens have white filaments and pinkish anthers.

LEAVES: Opposite. Blades elliptic to linear-lance-shaped, to 1⅜ inches long (35 mm) by ⅝ inch wide (14 mm); surfaces minutely hairy, margins entire with ciliate hairs, tip blunt to pointed; the bottom has a prominent center vein.

HABITAT: Talus slopes, dry meadows, forest understory; foothills, montane, subalpine. Elevation 5,600–10,900 feet (1,701–3,322 m).

SIMILAR SPECIES: Fendler's Sandwort, *Eremogone fendleri*, in much the same range, forms a dense mat with grass-like leaves.

Field Chickweed

Cerastium arvense, Pink Family, Caryophyllaceae; Perennial herb

QUICK ID: Look for mats or mounds of branching stems and erect stems with clusters of small white flowers with deeply notched petals.

RANGE: NR, MR, SR, Canada; widespread, common

STEM: Branched, clump forming, 4–16 inches wide (10–40 cm), hairy.

FLOWERS: May–September. Clusters have 1–20 flowers with 5 petals, each oval, deeply notched, ⁵⁄₁₆–½ inch long (8–12 mm), throat greenish yellow; sepals hairy, pointed, only half as long as petals.

LEAVES: Opposite. Blades linear to lance-shaped, ⅜–1¼ inches long (1–3 cm), with bundles of small secondary leaves in lower leaf axils; edges ciliate, surfaces slightly to softly hairy, tips pointed.

HABITAT: Coarse soils, moist areas; grasslands, foothills, montane, subalpine forests, alpine. Elevation 6,000–12,600 feet (1,839–3,840 m).

SIMILAR SPECIES: Bering Chickweed, *C. beeringianum*, in alpine areas, doesn't have clusters of small leaves in the axils.

Alpine Sandwort

Cherleria obtusiloba (Minuartia obtusiloba), Pink Family, Caryophyllaceae; Perennial herb

QUICK ID: Look for dense cushion-mats covered with small white flowers on short stalks with 5 rounded petals and yellowish throats.

RANGE: NR, MR, SR, Canada; widespread, common

STEM: Mounding mats to 16 inches across (40 cm), glandular-hairy.

FLOWERS: July–August. Solitary flower on short, glandular-hairy stalk; 5 petals, oval, ⅛–⅜ inch long (4–10 mm), throat greenish yellow. Sepals 5, shorter than petals, 3⁄16 inch long (4–5 mm), tips rounded, purplish, glandular-hairy.

LEAVES: Basal, erect, tightly overlapping; blades 3-angled, oblong to linear, ⅛–⅜ inch long (3–8 mm), less than 1 mm wide, 1-nerved, smooth to glandular-hairy or with hairy edges; axillary leaves bundled in axils of primary leaves. Stem leaves similar, opposite.

HABITAT: Dry slopes. meadows, fell-fields; subalpine, alpine. Elevation 9,000–13,000 feet (2,743–3,962 m).

SIMILAR SPECIES: Nuttall's Sandwort, *Sabulina nuttallii*, (NR, MR) has several flowers per stem.

Ballhead Sandwort

Eremogone congesta, Pink Family, Caryophyllaceae; Perennial herb

QUICK ID: Look for grass-like mats of needle-like leaves with tall stems tipped with dense, rounded clusters of small white flowers.

RANGE: NR, MR, SR (absent NM), Canada; widespread, common

STEM: Erect, slender, mostly leafless, 3–16 inches tall (8–40 cm).

FLOWERS: May–August. Densely packed, head-like clusters of star-shaped flowers, each with 5 oval petals ¼–⅜ inch long (5–8 mm), about twice as long as sepals; 10 white stamens protrude from the throat, anthers white to pink.

LEAVES: Basal grass-like, present or not; stem leaves 3–5 pairs, similar to basal but smaller. Blades erect to spreading, needle-like, ¾–4⅜ inches long (2–11 cm) by 1⁄16 inch wide (2 mm), flexible or rigid.

HABITAT: Dry soils of sagebrush, pinyon-juniper foothills, montane, subalpine forests. Elevation 4,000–9,850 feet (1,200–3,300 m).

Fendler's Sandwort

Eremogone fendleri, Pink Family, Caryophyllaceae; Perennial herb

QUICK ID: Look for mats of grass-like, flexible (not prickly) leaves with tall stems and open clusters of small, white, star-shaped flowers.

RANGE: SR; widespread, common

STEM: Erect, slender, 4–12 inches tall (10–30 cm), glandular-hairy.

FLOWERS: May–July. Spreading clusters have 3–35 flowers, each with 5 linear, white petals, ¼–⅜ inch long (5–8 mm), tips rounded; petals longer than sepals; sepals glandular-hairy with pointed tips; 10 stamens tipped with reddish anthers, fading to yellow. Note that stalks and sepals are covered with sticky, glandular hairs.

LEAVES: Basal and opposite on stem. Thick mat of flexible, linear, grass-like basal leaves ⅜–4 inches long (1–10 cm); 2–6 pairs if stem leaves similar, opposite.

HABITAT: Pinyon-juniper, ponderosa, spruce-fir forests, alpine meadows. Elevation 6,500–13,000 feet (1,980–3,965 m).

SIMILAR SPECIES: Prickly Sandwort, *E. aculeata*, (NR) has a prickly mat of leaves.

Hooker's Sandwort

Eremogone hookeri, Pink Family, Caryophyllaceae; Perennial herb

QUICK ID: Look for dense, hemispheric clumps with needle-like leaves covered with clusters of small flowers with 5 star-like petals.

RANGE: MR, SR; widespread, infrequent

STEM: Erect, unbranched, to 8 inches tall (20 cm), mat forming.

FLOWERS: May–August. Crowded clusters on stem tips have flowers about ⅜–¾ inch wide (9–17 mm) with spreading, oval petals with round-to-pointed tips; 10 protruding white stamens have white anthers; sepals lance-shaped, hairy, sharply pointed.

LEAVES: Basal; blades needle-like, stiff, ¼–⅝ inch long (5–15 mm). Stem leaves opposite with 1–4 pairs.

HABITAT: Grasslands, sagebrush, foothills, montane forests; Elevation 3,050–9,515 feet (1,200–2,900 m).

Bluntleaf Sandwort

Moehringia lateriflora, Pink Family, Caryophyllaceae; Perennial herb

QUICK ID: Look for delicate stems; opposite, elliptic leaves; and upper branches with small flowers with 5 rounded, white petals.

RANGE: NR, MR, SR, Canada; widespread, common

STEM: Erect to prostrate, typically branched, 2–10 inches tall (5–30 cm), short-hairy, rhizomatous, colony forming.

FLOWERS: April–July. Terminal clusters have 2–6 flowers; each flower ⅜ inch wide (8 mm) with 5 egg-shaped petals; 5 sepals with blunt tips. Note the petals are ¾–1½ times longer than sepals.

LEAVES: Opposite, 3–7 pairs; blades elliptic, ½–1½ inches long (12–40 mm) by ⅛–⅜ inch wide (3–10 mm); 1–3 veins, surfaces smooth to short-hairy below; edge minutely hairy, tip blunt.

HABITAT: Open woodlands, meadows, prairies; foothills, montane forests. Elevation 6,000–9,000 feet (1,828–2,743 m).

SIMILAR SPECIES: Largeleaf Sandwort, *M. macrophylla*, (SR, NR, Canada) has sharp-pointed sepals ¾–1½ times shorter than petals.

Largeleaf Sandwort

Moehringia macrophylla, Pink Family, Caryophyllaceae; Perennial herb

QUICK ID: Look for delicate stems with evenly spaced, opposite leaves, and small, white flowers in open, short-branching clusters.

RANGE: NR, SR, Canada; widespread, common

STEM: Erect, simple or branching, 2–8 inches tall (5–20 cm), minutely hairy, rhizomatous, colony forming.

FLOWERS: May–July. Clusters have 1–5 flowers on short branches. Flowers ¼–½ inch wide (6–12 mm) with 5 white, rounded petals ⅛–¼ inch long (3–6 mm); sepals pointed. Note the petals are ¾ to 1½ times longer than the sepals.

LEAVES: Opposite. Blades thin, lance-shaped to elliptical, ⅝–2 inches long (15–50 mm), to ½ inch wide (12 mm), 1–3 veined; surfaces minutely hairy, margins entire, tips pointed.

HABITAT: Moist, forest understory, riparian; montane, subalpine forests. Elevation 7,300–10,500 feet (2,225–3,200 m).

SIMILAR SPECIES: Bluntleaf Starwort, *M. lateriflora*, (all regions) has blunt-tipped sepals about half as long as the petals.

Tuber Starwort

Pseudostellaria jamesiana, Pink Family, Caryophyllaceae; Perennial herb

QUICK ID: Look for clumps of slender stems with narrow, opposite leaves and small white flowers with 5 notched petals.

RANGE: NR, MR, SR; widespread, common

STEM: Erect, 4–17 inches tall (10–43 cm), 4-angled, hairless or glandular-hairy, rhizomatous.

FLOWERS: May–August. Flowers ¾ inch wide (2 cm) on glandular stalks; 5 petals, tips rounded, V-shaped notched; 10 anthers dark brown to purple. Capsule oblong, ¼ inch long (5 mm).

LEAVES: Opposite, stalkless, widely spaced, perpendicular to stem. Blades linear to lance-shaped, ¾–4 inches long (2–10 cm) by 1⁄16–¾ inch wide (2–20 mm); edges entire, tip pointed, surfaces smooth to glandular-hairy, with one prominent vein.

HABITAT: Meadows, drainages, disturbed areas; grasslands to montane forests. Elevation 6,500–10,500 feet (1,980–3,200 m).

SIMILAR SPECIES: Long-stalk Starwort, *Stellaria longipes*, (common throughout) has five petals so deeply notched that they look like 10.

Nuttall's Sandwort

Sabulina nuttallii (Minuartia nuttallii), Pink Family, Caryophyllaceae; Perennial herb

QUICK ID: Look for mat-forming clumps, narrow leaves, and flowering stalks with loose clusters of star-like flowers with 5 white petals.

RANGE: NR, MR, Canada (rare); widespread

STEM: Much branched from base, spreading to 1 foot wide (30 cm), densely glandular-hairy, rhizomatous.

FLOWERS: May–September. Open clusters with 6–30 flowers on erect stalks to 1–4 inches tall (3–10 cm) and very brittle; 5 star-like, oblong, pointed petals, 3⁄16 inch long (4 mm), separated by 5 longer, brownish, pointed sepals; 10 stamens, spreading.

LEAVES: Opposite. Blades linear to narrowly lance-shaped, ¼–½ inch long (6–12 mm) by 1 mm wide, lying flat against the stem, overlapping adjacent leaves; tips pointed, surfaces glandular-hairy; secondary leaves clustered in axils of primary leaves.

HABITAT: Sandy, rocky soils; sagebrush, foothills, montane, subalpine forests, alpine. Elevation 4,500–12,000 feet (1,312–3,656 m).

Beautiful Sandwort

Sabulina rubella (Minuartia rubella), Pink Family, Caryophyllaceae; Perennial herb

QUICK ID: Look in tundra for mat-forming plants with glandular-hairy flower stems to 6 inches tall (15 cm) with small white flowers.

RANGE: NR, MR, SR, Canada; widespread, locally common

STEM: Branching from root crown, 1½–8 inches across (4–20 cm), glandular-hairy.

FLOWERS: June–September. Loose clusters with 3–7 flowers on densely glandular-hairy, leafy stalks; 5 petals, elliptic, ⅛–¼ inch long (3–5 mm); 5 sepals, about equal to the petals, tips pointed, green to purple.

LEAVES: Basal, erect, crowded, overlapping; blades needle-like, straight to curved outward, to ⅜ inch long (10 mm), flat to 3-angled; surface often hairy, bottom side 3-veined. Stem leaves opposite, smaller.

HABITAT: Open woods, meadows, slopes, fellfields; subalpine, alpine. Elevation 7,875–13,000 feet (2,400–3,962 m).

SIMILAR SPECIES: The alpine Large-flowered Sandwort, *S. macrantha*, (MR, SR) is hairless throughout.

Sleepy Catchfly

Silene antirrhina, Pink Family, Caryophyllaceae; Annual herb

QUICK ID: Look for thin stems with reddish sticky bands (often with trapped insects), narrow leaves, and tiny white-to-pink-tinted flowers.

RANGE: NR, MR, SR, Canada; widespread, infrequent

STEM: Erect, often branched, 4–32 inches tall (10–80 cm), smooth with red-to-brown sticky bands.

FLOWERS: March–May. Flowers ¼ inch wide (6 mm) with 5 small petals, white to pink, or bicolored with interior white, exterior red, tips pointed or lobed; calyx oval, hairless with 10 longitudinal ribs.

LEAVES: Basal, stalkless; blades linear to lance-shaped, 1–2 inches long (3–5 cm) by 1⁄16–½ inch wide (2–12 mm); surfaces hairless, rough; margins entire. Stem leaves few, opposite, lower leaves lined with ciliate hairs.

HABITAT: Dry, coarse soils, disturbed areas; arid grasslands, sagebrush, foothills, montane forests. Elevation 3,600–8,450 feet (1,100–2,575 m).

Drummond's Campion

Silene drummondii, Pink Family, Caryophyllaceae; Perennial herb

QUICK ID: Look for tall stems with few leaves, flowers with white-to-reddish petals, and a glandular-hairy calyx with 10 dark ribs.

RANGE: NR, MR, SR, Canada; widespread, common

STEM: Erect, branched or not, 8–20 inches tall (20–50 cm); short-hairy to glandular.

FLOWERS: June–September. Loose clusters have 1-20 glandular or hairy flowers; calyx (below petals) tubular, ⅜–⅝ inch long (10–15 mm), glandular-hairy, with 10 dark ribs; 5 notched petals equal or 1½ times the length of the calyx.

LEAVES: Mostly basal rosette, stalked; blades elliptic to lance-shaped, 1-4 inches long (3-10 cm); surfaces with stiff, flat-lying hairs. Stem leaves opposite, 2-5 pairs, stalkless, much smaller.

HABITAT: Dry prairies, open woods; sagebrush to alpine. Elevation 7,000–12,500 feet (2,134–3,810 m).

SIMILAR SPECIES: White Campion, *S. latifolia*, (exotic) has separate male flowers with yellow stamen, and female flowers with white pistils.

White Campion

Silene latifolia, Pink Family, Caryophyllaceae; Annual, biennial, short-lived perennial herb, introduced

QUICK ID: Look for stems with opposite leaves and unisexual white flowers: males with yellow stamen, females with white pistils.

RANGE: NR, MR, SR, Canada; widespread, common, naturalized

STEM: Erect, branched from base, 16–40 inches tall (40–100 cm), lower stem stiff-hairy, upper glandular, sticky.

FLOWERS: May–September. Clusters branched; flowers have 5 white petals, entire or 2-lobed, ¾–1⅝ inch long (2-4 cm), longer than calyx; calyx short-hairy to glandular, ⅜–1 inch long (1-3 cm). Male tubular with 10 dark ribs; female inflated, urn-shaped, with 20 dark ribs.

LEAVES: Basal usually wither by flowering. Stem leaves stalkless, opposite, 3-8 pairs; blade lance-shaped to elliptic, 1-5 inches long (3–12 cm); edges entire, surfaces short-hairy.

HABITAT: Invasive; roadsides, disturbed areas; grasslands to montane forests. Elevation 6,000–9,500 feet (1,800–2,900 m).

Long-stalk Starwort

Stellaria longipes, Pink Family, Caryophyllaceae; Perennial herb

QUICK ID: Look for mats or clumps with small white flowers with 5 pointed petals split to base to appear to be 10 petals.

RANGE: NR, MR, SR, Canada; widespread, common

STEM: Erect, branched or not, 1–12 inches long (3–30 cm), 4-angled, usually hairless or only soft hairs.

FLOWERS: May–August. Flowers from stem tips, single or in open clusters, ¼–⅜ inches wide (5–10 mm); 5 slender, pointed petals divided to the base; 5–10 stamens, 3 styles curled at the tip.

LEAVES: Opposite, stalkless. Blades linear to narrowly lance-shaped, ⅜–1 inch long (1–3 cm), to 3⁄16 inch wide (4 mm), prominent midrib; tips pointed, edges entire, surfaces smooth to sparsely hairy.

HABITAT: Moist meadows, stream banks, drainages; montane, subalpine forests, alpine. Elevation 7,300–11,625 feet (2,225–3,543 m).

SIMILAR SPECIES: Tuber Starwort, *Pseudostellaria jamesiana*, has shallow notched petals.

Fringed Grass of Parnassus

Parnassia fimbriata, Bittersweet Family, Celastraceae; Perennial herb

QUICK ID: Look in wet areas for rosettes of glossy rounded leaves, stalks with a single white flower, and 5 petals fringed on lower half.

RANGE: NR, MR, SR, Canada (infrequent); widespread, common

STEM: Flower stalk erect, 1 to several, 6–12 inches tall (15–30 cm).

FLOWERS: July–September. Single flower on a leafless stalk; 5 petals, oblong, ⅜–½ inch long (8–12 mm), fringed, 5–7-veined. Bract near mid-stem, heart-shaped, ⅝ inch long (15 mm), clasping.

LEAVES: Basal, long-stalked to 4 inches long (10 cm), base heart-shaped; blades heart- to kidney-shaped, ⅜–2 inches wide (1–5 cm); edges entire, surfaces smooth, glossy green, tip rounded.

HABITAT: Wet meadows, bogs, seeps; foothills, montane, subalpine forests, alpine. Elevation 3,000–12,000 feet (915–3,656 m).

Marsh Grass of Parnassus

Parnassia palustris, Bittersweet Family, Celastraceae; Perennial herb

QUICK ID: Look for rosettes of oval long-stalked leaves, a leafless stalk with 1 white flower, and petals with 5–13 veins and no fringe.

RANGE: NR, MR, SR, Canada; widespread, common

STEM: Flower stalk erect, unbranched, 3–16 inches tall (8–40 cm).

FLOWERS: July–August. Single flower on leafless stalk with 5 petals 7–13 veined, round-oval, ⅜–¾ inch long (8–20 mm). Bract near mid-stem, heart-shaped, 1 inch long (3 cm), clasping.

LEAVES: Basal, long-stalked to 4 inches long (10 cm), base rounded to heart-shaped; blades oval to elliptic, ⅝–1¼ inch long (15–30 mm); edges and surfaces smooth, tip pointed.

HABITAT: Wet meadows, seeps, wetlands; foothills, montane, subalpine forests. Elevation 1,400–11,000 feet (425–3,353 m).

SIMILAR SPECIES: Smallflower Grass of Parnassus, *P. parviflora*, has petals to ⅜ inch long (10 mm). The rare Kotzebue's Grass of Parnassus, *P. kotzebuei*, has petals with 3 veins, is often bractless.

Smallflower Grass of Parnassus

Parnassia parviflora, Bittersweet Family, Celastraceae; Perennial herb

QUICK ID: Look in wetlands for rosettes of oval long-stalked leaves, a slender stalk with a leafy bract below mid-stem, and 1 white flower with small petals with 5–13 veins.

RANGE: NR, MR, SR, Canada; scattered, infrequent

STEM: Flower stalk erect, solitary, 4–14 inches tall (10–35 cm).

FLOWERS: July–September. Single flower on leafless stalk, 5 petals, 5–13 veined, oblong to elliptic, ⅛–⅜ inch long (4–8 mm). Bract leaf-like, ¼–¾ inch long (7–18 mm), stalkless, on bottom half of stem.

LEAVES: Basal, long stalked, to ¾ inch long (2 cm); blades egg-shaped to elliptic, to 1⅜ inches long (35 mm); base tapering, tip pointed.

HABITAT: Wet meadows, seeps, wetlands; foothills, montane, subalpine forests. Elevation 2,625–11,000 feet (800–3,353 m).

SIMILAR SPECIES: Marsh Grass of Parnassus, *P. palustris*, has petals ⅜–¾ inch long (8–20 mm).

Redwhisker Clammyweed

Polanisia dodecandra, Beeplant Family, Cleomaceae; Annual herb

QUICK ID: Look for sticky, smelly stems with 3 leaflets; compact heads of small white flowers; long purple stamens; erect seed pods.

RANGE: NR, MR, SR, Canada; widespread, common

STEM: Erect, branched, 8-30 inches tall (20-80 cm), glandular-hairy.

FLOWERS: May-October. Dense, rounded clusters on stem ends with 4 petals white to pinkish, ¼-⅜ inch (5-10 mm) long, 10-20 purple stamens extending 1 inch (25 mm) beyond the petals. Seed pods 1½-2¾ inches long (4-7 cm), upright around stem.

LEAVES: Alternate; blade palmately divided into 3 elliptic, pointed leaflets ¾-2 inches long (19-50 mm); foliage covered with sticky, smelly, glandular hairs.

HABITAT: Coarse soils, drainages, disturbed areas; arid grasslands, sagebrush, foothills, montane forests. Elevation 3,500-7,000 feet (1,068-2,134 m).

Field Bindweed

Convolvulus arvensis, Morning Glory Family, Convolvulaceae; Perennial vine; introduced, invasive

QUICK ID: Look for a twining to prostrate, often wide-spreading vine with white-to-pink, morning glory-like flowers that last only one day.

RANGE: NR, MR, SR, Canada; widespread, common

STEM: Slender, branching, spreading to 6 feet (2 m); taproots 2-10 feet deep (0.6-3 m), rhizomes can spread 20 feet (6 m).

FLOWERS: April-October. Clusters of 1-3, white-to-pink-tinged flowers, 1-1½ inches (25-40 mm) wide, on stalks (peduncles) from leaf axils, petals fused to form funnel-shaped flower.

LEAVES: Alternate. Blade variable, ½-4 inches long (1-10 cm), oval to lance-shaped, often with two, opposite spreading lobes at the base; surfaces hairless or nearly so.

HABITAT: Fields, roadsides, disturbed areas; grasslands, sagebrush, foothills, montane forests. Elevation 1,100-7,700 feet (335-2,350 m).

Bunchberry

Cornus canadensis, Dogwood Family, Cornaceae, Perennial herb

QUICK ID: Look for low stems with a whorl of large leaves; 4 oval, white bracts around a cluster of small flowers; and bright-red fruit.

RANGE: NR, MR, SR, Canada; widespread, locally common

STEM: Erect, slender, 2–8 inches tall (5–20 cm), spreads by rhizomes.

FLOWERS: May–August. Have 4 showy, petal-like bracts, 2–6 inches long (5–15 cm), surrounding a tight cluster of 12–40 small flowers, each with tiny creamy-to-purple petals and sepals. Fruit a tight bunch of 5–20 red drupes, ¼–⅜ inch diameter (6–9 mm).

LEAVES: Whorls of 4–6 just below the flower cluster. Blades elliptic to oval, 1–3 inches long (3–8 cm); surfaces hairless, tip pointed.

HABITAT: Dry to moist hardwood, conifer forests; montane to subalpine. Elevation sea level to 11,000 feet (3,400 m).

NOTE: *C. canadensis* is common from NR Idaho to Alaska, scattered in MR, SR. Western Bunchberry, *C. unalaschensis,* minutely different, is common from Idaho to Alaska.

Red-osier Dogwood

Cornus sericea, Dogwood Family, Cornaceae; Deciduous shrub

QUICK ID: Look for a dense shrub with reddish stems, flat-topped clusters of small white flowers, and opposite oval leaves.

RANGE: NR, MR, SR, Canada; widespread, common

STEM: Woody, multi-stemmed, 3–10 feet tall (1–3 m), maroon red (esp. winter), thicket forming.

FLOWERS: May–July. Flat to curved clusters to 3 inches wide (8 cm), dense with white flowers, each ¼–⅜ inch wide (7–9 mm) with 4 lance-shaped petals; stamens spreading, longer than petals. Fruit a round, white-to-bluish drupe, to ⅜ inch diameter (9 mm).

LEAVES: Opposite. Blades lance-shaped to oval, 2–4 inches long (5–10 cm), tip tapered; edges smooth, top surface hairless or nearly so, bottom sparsely covered with fine, white hairs.

HABITAT: Moist woods, along streams; wetlands, foothills, montane, subalpine forests. Elevation 4,500–10,000 feet (1,372–3,048 m).

Cockerell's Stonecrop

Sedum cockerellii, Stonecrop Family, Crassulaceae; Perennial succulent herb

QUICK ID: Look for compact rosettes of succulent leaves, clusters of star-shaped flowers with whitish-pink petals, filaments, red anthers.

RANGE: SR (NM); widespread, common

STEM: Erect, clumped, upper branched, 2-8 inches tall (5-20 cm)

FLOWERS: June–September. Flat-topped clusters have flowers ⅝–¾ inch wide (15–20 mm); 5 petals, white to pinkish, lance-shaped, pointed, ¼–⅜ inch long (6–9 mm); 10 stamens, have white-to-pinkish filaments, reddish-brown anthers; pistils erect, pinkish.

LEAVES: Dense basal rosette; blades succulent, slightly flat (not cylindric), oval to spatula-shaped, ¼ inch (1-6 mm) long. Stem leaves alternate, crowded, narrow, linear to elliptic, flattish to cylindric, succulent, ¼–¾ inch (5–18 mm) long.

HABITAT: Rocky outcrops, crevices; foothills, montane forests. Elevation 5,700-10,600 feet (1,737-3,230 m).

SIMIAR SPECIES: Wright's Stonecrop, *S. wrightii*, (SR) has erect petals that open near the tip.

Dodder

Cuscuta species, Dodder Family, Cuscutaceae; Perennial, parasitic vine

QUICK ID: Look for yellow-orange, spaghetti-like vine tangled in vegetation, and dense clusters of up to 300 tiny white flowers.

RANGE: NR, MR, SR, Canada; widespread, locally common

STEM: Slender, delicate twinning vine.

FLOWERS: Summer. Clusters of white flowers, ⅛ inch long (3 mm), star-shaped with 5 pointed petals; yellow anthers extend beyond the petals, styles unequal length.

LEAVES: Absent. This parasitic vine needs no chlorophyll or leaves; it drains its nutrients from the stems of the forbs it attacks.

HABITAT: Sandy, gravelly soils of disturbed areas; sagebrush, pinyon-juniper foothills. Elevation 3,800–7,000 feet (1,158–2,134 m).

Kinnikinnick, Bearberry

Arctostaphylos uva-ursi, Heath Family, Ericaceae; Perennial woody subshrub

QUICK ID: Look for a woody groundcover with small evergreen leaves, whitish urn-shaped flowers, and red berries.

RANGE: NR, MR, SR, Canada; widespread, locally common

STEM: Dense, sprawling, 5–12 inches high (12–30 cm).

FLOWERS: May–August. Flowers, nodding, to ⅜ inch long (10 mm), white-to-pinkish-tinged; fruit a round, bright-red drupe, ¼–½ inch diameter (6–12 mm), devoured by animals.

LEAVES: Alternate. Blades oval, ⅜–1 inch long (10–25 mm), dark green above, lighter below, leathery, margins entire, often cupped; surfaces smooth to slightly hairy.

HABITAT: Dry to moist soils of pinyon-juniper foothills, montane, subalpine forests, alpine. Elevation 7,000–12,000 feet (2,133–3,658 m).

White Mountain Heather

Cassiope mertensiana, Heath Family, Ericaceae; Evergreen shrub

QUICK ID: Look for dense mats with short leaves in crowded rows on 4 sides of stem; clusters of bell-shaped, white flowers on stem ends.

RANGE: NR, Canada; widespread, common

STEM: Mat forming, 2–12 inches tall/long (5–30 cm), concealed by leaves.

FLOWERS: June–August. Several smooth to short-hairy flower stalks to 1 inch long (3 cm) near stem tip; flowers nodding, 3/16–5/16 inch long (5–8 mm) with 5 lobes with curled tips; stamens inside petals; sepals oval, reddish.

LEAVES: Opposite, overlapping in 4 distinct rows along stem; blades oval, lance-shaped, 1/16–3/16 inch long (2–5 mm); edges and surfaces hairless, no groove on bottom.

HABITAT: Meadows, slopes; subalpine forests, alpine. Elevation 330–10,500 feet (100–3,200 m).

SIMILAR SPECIES: Arctic White Heather, *C. tetragona* (same range), has leaves with deeply grooved undersides.

Wood Nymph

Moneses uniflora (Pyrola uniflora), Heath Family, Ericaceae; Perennial herb

QUICK ID: Look in shady, high-elevation forests for a short, leafless stalk with a nickel-size, nodding flower with creamy-white petals.

RANGE: NR, MR, SR, Canada; widespread, common

STEM: Erect, unbranched, leafless, 2–6 inches tall (5–15 cm).

FLOWERS: June–August. Flowers ½–1 inch diameter (12–25 mm) with 5 wide-spreading, oval petals. The style in the center of flower is cylindrical, green, tipped with 5 pointed, auger-like stigma lobes; 10 stamens spread against petals like hands on a clock, anthers curve inward. Seed capsule erect with about 1,000 tiny seeds.

LEAVES: Appearing basal or whorled around base of stem. Blade 1–2 inches long (3–5 cm), oval to round; edges lined with tiny, sharp-to-rounded teeth.

HABITAT: Moist soils; shady, cool, damp woods; meadows; subalpine forests. Elevation 9,200–11,150 feet (2,800–3,400 m).

Lesser Wintergreen

Pyrola minor, Heath Family, Ericaceae; Perennial subshrub

QUICK ID: Look for rosettes of rounded, solid-green leaves, and flower stalks lined with white-to-pinkish, nodding flowers with the style not protruding.

RANGE: NR, MR, SR, Canada; widespread, common

STEM: Flower stalk erect, unbranched, 4¾–8 inches tall (12–20 cm).

FLOWERS: June–August. Cylindrical with 3–11 flowers along stem on 1⁄16-inch-long (2 mm) stalks; 5 petals curved downward. Note the style is straight and equal or shorter than the petals.

LEAVES: Basal stalked; blades oblong to elliptic or round ¾–1 inch long (2–3 cm); edges with shallow, round teeth, hairless.

HABITAT: Moist woods, stream banks; montane, subalpine forests. Elevation 7,000–11,200 feet (2,133–3,420 m).

SIMILAR SPECIES: Pink Wintergreen, *P. asarifolia*, reaches 17 inches tall (43 cm) and has a curved style much longer than the petals.

White-vein Wintergreen

Pyrola picta, Heath Family, Ericaceae; Perennial herb

QUICK ID: Look for oval basal leaves streaked with white veins, and stems lined with small, nodding, creamy flowers with a curved style.

RANGE: NR, MR, SR, Canada; scattered, locally common

STEM: Flower stalk erect, unbranched, 2⅜–12 inches tall (6–30 cm).

FLOWERS: June–September. Elongated clusters have 4–25 creamy-to-pale-green or pinkish flowers, ⅜ inch wide (1 cm); flowers nod like inverted cups; style curved, longer than petals.

LEAVES: Basal on stalk ⅜–1¾ inches long (1–5 cm), evergreen. Blades oval to elliptic, 1–3 inches long (3–8 cm); surfaces green, mottled with white along the veins; margins entire or with minute, rounded teeth.

HABITAT: Moist to dry forest floors; foothills, montane, subalpine forests. Elevation 7,900–10,200 feet (2,407–3,110 m).

SIMILAR SPECIES: Lesser Wintergreen, *P. minor*, and other wintergreens have solid-green leaves.

Western Labrador Tea

Rhododendron columbianum, Heath Family, Ericaceae; Evergreen shrub

QUICK ID: Look for large, spreading shrubs with broad leaves and rounded clusters of small white flowers; leaves fragrant when crushed.

RANGE: NR, MR, Canada; widespread, locally common

STEM: Upright, branching, woody, to 6 feet tall/ wide (2 m).

FLOWERS: June–August. Dense, rounded clusters at branch tips have flowers ⅜–⅝ inch wide (10–15 mm); 5 petals, oblong, spreading; stamens extend beyond petals.

LEAVES: Alternate, long-stalked, evergreen, leathery; blades elliptic to oblong, ¾–2 inches long (2–5 cm); edges entire, slightly rolled under; top surface smooth, deep green, bottom whitish fine-hairy, densely glandular.

HABITAT: Wet meadows, bogs, open woods; montane, subalpine forests. Elevation 5,500–10,000 feet (1,676–3,048 m).

Snow-on-the-Mountain

Euphorbia marginata, Spurge Family, Euphorbiaceae; Annual herb

QUICK ID: Look for tall stems branching in sets of three; broad, oval, green leaves; and green-and-white bracts around clusters of tiny white flowers. Toxic milky sap can cause dermatitis.

RANGE: SR; widespread, locally common

STEM: Erect, branching, 1–3 feet tall (30–90 cm), hairy.

FLOWERS: July–October. Rounded clusters on stem tips, flowers tiny with 5 white, petal-like appendages on the rim of a ¼-inch wide (6 mm), cup-like structure containing the tiny true flowers. Fruit a hairy, green, 3-sided capsule on a short, nodding stalk in the center of the female flower. Bi-colored, leaf-like bracts below the flowers may be opposite or whorled.

LEAVES: Alternate, whorled around the branching nodes, opposite and bicolored on upper branches. Blades broad, oblong, 1–3 inches long (3–8 cm), narrower near stem tip.

HABITAT: Pastures, disturbed areas; grasslands, sagebrush, foothills. montane forests. Elevation 3,700–8,360 feet (1,128–2,550 m).

Alpine Milkvetch

Astragalus alpinus, Legume Family, Fabaceae; Perennial herb

QUICK ID: Look for sprawling colonies at upper altitudes with loose clusters of purple-and-white, pea-like flowers and hairy pods.

RANGE: NR, MR, SR, Canada, circumpolar; widespread, common

STEM: Erect to mat forming, 2–18 inches long (5–45 cm).

FLOWERS: April–September. Flower stems erect, leafless, with loose spreading clusters of 5–35 bicolored flowers, each to ½ inch long (12 mm) with 5 petals: 1 upper banner petal light lavender with darker streaks into the throat, 2 white side wing petals, 2 keel petals with a white base and purple tip. Pods oblong, drooping, to ¾ inch long (19 mm), deeply grooved, densely hairy.

LEAVES: Alternate, pinnately compound. Leaflets 15–35, oval to elliptic, to ⅜–¾ inch long (8–20 mm), tips rounded.

HABITAT: Open slopes, rocky areas, moist meadows; montane, subalpine forests, alpine. Elevation 8,300–12,500 feet (2,530–3,810 m).

Canada Milkvetch

Astragalus canadensis, Legume Family, Fabaceae; Perennial herb

QUICK ID: Look for tall, leafy stems; spikes of creamy-to-yellowish, tubular flowers; and compound leaves with 15–35 oval leaflets.

RANGE: NR, MR, SR, Canada; widespread, locally common

STEM: Leafy, branching, 1–4 feet tall (30–122 cm), colony forming.

FLOWERS: May–August. Dense, spike-like clusters to 6 inches long (15 cm) with whorls of 30–100 creamy-to-greenish-white flowers, each ½–¾ inch long (12–20 cm) with 5 petals: 1 upturned banner petal, 2 tight-fitting side petals around 2 central keel petals. Pods oval, crowded, erect, ⅜–⅝ inch long (10–15 mm), hairless.

LEAVES: Alternate, pinnately compound. Leaflets oblong to elliptic, ⅜–1⅝ inches long (1–4 cm); top smooth, bottom with short hairs.

HABITAT: Prairies, woodlands, stream sides; grasslands, sagebrush, foothills, montane forests. Elevation 110–7,000 feet (34–2,130 m).

Drummond's Milkvetch

Astragalus drummondii, Legume Family, Fabaceae; Perennial herb

QUICK ID: Look for bushy clumps; spikes of nodding, tubular, white flowers; compound leaves with 6–16 pairs of shaggy-hairy leaflets.

RANGE: NR, MR, SR, Canada; widespread, common

STEM: Erect, 16–28 inches tall (40–70 cm), hairy.

FLOWERS: May–August. Elongated clusters have 14–35 white-to-creamy flowers, each with 1 erect to sightly reflexed banner petal to 1 inch long (25 mm), 2 small white wing petals spreading to the sides, and 2 often lilac-tinted petals that form a keel in the center. Pods are hairless, drooping, ¾–1½ inches long (2–4 cm) by ¼ inch thick (6 mm), with a deeply indented groove down the middle.

LEAVES: Alternate, pinnately compound. Leaflets oval to spatula-shaped, ⅛–1⅜ inches long (4–33 mm) by 1⁄16–½ inch wide (2–12 mm); surfaces nearly hairless on top, long-hairy on the bottom.

HABITAT: Dry to damp coarse soils; grasslands, sagebrush, foothills, montane forests. Elevation 2,200–8,600 feet (670–2,650 m).

White Prairie-Clover

Dalea candida, Legume Family, Fabaceae; Perennial herb

QUICK ID: Look for dense clumps with tall flower stalks topped with rounded-to-elongated cones of small, tubular, white flowers.

RANGE: NR, MR, SR, Canada; widespread, common

STEM: Erect to arching, hairless, 1–3 feet tall and wide (30–90 cm).

FLOWERS: May–September. Dense cylindric clusters; flowers ¼ inch long (6 mm) with 5 similar-shaped petals, 5 stamens, 5 showy yellow anthers; blooms in a ring around the spike that advances up to the apex. The ⅛-inch long (3 mm) pod doesn't split open when dried.

LEAVES: Alternate. Blade has 5–9 linear-to-oblong leaflets, each ⅜–1¼ inches long (1–3 cm); surfaces hairless, tips pointed.

HABITAT: Disturbed areas; grasslands, pinyon-juniper foothills, montane forests. Elevation 4,000–9,000 feet (1,220–2,745 m).

SIMILAR SPECIES: Large-spike Prairie-Clover, *D. cylindriceps* (SR), has hairless leaves and a flower cluster 1–7 inches long (3–18 cm).

Wild Licorice

Glycyrrhiza lepidota, Legume Family, Fabaceae; Perennial herb

QUICK ID: Look for colonies of leafy plants with dense spikes of creamy, pea-like flowers and brown, bur-like seed pods.

RANGE: NR, MR, SR, Canada; widespread, common

STEM: Erect, colony forming, 1–4 feet tall (30–120 cm), rhizomatous.

FLOWERS: May–August. Spikes have 20–50 white to creamy, tubular flowers, each ⅜–½ inch long (9–13 mm); 5 petals: 1 narrow, upper banner, 2 side wings, and 2 forming a short keel. Seedpods oblong, ½–¾ inch long (12–20 mm), densely covered with hooked prickles.

LEAVES: Alternate. Blade 3–7½ inches long (8–19 cm), pinnately compound with 13–19 leaflets along the midrib, each 5⁄16–2⅛ inches long (8–53 mm), lance-shaped to oblong. Note glandular dots on bottom of leaflets.

HABITAT: Periodically moist soils, disturbed areas; grasslands, sage, pinyon-juniper foothills. Elevation 3,500–8,400 feet (1,066–2,560 m).

SIMILAR SPECIES: White-flowered milkvetches, *Astragalus* species, have smooth pods.

White Sweetvetch

Hedysarum sulphurescens, Legume Family, Fabaceae; Perennial herb

QUICK ID: Look for tall stems; compound leaves with large, elliptic leaflets; erect spikes of creamy, pea-like flowers; and flat, oval pods.

RANGE: NR, MR, Canada; locally common

STEM: Erect to spreading, branching above, 8–36 inches tall (20–90 cm), sparsely short-stiff-hairy.

FLOWERS: May–September. Spike-like clusters, often one-sided, with 20–100 slightly drooping, white-to-creamy-yellow flowers. Petals 5: a lobed banner curving upward; 2 side petals; and 2 longer, fused keel petals pointing forward; 5 sepals with short, pointed tips. Fruit a chain of 2–4 oval, disk-like pods.

LEAVES: Alternate. Blades pinnately compound, 3–8 inches long (8–20 cm), with 9–17 leaflets, elliptic to lance-shaped, ⅝–1¼ inch long (15–30 mm), to ⅜ inch wide (10 mm); top surface sparsely hairy, bottom hairless; tips with a tiny sharp point.

HABITAT: Dry, open forests; grasslands, sagebrush, foothills, montane to alpine. Elevation 3,500–10,500 feet (1,067–3,200 m).

Nevada Peavine

Lathyrus lanszwertii (includes L. leucanthus), Legume Family, Fabaceae; Perennial herb

QUICK ID: Look for erect to sprawling stems with clusters of small, pea-like, white flowers with red veins on the upper banner petal.

RANGE: NR, MR, SR, Canada; widespread, common

STEM: Slender, arching or climbing, 8–24 inches tall (20–60 cm).

FLOWERS: June–September. Loose clusters with 2–5 flowers, each ⅔–1 inch long (12–22 mm); 5 white petals: an upper banner with reddish-pink streaks, 2 side wings, and 2 fused petals forming the keel. Pods straight, flat, smooth, 1¼–2½ inches long (3–6 cm).

LEAVES: Alternate. Pinnately compound with 4–10 leaflets in pairs along midrib; leaflets elliptic, oblong, to lance-shaped, ½–3 inches long (12–75 mm), to ¾ inch wide (18 mm); surfaces smooth or hairy, edges entire, tips pointed. The tip of the midrib may or may not have a coiled or bristle-like tendril.

HABITAT: Clearings, open forests; sagebrush, montane, subalpine forests, alpine meadows. Elevation 7,600–10,500 feet.

Cream Pea

Lathyrus ochroleucus, Legume Family, Fabaceae; Perennial herb

QUICK ID: Look for compound leaves with tendrils; broad, elliptic, thin leaflets; and elongated clusters of creamy, pea-like flowers.

RANGE: NR, Canada; widespread, common

STEM: Erect to sprawling, 1-3 feet long (30-100 cm), smooth.

FLOWERS: May–September. Loose, spike-like clusters from leaf axils have 6–14 creamy-to-greenish-white, pea-like flowers, each ½–¾ inch long (12–18 mm); petals 5: 1 erect banner, 2 wings enclose the 2 keel petals. Pods straight, flat, 1¼–3 inches long (3–8 cm).

LEAVES: Alternate. Blades pinnately compound with 6–8 leaflets in pairs, each elliptic to oval, 1–2¾ inches long (3–7 cm) by ⅜–1½ inches wide (1–4 cm); edges entire, surfaces smooth; branching tendril on midrib well-developed, clasping.

HABITAT: Open forests, meadows; foothills, montane forests. Elevation sea level to 7,875 feet (2,400 m).

White Locoweed

Oxytropis sericea, Legume Family, Fabaceae; Perennial herb

QUICK ID: Look for basal clumps with silvery-hairy leaflets, hairy stalks with spikes of white pea-like flowers, and hairy bean-like pods.

RANGE: NR, MR, SR, Canada; widespread, common

STEM: Flower stalk erect, clumped, 4–20 inches tall (10–50 cm), hairy.

FLOWERS: March–August. Dense spike has 6–25 flowers, each ⅝–1 inch long (15–25 mm) with 5 petals: 1 upturned banner, may be dark lined; 2 wings around a pointed keel of 2 fused petals, tip often purple tinted or spotted; calyx beneath petals has long white or dark hairs. Pods erect, ⅝–1 inch long (15–25 mm), silky-hairy, tip pointed.

LEAVES: Basal, pinnately compound, 9–23 narrowly oval leaflets ⅜–1⅝ inches long (1–4 cm); surfaces dense with flat-lying, silky hairs.

HABITAT: Dry, coarse soils, open sites; throughout all zones. Elevation 3,000–11,000 feet (914–3,353 m).

SIMILAR SPECIES: Yellow Locoweed, *O. campestris*, (all regions) has pale-yellow flowers.

White Clover

Trifolium repens, Legume Family, Fabaceae; Perennial herb; introduced

QUICK ID: Look for leaves with three leaflets (four if you're lucky), and spherical, terminal clusters of small, white, pea-like flowers.

RANGE: NR, MR, SR, Canada; widespread, common, naturalized

STEM: Creeping, rooting, reaching 2 feet long (60 cm).

FLOWERS: June–September. Spherical, many-flowered heads, 1 inch diameter (25 mm), on stalks 4–10 inches tall (10–25 cm); each tubular flower ¼–½ inch long (6–11 mm), with 1 banner, 2 side wings, and 2 keel-shaped petals.

LEAVES: Alternate or clustered with 2–8-inch-long (5–20 cm) stalks; palmate with 3 oval to elliptic leaflets ⅜–¾ inch long (1–2 cm); edges with tiny teeth, surfaces hairless, top with a light-green V mark.

HABITAT: Meadows, lawns, disturbed areas; grasslands to subalpine forests. Elevation 3,500–11,300 feet (1,066–3,444 m).

Whitestem Frasera

Frasera albicaulis, Gentian Family, Gentianaceae; Perennial herb

QUICK ID: Look for narrow, white-lined basal leaves and elongated clusters of flowers with 4 whitish-blue, often mottled, pointed petals.

RANGE: NR, Canada; scattered, locally common

STEM: Erect, branching from base, 4–28 inches tall (10–70 cm), hairy or not.

FLOWERS: May–July. Dense to loose clusters spaced along stem end; 4 petal-like lobes, pointed, spreading, each ¼–½ inch long (5–11 mm), oval, white to light blue or purple, often mottled or lined; have 4 long, spreading stamens.

LEAVES: Basal; blades erect, narrowly lance-shaped, 1⅝–10 inches long (4–25 cm); prominently 3 nerved, edges white lined, surfaces densely hairy or not. Stem leaves opposite, smaller.

HABITAT: Plains, open areas; sagebrush, foothills, montane, subalpine forests. Elevation 2,000–7,000 feet (610–2,133 m).

Whitish (Arctic) Gentian

Gentiana algida, Gentian Family, Gentianaceae; Perennial herb

QUICK ID: Look in high-elevation, moist habitats for dense clumps of basal leaves with showy white, trumpet-shaped flowers with purplish markings.

RANGE: NR, MR, SR; scattered, locally common

STEM: Erect, 1 to clustered, leafy, 2–4 inches tall (5–20 cm), hairless.

FLOWERS: July–September. Upright, often in terminal pairs, 1⅜–2 inches long (4–5 cm), 5 united lobes with short points, creamy-to-greenish-white with purplish lines, dots, and blotches.

LEAVES: Basal blades linear to lance-shaped, narrow, 1½–4¾ inches long (4–12 cm); edges entire, surfaces hairless. Stem leaves opposite, 3–5 pairs, lance-shaped, 1–5 inches long (3–5 cm).

HABITAT: Meadows, stream sides, fellfields; subalpine forests, alpine. Elevation 9,500–13,000 feet (2,895–4,115 m).

Richardson's Geranium

Geranium richardsonii, Geranium Family, Geraniaceae; Perennial herb

QUICK ID: Look for stems with reddish-purple hairs, flowers with whitish petals with reddish lines, and lobed leaves with pointed teeth.

RANGE: NR, MR, SR, Canada; widespread, common

STEM: Erect, 7–32 inches tall (18–81 cm), hairy.

FLOWERS: June–August. Flowers 1 inch wide with 5 white-to-pinkish petals lined with dark veins, each petal ⅜–¾ inch long (10–18 mm), tips rounded, base sparsely hairy; 10 arching stamens, 5 sepals to ½ inch long (12 mm), bristle-tipped. Fruit is a slender capsule, ¾–1 inch long (20–25 mm), pointed like a crane's bill.

LEAVES: Basal on long stalks, blades palmate with spreading segments, 2–6 inches wide (5–15 cm), with 3–7 broad lobes, each with coarse, pointed teeth; surfaces sparsely short-hairy. Stem leaves opposite, smaller.

HABITAT: Meadows, stream sides, openings; foothills, montane, subalpine forests. Elevation 7,000–10,900 feet (2,134–3,322 m).

Wax Currant

Ribes cereum, Currant Family, Grossulariaceae; Deciduous shrub

QUICK ID: Look for shoulder-high, thornless shrubs with rounded toothed leaves, small pinkish-white tubular flowers, and red berries.

RANGE: NR, MR, SR, Canada; widespread, common

STEM: Upright, open branching, 2–4 feet tall (60–120 cm).

FLOWERS: April–July. Clusters have 2–3 tubular flowers, ¼–⅜ inch long (6–10 mm), white to creamy or pink tinged, glandular-hairy, with 5 spreading petal-like sepals and 5 smaller interior petals. Fruit a round, red-to-orange berry to ⅜ inch diameter (10 mm) with scattered short glandular hairs; edible, rather tasteless.

LEAVES: Alternate or crowded on short branchlets. Blades rounded, 3–7 shallow lobes, ⅜–1 ½ inches long and wide (9–38 mm); edges coarsely toothed, surfaces with short hairs, glandular hairs, or hairless.

HABITAT: Ridges, slopes, riparian sites, woodlands; sagebrush to alpine. Elevation 4,200–11,850 feet (1,280–3,595 m).

Whitestem Gooseberry

Ribes inerme, Currant Family, Grossulariaceae; Deciduous shrub

QUICK ID: Look for open shrubs, branches often with 1–3 thorns at leaf nodes, 3-lobed leaves, and white-to-greenish, tubular flowers.

RANGE: NR, MR, SR, Canada; widespread, common

STEM: Upright to sprawling, branched, 3–6 feet tall (1–2 m), often armed with spines and prickles.

FLOWERS: April–June. Drooping clusters have 1–4 tubular flowers with 5 spreading, petal-like sepals, white, greenish or pink tinged, hairless; 5 smaller erect, white petals; stamens 2 times size of petals. Berries greenish to red-purple, to ½ inch diameter (12 mm), hairless.

LEAVES: Alternate, stalked; blades oval, ¾–3 inches long (2–8 cm) with 3 lobes cut nearly ½ to midrib, lobes oval to rounded, tips sharp to coarsely toothed, surfaces smooth or sparsely short-hairy.

HABITAT: Stream banks, meadows, open woods; foothills, montane, subalpine forests. Elevation 6,200–10,800 feet (1,985–3,290 m).

SIMILAR SPECIES: Trumpet Gooseberry, *R. leptanthum*, (SR) has black berries and leaves.

Wolf's Currant

Ribes wolfii, Currant Family, Grossulariaceae; Deciduous shrub

QUICK ID: Look for spreading, unarmed branches, maple-like leaves, clusters of small cup-shaped white flowers, and black berries.

RANGE: NR, rare; MR (UT), SR; widespread, common

STEM: Erect, spreading, freely branching, 3-10 feet tall/wide (1-3 m).

FLOWERS: May–June. Crowded clusters with 7-25 whitish-to-greenish flowers, cup-shaped with green, yellow, or clear short glandular hairs; 5 petal-like sepals, 5 smaller interior petals. Fruit a round, black berry ½–1½ inches diameter (12–38 mm), glandular-hairy.

LEAVES: Alternate or whorl-like on short branchlets, long stalked. Blade 1½–3½ inches long and wide (4–8 cm) with 3-5 pointed lobes; edges toothed, surfaces with minute clear glands.

HABITAT: Stream sides, slopes, forest openings; montane, subalpine forests. Elevation 8,700–12,000 feet (2,650–3,657 m).

SIMILAR SPECIES: Trailing Black Currant, *R. laxiflorum*, (SR, NR, Canada–infrequent) is low-growing, thornless with pink flowers.

Phlox Heliotrope

Euploca convolvulacea, Heliotrope Family, Heliotropiaceae; Annual herb

QUICK ID: Look in sandy habitats for white, funnel-shaped flowers with a 5-sided, crape-paper-like disk and a tiny yellow throat.

RANGE: MR, SR; widespread, locally common

STEM: Erect, sprawling, branched, 4–16 inches tall (10–40 cm), hairy.

FLOWERS: May–September. Flowers solitary in leaf axils, fragrant, ⅝–1 inch wide (15–25 mm) with 5 united, petal-like lobes; stamens and style hidden inside the yellow throat; stem and sepals very hairy.

LEAVES: Alternate. Blade lance-shaped to elliptic, ⅜–1½ inches long (1–4 cm), ⅜–⅝ inch wide (10–15 mm); margins entire, long-hairy; surfaces with flat-lying hairs, tip rounded to pointed.

HABITAT: Sandy soils, dunes, disturbed areas; grasslands, sagebrush, juniper foothills. Elevation 2,000–6,300 feet (610–1,920 m).

Salt Heliotrope

Heliotropium curassavicum, Heliotrope Family, Heliotropiaceae; Annual, perennial herb

QUICK ID: Look where evaporating water concentrates mineral salts for coiled arrays of tiny white flowers with yellow-to-purple throats.

RANGE: NR, MR, SR, Canada; scattered, locally common

STEM: Erect, branching to trailing, 1-2 feet long (10-60 cm), hairless.

FLOWERS: May-September. Dense, hooked clusters have double rows of flowers along one side of the branch ends; flowers trumpet-shaped, ¼-⅝ inch wide (6-16 mm) with 5 white lobes and yellow or purple throats.

LEAVES: Alternate. Blades green to glaucous, succulent, narrowly elliptic to lance-shaped, ¾-3 inches long (2-8 cm), ⅛-¾ inch wide (3-18 mm); surfaces hairless, edges entire, tips blunt to pointed.

HABITAT: Moist, alkaline soils; alkali flats, wetlands, badlands; grasslands, sagebrush. Elevation 3,320-8,500 feet (1,010-2,590 m).

Cliff Fendlerbush

Fendlera rupicola, Hydrangea, Family, Hydrangeaceae; Deciduous shrub

QUICK ID: Look for a head-high, dense shrub with leaves in bundled clusters, and white flowers with 4 spreading, spoon-shaped petals.

RANGE: SR; widespread, common

STEM: Erect, 6-9 feet tall (2-3 m), 4 feet wide (122 cm).

FLOWERS: March-June. Solitary or clustered at branch tips; 4 white petals, ⅜-¾ inch long (1-2 cm), tapering to a narrow base, tips pointed; stamens grouped in erect column. Fruit a woody, brown, oval, pointed capsule ⅝ inch long (15 mm).

LEAVES: Opposite or in pairs of fascicled clusters. Blade lance-shaped to oval, ⅜-1½ inch long (1-4 cm) to ⅜ inch wide (10 mm); edges entire, often rolled under; top surface shiny green, bottom dull green with midvein, densely hairy or not.

HABITAT: Rocky slopes, canyons; sagebrush, pinyon-juniper foothills. Elevation 3,000-8,400 feet (914-2,560 m).

Cliffbush

Jamesia americana, Hydrangea Family, Hydrangeaceae; Deciduous shrub

QUICK ID: Look for rounded bushy shrubs with opposite, strongly veined leaves, and clusters of small flowers with 5 white petals.

RANGE: SR; widespread, common

STEM: Upright, branching 3–6½ feet tall (1–2 m), hairy.

FLOWERS: May–August. Rounded clusters have 15–35 flowers with 5 white to pinkish, oval petals, ¼–½ inch long (6–12 mm), sparsely to densely hairy, 10 white stamens form an erect column.

LEAVES: Opposite, stalked; blades oval, ⅜–3 inches long (1–8 cm); edges toothed, top surface smooth, green, strongly veined; bottom whitish-hairy.

HABITAT: Rocky slopes, canyons, cliffs; foothills, montane forests. Elevation 4,930–9,850 feet (1,500–3,000 m).

Lewis Mock Orange

Philadelphus lewisii, Hydrangea Family, Hydrageaceae; Deciduous shrub

QUICK ID: Look for leafy shrubs with large, opposite leaves and clusters of showy white flowers with 4 petals and clustered stamens.

RANGE: NR, Canada; widespread, common

STEM: Erect, open branching, 5–10 feet tall (1.5–3 m).

FLOWERS: April–September. Clusters have 3–15 fragrant flowers with spreading, pure-white petals, each oblong, ⅜–1 inch long (10–25 mm); stamens many, radiating, white, tipped with yellow anthers.

LEAVES: Opposite, stalked; blade broadly lance-shaped to elliptic, 1–2⅜ inches long (3–6 cm) by ⅜–1 inch wide (1–3 cm); edges entire to toothed, surfaces smooth to slightly short-hairy.

HABITAT: Moist woods, rocky slopes, canyons; grasslands, sagebrush, foothills, montane forests. Elevation 900–5,300 feet (275–1,615 m).

SIMILAR SPECIES: Little-leaf Mock Orange, *P. microphyllus*, replaces *P. lewisii* in the Middle and Southern Rockies.

Fendler's Waterleaf

Hydrophyllum fendleri, Waterleaf Family, Hydrophyllaceae; Perennial herb

QUICK ID: Look for loose clusters of white-to-lavender flowers blooming above large compound leaves with sharp-toothed leaflets.

RANGE: NR, MR, SR, Canada; widespread, common

STEM: Erect, solitary, 7-32 inches tall (18–80 cm), hairy, rhizomatous.

FLOWERS: June–July. Hairy clusters on stalks to 6¾ inches long (17 cm) surpassing leaves. Flowers bell-shaped, ¼–⅜ inch long (6–10 mm); 5 petals, whitish to lavender, with protruding stamens; calyx lobes beneath the petals pointed, covered with long hairs.

LEAVES: Alternate, on long stalks. Blades to 12 inches long (30 cm), pinnately compound with 9–13 lance-shaped leaflets with 4–8 sharp teeth per side; surfaces with stiff hairs, tips pointed.

HABITAT: Moist, open woods, stream banks; foothills, montane, subalpine forests. Elevation 6,500–10,700 feet (1,980–3,260 m).

White Scorpionweed

Phacelia alba, Waterleaf Family, Hydrophyllaceae; Annual herb

QUICK ID: Look for hairy, leafy stems; deeply lobed leaves; and small, bell-shaped, white flowers crowded along one side of a stem with the tip coiled like a scorpion's tail.

RANGE: SR, widespread, common

STEM: Erect, 1-few, 2–28 inches tall (5–70 cm), hairy.

FLOWERS: May–September. Densely hairy, branched clusters have multiple, coiled arrays with bell-shaped flowers; 5 white-to-pale-blue petals with ragged edges, ⅛–3⁄16 inch long (3–4 cm); stamens extend 2–4 cm beyond petals, style equal or longer than stamens.

LEAVES: Basal, alternate on stem. Blades pinnately compound, ¾–4 inches long (2–10 cm); leaflets ¾–3 inches long (2–8 cm), cut to midrib and irregularly lobed; surfaces hairy, may be glandular.

HABITAT: Coarse soils, open lands; sagebrush, foothills, montane, subalpine forests. Elevation 6,100–12,000 feet (1,860–3,658 m).

SIMILAR SPECIES: New Mexico Scorpionweed, *P. neomexicana*, (SR) has blue flowers.

Silverleaf Scorpionweed

Phacelia hastata, Waterleaf Family, Hydrophyllaceae; Perennial herb

QUICK ID: Look for sprawling plants with prominently veined, silvery-hairy leaves, tightly coiled clusters of small white flowers, and long stamens.

RANGE: NR, MR, SR, Canada; widespread, common

STEM: Trailing to erect, branched from base, 2–20 inches tall/long (5–50 cm), loose-hairy.

FLOWERS: May–September. Densely hairy clusters have white-to-pale-lavender flowers with 5 oval petal-lobes, each ⅛–3⁄16 inch long (2–4 mm); stamens longer that petals, style deeply divided.

LEAVES: Basal, stalked; blades narrowly to broadly elliptic, ½–4 inches long (1–10 cm); edges entire, surfaces with fine, short, silvery hairs. Stem leaves similar, alternate, smaller, unstalked up the stem.

HABITAT: Dry, coarse soils, open woods, fellfields; grasslands to alpine. Elevation 1,000–11,000 feet (304–3,353 m).

Varileaf Scorpionweed

Phacelia heterophylla, Waterleaf Family, Hydrophyllaceae; Perennial, biennial herb

QUICK ID: Look for hairy stems, strongly veined leaves with and without pointed basal leaflets, and one-sided clusters of coiled rows with small white flowers with long stamens.

RANGE: NR, MR, SR, Canada; widespread, common

STEM: Erect, branched, 8–48 inches tall (20–120 cm), bristly hairy.

FLOWERS: June–October. Small, bell-shaped, white-to-pinkish flowers grow in elongated, densely bristly, coiled clusters; have 5 petals, 3⁄16–5⁄16 inch long (4–7 mm); stamens and style longer than petals.

LEAVES: Basal, long-stalked; blades elliptic, pointed, 2–6 inches long (50–150 mm); edges entire or with 1 to 4 pairs of small lobes at the base of the blade; surface hairy with pronounced veins. Stem leaves alternate, entire to basely lobed.

HABITAT: Coarse soils, open areas; sagebrush, foothills, montane, subalpine forests. Elevation 3,000–10,500 feet (915–3,200 m).

Ives Phacelia

Phacelia ivesiana, Waterleaf Family, Hydrophyllaceae; Annual herb

QUICK ID: Look in sandy soils for low-growing, hairy stems; pinnately lobed leaves; and loose clusters of tiny flowers with 5 white petals and yellow throat.

RANGE: MR, SR; widespread common

STEM: Prostrate to erect, branched from base 2–12 inches tall/wide (5–30 cm), glandular-hairy throughout.

FLOWERS: February–June. Few-flowered, densely hairy clusters have small, bell-shaped flowers ⅛ inch long (2–4 mm), with 5 spreading, rounded petal-lobes; stamens and style wholly within yellow throat.

LEAVES: Basal and alternate on stem; blades deeply pinnately lobed, ⅝–2 inches long (15–50 mm); lobes oblong, densely hairy, tips round.

HABITAT: Dry open, sandy areas; arid grasslands, sagebrush, pinyon-juniper foothills. Elevation 5,000–7,500 feet (1,500–2,286 m).

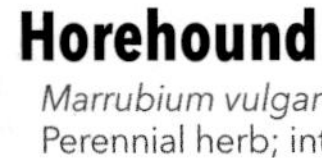

Horehound

Marrubium vulgare, Mint Family, Lamiaceae; Perennial herb; introduced, naturalized

QUICK ID: Look for woolly stems, scented wrinkled leaves, and whorled clusters of tiny white flowers along the stem leaf nodes.

RANGE: NR, MR, SR, Canada; widespread, common

STEM: Erect, square, 1–2 feet tall (30–60 cm), white-woolly

FLOWERS: April–July. Dense whorls of tiny white flowers bloom in the leaf nodes. Flowers tubular, $\frac{3}{16}$ inch long (5 mm) with 2 lips: the upper erect with 2 lobes, the lower drooping with 3 lobes. Fruit small burrs with hooked spines, 4 seeds.

LEAVES: Opposite. Blades oval, ¾–2⅜ inches long (2–6 cm); edges with rounded teeth, surfaces prominently veined, wrinkled, hairy above, woolly below.

HABITAT: Disturbed areas; prairies, grasslands, sagebrush, foothills, montane forests. Elevation 2,000–8,400 feet (609–2,560 m).

Wild Mint

Mentha arvensis, Mint Family, Lamiaceae; Perennial herb

QUICK ID: Look in moist soils for rooting stems, aromatic leaves, and erect flower stalks with whorled clusters of small, pale-blue flowers.

RANGE: NR, MR, SR, Canada; widespread, common

STEM: Erect, 6–32 inches tall (15–80 cm), square, hairy, rhizomatous.

FLOWERS: June–September. Flowers in dense clusters in the leaf axils (not spikes on the branch tips); each whitish-blue to pale-lavender flower is tubular, 3/16–1/4 inch long (4–6 mm), with 2 lips.

LEAVES: Opposite, on short stalks with minty aroma, separated along stem. Blades elliptic to lance-shaped, 1/2–3 inches long (1–8 cm), margins serrated, surfaces pitted with glands, lower surface (especially veins) short-hairy.

HABITAT: Moist areas, stream sides; foothills, montane, subalpine forests. Elevation 3,400–9,700 feet (1,036–2,960 m).

Pointed-tip Mariposa Lily

Calochortus apiculatus, Lily Family, Liliaceae; Perennial herb

QUICK ID: Look for slender stems, a solitary basal leaf, and bowl-shaped flowers with 3 creamy, hairy petals and a throat lined with yellow hair.

RANGE: NR, Canada; widespread, common

STEM: Erect, unbranched, 4–12 inches tall (10–30 cm), smooth.

FLOWERS: March–September. Terminal clusters have 1–5 flowers with 3 triangular to rounded, creamy petals, sometimes penciled with purple, typical with a dark spot (nectary) at base; top surface densely hairy, edges fringed, throat with yellow hairs; 3 sepals shorter than petals, pointed.

LEAVES: Basal from bulb, flat, linear to lance-shaped, 4–12 inches long (10–30 cm) to 3/4 inch wide (18 mm), both ends taper, surfaces smooth; usually shorter than flower stem.

HABITAT: Dry meadows, rocky slopes; grasslands, foothills, montane forests. Elevation 2,000–6,000 feet (610–1,928 m).

White Mariposa Lily

Calochortus eurycarpus, Lily Family, Liliaceae; Perennial herb

QUICK ID: Look for slender stems with 1–5 white, cup-shaped flowers. Petals have a central purple mark and yellow basal spot.

RANGE: MR, NR; widespread, locally common

STEM: Erect, single, branching near top, 6–24 inches tall (15–60 cm).

FLOWERS: June–August. Flowers 2 inches wide (5 cm). Petals 1–1½ inches long (3–4 cm), creamy white to lavender with a large purple blotch halfway and a fringed yellow nectar gland at base; between petals are 3 lance-shaped, pointed sepals; anthers oblong with blunt tip. Seed capsule oblong, erect, 3-angled, ¾–1¼ inches long (2–3 cm). Often grows in masses.

LEAVES: Basal from bulb, 1 blade, flat, 8–12 inches long (20–30 cm), to ⅜ inch wide (10 mm); 1 mid-stem leaf, small, bract-like.

HABITAT: Open slopes, meadows; grasslands, sagebrush, foothills, montane forests. Elevation 4,000–8,500 feet (1,220–2,590 m).

Gunnison's Mariposa Lily

Calochortus gunnisonii, Lily Family, Liliaceae; Perennial herb

QUICK ID: Look for white-to-purple-tinted, cup-shaped flowers with 3 petals with purple band and yellow, beard-like hairs circling the throat.

RANGE: SR, MR; widespread, common

STEM: Single, 8–20 inches tall (20–51 cm).

FLOWERS: May–July. Flowers 3 inches wide (8 cm). Petals separated by 3 lance-shaped, pointed sepals. A thin, continuous purple band usually circles the hairy, yellowish lower half of each petal, and a purple blotch dots the base. Note the 6 anthers are broad with sharp points. Fruit is an erect, 3-angled, linear capsule. Yellow and magenta flowering forms grow in the mountains of NM.

LEAVES: Basal from bulb (wither early); blades 2–4, channeled (not flat), narrow-linear, 7–14 inches long (18–35 cm). Stem blades alternate, smaller.

HABITAT: Coarse soils, open slopes, meadows; montane, subalpine forests. Elevation 6,900–10,800 feet (2,100–3,300 m).

Sego Lily

Calochortus nuttallii, Lily Family, Liliaceae; Perennial herb

QUICK ID: Look for stems with 1-4 cupped-shaped, white flowers with 3 petals that have a maroon crescent band above the hairy, yellow base.

RANGE: NR, MR, SR; widespread, common

STEM: Slender, branching near top, 12 inches tall (30 cm).

FLOWERS: May–June. Flowers 3 inches wide (8 cm); petals white (often tinged with lilac or pale yellow), or occasionally pink, separated by 3 lance-shaped, pointed sepals. A purple-to-brown, crescent band often circles the hairy, yellow base; 6 yellowish-to-pinkish anthers are narrow with blunt tips. Fruit is an erect, 3-angled capsule.

LEAVES: Basal from bulb; blades linear, channeled (not flat), 4–8 inches long (10–20 cm), narrow (2–4 mm wide). Stem blades alternate, smaller.

HABITAT: Sandy, gravelly, alluvial loam soils; sagebrush and creosote scrub, pinyon-juniper foothills, lower montane forests. Elevation 4,800–9,800 feet (1,463–2,990 m).

Bride's Bonnet, Queen's Cup

Clintonia uniflora, Lily Family, Liliaceae; Perennial herb

QUICK ID: Look for low plants with star-like flowers with 6 white petals; broad, sword-like leaves; and round, bright-blue berries.

RANGE: NR, Canada; widespread, common

STEM: Erect, hairy flower stem (scape) 6–10 inches tall (15–25 cm).

FLOWERS: June–September. Solitary flower 1–2 inches wide (3–5 cm), with 6 narrow petals (tepals), anthers yellow. Fruit a smooth, blue berry ¼–½ inch diameter (6–13 mm).

LEAVES: Basal rosette from rhizome. Blades 2-3, oblong, flat, 3-6 inches long (7–15 cm) by 1–2¾ inches wide (3-7 cm); margins entire, tip pointed.

HABITAT: Moist montane forests to lower subalpine. Elevation sea level–8,330 feet (2,600 m).

Alpine Lily

Lloydia serotina, Lily Family, Liliaceae; Perennial herb

QUICK ID: Look for this petite lily on treeless alpine tundra, rocky fellfields, and stream banks in dense conifer forests. Note the grass-like leaves and 6 white, petal-like tepals lined with pencil-like marks.

RANGE: NR, MR, SR, Canada; widespread, locally common

STEM: Erect, slender, 2–8 inches tall (5–20 cm), smooth.

FLOWERS: June–September. Flowers erect, ¾ inch wide (20 mm), usually solitary; 6 petal-like tepals (3 sepals and 3 petals all alike), are white with a yellowish base and dark veins.

LEAVES: 2 basal leaves, grass-like, 1½–4 inches long (4–10 cm); 2–4 alternate stem leaves much shorter; surfaces smooth.

HABITAT: Rocky ridges, grassy slopes; upper subalpine forests, alpine tundra. Elevation 9,000–13,000 feet (2,743–3,962 m).

Roughfruit Fairybells

Prosartes trachycarpa, Lily Family, Lilaceae; Perennial herb

QUICK ID: Look for 1–2 bell-shaped, creamy-white flowers drooping at branch tips on stout, hairy stalks; fruit a round, bumpy, red berry.

RANGE: NR, MR, SR, Canada; widespread, common

STEM: Erect, few-branched, 12–32 inches tall (30–80 cm), hairy.

FLOWERS: May–July. 1–2 flowers with 6 tepals, each ⅜–⅝ inch long (9–15 mm), spreading, pointed; 6 stamens longer than petals. Fruit a rounded berry ⅜–⅝ inch long (9–15 mm), surface warty, green maturing red.

LEAVES: Alternate, clasping; blades oval, pointed, 1½–4¾ inches long (4–12 cm) by ¾–2 inches wide (2–5 cm); edges entire, lined with spreading hairs, top surface smooth, bottom short-hairy.

HABITAT: Moist to dry, shady woods; grasslands, foothills, montane, subalpine forests. Elevation 7,000–9,400 feet (2,132–2,895 m).

Claspleaf Twistedstalk

Streptopus amplexifolius, Lily Family, Liliaceae; Perennial herb

QUICK ID: Look in moist forests for arching stems; broad, oval, clasping leaves; and white-to-greenish-yellow flowers dangling on slender stalks with a sharp bend.

RANGE: NR, MR, SR, Canada; widespread, common

STEM: Arching, freely branched, 20–48 inches tall (50–120 cm).

FLOWERS: June–August. 1–2 bell-shaped flowers, dangle from leaf axils on stalks ¾–2 inches long (2–5 cm) with a sharp bend or twist; flowers have 6 narrow tepals, ⅜ inch long (1 cm), tips curved. Fruit bright red to yellowish-orange, oval berry, ½ inch long (12 mm).

LEAVES: Alternate with clasping base. Blades oval to oblong, 2–6 inches long (5–15 cm), ¾–2 inches wide (2–5 cm); tips pointed, base with heart-shaped lobes around stem.

HABITAT: Dense forests, stream sides, marshy areas; montane, subalpine forests. Elevation 7,500–11,000 feet (2,286–3,353 m).

SIMILAR SPECIES: Roughfruit Fairybells, *Prosartes trachycarpa*, has 1–2 flowers on straight stems and straight petals.

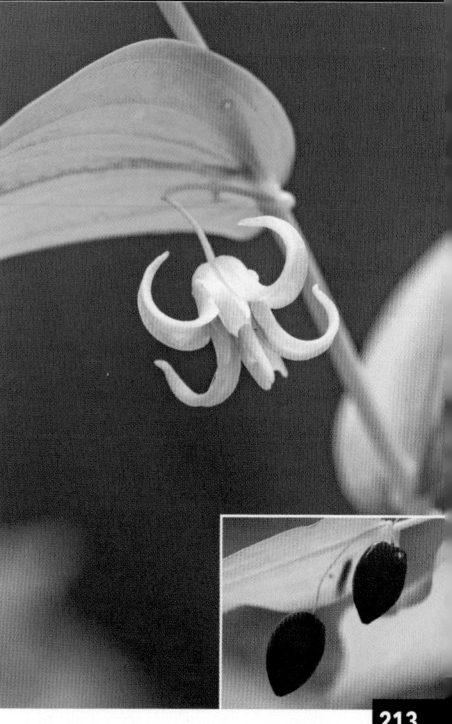

Ten-petal Blazingstar

Mentzelia decapetala, Blazingstar Family, Loasaceae; Biennial, perennial herb

QUICK ID: Look in rocky soils for bushy clumps; rough, clinging leaves with narrow, pointed lobes; and large flowers with 10 white petals and 100–200 long stamens. Opens at dusk for moth pollinators.

RANGE: NR, MR, SR, Canada; widespread, common

STEM: Erect, branches from base, 12–40 inches tall (30–100 cm).

FLOWERS: June–October. Clusters on branch tips. Flowers white to cream; 5 petals, 1–2⅜ inches long (3–6 cm) by ½ inch wide (12 mm), and 5 similar petal-like stamens; stamen cluster cream to yellow; base narrow, tip pointed. Capsule 1–2 inches long (3–5 cm).

LEAVES: Alternate; blades lance-shaped, 2–6 inches long (5–15 cm), edges serrated or with 9–20 narrow, wavy, pointed lobes along mid-rib; tips tapering, both surfaces rough-hairy.

HABITAT: Dry, rocky soils, plains, disturbed areas; grasslands, sagebrush, foothills. Elevation 1,000–7,858 feet (300–2,400 m).

Bractless Blazingstar

Mentzelia nuda, Blazingstar Family, Loasaceae; Biennial, perennial herb

QUICK ID: Look in sandy soils for branching stems, clinging leaves, and showy white flowers with long stamens that open near dusk.

RANGE: MR, SR; widespread, common

STEM: Erect, stiff, upper branching, 1-3 feet tall (30–90 cm), hairy.

FLOWERS: July–September. Flowers 1½–3½ inches wide (3–9 cm) with 5 white petals, narrow, lance-shaped 1–2 inches long (3–5 cm) by ⅜ inch wide (10 mm), and 5 similar petal-like, modified stamens; stamen cluster white. Capsule cylindrical ¾–1⅛ inches long (2–3 cm), tipped with dried finger-like lobes.

LEAVES: Alternate; lower leaves short-stalked, upper leaves clasp the stem. Blades lance-shaped, 1½–4 inches long (4–10 cm); edges coarsely toothed, tips pointed, surfaces have short, barbed hairs.

HABITAT: Sandy soils, fields, disturbed areas; grasslands, sagebrush, foothills. Elevation 3,300–7,000 feet (1,005–2,134 m).

SIMILAR SPECIES: Ten-petal Blazingstar, *M. decapetala*, has a yellow stamen cluster.

Streambank Wild Hollyhock

Iliamna rivularis, Mallow Family, Malvaceae; Perennial herb

QUICK ID: Look for tall, stout stems (usually clustered) with white-to-pink, cup-shaped flowers in spaced clusters along the upper stem.

RANGE: NR, MR, SR (absent NM), Canada; widespread, common

STEM: Erect, branching, 2–6 feet tall (60–182 cm), sparsely hairy.

FLOWERS: June–August. Flowers 1–3 inches wide (3–8 cm); petals 5, white to pinkish or rose-purple, each ¾–1 inch long (18–25 mm).

LEAVES: Alternate on stalks 2–4 inches long (5–10 cm). Blades 2–8 inches long (5–20 cm), palmately 3-7 lobed (maple-like); edges coarsely-toothed, tips pointed, surfaces hairy.

HABITAT: Moist soils, open areas, meadows, stream banks; wetlands, foothills, montane forests. Elevation 2,000–9,515 feet (610–2,900 m).

Common Mallow, Cheeseweed

Malva neglecta, Mallow Family, Malvaceae; Annual herb; introduced, invasive

QUICK ID: Look for spreading stems with rounded, shallow-lobed leaves, and lined, white-to-pink flowers with a showy stamen column.

RANGE: NR, MR, SR, Canada; widespread, common

STEM: Erect to sprawling, branching, to 3 feet long (1 m), hairy.

FLOWERS: May–October. Flowers ½–1 inch wide (12–25 mm) with 5 petals, slightly notched, with dark lines.

LEAVES: Alternate on stalks to 4 inches long (10 cm). Blades palmate, rounded, ½–3 inches across (12–80 mm); margins with 5-7 shallow lobes with teeth, surfaces with indented veins, short hairs

HABITAT: Disturbed areas. Elevation sea level-6,000 feet (1,828 m).

White Checkermallow

Sidalcea candida, Mallow Family, Malvaceae; Perennial herb

QUICK ID: Look for single stalks with palmate leaves, and spikes of showy flowers with 5 white, spreading petals and a white stamen column topped with purple anthers.

RANGE: MR (UT), SR; widespread, common

STEM: Erect, single, clustered, 1–3 feet tall (30–100 cm), smooth to sparsely hairy.

FLOWERS: May–September. Terminal spike-like clusters of buds have several 2-inch wide (5 cm) flowers in bloom at once; 5 white-to-pinkish, oval petals ½–1 inch long (12–25 mm) with narrow bases.

LEAVES: Basal, few. Alternate on stem, long stalked; blade 2–8 inches wide (5–20 cm), palmately divided into 5-7 lance-shaped-to-narrow segments, edges toothed; upper leaves edges entire.

HABITAT: Wet meadows, riparian areas, plains; foothills, montane, subalpine forests. Elevation 6,000–10,000 feet (1,828–3,048 m).

SIMILAR SPECIES: New Mexico Checkermallow, *S. neomexicana*, (SR) has pink flowers.

Mountain Death Camas

Anticlea elegans, Death Camas Family, Melanthiaceae; Perennial herb from bulb

QUICK ID: Look for creamy flowers with heart-shaped, yellow-to-green glands at the base of the petals; basal leaves grass-like.

RANGE: NR, MR, SR, Canada; widespread, common

STEM: Flower stalk 1-2 feet tall (30-60 cm); roots deadly poisonous.

FLOWERS: June–July. A loose spike has 10–30 creamy-to-greenish-white flowers alternating up the bloom stalk. Flowers spread open ⅝–¾ inch wide (15-20 mm) with 6 petal-like tepals ¼–½-inch long (7-12 mm) with yellow-to-green, heart-shaped glands at base, tips rounded to notched; 6 erect stamens as long as the tepals.

LEAVES: Basal from bulbs. Blades linear, grass-like, 4–12 inches long (10–30 cm) by ⅛–⅝ inch wide (3-15 mm); stem leaves smaller.

HABITAT: Mountain meadows, open forests; montane, subalpine forests. Elevation 6,500–12,500 feet (1,980–3,810 m).

SIMILAR SPECIES: Meadow Death Camas, *Toxicoscordion venenosum*, has oval basal spots on the petals.

Meadow Death Camas

Toxicoscordion venenosum, Death Camas Family, Melanthiaceae; Perennial herb from bulb

QUICK ID: Look for grass-like leaves, dense clusters of small white flowers, and petals with a yellow-greenish, oval basal spot. The bulb and seeds are deadly poisonous.

RANGE: NR, MR, SR, Canada; widespread, common

STEM: Erect, 1-2 from bulb, 6–18 inches tall (15-45 cm), smooth.

FLOWERS: April–June. Clusters have either short branching stalks from the stem with several flowers (var. *gramineus*), or unbranching stalks with 1 flower (var. *venenosus*); flowers to ⅜ inch wide (10 mm), with 6 tepals. The tepal base usually abruptly narrows into a "claw."

LEAVES: Basal from bulb; blades grass-like, 4–16 inches long (10–40 cm), ⅛–⅜ inch wide (4–10 mm). Stem leaves alternate, smaller.

HABITAT: Meadows, open woods; arid grasslands, sagebrush, foothills, montane forests. Elevation 5,000–8,000 feet (1,524–2,438 m).

SIMILAR SPECIES: Foothills Death Camas, *T. paniculatum*, (all regions), usually has outer petals without claws.

Western Trillium

Trillium ovatum, Death Camas Family, Melanthiaceae; Perennial herb

QUICK ID: Look in conifer forests for stems tipped with 3 large whorled leaves and a single flower with lance-shaped, white petals.

RANGE: NR, Canada: widespread, common; SR (CO, WY): rare

STEM: Erect, stout, 8–18 inches tall (20–45 cm), rhizomatous.

FLOWERS: April–July. Solitary on short stalk at stem tip, petals 1–2⅛ inches long (3–5 cm), white, aging dark red.

LEAVES: Whorl of 3 at stem tip, egg- to diamond-shaped, pointed, 3–6 inches long (5–18 cm), hairless, edges entire.

HABITAT: Dry to moist soils, meadows, shady understory; montane, subalpine forests. Elevation 2,093–9,500 feet (668–2,895 m).

Corn Lily

Veratrum californicum, Death Camas Family, Melanthiaceae; Perennial herb

QUICK ID: Look in moist meadows for tall stems with erect, broad, corn-like leaves and long, branching clusters with tiny white flowers.

RANGE: NR, MR, SR; widespread, common

STEM: Erect, 3–6 feet tall (1–2 m), colony forming.

FLOWERS: July–August. Elongated terminal clusters 1–2 feet long (30–60 cm) have horizontal to upward-angled branches packed with star-shaped flowers with 6 creamy-greenish petal-like tepals, each 5⁄16–⅝ inch long (8–15 mm) with a green base.

LEAVES: Dense basal rosette; blades broad, elliptic to lance-shaped, strongly parallel veined, often pleated, sheathing the stem. Stem leaves alternate, 7–16 inches long (20–40 cm) by 3–8 inches wide (8–20 cm), smaller upward.

HABITAT: Moist meadows, bogs, seeps; montane, subalpine forests. Elevation 8,000–11,800 feet (2,438–3,600 m).

SIMILAR SPECIES: Green Corn Lily, *V. viride*, (NR, Canada) has green flowers and woolly herbage.

Beargrass

Xerophyllum tenax, Death Camas Family, Melanthiaceae; Perennial evergreen herb

QUICK ID: Look for dense, mounding clumps of wiry grass-like leaves, and tall bloom stalks topped with dense clusters of small white flowers.

RANGE: NR, MR, Canada; widespread, common

STEM: Flowering stems erect, 20–60 inches tall (50–150 cm).

FLOWERS: May–August. Dense terminal conical clusters elongate to club-shaped; flowers small, saucer-shaped, with 6 narrow spreading tepals, ¼–⅜ inch long (5–10 mm), white to creamy; stamens long.

LEAVES: Mainly basal; blades grass-like, 6–24 inches long (15–60 cm) by ⅛ inch wide (3 mm); edges with sharp, fine teeth. Stem leaves alternate, shorter.

HABITAT: Meadows, open woods; montane and subalpine forests. Elevation 5,700–8,250 feet (1,737–2,515 m).

Mt. Hood Pussypaws

Cistanthe umbellata, Miner's Lettuce Family, Montiaceae; Perennial herb

QUICK ID: Look for mat-forming basal rosettes with spreading-to-erect flower stalks tipped with spherical clusters of white flowers.

RANGE: NR, MR, Canada; widespread, locally common

STEM: Erect to prostrate flower stalks from root crown.

FLOWERS: May–October. Clusters ⅜–1½ inches diameter (1–4 cm) on reddish stalks ⅜–4 inches tall (1–10 cm); 4 pointed petals white to pinkish that fade early to reddish; 2 showy, rounded sepals white to pinkish, persistent and drying pinkish red; anthers red or yellow.

LEAVES: Basal rosettes, usually 2 or more clustered together forming mats to 6 inches wide (15 cm). Blades spatula-shaped, fleshy, ¾–2 ¾ inches long (2–7 cm).

HABITAT: Sandy, rocky, exposed soils; montane, subalpine forests, alpine. Elevation 3,950–14,100 feet (1,500-4,300 m).

Western Springbeauty

Claytonia lanceolata, Miner's Lettuce Family, Montiaceae; Perennial herb

QUICK ID: Look for 1–10 stems with 2 opposite leaves and small, white-to-pink flowers, often with pink lines and yellow throat.

RANGE: NR, MR, SR, Canada; widespread, common

STEM: Erect, slender, 2–6 inches high (5–15 cm), from tubers.

FLOWERS: April–July. Loose clusters of 3–5 flowers on spreading pedicles. Flowers ⅜–⅝ inch wide (8–14 mm), 5 notched petals white to pinkish; 5 white stamens with pink anthers.

LEAVES: Basal, linear, stemless, often absent at flowering; stem leaves opposite 1 pair. Blade linear to oval, pointed, ⅜–2 ¾ inches long (1–7 cm), stemless (sessile).

HABITAT: Often after snowmelt; grasslands to alpine zones. Elevation 1,640–9,850 feet (500–3,000 m).

SIMILAR SPECIES: Other springbeauties: *C. rosea*, (scattered in SR) has pink to magenta petals; *C. multiscapa*, (NR, MR) has yellow, orange, or creamy flowers without yellow spots.

Candyflower

Claytonia sibirica, Miner's Lettuce Family, Montiaceae; Perennial herb

QUICK ID: Look for a basal rosette with 1–3 short stems with clusters of small flowers with 5 white-to-pink petals with pink stripes.

RANGE: NR, Canada; widespread, locally common

STEM: Erect to spreading, few to several, 4–16 inches tall (10–40 cm).

FLOWERS: March–September. Note the pair of small leaf-like, elliptical bracts at base of each elongated cluster; flowers on spreading pedicels ⅜–1½ inches long (1–4 cm). Flowers ⅜–¾ inch wide (8–20 mm) with 5 notched petals, white occasionally pink; anthers pink.

LEAVES: Basal egg-shaped with long stalks (petioles). 2 stem leaves, opposite; blades stalkless (sessile), lance-shaped to broadly oval, ¾–3 inches long (2–8 cm).

HABITAT: Moist, shaded forests, stream sides, meadows, thickets; montane, subalpine forests. Elevation sea level–6,500 feet (2,000 m).

Threeleaf Lewisia

Lewisia triphylla, Miner's Lettuce Family, Montiaceae; Perennial herb

QUICK ID: Look in seasonally wet soils for tiny ground-level plants with loose clusters of tiny, white, dime-size flowers.

RANGE: NR, MR, SR, Canada; scattered, infrequent to locally common

STEM: Erect to trailing, 1 to several, 1-4 inches tall (3-10 cm).

FLOWERS: May–August. Loose clusters of 2-25 tiny flowers with 5-9 white-to-pinkish petals with pink veins, each petal to ¼ inch long (7 mm), tips rounded.

LEAVES: Basal, wither by flowering; blades narrowly linear, ⅜-2 inches long (1-5 cm), edges entire, round in cross section. Stem leaves similar, 2-3, opposite or whorled, just above ground level.

HABITAT: Moist sandy, gravelly soils, open places; montane, subalpine, alpine. Elevation 4,500-10,500 feet (1,370-3,200 m).

Fragrant (Snowball) Sand-Verbena

Abronia fragrans, Four-O'Clock Family, Nyctaginaceae; Perennial herb

QUICK ID: Look for sprawling stems with sticky, glandular hairs; sticky leaves; and snowball-like clusters of fragrant, white, tubular flowers.

RANGE: MR, SR; widespread, locally common

STEMS: Branching, spreading, 10–40 inches high (25–100 cm).

FLOWERS: March–May. Spherical clusters, 2-3 inches wide (5–7.5 cm), have 30–80 tubular flowers, each ⅜–1 inch long (1–2.5 cm); tube green to reddish; 5 petal lobes open ¼–⅜ inch wide (6–10 mm), white, occasionally pink, edges wavy, lobed. Flowers open late afternoon for nighttime pollination.

LEAVES: Opposite, unequal. Blades hairy, oval to lance-shaped, 1–4¾ inches long (3–12 cm), ⅜–3 inches wide (1–8 cm), on long stems; edges entire to wavy; surfaces sticky-hairy.

HABITAT: Dunes, arid grasslands, sagebrush, pinyon-juniper foothills. Elevation 1,300–7,200 feet (400–2,200 m).

White-stem Evening Primrose

Oenothera albicaulis, Evening Primrose Family, Onagraceae; Annual herb

QUICK ID: Look for mounds with hairy, lobed leaves; flowers with 4 white, notched petals; and nodding, red-striped, torpedo-shaped buds.

RANGE: SR; widespread, common

STEM: Erect to sprawling, 2–12 inches tall (5–30 cm), hairy.

FLOWERS: April–May. Flowers 1½–3 inches wide (38–76 mm) in axils of upper leaves; floral tube, ⅝–1⅛ inches long (15–30 cm), inside hairless; stamens equal, style has 4 cross-shaped lobes and extends beyond the 8 anthers; 4 sepals beneath the flower, ½–1 inch long (12–25 mm), margins red, bent back against the stem; tips of buds fully united. Fruit a ribbed, cylindrical capsule 1½ inches long (4 cm).

LEAVES: Basal stalked; blades lance-shaped. Stem leaves alternate, stalkless; blades ½–4 inches long (1–10 cm); margins wavy to deeply lobed.

HABITAT: Coarse soils, disturbed areas; arid grasslands, foothills, montane forests. Elevation 4,000–8,000 feet (1,220–2,438 m).

Tufted Evening Primrose

Oenothera caespitosa, Evening Primrose Family, Onagraceae; Perennial herb

QUICK ID: Look for leafy, nearly hairless, sprawling stems; long-tubed flowers with 4 white petals; and erect, ribbed, hairy buds.

RANGE: NR, MR, SR, Canada; widespread, common

STEM: Absent, or sprawling to matted, to 16 inches long (40 cm).

FLOWERS: April–September. Erect floral tubes 1½–5½ inches long (4–14 cm) sprout from roots or leaf axils; buds erect, hairy, with red stripes, tips at point united (not spreading); petals ¾–1¾ inches long (2–5 cm), heart shaped; stamens unequal, stigma with 4 slender, cross-shaped lobes; 4 sepals bend backward. Fruit a strongly ribbed cylindrical capsule ⅝–2⅜ inches long (15–60 mm).

LEAVES: Basal rosette; alternate on stem. Blades highly variable on same plant, ¾–10 inches long (2–25 cm), elliptic, hairy, margins entire or with irregular teeth or lobes.

HABITAT: Coarse soils, roadsides; arid grasslands, sagebrush, foothills, montane, subalpine forests. Elevation 4,300–8,500 feet (1,310–2,590 m).

Crownleaf Evening Primrose

Oenothera coronopifolia, Evening Primrose Family, Onagraceae; Perennial herb

QUICK ID: Look for coarsely hairy stems, leaves with narrow comb-like lobes, nodding buds, and white flowers with a very hairy throat.

RANGE: MR (UT): scattered; SR: widespread, common

STEM: Erect, rigid, branching or not, 1-2 feet tall (30-90 cm).

FLOWERS: June–September. Flowers solitary from leaf axils, 2 inches across (5 cm); note the floral tube throat is dense with long hairs; 4 petals, white, notched ⅜–¾ inch long (1-2 cm); style longer than stamens with cross-shaped lobes at tip; buds nod, tips at point united (not spreading). Fruit a cylindrical capsule to ¾ inch long (2 cm).

LEAVES: Basal rosette. Stem leaves alternate, ¾–2¾ inches long (2–7 cm), deeply cut into narrow lobes evenly spaced like teeth on a comb, no wider than 2 mm (especially upper leaves).

HABITAT: Coarse soils, open areas; grasslands, foothills, ponderosa montane forest. Elevation 5,000-9,843 feet (1,524–3,000 m).

Nuttall's Evening Primrose

Oenothera nuttallii, Evening Primrose Family, Onagraceae; Perennial herb

QUICK ID: Look in dry soils for plants with hairless stems, long narrow leaves, white flowers with 4 notched petals, and nodding buds.

RANGE: NR, MR, SR (absent NM), Canada; widespread, common

STEM: Erect, reddish aging white, often branched, 1–3 feet tall (30–100 cm), hairless, rhizomatous.

FLOWERS: June–September. Flowers 1–2 inches wide (3-5 cm); petals ⅝–1¼ inches long (15–30 mm), floral tube ⅝–1⅝ inches long (15–40 mm), throat yellowish, hairless; buds red or striped, with tiny, spreading tips 1⁄16 inch long (1–2 mm); stigma with 4 lobes extends beyond stamens. Capsule erect, ¾–1 inch long (2–3 cm).

LEAVES: Basal absent by flowering. Stem leaves alternate, linear to narrowly oblong, ¾–4 inches long (2–10 cm) by ¼ inch wide (6 mm); edges entire to weakly toothed.

HABITAT: Dry, coarse soils, open areas; grasslands, sagebrush, foothills, montane forests. Elevation 1,000–9,000 feet (304–2,743 m).

Pale Evening Primrose

Oenothera pallida, Evening Primrose Family, Onagraceae; Perennial, annual herb

QUICK ID: Look in dry areas for leafy stems, lance-shaped to deeply cut leaves, white flowers with 4 notched petals, and nodding buds.

RANGE: NR, MR, SR, Canada; widespread, common

STEM: Erect, reddish aging white, often branching, 4–20 inches (10–50 cm), smooth to short-hairy, rhizomatous.

FLOWERS: April–September. Floral tube ⅝–1⅜ inches long (15–35 mm), throat yellowish hairless; petals to 1 inch long (3 cm); 4 reddish sepals fused, bending sidewards; stigma with 4 lobes extends beyond stamens; buds red or striped with tiny spreading tips. Capsule spreading to curved, cylindrical, 1⅜ inches long (4 cm).

LEAVES: Basal rosette usually absent. Stem leaves alternate oblong to lance-shaped, ⅜–2⅜ inches long (1–6 cm), ⅝ inch wide (15 mm); margins entire, wavy, toothed or deeply cut; surfaces hairless to short-hairy.

HABITAT: Dry, coarse soils; arid grasslands, sagebrush, pinyon-juniper foothills, montane forests. Elevation 3,800–8,000 feet (1,158–2,438 m).

Scarlet Beeblossom

Oenothera suffrutescens (Gaura coccinea), Evening Primrose Family, Onagraceae; Perennial herb

QUICK ID: Look for slender stems with narrow leaves, spikes of small flowers with 4 white, fading-to-pink, spoon-shaped petals, and dangling stamens with reddish anthers.

RANGE: NR, MR, SR, Canada; widespread, common

STEM: Erect, branching near base, 1–4 feet tall (30–120 cm), smooth to densely short-hairy.

FLOWERS: May–August. Terminal spikes 2–8 inches long (5–20 cm); petals, ⅛–¼ inch long (3–7 mm), white fading to red; 8 white filaments hang down with red anthers, yellow pollen; stigma lobes 4. Capsule cylindrical, ⅜ inch long (9 mm).

LEAVES: Alternate. Blades linear to oblong or lance-shaped, ¼–2 ½ inches long (1–6 cm) to ⅝ inch wide (15 mm); edges entire to shallowly toothed, tips pointed.

HABITAT: Dry, coarse soils, roadsides, disturbed areas; arid grasslands, sagebrush, pinyon-juniper foothills, montane forests. Elevation 2,000–8,500 feet (610–2,438 m).

Early Coralroot Orchid

Corallorhiza trifida, Orchid Family, Orchidaceae; Perennial herb

QUICK ID: Look for short, leafless, yellow-to-greenish stems with small yellowish-green-to-white flowers; lip is white with spots or not.

RANGE: NR, MR, SR, Canada; scattered, infrequent

STEM: Erect, single or clusters, 2–10 inches tall (5–25 cm).

FLOWERS: June–August. Spike-like clusters of 3–18 flowers, about ⅝ inch wide (15 mm), along upper stem (scape). Sepals petal-like, narrow, about ¼ inch long (6 mm): 2 spread forward, 1 arches upward with 2 petals to form the hood; 1 lower petal (lip) oblong, white, sometimes red-spotted, with 2 short parallel ridges on the top.

LEAVES: None. Lacking chlorophyll, coralroots depend on root fungi to absorb nutrients from decomposing organic material.

HABITAT: Moist forest leaf litter, along streams; montane forests. Elevation sea level–6,270 feet (1,910 m).

Spring Coralroot Orchid

Corallorhiza wisteriana, Orchid Family, Orchidaceae; Perennial herb

QUICK ID: Look for leafless, reddish-to-brownish stems with spikes of small flowers with a white, down-curved lip, with or without spots.

RANGE: NR, MR, SR; scattered, infrequent

STEM: Erect, single or clustered, 4–16 inches tall (10–40 cm).

FLOWERS: April–June. Elongated, loose cluster has 10–15 flowers to ¾ inch long (2 cm). Has 3 sepals, petal-like, purplish brown to greenish yellow, all arch upward to form the hood with 2 upper petals; 1 lower petal (lip) oval, to ¼ inch long and wide (7 mm), pure white or purple-spotted, edges finely fringed, base without lateral lobes.

LEAVES: None. Lacking chlorophyll, coralroots depend on root fungi to absorb nutrients from decomposing organic material.

HABITAT: Damp forest leaf litter; juniper, pine-fir, montane forests. Elevation 5,500–9,000 feet (1,675–3,000 m).

SIMILAR SPECIES: The lip of Spotted Coralroot, *C. maculata*, (all) is white with reddish spots.

Mountain Lady's Slipper Orchid

Cypripedium montanum, Orchid Family, Orchidaceae; Perennial herb

QUICK ID: Look for stems with broad, sword-like leaves and 1-3 white flowers with a slipper-shaped, 1-inch-long (3 cm) lower lip.

RANGE: NR, Canada; rare, localized

STEM: Erect, leafy 8–24 inches tall (20–60 cm).

FLOWERS: May–August. Flowers 1–3 near stem tip. Sepals and petals are brownish purple: 2 twisted petals, each 1½–2¾ inches long (4–7 cm), spread sideways; 1 sepal arcs above and 2 fused into 1 curl below the flower. The small, pouch-like lip typically has purple-tinged opening and spots on the yellow stamen column that arches over the opening. A sweet scent attracts small bees into the pouch, but they find no nectar (orchids lie!), then get covered with pollen as they escape through tiny openings under the anthers.

LEAVES: Alternate, broadly oval-elliptic to, 2–6 inches long (5–15 cm) and up to 2¾ inches wide (7 cm), sheathing.

HABITAT: Moist to dry shady forests; montane, subalpine forests. Elevation 1,500–6,900 feet (495–2,100 m).

Rattlesnake Plantain Orchid

Goodyera oblongifolia, Orchid Family, Orchidaceae; Perennial evergreen herb

QUICK ID: Look for a rosette of broad, oval leaves with white midribs, and small, hairy, white flowers on one side of a delicate bloom stalk.

RANGE: NR, MR, SR, Canada; widespread, common

STEM: Erect, 8–16 inches tall (20–40 cm), hairy.

FLOWERS: July–September. Spike-like clusters with 10–48 flowers bloom from the top down along one side of the stem. Each ½-inch-long (12 mm) flower has a white hood and boat-shaped lip. Note the petals and sepals are green and hairy.

LEAVES: Basal rosette. Blades 1–4 inches long (2.5–10 cm), elliptic to oval, midrib white, often spreading into lateral veins; margins entire.

HABITAT: Rich, forest soils; foothills, montane, subalpine forests. Elevation 8,000–10,500 feet (2,438–3,200 m).

SIMILAR SPECIES: Dwarf Rattlesnake Plantain, *G. repens* (NM, Canada: common; CO, NR: rare) is 4–6 inches tall (10–15 cm), has ¼-inch (6 mm) flowers, white sepals, and leaves green or white-mottled.

White Bog Orchid

Platanthera dilatata, Orchid Family, Orchidaceae; Perennial herb

QUICK ID: Look in wet soils for pencil-thin stems with spikes of tiny bright-white, clove-scented orchid flowers with short rear spurs.

RANGE: NR, MR, SR, Canada; widespread, common

STEM: Erect, slender, 5–32 inches tall (12–90 cm).

FLOWERS: June–August. Dense to loose spike has pure-white flowers (not greenish), ¾ inch diameter, 3 petal-like white sepals: 2 spread sideways or bending backwards; 1 arches upwards with 2 upper petals to form a hood over the stamen column; the third petal forms a lower lip to ⅜ inch long (1 cm), curved down with a broad base and pointed tip; rear spur cylindrical, curved, tip rounded, about as long as the lip.

LEAVES: Alternate, 4–6 erect blades, sheathing stem, stalkless, linear to narrowly lance-shaped, 1⅜–12 inches long (4–30 cm), smaller upwards; hairless, edges entire.

HABITAT: Wet soils, meadows, seeps, drainages; grasslands to subalpine forests. Elevation 6,000–11,200 feet (1,828–3,400 m).

Hooded Lady's Tresses Orchid

Spiranthes romanzoffiana, Orchid Family, Orchidaceae; Perennial herb

QUICK ID: Look in moist areas for clumps of blade-like basal leaves and spikes with spiraling rows of small, pearl-white flowers.

RANGE: NR, MR, SR, Canada; infrequent, locally common

STEM: Erect, stiff, 3–21 inches tall (8–55 cm), green, smooth.

FLOWERS: July–September. Dense spikes have 1–4 tight rows spiraling around the stem with up to 45 white flowers, each ½ inch long (12 mm) and bilaterally-symmetrical; white sepals and upper petal form a hood over the stamen column; the lower lip petal curves abruptly downward with a narrow middle. Bumblebees are the primary pollinators.

LEAVES: Basal, erect, present while flowering; blades slender, 3–12 inches long (8–30 cm). Stem leaves alternate scale-like.

HABITAT: Wet meadows, bogs, seeps, stream banks; montane, subalpine forests. Elevation 7,650–10,600 feet (2,332–2,230 m).

Coiled Lousewort

Pedicularis contorta, Broomrape Family, Orobanchaceae; Perennial herb, hemiparasitic

QUICK ID: Look for fern-like basal and stem leaves, and spikes lined with tubular creamy-white flowers with an arching hooded upper lip that narrows into a slender, curved beak.

RANGE: NR, MR: widespread, common; Canada: infrequent

STEM: Erect, clustered, unbranched, 6–24 inches tall (15–60 cm), smooth throughout.

FLOWERS: Loose spikes of tubular flowers with a hood-like upper lip (often purple-spotted) that narrows into a semicircular beak, and a spreading 3-lobed lower lip.

LEAVES: Basal, long stalked; blade oblong to lance-shaped, 2-7 inches long (5–18 cm), deeply pinnately cut into 25–41 linear, toothed lobes. Stem leaves alternate, smaller, unstalked up the stem.

HABITAT: Dry rocky slopes, meadows, open forests; montane, subalpine forests, alpine. Elevation 5,000–10,000 feet (1,524–3,048 m).

Sickletop Lousewort

Pedicularis racemosa, Broomrape Family, Orobanchaceae; Perennial herb, hemiparasitic

QUICK ID: Look for unlobed, serrated leaves, and creamy-white flowers with a distinct curved beak and a broad 3-lobed lower lip.

RANGE: NR, MR, SR, Canada; widespread, common

STEM: Erect, often in clusters, 4–20 inches tall (10–50 cm), hairless.

FLOWERS: June–August. Loose, elongated clusters have 3–25 white-to-pinkish flowers interspaced with leaf-like bracts; flowers ⅜–⅝ inch long (10–15 mm) with 2 lips: hooded upper lip arches down and narrows into a thin, semicircular tube or beak that often rests on the 3 broad, spreading lobes of the lower lip.

LEAVES: Alternate. Blades linear to lance-shaped, 1½–4 inches long (4–10 cm), edges lined with fine teeth. Stem, leaves often turn red.

HABITAT: Meadows, forest openings; montane, subalpine forests, alpine. Elevation 4,000–13,000 feet (1,220–3,962 m).

SIMILAR SPECIES: Coiled Lousewort, *P. contorta*, (NR, MR) has fern-like leaves.

Rough Prickly Poppy

Argemone hispida, Poppy Family, Papaveraceae; Perennial herbs

QUICK ID: Look for tall, prickly stems, deeply lobed leaves with prickly surfaces and veins, large crinkly flowers with yellow stamens, and densely prickly seed capsules.

RANGE: SR; widespread, common

STEM: Erect, 1–2 feet tall (30–60 cm), densely prickly

FLOWERS: April–September. Flower buds egg-shaped, ⅝–¾ inch long (16–20 mm), densely prickly, tipped with ¼-inch-long (4–7 mm) horns, end horn flattened. Flowers 2¾–4 inches across (7–10 cm) with 6 delicate, white petals; many yellow stamens. Seed capsule egg-shaped, surface obscured with dense prickles.

LEAVES: Alternate. Blades deeply lobed and toothed, veins prickly (especially on bottom side), surfaces sparsely to densely prickly between veins; upper leaves not clasping.

HABITAT: Prairies, roadsides, disturbed areas; grasslands, sagebrush, pinyon-juniper foothills. Elevation 4,900–7,500 feet (1,494–2,286 m).

Crested Prickly Poppy

Argemone polyanthemos (A. albiflora), Poppy Family, Papaveraceae; Annual, biennial herb

QUICK ID: Look for spine-tipped leaves with prickly veins, flowers with white crinkly petals, bright-yellow stamens, and orange latex sap.

RANGE: SR; widespread, common

STEM: Erect, 2–4 feet tall (60–120 cm) with scattered prickles.

FLOWERS: March–August. Flower buds egg-shaped with widely spaced prickles and tipped with ⅜-inch-long (9 mm), round, tapering horns; flowers have 6 delicate, white (occasionally lavender) petals; seed capsule egg-shaped with widely spaced prickles.

LEAVES: Alternate, upper leaves clasp stem. Blades to 8 inches long (20 cm), deeply lobed ⅔ to the white midrib; top smooth, bottom main veins prickly.

HABITAT: Grassy plains, disturbed areas; grasslands, sagebrush, pinyon-juniper foothills. Elevation 1,000–7,500 feet (304–2,286 m).

SIMILAR SPECIES: Rough Prickly Poppy, *A. hispida,* (SR foothills) has densely prickly stems, leaf surfaces, buds, and capsules.

Longhorn Steer's Head

Dicentra uniflora, Poppy Family, Papaveraceae; Perennial herb

QUICK ID: Look for a single basal leaf and a delicate flower stalk with a single white-to-pink flower shaped like a tiny steer head.

RANGE: NR, MR, Canada; scattered, infrequent

STEM: Erect, slender, leafless, 1½–4 inches tall (4–10 cm).

FLOWERS: April–July. Solitary flower on stalk, slightly longer than leaf; flower erect to nodding with 2 outer petals flat, bent back to form steer's horns, 2 inner petals point forward arrowhead-like, ½ inch long (12 mm), to form steer's head.

LEAVES: Single basal leaf 1½–2¾ inches long (4–7 cm) including stalk; blade divided into 3-4 leaflets with divided lobes.

HABITAT: Gravelly soil, meadows, typically near snowmelt; montane, subalpine forests. Elevation 5,000–10,000 feet (1,524–3,048 m).

White Penstemon

Penstemon albidus, Plantain Family, Plantaginaceae; Perennial herbaceous

QUICK ID: Look for clustered stems with opposite leaves, white flowers with black anthers, and beardtongue tipped with yellow hairs.

RANGE: NR, MR, SR, Canada; widespread, common

STEM: Erect, 1–5 from base, 6–20 inches tall (15–19 cm), upper stem glandular-hairy.

FLOWERS: May–August. Cylindrical clusters have 4–24 whorls of slightly inflated, tubular flowers ¾ inch long (20 mm) with 2 lips: lower lip 3 lobed, upper lip 2 lobed; red guidelines in throat; glandular-hairy throughout.

LEAVES: Basal, short stalked; blades lance-shaped to oblong, ¾–3 inches long (2–8 cm); edges smooth to irregular toothed, surfaces smooth to short-hairy. Stem leaves, similar, opposite, 2–5 pairs.

HABITAT: Dry prairies, hillsides; grasslands, sagebrush, foothills. Elevation 1,000–7,700 feet (304–2,350 m).

Hotrock Penstemon

Penstemon deustus var. *deustus*, Plantain Family, Plantaginaceae; Perennial herb

QUICK ID: Look for clumps of stems with sharp-toothed leaves, and elongated clusters of tubular flowers with white lobes and red stripes.

RANGE: NR, MR; widespread, common

STEM: Erect, much-branched from base, 8–24 inches tall (20–60 cm), hairless to short-hairy

FLOWERS: May–July. Cylindrical clusters have flowers ½–¾ inch long (11–18 mm) with 5 spreading petal-like lobes, white to yellowish-brown or pinkish-lavender tinted; flora tube glandular-hairy externally and internally; throat red striped, slightly 2-ridged; beardtongue tip smooth to sparsely yellow- or white-hairy.

LEAVES: Opposite, 5-9 pairs; blades egg-shaped, ⅜–2 inches long (10–50 mm) to ¾ inch wide (20 mm); edges sharply serrate, surfaces smooth to short-hairy.

HABITAT: Rocky outcrops, dry open areas; sagebrush, grasslands, foothills, montane forests. Elevation 1,312–8,530 feet (400–2,600 m).

Woolly Plantain

Plantago patagonica, Plantain Family, Plantaginaceae; Annual herb

QUICK ID: Look for basal rosettes of densely hairy, narrow leaves, and woolly-hairy spikes of tiny flowers with 4 whitish-tan petals.

RANGE: NR, MR, SR, Canada; widespread, common

STEM: Flower stalk erect, 2–8 inches tall (5–20 cm), white-woolly.

FLOWERS: February–July. Flowers have 4 petal lobes, spreading, oval, 1⁄16–⅛ inch long (1–3 mm), often nearly transparent, separated by narrow, leaf-like bracts.

LEAVES: Basal rosette. Blades linear, narrow, to 6 inches long (15 cm), ⅜ inch wide (10 mm); margins entire, surfaces densely hairy.

HABITAT: Dry coarse soils, disturbed areas; arid grasslands, sagebrush, foothills. Elevation 3,000–8,200 feet (915–2,438 m).

SIMILAR SPECIES: Introduced Narrowleaf Plantain, *P. lanceolata*, has linear-elliptic, 5-veined leaves that reach 10 inches long (25 cm) with few to no surface hairs. Introduced Common Plantain, *P. major*, has broad, oval, pointed basal leaves.

Ballhead Gilia

Ipomopsis congesta, Phlox Family, Polemoniaceae; Perennial herb

QUICK ID: Look for sprawling to erect, rounded clumps of woody stems tipped with dense spherical heads of small white flowers.

RANGE: NR, MR, SR; widespread, common; Has 8 subspecies across West with variable features.

STEM: Woody base, branching, 4–24 inches tall (10–60 cm) with short, white, curly or woolly hairs, depending on subspecies.

FLOWERS: May–September. Flower tubular, ⅛–¼ inch long (3–5 mm), spreading open to 5 rounded to pointed, petal-like lobes, sometimes with pink splotches; stamens protruding.

LEAVES: Basal rosette; blades ⅜–2⅜ inches long (1–6 cm); edges entire or divided palmately to pinnately into narrow, pointed lobes; surfaces smooth to short-woolly. Stem leaves alternate, smaller.

HABITAT: Rocky, sandy soils; arid scrublands, sagebrush, foothills. montane forests. Elevation 4,000–8,500 feet (1,220–2,590 m).

SIMILAR SPECIES: Spiked Ipomopsis, *I. spicata*, (all regions) has a single stem and narrow linear leaves, with or without lobes.

Spiked Ipomopsis

Ipomopsis spicata, Phlox Family, Polemoniaceae; Perennial herb

QUICK ID: Look for single, woolly stems with narrow, linear leaves, and spherical to elongated clusters of small white flowers.

RANGE: NR, MR, SR; widespread, common; 5 subspecies across West with variable features

STEM: Erect, branched or not, 2–12 inches tall (5–30 cm), woolly hairy, sticky resin glands.

FLOWERS: June–August. Terminal clusters, often nodding, packed with small, tubular flowers ¼–⅜ inch long (5–9 mm); 5 petal lobes, spreading, pointed, white to creamy; stamens inside throat.

LEAVES: Basal rosette usually dense; blades narrow, linear, ⅜–2 inches long (1–5 cm); 3-lobed to entire, depending on subspecies. Stem leaves alternate, smaller.

HABITAT: Dry open areas; sagebrush, foothills, montane, subalpine forests. Elevation 4,500–12,000 feet (1,372–3,658 m).

SIMILAR SPECIES: Ballhead Gilia, *I. congesta*, (all regions) has multiple, erect-to-sprawling stems and spherical flower clusters.

Nuttall's Linanthus

Leptosiphon nuttallii, Phlox Family, Polemoniaceae; Perennial herb

QUICK ID: Look for dense, leafy clumps with narrow, linear, whorled leaves, and rounded clusters of white, tubular flowers with 5 petals.

RANGE: NR, MR, SR; widespread, common

STEM: Erect, branching from base, 4–12 inches tall (10–30 cm).

FLOWERS: May–September. Rounded clusters with 2-5 tubular flowers, each ⅜–⅝ inch long (9–15 mm); 5 white, oval petals open ½ inch wide (12 mm); stamens and style extend slightly beyond the yellow throat; tapering sepals enclose most of the floral tube.

LEAVES: Opposite, whorl-like at stem nodes. Blade cut into 5-9 thread-like, linear to lance-shaped, lobes ⅜–¾ inch long (10–20 mm); tips spiny, surfaces with short hairs.

HABITAT: Dry coarse soils, meadows, open woodlands; foothills, montane, subalpine forests. Elevation 5,700–10,000 feet (1,757-3,048 m).

Desert Mountain Phlox

Phlox austromontana, Phlox Family, Polemoniaceae; Perennial herb

QUICK ID: Look in arid habitats for loose to dense mats of stiff, prickly leaves covered with showy flowers with 5 white-to-pink petals.

RANGE: NR, MR; widespread, common

STEM: Mat forming, 2–4 inches tall (5–10 cm), obscured by leaves.

FLOWERS: May–June. Flowers ½–¾ inch across (1-2 cm) with a floral tube ¼–¾ inch long (8–18 mm); 5 spreading petal-like lobes white to pink, stamens inside tube; vase-like calyx beneath the flower is hairy to hairless.

LEAVES: Opposite, crowded, gray green, firm. Blades narrow, linear to ⅝ inch long (8–15 mm), smooth to sparsely hairy but not woolly or cobwebby; tips sharply pointed.

HABITAT: Rocky, sandy soils; arid grasslands, sagebrush, pinyon-juniper foothills. Elevation 4,300–8,000 feet (1,310–2,438 m).

SIMILAR SPECIES: Carpet Phlox, *P. hoodii* ssp. *canescens*, (widespread) has cobwebby leaves.

Dwarf Phlox

Phlox condensata, Phlox Family, Polemoniaceae; Perennial herb

QUICK ID: Look at high elevations for tight mounds with stiff, bristle-tipped leaves, and small white flowers with 5 oval lobes. Leaves obscure the stem; flowers can cover the leaves.

RANGE: SR; widespread, common

STEM: Mat forming, ⅜–2 inches tall/long (1–5 cm).

FLOWERS: June–August. Solitary tubular flowers have white-to-pale pink, oblong petal-lobes; floral tube ¼–⅜ inch long (6–10 mm), anthers yellow; sepals (calyx) cupping petals glandular-hairy, much shorter than floral tube.

LEAVES: Opposite, crowded, erect or against the stem (not spreading). Blades rigid, linear to oblong, ¼–⅜ inch long (6–10 mm); surfaces smooth to glandular-hairy, edges lined with stiff hairs.

HABITAT: Coarse soils, scree, tundra; subalpine forests, alpine. Elevation 9,000–13,000 feet (2,700–3,960 m).

SIMILAR SPECIES: Cushion Phlox, *P. pulvinata*, (widespread) forms looser mats with tangled stems and spreading leaves.

Spiny Phlox

Phlox hoodii, Phlox Family, Polemoniaceae; Perennial herb

QUICK ID: Look for dense mats with short, narrow, bristle-tipped leaves, and tubular flowers with spreading white-to-pink petals.

RANGE: NR, MR, SR, Canada; widespread, common with 6 subspecies with varying features.

STEM: Prostrate to ascending, ⅜–2⅜ inches tall/long (1–6 cm).

FLOWERS: April–July. Solitary tubular flowers ¼–½ inch long (6–12 mm) with 5 spreading petal lobes, white to pink; sepals (calyx) cobwebby-hairy. Dense flowering can conceal leaves.

LEAVES: Opposite, crowded; blade stiff, linear, ¼–⅜ inch long (6–10 mm) by 1 mm wide; base and edges with tangled hairs; surfaces generally hairy, tip sharp-pointed.

HABITAT: Open woods, plains, disturbed sites; arid grasslands, sagebrush, foothills montane. Elevation 4,920–8,858 feet (1,500–2,700 m).

SIMILAR SPECIES: Hard to separate in the field from Desert Mountain Phlox, *P. austromontana*. Moss Phlox, *P. hoodii* ssp. *muscoides*, has congested, overlapping, woolly-hairy leaves.

Longleaf Phlox

Phlox longifolia, Phlox Family, Polemoniaceae; Perennial herb

QUICK ID: Look for loose clumps of erect slender stems, widely spaced narrow leaves, and clusters of 2–3 white-to-pink flowers with 5 oval petals; herbage hairless to short-hairy or glandular-hairy.

RANGE: NR, MR, SR, Canada; widespread, common; highly variable across range

STEM: Erect, 3–10 from base, unbranched, 4–12 inches tall (10–30 cm), hairless below, short-hairy to glandular upward.

FLOWERS: April–June. Clusters of 2–3 on branch tips; floral tube ⅜–¾ inch long (10–18 mm), spreading open 1 inch wide (25 mm) with 5 oblong petal lobes, both white to deep pink common. Sepals (calyx) much longer than floral tube.

LEAVES: Opposite, widely spaced on stem; blades narrow, linear, ½–4 inches long (1–10 cm) to ¼ inch wide (6 mm); edges entire, surfaces hairless to short-hairy or glandular-hairy.

HABITAT: Coarse soils, open sites; grasslands, sagebrush, foothills, montane, subalpine forests. Elevation 3,200–8,000 feet (980–2,438 m).

Rocky Mountain Phlox

Phlox multiflora, Phlox Family, Polemoniaceae; Perennial herb

QUICK ID: Look for loose mats; stems with hairless, closely-spaced leaves; and clusters on stem tips with 1–3 flowers with 5 white petals.

RANGE: NR, MR, SR; widespread, common

STEM: Mats to mounds, branched from base, 2–6 inches tall/long (5–15 cm), hairless.

FLOWERS: May–August. Clusters of 1–3 at stem ends; tubular flowers ⅜–⅝ inch long (1–2 cm), spreading open with 5 petal lobes, white to occasionally pinkish; sepals (calyx) cupping the petals generally hairless and slightly shorter than floral tube.

LEAVES: Opposite; blades linear, thin, ⅜–1 inch long (1–3 cm), edges slightly hairy, surfaces hairless; leaves closely spaced on stem.

HABITAT: Coarse soils, open woods; arid grasslands, sagebrush, to above timberline. Elevation 7,000–10,700 feet (2,133–3,261 m).

Cushion Phlox

Phlox pulvinata, Phlox Family, Polemoniaceae; Perennial herb

QUICK ID: Look near timberline soon after snowmelt for dense mats of woody stems with short, thin leaves often obscured by small flowers with 5 white petals.

RANGE: NR, MR, SR; widespread, common

STEM: Mat or cushion forming, ¾–4 inches tall/long (2–10 cm), glandular-hairy.

FLOWERS: July–August. Solitary on stem end; tubular flowers ⅜–½ inch long (9–13 mm) with 5 spreading white-to-bluish petal lobes; sepals (calyx) cupping flowers glandular-hairy, less than half the length of floral tube.

LEAVES: Opposite, crowded; blades narrow, linear, 3⁄16–½ inch long (5–12 mm); edges short-hairy, top spiny, surfaces smooth, hairy, or glandular.

HABITAT: Fellfields, dry meadows; subalpine forests, alpine. Elevation 9,000 and 13,000 feet (2,472–2,962 m).

American Bistort

Bistorta bistortoides, Buckwheat Family, Polygonaceae; Perennial herb

QUICK ID: Look for short, slender stems topped with dense, cylindrical spikes of small white-to-pale-pink flowers.

RANGE: NR, MR, SR, Canada; widespread, common

STEM: Erect, often reddish, 7–16 inches tall (18–40 cm), colony forming.

FLOWERS: July–September. Erect flower stems have densely packed spikes ¾–1 ½ inches long (2–4 cm); petals (tepals) 3⁄16 inch long (5 mm), white stamens protrude beyond the flower.

LEAVES: Mostly basal with stalks 1–2¾ inches long (3–7 cm); blades elliptic to lance-shaped, 2–10 inches long (5–25 cm), surfaces hairless, margins entire, tip usually pointed. Stem leaves few, alternate, much smaller.

HABITAT: Moist soils; montane, subalpine forests, alpine meadows. Elevation 7,000–12,500 feet (2,130–3,660 m).

SIMILAR SPECIES: Alpine Bistort, *B. vivipara*, has spikes of sterile flowers above rows of bulblets that fall off and sprout.

Annual Buckwheat

Eriogonum annuum, Buckwheat Family, Polygonaceae; Annual herb

QUICK ID: Look for tall, thin, densely hairy stems with spreading branches tipped with rounded clusters of tiny white-and-red flowers.

RANGE: MR, SR; widespread, common

STEM: Erect, slender, 1–3 feet tall (30–90 cm), woolly hairy.

FLOWERS: April–November. Dense, hairy clusters have flowers ⅛ inch (3 mm) wide with two rows of white-to-pink-tinted sepals.

LEAVES: Basal rosette usually withers by blooming. Stem leaves alternate, dense on lower stem, fewer upward; blades oblong to club-shaped, ⅜–1¾ inches long (10–45 mm) by ⅛–⅝ inch wide (3–15 mm), with one prominent vein; edges entire or with a few rounded teeth, small leaf clusters often grow in the leaf axils. White, woolly, tangled tufts of hairs cover the stems and both leaf surfaces.

HABITAT: Grasslands, sagebrush, pinyon-juniper foothills, montane forests. Elevation 3,800–7,200 feet (1,160–2,195 m).

SIMILAR SPECIES: Compare to Redroot Buckwheat, *E. racemosum*, (SR).

Parsnip-flower Buckwheat

Eriogonum heracleoides var. *heracleoides*, Buckwheat Family, Polygonaceae; Perennial herb

QUICK ID: Look for woolly-hairy stems with a whorl of leaf-like bracts at mid-stem and clusters of small, creamy flowers on the branch tips.

RANGE: NR, MR; widespread, common

STEM: Erect, unbranched, 4–16 inches tall (10–40 cm), white-woolly.

FLOWERS: May–August. A long, single flower stalk rises from a whorl of leaf-like bracts to a smaller whorl beneath an umbrella-like cluster of flowers; each flower ¼ inch long (6 mm), creamy to white, sometimes pinkish, hairless; a short stalk-like stipe at base of each flower is ⅛ inch long (3 mm).

LEAVES: Basal in loose mat, stalks (petioles) longer than blade; blades linear to lance-shaped, 1–2 inches long (3–5 cm), bottom surface densely gray-woolly, top mostly hairless; edges entire, flat.

HABITAT: Coarse soils; grasslands, sagebrush, foothills, montane, subalpine forests. Elevation 1,968–10,170 feet (600–3,100 m).

James Buckwheat

Eriogonum jamesii, Buckwheat Family, Polygonaceae; Perennial subshrub

QUICK ID: Look for mats of hairy basal leaves; compact clumps of erect, densely hairy flower stems; and whorls of leaf-like bracts below rounded clusters of small white flowers.

RANGE: MR, SR; widespread, common

STEM: Erect, 4–10 inches tall (10–25 cm) by 6 inches (15 cm) wide.

FLOWERS: June–October. A long stem leads to a cluster of hairy, leaf-like bracts; several flower stalks rise from the whorl to another whorl of leaf-like bracts below each umbrella-like cluster of flowers; flowers creamy white, ⅜ inch wide (10 mm).

LEAVES: Basal; blades narrowly elliptic, ⅜–1 inch long (10–25 mm) by ⅛–⅜ inch wide (3–10 mm), densely hairy on the bottom, moderately on top.

HABITAT: Grasslands, sagebrush, pinyon-juniper foothills, montane forests. Elevation 4,800–7,500 feet (1,463–2,286 m).

SIMILAR SPECIES: Redroot Buckwheat, *E. racemosum*, (SR) has woolly, leafless stems and spike-like clusters of white flowers.

Simpson's Buckwheat

Eriogonum microthecum var. *simpsonii*, Buckwheat Family, Polygonaceae; Perennial subshrub

QUICK ID: Look for scraggly, woody subshrubs with reddish branches, often flat-topped, clusters of small white-to-pink flowers.

RANGE: MR, SR; widespread, common

STEM: Spreading, 8–60 inches tall/wide (20–150 cm), hairy.

FLOWERS: June–October. Spreading, usually flat-topped clusters of white, pink, rose, or yellow flowers, each ⅛ inch long (3 mm); stamens longer than petals; flowers and stems thinly to densely hairy.

LEAVES: Alternate or (usually) in bundles on stem. Blade narrowly elliptic to linear, to ⅝ inch long (15 mm) by 1⅛ inch wide (3 mm), margins entire, rolled under; bottom surface densely gray-woolly, top slightly white-hairy.

HABITAT: Grasslands, sagebrush, pinyon-juniper, montane forests. Elevation 4,600–8,700 feet (1,400–2,650 m).

SIMILAR SPECIES: Slender Buckwheat, *E. microthecum* var. *laxiflorum*, (NR, MR, SR) has leaves with flat edges (not rolled under).

Redroot Buckwheat

Eriogonum racemosum, Buckwheat Family, Polygonaceae; Perennial herb

QUICK ID: Look for woolly, leafless stems with upper half branching 2-3 times, and erect spikes with whorls of small white flowers.

RANGE: MR, SR; widespread, common

STEM: Erect, 1-3 feet tall (30-91 cm), hairy.

FLOWERS: June-October. A series of dense whorled clusters blooms along densely hairy upper stems; flowers white to pinkish, ⅛ inch wide (3 mm), 6 petal-like sepals have red-to-green midstripes; stamens with red anthers extend beyond the flower.

LEAVES: Basal in a crowded rosette. Leaves spoon-shaped on slender stalks 1-4 inches long (3-10 cm); blades elliptic to oval or round, ¾-2⅜ inches long (2-6 cm) by ⅜-1½ inches wide (1-4 cm); margin entire, surfaces woolly.

HABITAT: Grasslands, sagebrush, pinyon-juniper foothills, montane conifer forests. Elevation 6,500-10,500 feet (1,980-3,200 m).

Subalpine Sulphur Flower

Eriogonum umbellatum var. *majus*, Buckwheat Family, Polygonaceae; Perennial herb

QUICK ID: Look for basal leaves with woolly bottoms and green tops, and hairy, leafless stems topped with rounded clusters of white flowers.

RANGE: NR, MR, SR, Canada; widespread, common

STEM: Erect, 6-12 inches tall (15-30 cm), with loose hairs.

FLOWERS: June-September. Rounded, clusters have 3-9 umbrella-like stalks joined at a whorl of small bracts on the tip of the flower stem; flowers ¼ inch long (4 mm), creamy white, hairless. A whorl of mid-stem, leaf-like bracts not present.

LEAVES: Basal in loose mat. Blade elliptic to oblong, tip pointed, ¼-¾ inch long (5-20 mm); edges entire, flat; bottom surface densely woolly-hairy, top hairless, bright green.

HABITAT: Grasslands, sagebrush, foothills, montane, subalpine conifer forests, alpine. Elevation 3,940-9,190 feet (1,200-2,800 m).

Nodding Smartweed

Persicaria lapathifolia (Polygonum lapathifolium), Buckwheat Family, Polygonaceae; Annual herb

QUICK ID: Look in moist soils for tall stems with large leaves and dense, long, nodding spikes of small white-to-pinkish flowers.

RANGE: NR, MR, SR, Canada (introduced); widespread, common

STEM: Erect, branching, 2–4 feet tall (60–120 cm), colony forming.

FLOWERS: April–October. Branches erect to arching with erect to nodding, densely packed cylindrical clusters of tiny white-to-pinkish flowers ⅛ inch long (3 mm) with 4 petal-like tepals that barely open.

LEAVES: Alternate. Blades linear to lance-shaped, 2–8 inches long (5–20 cm) by 3/16–1½ inches wide (5–40 mm), sometimes with a red splotch, prominent mid-vein on upper side; margins entire, tip tapered; a sheath-like covering with a smooth upper edge (no bristles) wraps around the stem at the base of each leaf.

HABITAT: Moist soils, ditches, floodplains, marshes, shorelines, disturbed areas. Elevation 2,900–9,400 feet (885–2,865 m).

Sweetflower Rock Jasmine

Androsace chamaejasme, Primrose Family, Primulaceae; Perennial herb

QUICK ID: Look in rocky tundra for small, almost spherical, mat-forming rosettes of small leaves and a single flower stalk with clusters of small, white, fragrant flowers with a yellow throat.

RANGE: NR, MR, SR, Canada; widespread, common to infrequent

STEM: Erect, unbranched, leafless, ¾–4 inches tall (2–10 cm), sparsely to densely hairy with soft, shaggy hairs; stoloniferous.

FLOWERS: June–August. Clusters have 3–5 funnel-shaped flowers to ⅜ inch wide (5 mm) with 5 wide-spreading, rounded lobes; white aging pinkish.

LEAVES: Basal stacks of whorled rosettes forming spherical clumps; blades oblong, ⅛–⅝ inch long (3–15 mm); edges ciliate, surfaces smooth to sparsely shaggy-hairy.

HABITAT: Rocky ridges, open tundra; subalpine forests, alpine. Elevation 8,500–11,700 feet (2,590–3,566 m).

Rock Jasmine

Androsace septentrionalis, Primrose Family, Primulaceae; Annual herb

QUICK ID: Look for slender stems with erect, candelabra-like clusters of small white-to-pinkish flowers, and narrow, lance-shaped bracts at the base of the cluster.

RANGE: NR, MR, SR, Canada; widespread, common

STEM: Erect, upper branching, ¾–8 inches long (2–20 cm). Depending on elevation and habitat, plants vary from small and inconspicuous to robust and showy.

FLOWERS: April–September. Multiple stalks have umbrella-like clusters with 3–25 flowers with 5 petals, each ⅛ inch wide (3 mm), tip rounded; throat yellowish; bracts under each cluster narrow, pointed.

LEAVES: Basal rosette. Blades lance-shaped, 2–8 inches long (5–20 cm); surfaces hairy or not; margins entire or with small teeth.

HABITAT: Open woods, meadows; foothills, montane, subalpine forests, alpine tundra. Elevation 5,000–12,000 feet (1,524–3,658 m).

SIMILAR SPECIES: Western Rock Jasmine, *A. occidentalis*, below 6,000 feet, has broad, oval, leaf-like bracts beneath each cluster.

Baneberry

Actaea rubra, Buttercup Family, Ranunculaceae; Perennial herb

QUICK ID: Look for clumps of bushy stems with large, compound leaves, cylindrical clusters of white flowers, and red or white berries.

RANGE: NR, MR, SR, Canada; widespread, common

STEM: Upright, branching, leafy, 1–3 feet tall (30–100 cm), smooth.

FLOWERS: April–July. Erect, dense, bottlebrush clusters have ½-inch-wide (12 mm) flowers on stalks ½ inch long (12 mm), 5–10 spoon-shaped petals, many showy stamens. Fruit a cluster of small, rounded, shiny berries toxic to humans, loved by birds.

LEAVES: Alternate, long-stalked, pinnately divided 1–3 times, 1½ feet long (45 cm); leaflets lance-shaped, 1–4 inches long (3–10 cm), deeply lobed, coarsely toothed, sparsely hairy.

HABITAT: Shady woods, moist meadows; foothills, montane, subalpine forests. Elevation sea level to 11,000 feet (3,350 m).

Canada Anemone

Anemone canadensis, Buttercup Family, Ranunculaceae; Perennial herb

QUICK ID: Look for stems with deeply divided basal leaves, a whorl of similar leaf-like bracts midway up, and topped with a single, showy, white flower; can form dense colonies in moist soils.

RANGE: SR, Canada; widespread, common

STEM: Erect, hairy, 8–32 inches tall (20–80 cm).

FLOWERS: May–August. 5 petal-like sepals, oval, each 1–1½ inches wide (3–4 cm); 80–100 showy stamens with yellow anthers. Seeds develop spiky wings (not feathery plumes) embedded in a rounded head.

LEAVES: Basal; 1–5 blades, silky-hairy, toothed, with 4–8-inch-long (20–40 cm) stalks, palmately divided into 3 primary lobes, each lobe divided into 2–3 secondary lobes. Stem blades similar, smaller, opposite. The flowering stem produces 1–2 whorls of leaf-like bracts, similar to the basal leaves, that radiate around the stem.

HABITAT: Moist soils of meadows, marshes, springs, stream sides, ditches. Elevation 6,500–8,750 feet (1,980–2,670 m).

Candle Anemone, Thimbleweed

Anemone cylindrica, Buttercup Family, Ranunculaceae; Perennial herb

QUICK ID: Look for leaf-like bracts whorled at mid-stem and showy white flowers with a central thimble-like stamen cone; forms colonies in wet areas.

RANGE: NR, MR, SR, Canada; scattered locations, locally common

STEM: Erect, silky-hairy stems 1–3 feet tall (30–90 cm).

FLOWERS: May–July. Multiple flower stems (peduncles) 4–12 inches long (10–30 cm) branch from mid-stem, leaf-like bracts. Flowers ¾ inch wide (2 cm); 5 petal-like sepals have silky-hairy bottoms. As seeds mature, the stamen cone elongates up to ¾–1¾ inches long (2–5 cm), cottony-tufted seed head.

LEAVES: Basal, 5–10 blades on long stalks, shiny green, to 4 inches wide (10 cm), palmate with 3 lance-shaped, deeply cut lobes.

HABITAT: Moist to dry soils of meadows, prairies, open woods, stream sides, roadside ditches. Elevation 5,500–7,700 feet (1,676–2,350 m).

White Marsh Marigold

Caltha leptosepala, Buttercup Family, Ranunculaceae; Perennial herb

QUICK ID: Look in wet mountain meadows and seeps for flowers with many white, petal-like sepals around a mass of yellow stamens.

RANGE: NR, MR, SR, Canada; widespread, common

STEM: Erect, leafless with single flower, 6-12 inches tall (15-30 cm).

FLOWERS: May–September. Usually 1–2 stalks (scapes); flowers ⅝–1½ inches diameter (15–40 mm) with numerous white petal-like sepals with bluish-green undersides, stamens yellow. Bloom often follows the receding snow line.

LEAVES: Basal, erect from base with long stalks. Blades succulent, oval to oblong, to 4¾ inches long/wide (12 cm); margins entire to toothed.

HABITAT: Wet areas; open subalpine forests, meadows. Elevation 9,000–12,795 feet (2,743-3,900 m).

Western Virgin's Bower

Clematis ligusticifolia, Buttercup Family, Ranunculaceae; Perennial vine

QUICK ID: Look for tangled, climbing vines with showy clusters of small white flowers followed by seedheads with silky plumes.

RANGE: NR, MR, SR, Canada; widespread, common

STEM: Mounding, twining stems, typically to 20 feet long (6 m).

FLOWERS: April–September. Dense clusters of 7–20 flowers with 4 white, radiating, petal-like sepals, ¼–⅜ inch long (6–10 mm), slightly hairy; numerous showy stamens; seedhead like a dense feather duster of silky plumes.

LEAVES: Opposite. Blade compound with 4 (or more) oval-to-lance-shaped leaflets, 1⅜–3⅛ inches long (4–8 cm), lobed and/or with teeth, surfaces with few scattered hairs.

HABITAT: Dry to moist soils, meadows, slopes, roadsides; sagebrush, pinyon-juniper foothills, montane forests. Elevation 3,900–8,500 feet (1,188–2,590 m).

White Globeflower

Trollius albiflorus, Buttercup Family, Ranunculaceae; Perennial herb

QUICK ID: Look in high altitude, wet sites for dense clusters of palmately-lobed basal leaves, flowers with 5 showy, white sepals.

RANGE: NR, MR, SR (absent NM), Canada; widespread, common

STEM: Erect, 4–20 inches tall (10–50 cm), smooth throughout.

FLOWERS: May–August. Stem tip has solitary flower, 1–2 inches wide (3–5 cm) with 5–9 showy, petal-like, white sepals; petals 15–25, small, yellow, hidden under the cluster of longer stamens.

LEAVES: Basal, long stalked; blades deeply cut palmately into 5–7 oval segments with 3 coarsely toothed lobes. Stem leaves 1–3, similar, smaller, alternate with broad, clasping sheaths.

HABITAT: Wet meadows, open areas, wetlands; montane, subalpine forests, alpine. Elevation 3,950–12,500 feet (1,200–3,800 m).

Fendler's Ceanothus

Ceanothus fendleri, Buckhorn Family, Rhamnaceae; Evergreen shrub

QUICK ID: Look for rounded shrubs with clusters of white flowers, thorn-tipped branches, and small leaves with 3 obvious veins.

RANGE: SR; widespread, common

STEM: Woody, low, spreading to erect, 3–6½ feet tall (1–2 m).

FLOWERS: April–October. Numerous rounded clusters have 3–10 white flowers with 5 small, spoon-shaped petals. Fruit berry-like, red; dry brown capsules explode to expel the seeds.

LEAVES: Alternate, evergreen. Blades oval, ⅜–1 inch long (9–25 mm), with 3 prominent veins from leaf base; margins entire, surfaces dark green above, light green to whitish below, hairy or not, tips rounded to pointed.

HABITAT: Riparian areas, open forests; foothills, montane forests. Elevation 4,000–10,000 feet (1,220–3,048 m).

Snowbrush Ceanothus

Ceanothus velutinus, Buckhorn Family, Rhamnaceae; Evergreen shrub

QUICK ID: Look for dense, rounded, thornless shrubs with fragrant, evergreen leaves and showy, pyramidal clusters of white flowers.

RANGE: NR, MR, SR (absent NM), Canada; widespread, locally common

STEM: Spreading, 3–10 feet tall and wide (1–3 m), thicket forming. Also called Varnish-leaf Ceanothus, it is attractive in xeriscaping and pollinator gardens.

FLOWERS: May–September. Dense clusters 2–5 inches long (5–12 cm) have creamy flowers with 5 small petals. When dry, the 3-parted capsules explode to expel the seeds.

LEAVES: Alternate with stalks ⅜–¾ inch long (1–2 cm). Blades oval to elliptic, 2–4 inches long (5–10 cm); upper surface varnish-like shiny, lower grayish-hairy, 3-veined, edges finely toothed.

HABITAT: Shrublands, pinyon-juniper foothills, montane forests. Elevation 3,500–10,000 feet (1,066–3,050 m).

Western Serviceberry

Amelanchier alnifolia, Rose Family, Rosaceae; Deciduous shrub

QUICK ID: Look for a bush to small tree with strongly veined alternate leaves, short clusters of white flowers, and blackish berries.

RANGE: NR, SR, MR, Canada; widespread, common

STEM: Upright, branching, 3–16 feet tall (1–5 m).

FLOWERS: May–July. Short clusters erect to drooping, on branch tips with 5–15 flowers; 5 narrow petals, ¼–1 inch long (7–25 mm), white to pinkish. Fruit a fleshy pome ¼–⅜ inch diameter (7–10 mm), red becoming dark purple.

LEAVES: Alternate, stalked; blades oval to oblong, ¾–2 inches long (2–5 cm); edges upper half serrated, surfaces veined, surfaces hairy when young, usually hairless by flowering, tip rounded.

HABITAT: Riparian, meadows, open woods; sagebrush to subalpine forests. Elevation 6,000–11,000 feet (1,828–3,350 m).

SIMILAR SPECIES: Utah Serviceberry, *A. utahensis,* (MR, SR) has clusters with 3–6 flowers and hairy leaves when flowering.

Alderleaf Mountain Mahogany

Cercocarpus montanus, Rose Family, Rosaceae; Deciduous shrub

QUICK ID: Look on dry, rocky slopes for slender, leafy shrubs with small oval, veined leaves, and seeds with long, twisted, feathery tails.

RANGE: MR, SR; widespread, common

STEM: Erect, slender to rounded, 3–13 feet tall (1–4 m), bark smooth.

FLOWERS: March–August. Clusters along branches have 1–3 small flowers with a pinkish tube opening to a creamy cup lined with brownish stamens, 1 pistil, no petals. Seeds have a white, feathery, spiraled tail to 3 inches long (8 cm).

LEAVES: Alternate to clustered on spurs, short-stalked; blades ¼–2 inches long (6–50 mm); edges flat, serrated above middle, surfaces strongly veined, hairy.

HABITAT: Hills, ridges, canyons, open woods; sagebrush, foothills, montane, subalpine forests. Elevation 5,000–10,000 feet (1,524–3,048 m).

SIMILAR SPECIES: Curl-leaf Mountain Mahogany, *C. ledifolius*, (NR, MR) has leaves with the edges curled in.

Eight-petal Mountain Avens

Dryas hookeriana, Rose Family, Rosaceae; Perennial subshrub

QUICK ID: Look for mats of evergreen leaves, short stalks with erect white flowers, 8–10 wide-spreading petals, and many yellow stamens.

RANGE: NR, MR, SR (absent NM), Canada; widespread, common

STEM: Woody, rooting, mat forming, 6–35 inches long (15–90 cm).

FLOWERS: June–September. Solitary flowers, ¾–1¼ inch wide (2–6 cm), on erect, hairy stalks, ⅜–2½ inches tall (1–6 cm). Seeds have feathery tails to 1 inch long (25 mm) in dense clusters.

LEAVES: Alternate. Blades oblong to lance-shaped, 2–8 inches long (5–20 cm); edges flat to rolled under, coarsely toothed; top surface hairless, bottom densely woolly-white, tip blunt to pointed.

HABITAT: Open slopes, rocky areas, meadows; subalpine forests, alpine tundra. Elevation 4,920–12,800 feet (1,500–3,900 m).

Cream Cinquefoil

Drymocallis convallaria, Rose Family, Rosaceae; Perennial herb

QUICK ID: Look for densely hairy stems and leaves with clusters of creamy-white, cup-shaped flowers with 5 petals not overlapping.

RANGE: NR, MR, SR, Canada; widespread, infrequent

STEM: Slender, branching, 15–35 inches tall (40–90 cm), hairy.

FLOWERS: May–August. Hairy clusters have 10–40 flowers on upper stem; the 5 pointed, lance-shaped sepals separate the 5 oval, creamy to pale-yellow petals, each ¼–⅜ inch long (5–8 mm); yellow stamens surround a yellow receptacle in the center.

LEAVES: Basal 6–10 inches long (15–25 cm) with 3–4 pairs of side leaflets and a terminal leaflet, all oval with double teeth. Alternate stem leaves similar, with 3 pairs of side leaflets and a terminal one.

HABITAT: Seasonally wet meadows; grasslands, sagebrush, open montane forests. Elevation 1,000–9,000 feet (305–2,743 m).

Wild Strawberry

Fragaria vesca, Rose Family, Rosaceae; Perennial herb

QUICK ID: Look for basal leaves with 3 leaflets lined with teeth, small white flowers with many yellow stamens, and strawberry fruit.

RANGE: NR, MR, SR, Canada; widespread, common

STEM: Basal rosette 2–8 inches high (5–20 cm), spreads by runners.

FLOWERS: May–July. Clusters of up to 15 flowers with 5 white, oval petals, ⅜ inch long (9 mm). Fruit ⅜ inch wide (1 cm).

LEAVES: Basal. Leaves with three bright-green leaflets on 1–7-inch-long (3–18 cm) stalk covered with spreading hairs; leaflets stemless, oval, 1–2⅜ inches long (3–6 cm), veins distinctly prominent, margins coarsely toothed. Note the terminal tooth of the leaflets is usually equal or longer than adjacent teeth.

HABITAT: Moist, shady woods, meadows; foothills, montane, subalpine forests. Elevation 7,000–10,800 feet (2,134–3,292 m).

SIMILAR SPECIES: Virginia Strawberry, *F. virginiana*, have leaflets with the terminal tooth shorter than adjacent teeth.

Mountainspray

Holodiscus discolor, Rose Family, Rosaceae; Deciduous shrub

QUICK ID: Look for bushy shrubs, usually with long arching shoots, tipped with large, dense clusters of small white flowers.

RANGE: NR, MR, SR, Canada; widespread, common. In general, var. *dumosus* (mostly SR) tends to be smaller and favors lower, dryer habitats; var. *discolor* (mostly NR, Canada) is larger and favors higher, moister habitats.

STEM: Erect to arching, 5–18 feet tall (1.5–6 m), older bark peels.

FLOWERS: June–August. Dense, pyramidal clusters, often drooping, 4–10 inches long (10–25 cm). Flowers ¼ inch wide (6 mm), 5 petals, 5 sepals, white to creamy; stamens protruding.

LEAVES: Alternate, on 1-inch long (3 cm) stalks. Blades oval to elliptic, 1–3 inches long (3–8 cm); edges have 4–6 teeth per side, tip rounded, surfaces slightly to densely hairy. Leaf details variable depending on habitat and variety.

HABITAT: Forest edges and openings; foothills, montane, subalpine forests. Elevation sea level (BC) to 10,000 ft (3,048 m).

Partridge Foot

Luetkea pectinata, Rose Family, Rosaceae; Perennial, evergreen subshrub

QUICK ID: Look for extensive mats of long-trailing, leafy stems and erect flower stalks with dense spikes of small, white flowers.

RANGE: NR, Canada; scattered, locally common

STEM: Prostrate, mat forming, woody, rhizomatous.

FLOWERS: Flower stem erect, 2–10 inches tall (5–25 cm) with dense elongated clusters to 3 inches long (8 cm); flowers small, saucer-shaped, 5 petals, each ⅛ inch long (3–4 mm), about 20 stamens.

LEAVES: Basal numerous, crowded; blades fan-shaped, ¼–⅜ inch long (5–10 mm), divided finger-like into narrow lobes. Stem leaves alternate, smaller.

HABITAT: Moist forest openings, meadows, heath, scree, seepages; montane, subalpine forests, alpine. Elevation 3,500–8,200 feet (1,066–2,500 m).

Mountain Ninebark

Physocarpus monogynus, Rose Family, Rosaceae; Deciduous shrub

QUICK ID: Look in rocky forests for small shrubs with shredding bark and stem-tip clusters of white flowers with many long stamens.

RANGE: MR, SR, widespread, common

STEM: Much branched, 3 feet tall (1 m), brown, shredding bark.

FLOWERS: May–September. Rounded clusters have 9-25 flowers, each ⅜ inch diameter (10 mm) with 5 spreading petals; stamens many, longer than petals, anthers white to pink.

LEAVES: Alternate, stalked; blades 3–5 palmately lobed, ¼–1¼ inches long (5–30 mm); edges with rounded teeth, surfaces smooth to sparsely hairy below.

HABITAT: Slopes, canyons, open woods; montane, subalpine forests. Elevation 5,000–10,000 ft (1,524–3,048 m).

SIMILAR SPECIES: Twice as tall, Mallow Ninebark, *P. malvaceus*, replaces *P. monogunus* from the Middle Rockies into Canada.

Western Chokecherry

Prunus virginiana var. *demissa*, Rose Family, Rosaceae; Deciduous shrub

QUICK ID: Look for bushy shrubs with bright-green leaves, elongated clusters dense with small white flowers, and red-to-black berries.

RANGE: NR, MR, SR, Canada; widespread, common

STEM: Shrub to small tree to 25 feet tall (7.5 m), thicket forming.

FLOWERS: April–June. Blooms after leaves emerge. Elongated clusters 1⅝–8 inches long (4–20 cm) have 18–64 flowers, each ⅜–¾ inch wide (1–2 cm) with 5 petals, many stamens. Fruit clusters bright-red-to-black juicy drupes, ¼–½ inch diameter (6–8 mm).

LEAVES: Alternate, stalked; blades elliptic to oval, 1–4 inches long (3–10 cm); edges serrated, top surface bright green, bottom smooth to short-hairy, tip pointed to blunt.

HABITAT: Open woods, slopes, disturbed areas; grasslands, foothills, montane, subalpine forests. Elevation 5,575–9,500 feet (1,700–2,895 m).

SIMILAR SPECIES: American Plum, *P. americana*, (NR, SR) has bundles of 2–5 flowers.

Red Raspberry

Rubus idaeus, Rose Family, Rosaceae; Deciduous subshrub

QUICK ID: Look for slender, prickly stems; pinnate leaves with serrated leaflets; clusters of small white flowers; juicy, red berries.

RANGE: NR, MR, SR, Canada; widespread, common

STEM: Sprawling, vine-like canes with straight prickles, 2-6 feet long (0.6-2 m), thicket forming.

FLOWERS: May–August. Spike-like clusters have 1-4 white flowers with 5 spatula-shaped petals, each ¼ inch long (6 mm); stamens many, white, protruding; flower stalks and sepals have slender prickles and stalked glands. Fruit ½ inch diameter (12 mm), spherical, juicy aggregate of drupelets.

LEAVES: Alternate, stalked. Leaves pinnately compound with 3-7 lance-shaped leaflets, each 1 ⅝-4 inches long (4-10 cm); edges serrated, top surface smooth to sparsely hairy, bottom paler and greyish-woolly to nearly hairless.

HABITAT: Stream banks, rocky slopes, talus; montane, subalpine forests. Elevation 6,000-11,500 feet (1,828-3,505 m).

Thimbleberry

Rubus parviflorus, Rose Family, Rosaceae; Deciduous subshrub

QUICK ID: Look for spreading stems without prickles, dense maple-like leaves, clusters of showy flowers with 5 white petals, red berries.

RANGE: NR, MR, SR, Canada; widespread, common

STEM: Upright, leafy, branched 1½-6 feet tall/wide (0.5-2 m), thicket forming.

FLOWERS: June–August. Cluster of 2-10 white flowers have 5 oblong petals, each ⅜-1 inch long (10-25 mm), and a center with numerous yellow stamens. Fruit an aggregate of juicy, red drupelets, ¾ inch thick (20 mm), thimble shaped with a hollow center.

LEAVES: Alternate, stalked. Blade 4-8 inches long/wide (10-20 cm), palmately 5 lobed; tips pointed, edges coarsely toothed, top surface green, bottom pale, finely to densely hairy; turns yellow in autumn.

HABITAT: Moist soils, shaded woods, stream sides; montane, subalpine forests. Elevation 7,000-10,600 feet (2,134-3,230 m).

Rocky Mountain Ash

Sorbus scopulina, Rose Family, Rosaceae; Deciduous shrub

QUICK ID: Look for multi-stemmed shrubs with pinnate leaves, flat-topped clusters of small white flowers, and bundles of red berries.

RANGE: NR, MR, SR, Canada; widespread, common

STEM: Upright, freely branched, to 15 feet tall (5 m).

FLOWERS: June–July. Flat-topped clusters to 6 inches diameter (15 cm) have 40–400 small flowers, each ½ diameter (12 mm) with 5 petals. Fruit a bright-red pome, ¼–½ inch diameter (7–12 mm).

LEAVES: Alternate, pinnate with 7–15 opposite leaflets, each lance-shaped, 1½–3 inches long (4–8 cm), edges finely toothed, surfaces shiny, smooth to densely hairy, base and tip tapered; turns orange in autumn.

HABITAT: Moist, open woods, slopes; middle-upper montane, subalpine forests. Elevation 6,500–10,000 feet (2,000–3,011 m).

White Spirea

Spiraea betulifolia (Spiraea lucida), Rose Family, Rosaceae; Deciduous shrub

QUICK ID: Look for a low-growing plant with slender stems that may freeze to the ground and dense, flat-topped arrays of small white flowers.

RANGE: NR; widespread, common

STEM: Erect, woody, branched from base, 12–40 inches tall (30–100 cm), smooth, rhizomatous.

FLOWERS: May–August. Flat-topped clusters 1–6 inches wide (3–15 cm) on stem tips have small flowers to ¼ inch wide (6 mm); petals 5, stamens longer than petals.

LEAVES: Alternate, short stalked; blades oval, ¾–2¾ inches long (2–7 cm); edges coarsely toothed toward tip, surfaces smooth, green above, paler below.

HABITAT: Open woods, stream banks, meadows; foothills, montane, subalpine forests. Elevation 2,000–9,500 feet (610–2,895 m).

Cleavers

Galium aparine, Madder Family, Rubiaceae; Annual herb/vine

QUICK ID: Look for vine-like, brittle stems that cling with Velcro-like hooked prickles; narrow, whorled leaves; tiny white flowers.

RANGE: NR, MR, SR, Canada; widespread, common

STEM: Erect to prostrate, 4-sided, flexible, 1-5 feet long (30-150 cm); forms ground cover or climbs through vegetation.

FLOWERS: April-September. Clusters on short stalks from the leaf whorls; 1-3 tiny flowers to ⅛ inch wide (3 mm); 4 white, pointed petals. Bur-like capsules contain 1 nutlet with hooked hairs.

LEAVES: Whorled at widely separated nodes in sets of 6-8. Blades narrow, linear to lance-shaped, ½-1¼ inches long (13-31 mm) by ⅜ inch wide (1 cm), with one prominent central vein; the base tapers to the stem and the tip has a small, sharp point; margins lined with ciliate hairs, top surface bristly with hooked-tipped hairs.

HABITAT: Meadows, woods, disturbed areas; foothills, montane, subalpine forests. Elevation 4,600-10,000 feet (1,400-3,048 m).

Northern Bedstraw

Galium boreale, Madder Family, Rubiaceae; Perennial herb/subshrub

QUICK ID: Look for erect stems clumped from base; sets of 4 whorled leaves; and showy, dense clusters of white flowers with 4 tiny petals.

RANGE: NR, MR, SR, Canada; widespread, common

STEM: Branching, 4-angled, 1-3 feet tall (30-90 cm), hairs not hooked.

FLOWERS: June-September. Flowers to ⅜ inch wide (10 mm) in clusters on branch tips or on stalks from leaf axils. Fruit paired capsules ⅛ inch diameter (2 mm) with short, bristly hairs.

LEAVES: Whorled in 4s. Blades stiff, linear to lance-shaped, reaching 2 inches long (5 cm) by ½ inch wide (12 mm), with 3 distinct veins; margins lined with ciliate hairs, surfaces hairless or bottom with tiny, straight hairs.

HABITAT: Sagebrush, foothills, montane meadows and openings, subalpine forests. Elevation 5,300-11,150 feet (1,615-3,400 m).

SIMILAR SPECIES: Fragrant Bedstraw, *G. triflorum*, (all regions), has clusters of 3 flowers, 6 leaves per whorl, stem hairs not hooked.

Bastard Toadflax

Comandra umbellata, Sandalwood Family, Santalaceae; Perennial herb, hemiparasitic

QUICK ID: Look for leafy stems with rounded clusters of creamy, star-shaped flowers, and thick leaves; often forms dense colonies.

RANGE: NR, MR, SR, Canada; widespread, infrequent

STEM: Erect, 1 foot tall (30 cm), spreads by rhizomes.

FLOWERS: April–July. Rounded clusters with 3–6 white-to-greenish-white or pinkish flowers, above a leaf-like bract; 5 spreading, pointed petal lobes ⅛–¼ inch across (3–7 mm), 5 brown anthers.

LEAVES: Alternate, thick, whitish, gray green. Blade narrow, linear to lance-shaped to oblong, ¼–1½ inches long (5–30 mm), to ⅜ inch wide (10 mm); margins entire, tip acute. Though the green leaves photosynthesize, the roots parasitize over 200 plant species, making it the most widespread parasitic plant in North America.

HABITAT: Dry soils, open woodlands, meadows, disturbed areas; sea level to subalpine. Elevation 2,100–8,500 feet (640–2,590 m).

Rocky Mountain Alumroot

Heuchera bracteata, Saxifrage Family, Saxifragaceae; Perennial herb

QUICK ID: Look for clumps of rounded leaves with toothed lobes and spikes of small, creamy flowers on one side of the flower stalk.

RANGE: SR (absent NM); locally common

STEM: Erect, slender, to 1 foot tall (30 cm), glandular-hairy.

FLOWERS: May–July. Dense, elongated clusters have 50 or more small, urn-shaped flowers, ³⁄₁₆ inch long (5 mm); 5 erect petals and sepals, surfaces glandular-hairy. Note the stamens protrude outside the flower, anthers yellow.

LEAVES: Mostly basal. Blades broadly oval, ⅝–1⅝ inches long (15–40 mm), with 5–7 shallow, rounded lobes tipped with sharp teeth; surfaces have glandular hairs.

HABITAT: Rocky ledges, outcrops; foothills, montane, subalpine forests, alpine. Elevation 5,580–11,485 feet (1,700–3,500 m).

SIMILAR SPECIES: Front Range Alumroot, *H. hallii*, has stamens inside the flowers.

Roundleaf Alumroot

Heuchera cylindrica, Saxifrage Family, Saxifragaceae; Perennial herb

QUICK ID: Look for clusters of rounded leaves with toothed lobes and tall flower stalks with dense spikes of small, creamy flowers. Most features are highly variable across its range.

RANGE: NR, MR, Canada; widespread, locally common

STEM: Erect, 4–36 inches tall (10–90 cm), smooth to hairy.

FLOWERS: March–September. Dense, elongated clusters 1–5 inches long (3–12 cm). Urn-shaped flowers have 5 sepals ¼–⅜ inch long (6–10 mm), creamy white to greenish yellow, base often tinged red or green, surfaces glandular; 0–5 tiny petals; stamens inside flower.

LEAVES: Basal with long stalks. Blades oval to rounded, ¾–3 inches wide/long (2–8 cm) with 5–7 shallow, rounded lobes; edges toothed, surfaces smooth to glandular- or stiff-hairy.

HABITAT: Rocky soil, talus slopes; montane, subalpine, alpine. Elevation 3,280–11,155 feet (1,000–3,400 m).

SIMILAR SPECIES: Gooseberry-leaf Alumroot, *H. grossulariifolia* has 3–5 lobed leaves.

Little-leaf Alumroot

Heuchera parvifolia, Saxifrage Family, Saxifragaceae; Perennial herb

QUICK ID: Look for dense rosettes of 5–7 lobed basal leaves and tall, slender stalks with spikes of tiny flowers with white, spreading petals.

RANGE: NR, MR, SR, Canada; widespread, common

STEM: Erect, 4–28 inches tall (10–70 cm), finely glandular-hairy.

FLOWERS: May–August. Loose, elongated clusters of saucer-shaped flowers, ⅛ inch (3 mm) wide, with a yellowish-green center and 5 white, spreading petals, ⅛ inch long (3 mm), slightly longer than sepals; sepals green- or red-tipped, densely covered with glandular hairs.

LEAVES: Basal on long stalks, smooth or glandular-hairy. Blades heart-shaped to rounded, ⅜–2 inches long (1–5) cm, with 5–7 lobes with rounded teeth; surfaces smooth to glandular-hairy.

HABITAT: Rocky soils and outcrops; foothills, montane, subalpine forests. Elevation: 5,300–12,500 feet (1,615–3,810 m).

SIMILAR SPECIES: New Mexico Alumroot, *H. nova-mexican*, (SR) has erect (not spreading) petals.

Smallflower Woodland Star

Lithophragma parviflorum, Saxifrage Family, Saxifragaceae; Perennial herb

QUICK ID: Look for hairy, 3-lobed basal leaves and sticky stems with clusters of white-to-pinkish flowers with 3-lobed petals.

RANGE: NR, MR, SR (absent NM), Canada; widespread, common

STEM: Erect, 4–20 inches tall (20–50 cm), hairy, sticky, rhizomatous.

FLOWERS: April–June. Clusters of 5–11 flowers at stem tips, 5 petals, 3⁄16–3⁄8 inch long (5–10 mm), deeply 3-lobed, white to pinkish.

LEAVES: Mostly basal, on stalks 3⁄8–2 3⁄8 inches long (1–6 cm); blades 3⁄8–1 1⁄4 inches wide (1–3 cm), deeply palmately cut into 3–5 wedge-shaped segments that are divided again 2–3 times into pointed lobes; surfaces white-hairy, glandular. 2 stem leaves, much similar, alternate, deeply lobed, hairy, dark green.

HABITAT: Meadows, open woods; grasslands, sagebrush, foothills, montane forests. Elevation sea level to 8,000 feet (2,438 m).

SIMILAR SPECIES: Bulbous Woodland Star, *L. glabrum*, usually has tiny bulblets on the stem near the flowers.

Slender Woodland Star

Lithophragma tenellum, Saxifrage Family, Saxifragaceae; Perennial herb

QUICK ID: Look for sticky-hairy, deeply lobed basal leaves and 1–5 delicate stems topped with clusters of flowers with white, lobed petals.

RANGE: NR, MR, SR, Canada; widespread, common

STEM: Erect, unbranched, 6–12 inches tall (15–30 cm), sticky-hairy.

FLOWERS: April–August. Clusters have 3–5 flowers, each 1⁄2–3⁄4 inch wide (12–20 mm), 5 white-to-pinkish petals, deeply divided into 3–7 pointed lobes, the middle the longest.

LEAVES: Basal on stalks 3⁄8–2 3⁄4 inches long (1–7 cm); blades rounded, 5⁄8–3⁄4 inch wide (15–20 mm) with 3 lobes, each lobe again divided 2–3 times; surfaces short-hairy, glandular, edges hairy. 2 stem leaves, much smaller, alternate, deeply 3-lobed, hairy, bright green.

HABITAT: Meadows, open areas; grasslands, sagebrush, foothills, montane forests. Elevation 4,500–9,000 feet (1,372–2,743 m).

SIMILAR SPECIES: Bulbous Woodland Star, *L. glabrum*, usually has tiny bulblets on the stem.

Brook Saxifrage

Micranthes odontoloma, Saxifrage Family, Saxifragaceae; Perennial herb

QUICK ID: Look in moist habitats for rosettes of rounded, toothed leaves, and tall, elongated clusters along slender stems; small white flowers have 2 basal yellow-to-green spots.

RANGE: NR, MR, SR, Canada; widespread, locally common

STEM: Erect, leafless, branching, 8–24 inches tall (20–60 cm), rhizomatous.

FLOWERS: June–September. Open, elongated clusters with 10–30 flowers spread along the stem; 5 rounded, white petals, narrow at the base, have 2 green-to-yellow basal spots; 10 stamens white, club shaped, some longer than the petals, anthers reddish brown; ovary has two protruding, pointed, cone-shaped lobes.

LEAVES: Basal on round stalks to 12 inches long (30 cm); blades rounded, to 3 inches wide (8 cm); edges lined with even, coarse teeth.

HABITAT: Moist soils, wet meadows; montane, subalpine forests. Elevation 8,200–11,200 feet (2,500–3,114 m).

Bog Saxifrage

Micranthes oregana, Saxifrage Family, Saxifragaceae; Perennial herb

QUICK ID: Look in wet habitats for fleshy basal leaves, tall leafless flower stems, and conical-to-cylindrical clusters of small white flowers.

RANGE: NR, SR, Canada; widespread, locally common

STEM: Erect, slender, branching, 10–50 inches tall (25–125 cm), hairy, rhizomatous.

FLOWERS: March–September. Dense to loose clusters with gland-tipped hairs on branch tips; 5 petals, oval to elliptic, ⅛ inch long (2–4 mm); 10 stamens with showy anthers.

LEAVES: Basal rosette, stalks flattened, 1–4 inches long (3–10 cm); blade linear to lance-shaped, 2⅜–10 inches long (6–25 cm), fleshy; edges wavy to sharp-toothed, with ciliate hairs; surfaces smooth to sparsely stiff-hairy.

HABITAT: Bogs, marshes, wet meadows; montane, subalpine forests. Elevation 5,000–8,000 feet (1,524–2,500 m).

SIMILAR SPECIES: Brook Saxifrage, *M. odontoloma*, in wet habitats, has white petals with yellowish spots.

Diamond-leaf Saxifrage

Micranthes rhomboidea, Saxifrage Family, Saxifragaceae; Perennial herb

QUICK ID: Look for basal rosette of broad, fleshy leaves and flower stems topped with snowball clusters of white flowers with 5 petals.

RANGE: NR, MR, SR; widespread, common

STEM: Erect, solitary, 1½–12 inches tall (4–30 cm), densely covered with pale, yellow-tipped, glandular hairs.

FLOWERS: May–August. Rounded clusters have 10–40 small white flowers, each with 5 oblong petals, ½–3⁄16 inch long (1–4 mm).

LEAVES: Basal with flattened stalk to 1 inch long (3 cm). Blades fleshy, diamond-shaped to elliptic, ⅜–1⅝ inches long (1–4 cm); edges ciliate hairy, coarsely toothed; bottom with reddish-brown hairs.

HABITAT: Rocky soils, meadows, seeps; montane, subalpine forests, alpine tundra, ridges. Elevation 5,000–12,800 feet (1,524–3,900 m).

SIMILAR SPECIES: Wild Candytuft , *Noccaea fendleri*, in the mustard family, has a leafy stem and flowers with 4 petals.

Side-flowered Miterwort

Mitella stauropetala, Saxifrage Family, Saxifragaceae; Perennial herb

QUICK ID: Look for tufts of rounded basal leaves and slender, leafless stems lined on one side with tiny flowers with white sepals and thread-like petals divided into 3 segments.

RANGE: NR, MR, SR; widespread, locally common

STEM: Erect, unbranched, 4–22 inches tall (10–55 cm), glandular-hairy.

FLOWERS: April–September. Spike-like clusters 6–35 single flowers bloom along one side of a slender stem. Flowers a tiny cup with 5 white, oblong, petal-like sepals to ⅛ inch long (3 mm); 3 petals, white, thread-like, ends split into 3 segments.

LEAVES: Basal on stalks to 6 inches long (15 cm); blades rounded, 1–4 inches (3–10 cm) wide and almost as long; edges have 5 or 7 shallow, round-toothed lobes; surfaces smooth to sparsely glandular-hairy.

HABITAT: Moist woods, meadows; montane, subalpine forests, alpine. Elevation 3,000–11,000 feet (915–3,353 m).

Spotted Saxifrage

Saxifraga bronchialis ssp. *austromontana*, Saxifrage Family, Saxifragaceae; Perennial herb

QUICK ID: Look in high elevations for mats of small leaves, clumps of slender flower stems, flowers with small white petals with red-and-yellow dots, and white stamens and anthers.

RANGE: NR, MR, SR, Canada; widespread, common

STEM: Flower stalk erect, slender, 2–8 inches tall (5–20 cm).

FLOWERS: June–October. Rounded to flat-topped clusters have 3–15 flowers; 5 white, oblong petals, ¼ inch long (6 mm), with purple-to-red dots near tips, yellow dots near base; 5 white stamens.

LEAVES: Basal rosette mat-like; blades linear, lance-shaped or elliptic, ⅛–⅝ inch long (3–15 mm); margins lined with stiff, white ciliate hairs, tips bristly pointed; a few alternate stem leaves.

HABITAT: Meadows, talus slopes, ridges; foothills, montane, subalpine forests, alpine. Elevation 7,000–12,250 feet (2,136–3,718 m).

SIMILAR SPECIES: Three-toothed Saxifrage, *S. tricuspidata*, (Canada) has basal leaves tipped with 3 teeth or 1 long bristle.

Nodding Saxifrage

Saxifraga cernua, Saxifrage Family, Saxifragaceae; Perennial herb

QUICK ID: Look in the alpine zone for basal leaves with palmate, pointed lobes; hairy stalks with red, BB-size bulblets in the leaf axils; and white flowers with 5 small petals.

RANGE: NR, MR, SR, Canada; widespread, common

STEM: Flower stalk erect, 4–10 inches tall (10–25 cm), glandular-hairy.

FLOWERS: June–August. Flowers single, occasionally 2–5, on stem tip; 5 oval petals, white without spots, 3/16–7/16 inch long (5–12 mm); tiny red bulblets grow below flower and in leaf axils; 10 stamens have yellow anthers, sepals glandular-hairy; buds nod.

LEAVES: Basal, long stalked; blades rounded to kidney-shaped, ⅜–1 inch wide (10–25 mm), with 3-7 rounded lobes, tips with tiny points. Stem leaves alternate, oval, margins lobed to entire, smaller upwards.

HABITAT: Alpine scree, slopes, outcrops; alpine. Elevation 11,000–14,000 feet (3,352–4,262 m).

Tufted Alpine Saxifrage

Saxifraga cespitosa, Saxifrage Family, Saxifragaceae; Perennial herb

QUICK ID: Look for dense cushions of small basal leaves, slender flower stalks, and clusters of small flowers with white petals; glandular-hairy throughout.

RANGE: NR, MR, SR, Canada; widespread, locally common

STEM: Mat forming, flower stalk 2–10 inches tall (5–25 cm), densely glandular-hairy.

FLOWERS: July–August. Clusters have 1–5 flowers with 5 rounded petals, each ¼ inch long (6 mm), throat yellow green, often striped.

LEAVES: Basal in tight, round rosettes, base tapering, not stalked, fleshy; blades elliptic to spatula-shaped, ¼–¾ inch long (5–20 mm), 3–5 lobes at tip; edges entire, short-hairy, surfaces glandular-hairy. Stem leaves few, small, alternate.

HABITAT: Rocky outcrops, fellfields; tundra, alpine. Elevation 11,600–14,000 feet (3,535–4,270 m).

Three-leaf Foamflower

Tiarella trifoliata, Saxifrage Family, Saxifragaceae; Perennial herb

QUICK ID: Look in rich soils of shaded forests for groundcovers with large leaves with 3 lobes or leaflets, and slender stalks with loose clusters of tiny, white, nodding flowers.

RANGE: NR, Canada; widespread, common

STEM: Flowering stalks erect, 4–28 inches tall (10–70 cm), glandular-hairy.

FLOWERS: May–September. Elongated clusters on short stalks along upper stem, densely glandular-hairy; 5 petals, spreading, linear, ⅛ inch long (3 mm), tips pointed; stamens longer than petals.

LEAVES: Basal, long stalked; blades heart-shaped, 1–5 inches long/wide (3–12 cm), edges wavy-toothed, or with 3–5 lobes, or compound with 3 stalked leaflets; glandular-hairy. Stem leaves 1–4, smaller alternate.

HABITAT: Moist, shaded woods; montane, lower subalpine forests. Elevation 2,000–9,000 feet (610–2,750 m).

Blue Elderberry

Sambucus nigra ssp. *cerulea*, Virburnum Family, Virburnaceae; Deciduous shrub/small tree

QUICK ID: Look for a bushy shrub or small tree, pinnate leaves with toothed leaflets, showy flat-topped clusters of small white flowers, and small blue berries.

RANGE: NR, MR, SR, Canada; widespread, common

STEM: Upright, multibranched shrub 6–13 feet tall (2–4 m); occasionally a small tree, 7–26 feet tall (2–8 m).

FLOWERS: March–July. Clusters 2–8 inches wide (5–20 cm); flowers creamy white; fruit round, dark blue, fleshy, ¼ inch wide (6 mm) with a powdery white coating.

LEAVES: Opposite; blades 5–7 inches long (13–18 cm), pinnate with 5–9 leaflets, each lance-shaped to elliptic, 1–5 inches long (3–13 cm) by ⅜–2⅜ inches wide (1–6 cm); edges serrated; top surface smooth; bottom pale, smooth to sparsely hairy; tips pointed.

HABITAT: Stream sides, moist woods; grasslands, sagebrush, foothills, montane forests. Elevation 4,500–9,500 feet (1,372–2,896 m).

Red Elderberry

Sambucus racemosa, Virburnum Family, Virburnaceae; Deciduous shrub/small tree

QUICK ID: Look for a bushy shrub or small tree, pinnate leaves with toothed leaflets, showy pyramidal clusters of small white flowers, and small red berries.

RANGE: NR, MR, SR, Canada; widespread, common

STEM: Multibranched, 3–16 feet tall (1–5 m).

FLOWERS: March–July. Dense clusters pyramidal to rounded, 1⅝–3 inches wide (4–8 cm); flowers creamy white; fruit round, bright red, fleshy, ¼ inch wide (6 mm).

LEAVES: Opposite; blades 5–7 inches long (13–18 cm), pinnate with 5–9 leaflets, each elliptic to lance-shaped, 1–5 inches long (3–13 cm) by ¾–3 inches wide (2–8 cm); edges serrated, top surface smooth to sparsely hairy; bottom pale, smooth to short-hairy; tips tapered.

HABITAT: Forests, riparian, disturbed areas; sagebrush, foothills, montane, subalpine forests. Elevation 7,700–10,500 feet (2,300–3,100 m).

SIMILAR SPECIES: Variety melanocarpa has shiny black berries without a powdery white coating.

Canada White Violet

Viola canadensis, Violet Family, Violaceae; Perennial herb

QUICK ID: Look for heart-shaped basal leaves, branching stems, and white flowers with a yellow throat and a dark-lined lower petal.

RANGE: NR, MR, SR, Canada; widespread, common

STEM: Erect, branched, 8–15 inches tall (20-38 cm), smooth to short-hairy, colony forming.

FLOWERS: April–October. Leafless stalks have a single flower, ¾ inch wide (2 cm) with 5 white, elliptic-to-oval petals with a yellow base: upper 2 erect, 2 spreading side petals with tufts of white hairs, lower petal oval ⅝ inch long (15 mm) with purple lines in throat.

LEAVES: Basal 1–5, long stalked; blades oval to heart-shaped, 2–3½ inches long (5–9 cm), edges coarsely toothed, surfaces smooth to hairy, tips tapered. Stem leaves alternate, similar, oval to triangular.

HABITAT: Meadows, open to shaded woods; foothills, montane, subalpine forests. Elevation 7,500–11,500 feet (2,286–3,505 m).

SIMILAR SPECIES: Small White Violet, *V. macloskeyi*, (all regions) is stemless and colony forming, and has flowers with a rear spur.

Common Kochia

Kochia scoparia, Amaranth Family, Amaranthaceae; Annual herb; naturalized, noxious, invasive

QUICK ID: Look for tall, branching, reddish stems with long hairs; slender, hairy leaves; and spikes of tiny, greenish-yellow flowers. Widespread throughout North America, this aggressive plant invades agricultural and disturbed areas.

RANGE: NR, MR, SR, Canada; widespread, common

STEM: Erect, 2–5 feet tall (60–150 cm), forms impenetrable stands.

FLOWERS: May–October. Spikes are long-hairy (not woolly); flowers tiny, greenish, petals absent, 5 protruding stamens; short, leaf-like bracts grow in the spike beneath each flower.

LEAVES: Alternate. Blades linear to lance-shaped, flat, thin, ¾–4 inches long (2–10 cm) to ½ inch wide (12 mm); margins entire, surfaces with soft hairs.

HABITAT: Seasonally moist soils of croplands, pastures, disturbed areas; riparian, grasslands, sagebrush, foothills, montane forests. Elevation 3,700–9,000 feet (1,128–2,743 m).

Fragrant Sumac

Rhus aromatica (Rhus trilobata), Sumac Family, Anacardiaceae; Deciduous shrub

QUICK ID: Look for a low-spreading shrub, palmate leaves with 3 leaflets that turn red in fall, early creamy flowers, and reddish berries.

RANGE: NR, MR, SR; widespread, common; widely variable

STEM: Upright, much branched, 3–8 feet tall/wide (1–2.5 m).

FLOWERS: March–April. Dense, spike-like clusters have small, pale-yellow flowers before leaves emerge; male flowers 1-inch long (3 cm) catkins, female flowers have 5 petals ⅛ inch long (3 mm). Fruit a cluster of small, red-to-orange drupes, sticky, hairy, citric flavored.

LEAVES: Alternate, stalked; blades 3 leaflets each ⅜–2 inches long (1–5 cm), 3-lobed, edges lobed to round-toothed, ill-smelling.

HABITAT: Coarse soils, slopes, washes; arid grasslands, sagebrush, foothills, montane forests. Elevations 4,000–7,500 feet (1,219–2,286 m).

Fendler's Springparsley

Cymopterus glomeratus, Parsley Family, Apiaceae; Perennial herb

QUICK ID: Look for stemless plants with a rosette of thick parsley-like leaves, and flat-topped clusters of small yellow or white flowers.

RANGE: NR, MR, SR, Canada; widespread, common

STEM: Stemless with deep taproot.

FLOWERS: April–June. An umbrella-like cluster of 5–20 tiny flowers either yellow or white, depending on variety, forms on the end of a pinkish stalk (peduncle), 1¼–5½ inches long (3–14 cm). Fruit is a showy cluster of seeds with pink-tinted, papery wings.

LEAVES: Basal, erect to prostrate. Blade shiny, green, to 3 inches long (8 cm) including stem (petiole); edges deeply divided like parsley leaves,

HABITAT: Dry soils of grasslands, desert scrub, sagebrush steppe, pinyon-juniper. Elevation 4,900–7,500 feet (1,502–2,290 m).

Alpine False Springparsley

Cymopterus lemmonii, Parsley Family, Apiaceae; Perennial herb

QUICK ID: Look for basal clusters of parsley-like basal leaves, and stalks with rounded to flat, showy clusters of tiny yellow flowers.

RANGE: SR; widespread, common

STEM: Erect, leafy, 1-2 feet tall (30-60 cm).

FLOWERS: May–September. Stalks (peduncles) have 1-5 clusters, each to 2 inches wide (5 cm) with short, umbrella-like rays; small flowers, lemon-yellow, occasionally red to orange in NM.

LEAVES: Basal rosette with stalks (petioles) to 6 inches long (15 cm). Alternate, smaller leaves on flower stalks. Blades pinnately compound with 2-6 opposite leaflets, each with deeply cut, pointed segments; thin, linear leaflets occasionally occur.

HABITAT: Pinyon-juniper foothills, montane, subalpine forests, alpine meadows. Elevation 5,400-12,300 feet (5,400-3,759 m).

SIMILAR SPECIES: Mountain Springparsley, *C. longilobus* (SR, MR, NR) forms clumps covered with old stems.

Wyeth Biscuitroot

Lomatium ambiguum, Parsley Family, Apiaceae; Perennial herb

QUICK ID: Look for slender stems with compound, narrow leaflets and umbrella-shaped clusters of small, yellow flowers.

RANGE: NR, MR, Canada; widespread, common

STEM: Erect, branched or not, 4-32 inches tall (10-80 cm), smooth.

FLOWERS: May–August. Clusters at stem ends, umbrella-shaped with radiating stalks 1-4 inches long (3-10 cm), each tipped with a small cluster with tiny flowers with 5 yellow petals, but no tiny, leaf-like bractlets.

LEAVES: Basal, blades deeply divided 2-3 times along midrib into unequal, narrow, linear to thread-like segments, the largest ⅜-3 inches long (1-8 cm) by 1/16-3/16 inch wide (2-5 mm). Stem leaves few, alternate, similar.

HABITAT: Dry, stony open areas; grasslands, sagebrush, foothills, montane forests. Elevation 1,000-8,000 feet (305-2,438 m).

Cous Biscuitroot

Lomatium cous, Parsley Family, Apiaceae; Perennial herb

QUICK ID: Look for low-spreading plants, parsley-like basal leaves, and flower stalks with umbrella-like clusters of tiny, bright-yellow flowers.

RANGE: NR, MR, Canada; widespread, common

STEM: Stemless, flower stalks only, 6–14 inches tall (15–35 cm), smooth.

FLOWERS: March–August. Flower stalks directly from taproot with a dense, umbrella-like cluster with 5–20 radiating rays, each tipped with small, leaf-like bractlets 3⁄16 inch long (5 mm) with rounded tips, and a small cluster of yellow flowers with 5 small petals.

LEAVES: Basal. Blades pinnately cut into leaflets along midrib, each lined with parsley-like lobes; surfaces smooth, shiny, dark green.

HABITAT: Dry open, rocky areas; sagebrush, foothills, montane, subalpine forests, alpine. Elevation 2,000–12,000 feet (610–3,656 m).

Fernleaf Biscuitroot

Lomatium dissectum, Parsley Family, Apiaceae; Perennial herb

QUICK ID: Look for beds of fern-like basal leaves; smooth, robust stems; and umbrella-like clusters of small yellow flowers with 5 petals.

RANGE: NR, MR, Canada; widespread, common

STEM: Erect, several from taproot, 1–4 feet tall (30–120 cm).

FLOWERS: April–July. Umbrella-like clusters reach 5 inches wide (13 cm) with 10–30 radiating, spreading stalks; each stalk tipped with small, linear, leaf-like bractlets under a ¾-inch diameter (2 cm) spherical cluster of small, yellow (sometimes purple) flowers.

LEAVES: Basal on stalks 1–12 inches long (3–30 cm). Blade oval to rounded in outline, 6–12 inches wide (15–30 cm), pinnately compound with parsley- or fern-like leaflets lining the midrib; surfaces smooth to finely hairy. Stem leaves few, similar, alternate.

HABITAT: Wooded, brushy areas; grasslands, sagebrush, foothills, montane forests. Elevation sea level to 8,000 feet (2,438 m).

Desert Biscuitroot

Lomatium foeniculaceum, Parsley Family, Apiaceae; Perennial herb

QUICK ID: Look for parsley-like basal leaves often flat on the ground; stalks with umbrella-like clusters with bractlets beneath yellow flowers.

RANGE: NR, MR, Canada (rare); widespread, locally common

STEM: Stemless, flower stalks from taproot, 2–12 inches tall (5–30 cm), densely short-hairy.

FLOWERS: March–June. Hairy flower stalks have umbrella-like clusters of 7–27 spreading stalks, each tipped with small, leaf-like bractlets under a spherical cluster of tiny yellow flowers.

LEAVES: Basal; blades compound, finely dissected 3–4 times, oval to triangular in outline, 1–5 inches long (2–13 cm), final segments ⅛ inch long (3 mm); surfaces short-hairy, whitish to bluish green.

HABITAT: Open slopes, prairies; grasslands, sagebrush, foothills, montane forests. Elevation 3,900–9,000 feet (1,200–2,700 m).

Gray's Biscuitroot

Lomatium grayi, Parsley Family, Apiaceae; Perennial herb

QUICK ID: Look for beds of fern-like basal leaves and flower stalks with leaf-like bractlets under flat-topped clusters of tiny yellow flowers.

RANGE: NR, MR, SR, Canada; widespread, locally common

STEM: Stemless, erect to spreading flower stalks direct from taproot, 4–20 inches tall (10–50 cm), smooth.

FLOWERS: April–June. Dense, flat-topped clusters reach 6 inches wide (15 cm) with 10–26 spreading, radiating, smooth stalks, each tipped with 15–30 tiny yellow flowers above small, leaf-like bractlets.

LEAVES: Basal from taproot on stalks 1–5½ inches long (3–14 cm); blades compound, lance-shaped in outline, 3–10 inches long (8–25 cm); pinnately divided fern-like along midrib 3 times into hundreds of narrow segments; surfaces smooth to rough; strongly aromatic.

HABITAT: Dry, open, rocky areas; sagebrush, foothills, montane forests. Elevation 6,000–8,000 feet (1,830–2,440 m).

Nine-leaf Biscuitroot

Lomatium triternatum, Parsley Family, Apiaceae; Perennial herb

QUICK ID: Look for clusters of basal leaves with thread-like leaflets divided in sets of 3, and flower stems with spreading, spoke-like stalks tipped with clusters of small yellow flowers.

RANGE: NR, MR, SR, Canada; widespread, common

STEM: Absent or short; flower stalk erect, 6–32 inches tall (15–80 cm), smooth to finely soft-hairy.

FLOWERS: April–July. Flower stalks topped with 5–20 spreading, spoke-like stalks, each tipped with a rounded cluster of tiny, yellow flowers. Tiny bractlets below the small clusters linear to thread-like.

LEAVES: Basal on stalks, 2¾–8 inches long (7–20 cm); blade 2¾–8 inches long (7–20 cm), pinnately compound dividing into 3 leaflets that again divide three times; leaflets linear to lance-shaped, ⅝–5 inches long (15–127 mm); surfaces smooth to finely soft-hairy. Stem leaves few, similar.

HABITAT: Open hills, forest edges; grasslands, sagebrush, foothills, montane forests. Elevation 1,312–8,000 feet (400–2,440 m).

Leafy Wild Parsley

Musineon divaricatum, Parsley Family, Apiaceae; Perennial herb

QUICK ID: Look for rosettes with pinnately compound, parsley-like leaves; hairy flower stalks; and rounded clusters of tiny yellow flowers.

RANGE: NR, MR, SR (absent NM), Canada; widespread common

STEM: Appears stemless.

FLOWERS: April–July. Flower stalks hairy, ⅜–4 inches tall (1–10 cm), topped with rounded, umbrella-like clusters crowded with tiny flowers with 5 petals.

LEAVES: Basal; blades oval-pointed in outline, ¾–5 inches long (2–12 cm), pinnately divided into leaflets along midrib; leaflets deeply pinnately cut again into sharply lobed, parsley-like segments; surfaces smooth.

HABITAT: Dry soils, plains, valleys; arid grasslands, sagebrush. Elevation 2,000–7,000 feet (610–2,134 m).

Heartleaf Alexanders

Zizia aptera, Parsley Family, Apiaceae; Perennial herb

QUICK ID: Look in damp places for clusters of heart-shaped leaves on long stalks and stems topped with umbrella-like clusters of small yellow flowers.

RANGE: MR, NR, SR (absent NM), Canada; scattered, locally common

STEM: Erect, clustered, branched, 8–24 inches tall (20–60 cm), hairless throughout.

FLOWERS: April–August. Umbrella-like clusters have spreading rays 1–2 inches long (3–5 cm), each tipped with a flat-topped cluster of small, bright-yellow flowers.

LEAVES: Basal, very long stalked; blades heart-shaped, 1–4 inches long (3–10 cm); edges lined with small, rounded teeth, surfaces smooth, shiny. Stem leaves smaller, shorter stalked, divided into 3–5 palmate segments, sharp-toothed.

HABITAT: Wet meadows, open woods; grasslands, foothills, montane, lower subalpine forests. Elevation 5,200–9,300 feet (1,585–2,835 m).

Butterfly Milkweed

Asclepias tuberosa, Dogbane Family, Apocynaceae; Perennial herb

QUICK ID: Look for dense clusters of orange-to-yellow flowers, many narrow hairy leaves, and clear (not milky) sap.

RANGE: SR; locally common

STEM: Erect, hairy, 1½–3 feet tall (46–91 cm), unbranched.

FLOWERS: May–September. Orange-to-yellow flowers form loose, rounded clusters (umbels) 2–5 inches across (5–13 cm); 5 petal-like lobes bend backwards with the tips spreading, 5 erect hoods have needle-like horns arching toward the central column. Seed pods slender, hairy, to 6 inches long (15 cm).

LEAVES: Alternate, on short stalks (petioles), crowded on stem. Blades linear to lance-shaped, 1–4 inches long (3–10 cm) to 1¼ inches wide (3 cm); margins entire, surfaces variably hairy.

HABITAT: Moist soils; pinyon-juniper foothills, montane forests. Elevation: 3,600–8,200 feet (1,100–2,500 m).

Burnt-orange Dandelion

Agoseris aurantiaca, Aster Family, Asteraceae; Perennial herb

QUICK ID: Look for an orange, dandelion-like flower with leafless flower stalks; heads with ray flowers only; milky sap.

RANGE: NR, MR, SR, Canada; widespread, common

STEM: Flower stalks 4–20 inches tall (10–50 cm), hollow.

FLOWERS: June–August. Flower head ⅜–¾ inch wide (10–20 mm); 15–100 petal-like ray flowers, burnt orange, rarely pink, tips serrated; no disk flowers. Phyllaries beneath flower head hairy with purple-black blotches. Seeds feathery, dandelion-like.

LEAVES: All basal with purplish stem (petiole). Blades 2¾–15 inches long (7–38 cm), linear grass-like to lance-shaped; margins entire, occasionally with a few teeth or lobes.

HABITAT: Moist meadows, open forests; montane. subalpine forests. Elevation 7,000–12,500 feet (2,134–3,810 m).

Pale Agoseris

Agoseris glauca, Aster Family, Asteraceae; Perennial herb

QUICK ID: Look for unlobed basal leaves, yellow dandelion-like flower on leafless flower stalks, rays with serrated tips, and milky sap.

RANGE: NR, MR, SR, Canada; widespread, common

STEM: Flower stalks 4–24 inches tall (10–61 cm).

FLOWERS: April–September. Solitary flower heads 1-2 inches wide (3–5 cm), with up to 150 yellow rays (no disk florets); stamens radiate from center. Phyllaries beneath the head overlap with 2-3 rows, often with a rosy median line and spots or speckles, and usually are not hairy. Seeds feathery, dandelion-like.

LEAVES: Basal; blades erect to decumbent, narrow to lance-shaped, pointed, 1–18 inches long (2–46 cm); margins usually entire, often undulate, sometimes lobed; surfaces hairless or with woolly hairs.

HABITAT: Grasslands, montane, subalpine forests, alpine meadows. Elevation 5,400–11,400 feet (1,650–3,500 m).

SIMILAR SPECIES: Steppe Agoseris, *A. parviflora*, has basal leaves with backward pointing lobes.

Steppe Agoseris

Agoseris parviflora, Aster Family, Asteraceae; Perennial herb

QUICK ID: Look for basal leaf lobes angled backwards and stalks with solitary flower heads packed with yellow rays tipped with tiny teeth.

RANGE: NR, MR, SR; widespread, common

STEM: Erect, leafless, 2–10 inches long (5–25 cm).

FLOWERS: April–August. Solitary flower heads ¾–1½ inches wide (2–4 cm); slender rays 30–100 have serrated tips and stamens radiate from center. Phyllaries in 2–3 overlapping rows, narrow, tapering, with reddish midstripe, tips often reflexed.

LEAVES: Basal, erect to decumbent; blades linear to lance-shaped, 4–8 inches long (10–20 cm); edges have 5–8 pairs of lobes, mostly backward pointing, often some leaves unlobed; surfaces smooth or densely hairy.

HABITAT: Dry sandy soils; grasslands, sagebrush, foothills, montane forests. Elevation 6,500–10,000 feet (1,981–3,048 m).

SIMILAR SPECIES: Pale Agoseris, *A. glauca*, has basal leaves without lobes.

Ragleaf Bahia

Amauriopsis dissecta (Bahia dissecta), Aster Family, Asteraceae; Annual, biennial herb

QUICK ID: Look for branching stems, leaves with narrow, deeply cut lobes, and numerous yellow flower heads. Compared to the diameter of the yellow disk, the petal-like ray flowers seem stubby.

RANGE: MR (ID), SR; widespread

STEM: Erect, hairy, branching stems reach 3 feet tall (1 m).

FLOWERS: August–October. Flower stem (peduncle) to 2¾ inches long (7 cm) and densely hairy. Flower heads with 10–20 yellow rays, each 3⁄16–⅜ inch long (5–10 mm), tips notched with 2–3 points.

LEAVES: Alternate. Blades oval to lance-shaped in outline, ⅜–1⅜ inches long (10–35 mm), largest leaves near base; margins deeply divided into 3–25 lobed segments with narrow, linear final segments.

HABITAT: Grasslands and scrub, pinyon-juniper, ponderosa–Douglas-fir forests. Elevation 5,800–8,800 feet (1,770–2,680 m).

Leafy Arnica

Arnica chamissonis, Aster Family, Asteraceae; Perennial herb

QUICK ID: Look for clusters of 3–15 flower heads with showy, 2-inch-wide (5 cm), yellow flowers on stems with 5–10 pairs of leaves.

RANGE: NR, MR, SR, Canada; widespread, common

STEM: Erect, top-branching, 8–36 inches tall (20–90 cm), sparsely to densely hairy.

FLOWERS: April–September. Heads erect with 12–18 rays, each ⅜–¾ inch long (1–2 cm), tips shallowly notched to conspicuously toothed. Pappus hair surrounding the disk florets is yellowish white; phyllaries beneath the rays are narrow, white-hairy.

LEAVES: Basal leaves usually wither by flowering; stem leaves opposite. Blades lance-shaped to elliptic, 1–12 inches long (3–30 cm); lower leaves with stalks (petioles), upper leaves not stalked (sessile); edges entire to lightly toothed, surfaces smooth to densely woolly-hairy.

HABITAT: Stream sides, forest openings, meadows; foothills, montane, subalpine forests. Elevation 0–11,500 feet (0–3,500 m).

Heartleaf Arnica

Arnica cordifolia, Aster Family, Asteraceae; Perennial herb

QUICK ID: Look for a stem with 2–4 pairs of hairy, heart-shaped leaves, and a flower head with bright-yellow rays and disk.

RANGE: NR, MR, SR, Canada; widespread, common

STEM: Erect, 2 feet tall (60 cm) with a single flower head.

FLOWERS: May–August. Usually 1 flower head per stem, 1–2½ inches diameter (3–6 cm), with 6–13 yellow ray flowers and a yellow-orange disk; tawny (not white) pappus hairs in disk; phyllaries beneath the rays have a hairy surface and tufts at the tips.

LEAVES: Basal, with long stalks (petioles) usually wither by flowering; stem leaves opposite with stalks. Blades generally heart shaped, 1¼–4 inches long/wide (3–10 cm), smaller up the stem; surfaces hairy, margins entire or with shallow teeth.

HABITAT: Moist soils, riparian; subalpine meadows, forests. Elevation 7,000–11,000 feet (2,130–3,350 m).

Foothill Arnica

Arnica fulgens, Aster Family, Asteraceae; Perennial herb

QUICK ID: Look for unbranched stems with 2–4 pairs of hairy leaves and a single yellow flower head 1¾ inches wide (5 cm).

RANGE: NR, MR, SR, Canada; widespread, common

STEM: Erect, glandular-hairy stems 4–30 inches tall (10–75 cm).

FLOWERS: May–July. Heads have 10–23 rays, each ⅜–1 inch long (1–3 cm), tips with tiny, blunt teeth; the disk has spreading white hairs and whitish pappus bristles; phyllaries beneath the head are elliptic to narrow, pointed, glandular-hairy.

LEAVES: Basal, densely clustered with tufts of brown, woolly hair in axils; blades 2–6 inches long (5–15 cm) by ⅜–1⅝ inches wide (1–4 cm); edges entire with 3–5 prominent nerves. Stem leaves opposite, smaller, blades narrowly elliptic; surfaces glandular-hairy.

HABITAT: Grasslands, sagebrush, foothills, montane forests. Elevation 1,650–9,820 feet (500–3,000 m).

SIMILAR SPECIES: Twin Arnica, *A. soroia*, has no tufts of woolly brown hairs in the basal leaf axils.

Broadleaf Arnica

Arnica latifolia, Aster Family, Asteraceae; Perennial herb

QUICK ID: Look for unbranched stems with 1–5 showy, yellow flower heads, and 2–4 pairs of broad stem leaves with toothed edges.

RANGE: NR, MR, SR (absent NM), Canada; widespread, common

STEM: Erect, glandular-hairy, 4–20 inches tall (10–50 cm).

FLOWERS: June–September. Flower heads have 8–15 yellow rays, each ⅜–1⅛ inches long (10–30 mm) with tiny teeth on tips; disk yellow, slightly hairy; pappus bristles white. Phyllaries under the rays are lance-shaped, of equal length, generally with glandular hairs.

LEAVES: Basal with long stems (petioles). Stem leaves paired, blades lance-shaped, elliptic, to oval, ¾–5½ inches long (2–14 cm) by ⅜–3 inches wide (1–8 cm); surfaces smooth to sparsely hairy, margins toothed; mid-stem leaves are the largest.

HABITAT: Moist soils, stream sides; open montane, subalpine forests, alpine. Elevation 1,640–10,825 feet (500–3,300 m).

Longleaf Arnica

Arnica longifolia, Aster Family, Asteraceae; Perennial herb

QUICK ID: Look for unbranched stems with 5-7 pairs of long, narrow, hairy leaves and clusters of 1-20 showy yellow flower heads.

RANGE: NR, MR, SR (absent NM), Canada; widespread, common

STEM: Erect, 1-2 feet tall (30-60 cm), colony forming.

FLOWERS: June–October. Flower heads have 6-15 yellow rays, each ⅜-¾ inch long (10-20 mm), tipped with tiny teeth; disk yellow, pappus hairs whitish tan; phyllaries beneath the rays are all the same length, glandular-hairy, pointed.

LEAVES: Basal usually wither by blooming; stem leaves opposite, stalkless, blades lance-shaped to elliptic, 2-6 inches long (5-15 cm) by ⅝-1⅜ inches wide (15-35 mm), only slightly smaller up the stem; surfaces rough-hairy, margins entire, tip pointed.

HABITAT: Moist soils, stream sides, open montane, subalpine forests, alpine meadows. Elevation 4,265-12,140 feet (1,300-3,700 m).

Hairy Arnica

Arnica mollis, Aster Family, Asteraceae; Perennial herb

QUICK ID: Look for clumps of sticky, silky-hairy stems with 3-5 pairs of leaves and either 1 or a cluster of 3-7 showy, yellow flower heads.

RANGE: NR, MR, SR (rare NM), Canada; common

STEM: Erect, 6-28 inches tall (15-70 cm), clump forming.

FLOWERS: June–September. Heads have 12-22 yellow rays, each ⅝-1½ inches long (15-38 mm) with tiny teeth on the tips; disk yellow. Pappus hairs around florets tawny, silky, and slightly feathery; phyllaries broadly lance-shaped, green, often red tipped, all equal-sized, covered with short to long-silky hairs.

LEAVES: Opposite on stem, stalkless. Blades broad, elliptic to lance-shaped, 1½-8 inches long (4-20 cm) by ⅜-1½ inches wide (1-4 cm), slightly smaller up the stem; margins entire or irregularly toothed, surfaces moderately hairy, tips pointed.

HABITAT: Moist soils, stream sides; montane, subalpine forests, alpine meadows. Elevation 3,280-13,125 feet (1,000-4,000 m).

Nodding Arnica

Arnica parryi, Aster Family, Asteraceae; Perennial herb

QUICK ID: Look for unbranched stems with 3–4 pairs of leaves and 3–9 flower heads with yellow disks; usually no showy petal-like rays.

RANGE: NR, MR, SR (rare NM), Canada; widespread, common

STEM: Erect, 4–24 inches tall (10–60 cm), glandular-hairy.

FLOWERS: May–September. Buds nod, but flowers are erect. Disk has tawny, straw-colored pappus hairs. Phyllaries at base of head are in one row, narrow, equally sized, with long, glandular hairs, and slender, sharp-pointed tips.

LEAVES: Basal with or without stalks (petioles), round to oval, often withering by blooming. Stem blades oval to lance-shaped, 2–8 inches long (5–20 cm); edges usually entire, surfaces covered with few to many white hairs; upper leaves much smaller, stalkless (sessile).

HABITAT: Woodlands, open montane, subalpine forests, alpine meadows. Elevation 1,640–12,470 feet (500–3,800 m).

Twin Arnica

Arnica sororia, Aster Family, Asteraceae; Perennial herb

QUICK ID: Look for clustered basal leaves without brown tufts of hair in the axis and showy flower heads with yellow ray and disk florets.

RANGE: NR, Canada; widespread, common

STEM: Erect, simple or branched, 6–20 inches tall (15–50 cm), hairy.

FLOWERS: May–July. Clusters of 1–5 flower heads on stem ends and paired stalks from upper leaf axils; rays 9–17, each ⅜–1 inch long (1–3 cm); disk yellow with white pappus hairs; phyllaries narrow, hairy, uniform in length and width, tips pointed.

LEAVES: Basal, densely clustered, no brown tufts of hair in axils; blades narrowly oblong, 1–6 inches long (3–15 cm); edges entire, surfaces hairy with 3 or 5 prominent veins. Stem leaves smaller, 2–4 pairs, opposite.

HABITAT: Scrublands, open forests; grasslands, sagebrush, foothills, montane forests. Elevation 2,000–8,000 feet (610–2,438 m).

SIMILAR SPECIES: Foothill Arnica, *A. fulgens*, has long, woolly brown hairs in the basal leaf axils.

Silver Sage Wormwood

Artemisia ludoviciana, Aster Family, Asteraceae; Perennial subshrub

QUICK ID: Look for clusters of erect stems with narrow, white-woolly leaves and stalks with elongated clusters of tiny yellow flower heads.

RANGE: NR, MR, SR, Canada; widespread, common

STEM: Erect, leafy, branched or not, 8–32 inches tall (20–80 cm), rhizomatous, colony forming.

FLOWERS: August–November. Elongated, compact, leafy clusters have nodding to stalkless heads, each cup-shaped, ¼ inch wide (5 mm), with tiny disk flowers only.

LEAVES: Alternate. Blades linear to elliptic, ¾–4 inches long (2–10 cm); edges entire to lobed, surfaces gray green to white, woolly-hairy; highly aromatic with many traditional ceremonial and medicinal uses.

HABITAT: Open woodlands, plains, disturbed areas: grasslands, sagebrush, foothills, montane, subalpine forests. Elevation 920–10,000 feet (280–3,050 m).

Big Sagebrush

Artemisia tridentata, Asteraceae Family, Asteraceae; Evergreen shrub

QUICK ID: Look in brushlands for shrubs with small gray aromatic leaves with 3 tiny teeth, and elongated clusters of tiny yellow flowers.

RANGE: NR, MR, SR, Canada; widespread, common

STEM: Upright, short trunk to branched from base, 2–7 feet tall (0.6–2 m).

FLOWERS: July–September. Slender, erect arrays on branch tips have numerous tiny flowers with pale yellow, wind-pollinated disk florets.

LEAVES: Alternate, often clustered at nodes; blades wedge-shaped, ¼–1⅝ inch long (5–40 mm) to ½ inch wide (12 mm); surfaces greenish gray with silvery hairs, tips have 3 small teeth or lobes.

HABITAT: Dry plains, meadows, slopes; sagebrush, foothills, montane forests. Elevation 4,265–9,500 feet (1,300–2,900 m).

NOTES: Big Sagebrush and other *Artemisias* are the dominant plants of the Sagebrush Steppe biome that grows in arid, low- to mid-elevations throughout the Rocky Mountains and beyond.

Arrowleaf Balsamroot

Balsamorhiza sagittata, Aster Family, Asteraceae; Perennial herb

QUICK ID: Look for a dense rosette of silvery-hairy, arrowhead-shaped leaves and multiple stems topped with showy, yellow, sunflower-like heads.

RANGE: NR, MR, SR (absent NM), Canada; widespread, common

STEM: Multiple robust stems 1–2 feet tall (30–60 cm).

FLOWERS: April–September. Flower heads up to 3 inches wide (8 cm) with 8–25 rays, each 1–2 inches long (3–5 cm), surround a disk packed with tiny, tubular florets; phyllaries under the head are lance-shaped, hairy.

LEAVES: Basal, stalks longer than blades. Blades 2–12 inches long (5–30 cm) by ⅝–6 inches wide (15 to 150 mm), lance-triangular shaped with tapering tips, 2 rounded lobes at base; margins entire, surfaces (especially bottom) densely grayish- to white-woolly. Stem leaves much smaller, linear to elliptic, alternate.

HABITAT: Prairies, meadows, slopes; sagebrush, foothills, montane, subalpine forests. Elevation 3,500–9,000 feet (1,067–2,743 m).

Nodding Beggarticks

Bidens cernua, Aster family, Asteraceae; Annual herb

QUICK ID: Look in wet habitats for erect-to-spreading stems often branching near the base and long outer leaf-like phyllaries beneath the yellow flower heads.

RANGE: NR, MR, SR, Canada; widespread, common

STEM: Erect to sprawling, 8–40 inches tall (20–100 cm).

FLOWERS: August–October. Flower heads ½–1½ inches wide (12–38 mm) with 6–8 showy, oval ray florets, each ⅛–⅝ inch long (2–15 mm); 40–100 yellow disk flowers; 5–8 leaf-like outer bracts to ⅜ inch long (1 cm), about as long or longer than the rays. Flower heads are single or in loose, open clusters, erect to nodding with age, nodding when in fruit.

LEAVES: Opposite. Blades stalkless to clasping, lance-shaped, 1⅝–4 inches long (4–10 cm), tips pointed; margins coarsely toothed to serrated, surfaces hairless.

HABITAT: Moist, sandy soils; wet meadows, wetlands, floodplains, riparian. Elevation 3,900–8,800 feet (1,190–2,682 m).

Tassel-flower Brickellbush

Brickellia grandiflora, Aster family, Asteraceae; Perennial herbaceous subshrub

QUICK ID: Look for a 1-3-foot tall (30-90 cm) shrub with triangular leaves and clusters of nodding, tassel-like, white to yellow flower heads.

RANGE: NR, MR, SR, Canada; widespread, common

STEM: Subshrub erect to rounded, branching with fine, short hairs.

FLOWERS: July-October. Loose clusters of nodding, cylindrical-to-bell-shaped flower heads have 20-40 tiny, whitish-to-yellow-tinted, tassel-like florets ¼-⅜ inch long (6-8 mm); ray flowers absent.

LEAVES: Opposite, or nearly so, on stalks ⅜-2¾ inches long (10-70 mm). Blade triangular to lance-shaped, 1-4¾ inches long (3-12 cm); tips tapering, margins lined with small teeth, surfaces covered with minute hairs only visible with magnification.

HABITAT: Dry coarse soils; pinyon-juniper foothills, montane, subalpine forests. Elevation 4,800-10,300 feet (1,463-3,140 m).

Parry's Thistle

Cirsium parryi, Aster Family, Asteraceae; Biennial herb

QUICK ID: Look for stout stems with long, spiny leaves and cobwebby heads with yellow, filament-like disk florets.

RANGE: SR; widespread, common

STEM: Erect, branching or not, 2-7 feet tall (0.6-2 m), hairy.

FLOWERS: July-October. Flower heads, ⅝-1¼ inches wide (15-30 mm) have a dense network of spiny leaves and silver-hairy phyllaries around a dense cluster of thread-like disk florets.

LEAVES: Basal for the first year. Stem leaves alternate, clasping; blades highly variable, 4-12 inches long (10-30 cm), oblong to lance-shaped, edges prickly to spiny toothed to deeply dissected into pinnate lobes, variously armed with spines to ⅝ inch long (15 mm).

HABITAT: Mountain meadows, streams, open forests; montane, subalpine forests. Elevation 7,000-11,500 feet (2,133-3,500 m).

SIMILAR SPECIES: Yellow-spined Thistle, *C. ochrocentrum*, has pink, white, or purple flowers.

Tapertip Hawksbeard

Crepis acuminata, Aster Family, Asteraceae; Perennial herb

QUICK ID: Look for 1-5 stems with deeply-lobed leaves with long tapering tips and many flower heads with yellow rays with tiny teeth.

RANGE: NR, MR, SR; widespread, common

STEM: Erect, slender, branching, 4–26 inches tall (20–65 cm).

FLOWERS: May–August. Flat-topped clusters have 20–70 flower heads, each with 5–10 ray florets to ¾ inch long (18 mm), tipped with tiny teeth; beneath the flower are 5–8 phyllaries, narrow, evenly-sized, hairless, pointed.

LEAVES: Basal, alternate on stem. Blades elliptic, 5–16 inches long (12–40 cm) with 5–10 pairs of narrow, pointed lobes cut about halfway to the midrib; tips long, tapering.

HABITAT: Grassy flats, open woods; sagebrush, foothills, montane forests. Elevation 3,280-10,825 feet (1,000–3,300 m).

Fiddleleaf Hawksbeard

Crepis runcinata, Aster Family, Asteraceae; Perennial herb

QUICK ID: Look for basal rosettes with mostly entire leaves; tall, almost leafless, branching stems; and flower heads with yellow rays tipped with tiny teeth.

RANGE: NR, MR, SR, Canada; widespread, common

STEM: Erect, 1–3, upper branching, 6–26 inches tall (15–65 cm).

FLOWERS: May–September. Arrays on spreading branch tips, heads flat-topped, to 1 inch wide (3 cm) with 20–50 rays, each ⅜–¾ inch long (9–18 mm), tips with tiny teeth. Phyllaries 10–16 in 2 rows, lance-shaped, hairless to glandular-hairy, tapering to a slender tip.

LEAVES: Mostly in basal rosette; blades long-stalked, elliptic, linear to spatula-shaped, 1–12 inches long (3–30 cm); edges entire to few-toothed, surfaces smooth to hairy. Stem leaves small or absent, alternate, linear, to 2 inches long (5 cm) by 1 mm wide; edges entire.

HABITAT: Dry openings, disturbed areas; grasslands, sagebrush, foothills, montane forests. Elevation 2,000–10,000 feet (610–3,048 m).

Fetid Marigold

Dyssodia papposa, Aster Family, Asteraceae; Annual herb

QUICK ID: Look for a bushy plant with fetid-smelling leaves with narrow lobes and reddish flower heads with tiny yellow rays and disk.

RANGE: NR, MR, SR; widespread, common

STEM: Erect, slender, leafy, branched, 4–18 inches tall (10–45 cm).

FLOWERS: August–October. Numerous, small, reddish, bell-shaped flower heads, 3⁄16–3⁄8 inch diameter (4–10 mm); 8 or fewer tiny, yellow ray flowers with notched tips that barely extend beyond the yellow disk flowers.

LEAVES: Opposite below, often alternate above. Blades ¾–2 inches long (2–5 cm), pinnately divided into 11–15 narrow lobes along the midrib and often divided again at tips, dotted with oil-glands.

HABITAT: Meadows, roadsides, disturbed areas; grasslands, sagebrush, foothills. Elevation 4,000–8,700 feet (1,220–2,652 m).

Rubber Rabbitbrush

Ericameria nauseosa (Chrysothamnus nauseosus), Aster Family, Asteraceae; Perennial, evergreen shrub

QUICK ID: Look for a rounded shrub with compact, flexible branches with matted woolly-white hairs; narrow, gray leaves; and flat-topped clusters of small yellow, fall-blooming flowers.

RANGE: NR, MR, SR, Canada; widespread, common

STEM: Branching, 3–8 feet tall/wide (1–3 m), hairy.

FLOWERS: July–October. Dense clusters of yellow flower heads have no ray florets and 5 tubular disk flowers, each ½ inch long (12 mm), with a long protruding stigma; phyllaries below the head yellow with tapering tips, stacked in 3–5 spiraling rows.

LEAVES: Alternate, crowded on stem. Blade narrow, to 2¾ inches long (7 cm) by 3⁄8 inch wide (1 cm), tip pointed. The 21 varieties have gray or green leaves, white-woolly or not.

HABITAT: Coarse soils, disturbed areas; grasslands, sagebrush, pinyon-juniper foothills. Elevation 3,500–9,500 feet (1,066–2,895 m).

SIMILAR SPECIES: Parry's Rabbitbrush, *E. parryi*, has hairy stems, 5–20 disk florets, equal phyllaries.

Common Woolly Sunflower

Eriophyllum lanatum, Aster Family, Asteraceae; Perennial herb

QUICK ID: Look for dense clumps of multi-branching, hairy stems topped with flower heads with bright-yellow rays and disk.

RANGE: NR, MR, Canada; widespread, common, 10 varieties

STEM: Erect, branching, 1–24 inches tall (3–60 cm), hairy.

FLOWERS: May–August. Heads usually solitary with 8–13 rays, ⅜–¾ inch long (1–2 cm). Phyllaries in 2 rows, woolly, sticky-glandular.

LEAVES: Alternate to opposite. Blades narrow to lance-shaped, ⅜–3 inches long (1–8 cm); edges entire or with lobes along midrib depending on variety; surfaces woolly-hairy.

HABITAT: Dry meadows, slopes; sagebrush to alpine. Elevation sea level (Canada) to 11,500 feet (3,500 m).

Blanket Flower

Gaillardia aristata, Aster Family, Asteraceae; Perennial herb

QUICK ID: Look for clumps of slender flower stems with a single flower head with showy yellow or red-and-yellow-tipped rays, and a reddish-brown disk.

RANGE: NR, MR, SR, Canada; widespread, common

STEM: Much-branched, 8–27 inches tall (20–70 cm).

FLOWERS: May–September. Single on stem tip; flower head 1½–3 inches wide (4–8 cm) with 12–18 rays, each ⅝–1⅜ inches long (15–35 mm) with 3 broad, deep lobes, occasionally tubular with 3 lobes; rays solid yellow to red-tipped, or red with yellow tips; disk reddish brown.

LEAVES: Basal, alternate on stem. Blades lance-shaped, 2–6 inches long (5–15 cm), edges lobed or toothed along prominent midrib; surfaces sparsely to densely hairy.

HABITAT: Dry grasslands, sagebrush, foothills montane forests. Elevation 1,000–9,000 feet (304–2,743 m).

SIMILAR SPECIES: The look-alike blanket flower, *G. pinnatifida*, (SR) occurs in scrublands and foothills.

Curlycup Gumweed

Grindelia squarrosa, Aster Family, Asteraceae; Biennial, perennial herb

QUICK ID: Look for green, gray, or red stems; blunt-toothed leaves; buds white with resin; flowers with yellow rays and disk; and phyllaries with long, curled tips. This widespread species has many variations.

RANGE: NR, MR, SR, Canada; widespread, common

STEM: Erect, branched, 1–3 feet tall (30–90 cm), hairless.

FLOWERS: July–September. Flower heads in open arrays. Heads have either 24–36 rays or none. Disk ⅜–¾ inch wide (8–20 mm), often white with resin. Phyllaries densely resinous, tips curved to hooked.

LEAVES: Alternate. Blade oblong to lance-shaped, ⅝–2¾ inches long (15–70 mm) at mid-stem, smaller upward; surfaces hairless, strongly gland-dotted, margins entire or with irregular, blunt, rounded teeth; middle and upper leaf bases mostly clasp the stem.

HABITAT: Disturbed areas, grasslands, sagebrush, foothills, montane forests. Elevation 2,000–8,000 feet (610–2,438 m).

Subalpine Gumweed

Grindelia subalpina, Aster Family, Asteraceae; Biennial, perennial herb

QUICK ID: Look for reddish stems, sharp-toothed leaves, buds white with resin, yellow flower heads, and phyllaries with long, curled tips.

RANGE: MR (WY), SR (CO); widespread, common

STEM: Erect, branched, 6–12 inches tall (15–30 cm), hairless.

FLOWERS: July–September. Open arrays on branch tips. Heads have 18–28 yellow rays, each ⅜–⅝ inch long (10–15 mm). Disk ⅜–¾ inch wide (9–20 mm), often white with resin. Phyllaries slightly resinous, tips curved, hooked, or straight.

LEAVES: Alternate. Blades lance-shaped to oblong or spatula-shaped, ⅝–3 inches long (15–76 mm), edges usually have widely separated sharp teeth; surfaces hairless, sparsely or densely gland-dotted.

HABITAT: Disturbed areas; plains, foothills, montane, subalpine forests. Elevation 5,250–9,515 feet (1,600–2,900 m).

Snakeweed, Broomweed

Gutierrezia sarothrae, Aster Family, Asteraceae; Perennial subshrub

QUICK ID: Look for densely branching, mounding plants; small bright-green leaves; and flower heads with tiny yellow rays and disk.

RANGE: NR, MR, SR, Canada; widespread, common

STEM: Rounded, branching, 1-2 feet tall (30-60 cm), woody, twiggy.

FLOWERS: July–November. Compact, flat-topped clusters of 2–5 small flower heads almost obscure the foliage. Heads have 3-8 ray flowers ⅛–¼ inch long (3–6 mm); disk yellow with 3-9 tiny disk flowers.

LEAVES: Alternate. Blades resinous, bright green, thread-like, 3⁄16–2¾ inches long (5–70 mm) by 1⁄16 inch wide (2 mm).

HABITAT: Dry, disturbed areas; grasslands, sagebrush, foothills, montane pine forests. Elevation 3,200–8,500 feet (975–2,590 m).

Autumn Sneezeweed

Helenium autumnale, Aster Family, Asteraceae, Perennial herb

QUICK ID: Look for branching stems, leaves that attach with winged stalks, and all-yellow flower heads with notched rays and domed disks.

RANGE: NR, MR, SR, Canada; locally common

STEM: Erect, single, angled, winged, upper branching, 2-4 feet tall (60-130 cm), minutely to densely hairy or not.

FLOWERS: July–October. Stem tips have arrays of up to 70 flower heads 1-2 inches wide (3-5 cm) with 8–20 rays, ⅜–1 inch long (1-3 cm), fan-shaped, narrow at the base and broad at the tip with 3 lobes; disk yellow, domed, ⅜–¾ inch wide (1-2 cm).

LEAVES: Basal wither by flowering. Alternate on stem, lower leaves with winged stalks, upper stalkless; blades 1½–6 inches long (4–15 cm), 3⁄16–1½ inches wide (5–40 mm), elliptic to lance-shaped; edges often shallowly toothed, surfaces hairless or nearly so.

HABITAT: Wetlands, riparian, sagebrush, foothills, montane forests. Elevation 1,180–8,530 feet (360–2,600 m).

Parry's Dwarf Sunflower

Helianthella parryi, Aster Family, Asteraceae; Perennial herb

QUICK ID: Look for nodding, all-yellow flower heads with showy rays and disk, and narrow phyllaries lined with shaggy white hairs.

RANGE: SR; widespread, common

STEM: Erect, 8–20 inches tall (20–50 cm), hairy.

FLOWERS: June–September. Usually 1 per stem, nodding or sideways pointing, 3 inches diameter (8 cm), with 8–14 yellow rays, 1 inch long (25 mm) with 2 grooves; disk ⅝–13⁄16 inch wide (15–20 mm). Phyllaries linear to lance-shaped in 3 equal, loose rows, surfaces hairless, margins hairy, tips pointed.

LEAVES: Mostly basal rosette; blades spatula- to lance-shaped, 2⅝–4 inches long (6–10 cm); margins have ciliate hairs, surfaces rough with a conspicuous center vein and 2–4 side veins. Stem leaves smaller, few, opposite (lower) to alternate (upper).

HABITAT: Meadows, open forests; foothills, montane, subalpine forests. Elevation 7,400–11,800 feet (2,255–3,600 m).

Five-nerve Sunflower

Helianthella quinquenervis, Aster Family, Asteraceae; Perennial herb

QUICK ID: Look for tall stems, leaves with 3–5 strong veins, and nodding flower heads with showy yellow rays and disk.

RANGE: NR: infrequent; MR, SR: widespread, common

STEM: Erect, 2–5 feet tall (60–152 cm), hairy.

FLOWERS: June–September. Usually single, slightly nodding flower heads 1–2 inches wide (3–5 cm) with 13–25 ray flowers, each 1–1½ inches long (3–4 cm), tips notched; phyllaries oval to lance-shaped, loose and spreading, margins lined with ciliate hairs.

LEAVES: Basal rosette; blades strongly 3–5 nerved, elliptic to lance-shaped with pointed tips, 4–12 inches long (10–30 cm), ⅜–1½-inches wide (1–4 cm), leathery; margins entire, surfaces roughly hairy to smooth. Stem leaves few, opposite (mostly), upper sometimes alternate, largest below mid-stem.

HABITAT: Mountain meadows, foothills, montane, subalpine forests. Elevation 4,600–11,810 feet (1,400–3,600 m).

One-flower Sunflower

Helianthella uniflora, Aster Family, Asteraceae; Perennial herb

QUICK ID: Look for tall clustered stems, no basal leaves, and single erect flower heads with showy yellow rays and disk.

RANGE: NR, MR, SR, Canada; widespread, common

STEM: Erect, branched at base, 16–40 inches tall (40–100 cm), hairy.

FLOWERS: May–September. Single, erect or sideways heads on stem end; 11–20 rays, each ¾–1¾ inches long (2–5 cm); phyllaries lance-linear, tips pointed, surfaces and edges stiff-hairy.

LEAVES: Basal soon wither. Stem leaves opposite, largest at mid-stem with short stalk; blades elliptic to lance-shaped, 5–10 inches long (12–25 cm) by 2 inches wide (5 cm), edges entire; surfaces rough-hairy, or not depending on variety.

HABITAT: Grasslands, sagebrush, foothills, montane and subalpine forests. Elevation 4,000–9,000 feet (1,220–2,743 m).

Common Sunflower

Helianthus annuus, Aster Family, Asteraceae; Annual herb

QUICK ID: Look for tall, robust stems; large, rough, heart-shaped leaves; and many yellow flower heads on upper branches.

RANGE: NR, MR, SR, Canada; widespread, common

STEM: Erect, thick, upper branching, 3–9 feet tall (1–3 m), hairy.

FLOWERS: May–October. Flower heads 2–4 inches wide (5–10 cm) with 10–30 or more rays, each 1–2 inches long (3–5 cm); disk yellow to reddish-brown. Phyllaries hairy, oval to elliptic (not slender or lance-shaped) with long, thin tips; edges lined with ciliate hairs.

LEAVES: Stem leaves on stalks to 8 inches long (20 cm). Lower leaves opposite, upper alternate. Blades oval to heart-shaped, to 12 inches long/wide (30 cm); edges coarsely toothed, surfaces hairy.

HABITAT: Dry soils, disturbed areas; grasslands, sagebrush, foothills, montane forests. Elevation 1,000–8,400 feet (305–2,560 m).

SIMILAR SPECIES: Prairie Sunflower, *H. petiolaris*, has lance-shaped phyllaries with rough hairs.

Nuttall's Sunflower

Helianthus nuttallii, Aster Family, Asteraceae; Perennial herb

QUICK ID: Look for colonies of tall, branching stems topped with showy flower heads with yellow rays and disk.

RANGE: NR, MR, SR: widespread, locally common; Canada: rare

STEM: Erect, branched above, 3–9 feet tall (1–3 m), hairy or not.

FLOWERS: June–September. Arrays on stem tips have 1–6 flower heads with 10–21 rays, each 1 inch long (3 cm). Phyllaries loose, spreading, lance-shaped, surfaces and edges sparsely hairy or not.

LEAVES: Mostly opposite (ssp. *rydbergii*), lance-shaped to egg-shaped, tips rounded to pointed. Mostly alternate (ssp. *nuttallii*), lance-shaped, tips tapering. Both have blades, 1½–8 inches long (4–20 cm); edges entire to shallowly serrated, bottom surface stiff-hairy.

HABITAT: Moist open places; wetlands, grasslands, foothills, montane meadows. Elevation ssp. *nuttallii*, below 3,280 feet (1,000 m); ssp. *rydbergii*, 3,940–8,860 feet (1,200–2,700 m).

Prairie Sunflower

Helianthus petiolaris, Aster Family, Asteraceae; Annual herb

QUICK ID: Look for robust, branching stems tipped with flower heads with yellow rays and a brown disk with a whitish "eye" in the center.

RANGE: NR, MR, SR, Canada; widespread, common

STEM: Erect, branched, 1–3 feet tall (30–90 cm).

FLOWERS: May–October. Flower heads 2–3 inches wide on stalks 1½–6 inches long (4–15 cm); 10–30 rays, ⅝–1 inch long (15–25 mm); disk reddish-purple, ⅜–1 inch diameter (10–25 mm), and often with a white spot of hairs in the center when young. Phyllaries lance-shaped (not oval), surfaces rough-hairy, edges hairless.

LEAVES: Mostly alternate on stalks ⅜–1½ inches long (1–4 cm), lower leaves have longest stalks. Blades lance-shaped to triangular, 1½–6 inches long (4–15 cm) by ⅜–3 inches wide (1–8 cm), edges entire to serrated, tips pointed to rounded. Leaves gray green and densely hairy to green with short hair.

HABITAT: Grasslands, sagebrush, pinyon-juniper foothills. Elevation 3,800–7,800 feet (1,160–2,377 m).

Little Sunflower

Helianthus pumilus, Aster Family, Asteraceae; Perennial herb

QUICK ID: Look for bushy plants with rough, ashy-green, opposite leaves and large, all-yellow flower heads.

RANGE: SR (absent NM); widespread, infrequent

STEM: Erect, branched from base, 1–3 feet tall (30–100 cm), with short-rough and long-white hairs.

FLOWERS: June–September. Flower heads are 1–2½ inches wide (3–6 cm) with 8–13 rays, each ⅝–¾ inch long (15–20 mm); disk yellow with dark anthers. Phyllaries loosely stacked, faces have short and longer white hairs, tips pointed to tapering.

LEAVES: Opposite with stalks ¼–1 inch long (4–25 mm). Blades lance- to egg-shaped, 1⅝–6 inches long (4–15 cm), 3 veins from base, base tapering; edges entire to serrated, surfaces rough-hairy, gland-dotted.

HABITAT: Dry soils, open areas; grasslands, foothills, montane forests. Elevation 4,000–9,000 feet (1,220–2,743).

Showy Goldeneye

Heliomeris multiflora, Aster Family, Asteraceae; Perennial herb

QUICK ID: Look for bushy, leafy clumps of reddish stems; masses of golden-yellow flower heads; often blankets large, open areas.

RANGE: NR, MR, SR; widespread, locally common

STEM: Erect, branching, 1–4 feet tall (30–120 cm), sparsely hairy.

FLOWERS: July–October. Plants have many flower heads 1–2 inches wide (3–5 cm) on stalks 6 inches long (15 cm); rays 5–14, oval to oblong, ¾ inch (20 mm) long, tips fade with age, leaving a brighter center "eye." Phyllaries narrowly lance-shaped, curled backwards, covered with kinky, woolly hair.

LEAVES: Mostly opposite. Blades up to 3½ inches long (9 cm), margins with tiny hairs for ¼ the length. Variety *multiflora* (all regions) has oval-to-lance-shaped blades 3⁄16–¾ inch wide (5–20 mm) with flat margins; var. *nevadensis* (SR) has linear blades ¼ inch wide (6 mm) .

HABITAT: Open areas, forest understory; foothills, montane, subalpine forests. Elevation 5,300–11,800 feet (1,615–3,600 m).

Rockyscree False Goldenaster

Heterotheca fulcrata, Aster Family, Asteraceae; Perennial herb

QUICK ID: Look for stems with short hairs, leaves with long edge hairs, clusters of all-yellow flowers with leafy bracts below the head.

RANGE: MR, SR; widespread, locally common

STEM: Multiple branching stems, 6–10 inches tall (15-25 cm), hairy.

FLOWERS: June–September. Arrays on branch ends have 7–15 flower heads with 11–21 rays, each ⅜–½ inch long (9–13 mm); disk yellow. Bracts leaf-like, lance-shaped, hairy, often overtop the head.

LEAVES: Alternate, stalkless. Blades oblong to elliptic, ¾–2 inches long (2–5 cm), mid-leaves broad and lined with long hairs; surfaces sparsely to densely covered with short, stiff hairs; edges entire, wavy to straight, tips pointed. The number of long hairs on the leaf edges and short, stiff hairs on the surfaces vary from sparse to dense.

HABITAT: Grasslands, sagebrush, foothills, montane, subalpine forests. Elevation 4,500–10,400 feet (1,370–3,170 m).

Hairy False Goldenaster

Heterotheca villosa, Aster Family, Asteraceae; Perennial herb

QUICK ID: Look for bushy clumps of hairy stems, hairy leaves, and flat-topped clusters of all-yellow flower heads.

RANGE: NR, MR, SR, Canada; widespread common

STEM: Erect to sprawling, multiple stems, clump forming 6–16 inches tall and wide (15–40 cm), sparsely to densely hairy.

FLOWERS: May–October. Dense arrays of 1–1½ inches wide (3–4 cm), lemon-yellow flower heads with 10–20 rays, ¼–½ inch long (6–12 mm); disk yellow. Phyllaries stacked in 4-5 rows, pointed and often reddish tipped; edges long-hairy, surfaces short-hairy.

LEAVES: Alternate; upper leaves stemless. Blades lance-shaped to oblong, ⅜–1 inch long (10–25 mm), bases rounded to tapering, tip blunt to pointed; surfaces gray-green, rough, hairy; margins flat with no teeth, lined with ciliate to flat-lying hairs.

HABITAT: Grasslands, sagebrush, foothills, montane, subalpine forests. Elevation 4,000–10,500 feet (1,220–3,200 m).

Scouler's Hawkweed

Hieracium scouleri, Aster Family, Asteraceae; Perennial herb

QUICK ID: Look for slender stems with branching arrays of small, yellow flower heads; rays have tiny teeth, sap milky. Flower, leaf, and stem hair density varies from sparse to thick.

RANGE: NR, MR, Canada; widespread, common

STEM: Erect, upper branching, 14–24 inches tall (35–60 cm), hairy.

FLOWERS: May–September. Slender branches have 9–25 compact heads, each with 20–45 linear rays tipped with tiny teeth; no disk florets. Phyllaries linear, tips tapering, surfaces with bristly black hairs.

LEAVES: Basal; blades lance-shaped to elliptic, narrowing at base, 2–6 inches long (5–15 cm); edges entire to toothed, surfaces hairy or smooth. Stem leaves few, alternate, upper smaller.

HABITAT: Open sites; grasslands, sagebrush, foothills, montane, subalpine forests. Elevation 2,000–9,850 feet (610–3,000 m).

SIMILAR SPECIES: Narrow-leaf Hawkweed, *H. umbellatum*, (NR, MR-scattered) has no basal leaves.

Alpine Gold Hulsea

Hulsea algida, Aster Family, Asteraceae; Perennial herb

QUICK ID: Look at high elevations for clumps of narrow, hairy basal leaves with 1–15 stems, each with 1 large, all-yellow flower head.

RANGE: NR, MR; uncommon

STEM: Erect, slender, 8–16 inches tall (20–40 cm), sparsely woolly.

FLOWERS: July–August. Stems have 1 flower head, 1–2 inches wide (3–5 cm), with 25–60 narrow, yellow rays, each ⅜ inch long (1 cm), pointed; disk yellow. Phyllaries in 2–4 rows, narrowly oblong, woolly, shaggy-hairy, tips long, tapering.

LEAVES: Mostly basal rosette. Blades narrow, linear, 2–4⅜ inches long (5–11 cm); edges wavy, upturned, lobed or coarsely toothed; surfaces with long to short, sticky, glandular hairs. Stem leaves few, alternate, smaller.

HABITAT: Rocky outcrops, talus; upper subalpine forests to alpine. Elevation 8,500–13,000 feet (2,590–3,962 m).

Fineleaf Woollywhite

Hymenopappus filifolius, Aster Family, Asteraceae; Perennial herb

QUICK ID: Look for rosettes of thread-like leaves, multiple branching stems, and flower heads with a yellow disk but no petal-like rays.

RANGE: NR, MR, SR, Canada; widespread, common

STEM: Erect, multiple from root crown, 2–5 feet tall (60–150 cm), densely woolly near base.

FLOWERS: May–August. Loose arrays on branch tips; flower heads have a compact disk to ⅜ inch diameter (15 mm) with 10–50 yellow, tubular disk flowers with curled tips; no ray flowers.

LEAVES: Basal rosette. Blades 1–8 inches long (3–20 cm), divided into narrow, thread-like segments; surfaces smooth or woolly near base. Stem leaves alternate, up to 10, greatly reduced, widely spaced.

HABITAT: Coarse soils, disturbed areas; sagebrush, foothills, montane forests. Elevation 3,700–8,500 feet (1,128–2,590 m).

SIMILAR SPECIES: Yellow Plainsman, *H. flavescens*, (SR) has a single branching stem, many leaves, and 15–100 flower heads.

Brandegee's Four-nerve Daisy

Hymenoxys brandegeei, Aster Family, Asteraceae; Perennial herb

QUICK ID: Look in alpine regions for basal rosettes with unlobed leaves and woolly stems with a single large head with yellow-orange rays and disk.

RANGE: SR; widespread, locally common

STEM: Erect, 3–9 ½ inches tall (8–24 cm), dense tangled hairs.

FLOWERS: June–September. Heads to 1½ inches wide (4 cm), borne singly with 14–23 rays, each ½–1 inch long (1–3 cm), tips with 3 rounded notches. Phyllaries covered with dense, tangled, white hairs, in 2–3 rows, inner rows have tapering tips.

LEAVES: Basal rosette. Blades linear, narrow, 2–4 inches long (5–10 cm); entire, or some with 3–7 lobes, surfaces smooth or sparse to dense with long, white hairs. Stem leaves alternate, much smaller.

HABITAT: Subalpine meadows, alpine ridges, tundra. Elevation 9,190–13,450 feet (2,800–4,100 m).

Old Man of the Mountain

Hymenoxys grandiflora, Aster Family, Asteraceae; Perennial herb

QUICK ID: Look in alpine regions for basal rosettes with lobed leaves, woolly stems with a single head 2 inches wide (5 cm) with yellow rays and disk.

RANGE: NR, MR, SR; widespread, common

STEM: Erect, unbranched, 3-12 inches tall (8-30 cm), densely woolly.

FLOWERS: June–September. 1-10 flower stems per plant. Heads have 15-50 rays, ⅝-1⅜ inches long (15-35 mm), notched with 3 rounded tips. Phyllaries in 2-3 rows, covered with dense, tangled, white hairs. Plants grow for 12-15 years before flowering and dying.

LEAVES: Basal rosette; blades ¾-4¾ inches long (2-12 cm) with 3-7 linear lobes, surfaces smooth to woolly. Stem leaves alternate, smaller, lobed or not.

HABITAT: Meadows, rocky slopes; subalpine, alpine zones. Elevation 10,200–13,000 feet (3,100-3,965 m).

SIMILAR SPECIES: Brandegee's Four-nerve Daisy, *H. brandegeei*, (alpine zone SR) has unlobed basal leaves.

Orange Sneezeweed

Hymenoxys hoopesii, Aster Family, Asteraceae; Perennial herb

QUICK ID: Look in upper elevations for stout stems with large, unlobed leaves; yellow-orange flower heads with long, often drooping, slender rays; and a domed disk.

RANGE: NR: infrequent; MR, SR: widespread, common

STEM: Erect, upper branching, 2-3½ feet tall (60-106 cm).

FLOWERS: July–September. Plants have up to 12 flower heads on 1-4 stems; 14-26 rays, each ⅞-1¾ inches long (2-5 cm), drooping with age, tips with 3-4 shallow points; disk domes with age. Pointed green phyllaries often visible between the spaced rays.

LEAVES: Basal; blades linear to lance-shaped, to 12 inches long (30 cm), ⅜-2 inches wide (1-5 cm), clasping; edges entire, surfaces smooth to hairy. Stem blades alternate, similar, smaller upward.

HABITAT: Moist meadows, stream banks; montane, subalpine forests. Elevation 7,500-12,000 feet (2,286-3,600 m).

Colorado (Pingue) Rubberweed

Hymenoxys richardsonii, Aster Family, Asteraceae; Perennial herb

QUICK ID: Look for erect, dense clumps with filament-like leaves, and yellow flower heads with rays with three lobes on the tip.

RANGE: NR, MR, SR, Canada; widespread, common

STEM: Erect, upper branching, 4–12 inches tall (10–30 cm).

FLOWERS: May–October. Stems have 1–5 flower heads with 7–10 yellow rays, each ¼–½ inch long (7–11 mm), evenly spaced, not overlapping, slightly drooping, tipped with 3 rounded lobes; disk yellow. Phyllaries in 2 unequal rows, the inner longer with pointed tips.

LEAVES: Basal leaves have tufts of long, white hairs in the axils. Stem leaves alternate, to 6 inches long (15 cm), forked with 3–7 slender segments about 1⁄16 inch wide (2 mm), smooth to sparsely hairy.

HABITAT: Coarse soils, open areas; grasslands, sagebrush, foothills, montane forests. Elevation 5,500–10,700 feet (1,675–3,260 m).

Prickly Lettuce

Lactuca serriola, Aster Family, Asteraceae; Annual herb; introduced, naturalized

QUICK ID: Look for tall, leafy stems with milky sap, and clusters with dozens of small flower heads with yellow rays with teeth on tips.

RANGE: NR, MR, SR, Canada; widespread, common

STEM: Erect, branched above, 2–7 feet tall (0.6–2 m), smooth, sap milky.

FLOWERS: July–September. Spreading clusters along stem often have more than 100 flower heads; heads ⅜ inch wide (10 mm) with 12–20 rays, tips squared with 5 small teeth; no disk florets.

LEAVES: Alternate, stalkless, on lower ¾ of stem. Blade outline oblong to lance-shaped, 2–12 inches long (5–30 cm) by 4 inches wide (10 cm); entire or deeply lobed along midrib; surfaces smooth, edges lined with fine prickles; underside of midrib lined with prickles. Blades usually twist at base to point upward.

HABITAT: Waste places, disturbed areas; riparian, sagebrush, foothills, montane. Elevation 5,300–8,700 feet (1,600–2,700 m).

Mountain Tarweed

Madia glomerata, Aster Family, Asteraceae; Annual herb

QUICK ID: Look for slender stems with narrow leaves, all coated with smelly glandular hairs, and terminal clusters of small yellow flowers.

RANGE: NR, MR, SR, Canada; scattered, infrequent

STEM: Erect, branching, 4–24 inches tall (10–60 cm), glandular-hairy.

FLOWERS: June–September. Clusters dense, rounded arrays with small yellow flower heads; 1-3 rays, ⅛ inch long (3 mm), yellow to purplish, tipped with 3 lobes.

LEAVES: Opposite near base, alternate above. Blades linear to narrowly lance-shaped ¾-4 inches long (2–10 cm) to ¼ inch wide (6 mm), glandular, stiff-hairy.

HABITAT: Disturbed areas, roadsides; grasslands, sagebrush, foothills, montane forests. Elevation 4,000–10,000 feet (1,220–3,048 m).

Prairie False Dandelion

Nothocalais cuspidata, Aster Family, Asteraceae; Perennial herb

QUICK ID: Look in grasslands for rosettes of narrow leaves with wavy, white-fuzzy edges and flower heads packed with narrow, yellow rays with tiny teeth.

RANGE: NR: infrequent; SR (absent NM): widespread, common

STEM: Erect, leafless, 2–12 inches tall (5–30 cm), woolly near top.

FLOWERS: April–September. Solitary flower heads 1–2 inches across (3–5 cm) with 13–80 ray florets, narrow with 5 teeth on tip; no disk florets. Phyllaries in 2 overlapping rows, hairless, often red striped or dotted, tips pointed.

LEAVES: Basal. Blades narrow, linear, 3-12 inches long (7–30 cm); edges wavy, lined with fuzzy, white hairs.

HABITAT: Dry, coarse soils; grasslands, sagebrush, foothills. Elevation 985-7,500 feet (300–2,300 m).

SIMILAR SPECIES: The look-alike Sagebrush False Dandelion, *N. troximoides*, is more common in the NR.

Parry's Goldenrod

Oreochrysum parryi, Aster Family, Asteraceae; Perennial herb

QUICK ID: Look for hairy stems with clusters of 3-6 flower heads with yellow rays and disk; note the leaf-like bracts below the heads.

RANGE: MR, SR; widespread, common

STEM: Erect, leafy, base often purplish, 4–24 inches tall (10–60 cm).

FLOWERS: July–September. Flower heads 1 inch wide (3 cm) with 12–20 narrow, yellow ray florets not tightly crowded around the yellow disk; hair-like pappus around each floret is bristle-like; phyllaries in 3–4 unequal rows, tips green, pointed, curled back, hairy or not.

LEAVES: Basal on stalks, blades spatula-shaped to elliptic. Stem leaves alternate, elliptic, upper leaves clasping, 2⅜–6 inches long (6–15 cm); edges entire, surfaces smooth to scratchy, tips pointed.

HABITAT: Meadows, open woods, roadsides; montane, subalpine forests, alpine tundra. Elevation 7,000–12,800 feet (2,134–3,658 m).

SIMILAR SPECIES: Goldenrods, *Solidago* species, have crowded flower heads, tiny rays, and no leafy bracts.

Woolly Groundsel

Packera cana, Aster Family, Asteraceae; Perennial herb

QUICK ID: Look for basal rosettes with slender stems and flat-topped arrays of heads with yellow rays and disk; white woolly throughout.

RANGE: NR, MR, SR, Canada; widespread, common

STEM: Erect, branching, 4–12 inches tall (10–30 cm), woolly-hairy.

FLOWERS: May–August. Clusters have 8–15 flower heads ¾–1 inch wide (2–3 cm), each with 8–10 (or 13) rays; disk florets yellow; phyllaries 13 or 21, equally long, in single row, green, densely to sparsely hairy.

LEAVES: Basal, long-stalked; blades elliptic to lance-shaped, 1–2 inches long (25–50 mm), bases taper; edges entire to irregularly lobed, bottom woolly, top less so. Stem leaves alternate, similar, smaller upward.

HABITAT: Open plains, rocky slopes, meadows; all elevations grasslands to alpine.

SIMILAR SPECIES: Hoary Groundsel, *P. werneriifolia*, in alpine zones, usually has 1–2 flower heads per leafless stem.

Splitleaf Groundsel

Packera dimorphophylla, Aster Family, Asteraceae; Perennial herb

QUICK ID: Look for rounded, stalked basal leaves; hairless stems; clusters of flower heads with short, deep yellow rays and disk.

RANGE: NR (infrequent), MR, SR; widespread, common

STEM: Erect, usually single, 4–12 inches tall (10–30 cm), hairless.

FLOWERS: May–September. Tight clusters on stem tips have 1–6 flower heads, each with 8–13 rays, ¼ inch long (8 mm), yellow to orangish, disk yellow; phyllaries 13 or 21, equally long, in single row, green with green-to-dark tips, hairless.

LEAVES: Basal, stalked; blades thick, oval to spatula-shaped, ⅜–2 inches long/wide (1–5 cm); edges entire to shallowly toothed. Lower and mid-stem leaves large, stalkless to clasping or with tiny ear-like lobes, usually irregularly lobed; upper leaves small.

HABITAT: Coarse soils, moist meadows, seeps; subalpine forests, alpine. Elevation 7,000–13,000 feet (2,134–3,962 m).

Notchleaf Groundsel

Packera fenderi, Aster Family, Asteraceae; Perennial herb

QUICK ID: Look for leaves cut into even lobes, clusters of yellow flower heads, foliage densely covered with cobweb-woolly hair.

RANGE: SR; widespread, common

STEM: Erect, usually single, leafy, 4–16 inches tall (10–40 cm), hairy.

FLOWERS: June–September. Flat-topped clusters have 6–25 flower heads with 6–8 rays, each about ¼ inch long (7 mm), disk florets yellow; phyllaries 13, equally long, green, in one row, woolly.

LEAVES: Basal, alternate on stem. Blades lance-shaped, 1–3½-inches long (30–90 mm); edges cut evenly with lobes to the midrib, surfaces woolly. Lower stem leaves stalked, upper leaves smaller with no stalks. Note the basal leaf axils are not woolly.

HABITAT: Forest openings, disturbed areas; foothills, montane, subalpine forests. Elevation 6,000–11,800 feet (1,828–3,600 m).

SIMILAR SPECIES: Lobeleaf Groundsel, *P. multilobata*, (MR, SR) has multiple stems, 8–13 rays.

Lobeleaf Groundsel

Packera multilobata, Aster Family, Asteraceae; Perennial, biennial herb

QUICK ID: Look for single to clustered, branching stems; deeply lobed, hairless leaves; and flat-topped clusters of yellow flower heads.

RANGE: MR, SR; widespread, common

STEM: Erect, 1–5, branched, leafy, 8–16 inches tall (20–40 cm), hairless.

FLOWERS: May–August. Umbrella-like clusters have 10–30 flower heads, each with 8–13 yellow rays, ¼–⅜ inch long (7–10 mm), disk yellow; phyllaries 13–21, hairless, tips often yellow, red, or purplish.

LEAVES: Basal, stalked; blades oval to spatula-shaped, 1½–4 inches long (4–10 cm), deeply cut into angular, tooth-like lobes; surfaces hairless or nearly so. Stem leaves alternate, stalkless, similar, smaller upwards. Basal leaves have woolly hairs in the axils.

HABITAT: Coarse soils, open areas; sagebrush, foothills, montane, subalpine meadows. Elevation 5,000–11,000 feet (1,524–3,300 m).

SIMILAR SPECIES: Notchleaf Groundsel, *P. fendleri*, (SR) generally has single stems, woolly-hairy foliage, and 6–8 ray flowers.

New Mexico Groundsel

Packera neomexicana, Aster Family, Asteraceae; Perennial herb

QUICK ID: Look for narrow basal leaves, 1–3 stems with few leaves, and flat-topped arrays of yellow flower heads.

RANGE: SR; widespread, common

STEM: Erect, 8–20 inches tall (20–50 cm); foliage woolly-hairy to nearly hairless throughout.

FLOWERS: April–July. Open clusters have 3–20 flower heads, each with 8–13 yellow ray flowers to ⅜ inch long (10 mm); disk yellow; phyllaries 13 or 21 equally long, in 1 row, woolly to hairless.

LEAVES: Basal, long stalked; blades oval to lance-shaped, ¾–2⅜ inches long (2–6 cm); edges entire, toothed, or lobed; surfaces woolly, less so with age. Stem leaves alternate, similar, smaller up the stem.

HABITAT: Coarse soils, openings areas; pinyon-juniper foothills, ponderosa forests. Elevation 5,500–10,000 feet (1,676–3,048 m).

Balsam Groundsel

Packera paupercula, Aster Family, Asteraceae; Perennial herb

QUICK ID: Look for nearly hairless leaves and stems and flat-toped clusters with yellow flower heads with pale-yellow rays and disk; features highly variable across range.

RANGE: NR, MR, SR, Canada; widespread, common

STEM: Erect, usually solitary, weakly branched, 8–18 inches tall (20–45 cm), smooth to hairy near base.

FLOWERS: May–August. Loose clusters have 2–10 flower heads, ½–1 inch wide (1–3 cm), with 8–13 rays to ⅜ inch long (10 mm); phyllaries 13 or 21, green to purple-tipped, smooth, in 1 row.

LEAVES: Mostly basal, stalked; blades lance-shaped to narrowly elliptic, 1–2⅜ inches long (3–6 cm) by ⅜–¾ inch wide (1–2 cm); edges entire to coarsely toothed or serrated; surfaces hairless or nearly so. Stem leaves 2–4, alternate, not stalked, deeply toothed, much smaller up the stem.

HABITAT: Wet meadows, open woods; grasslands, sagebrush, foothills, montane forests. Elevation 500–7,050 feet (150–2,105 m).

Falsegold Groundsel

Packera pseudaurea, Aster Family, Asteraceae; Perennial herb

QUICK ID: Look for long-stalked, toothed basal leaves, and dense, flat-topped clusters of yellow flower heads; hairless throughout.

RANGE: NR, MR, SR, Canada; widespread, common

STEM: Erect, single or sometimes clustered, 8–28 inches tall (20–70 cm), smooth to slightly hairy near base.

FLOWERS: May–September. Tight clusters have 5–12 (SR) or 12–20 (NR) flower heads, each with 8 or 13 rays to ⅜ inch long (10 mm); 13 or 21 phyllaries, equally long, in 1 row, green, hairless.

LEAVES: Mostly basal, long-stalked equaling blade length; blades oval to broadly lance-shaped, ¾–3 inches long (2–8 cm); base rounded, edges sharp- to blunt-toothed. Lower stem leaves alternate, stalked, pinnately lobed; upper leaves stalkless.

HABITAT: Moist meadows, woodlands, wetlands; grasslands to subalpine forests. Elevation 5,900–8,860 feet (1,800–2,700 m).

Rocky Mountain Groundsel

Packera streptanthifolia, Aster Family, Asteraceae; Perennial herb

QUICK ID: Look for thick, long-stalked basal leaves; flat-topped arrays of yellow flower heads on hairy to hairless stalks.

RANGE: NR, MR, SR, Canada; widespread, common

STEM: Erect, single or clustered, 4–24 inches tall (10–60 cm), hairless or sparsely hairy near base.

FLOWERS: May–August. Loose arrays have 3–20 flower heads with 8 or 13 yellow rays 3⁄16–½ inch long (5–12 mm); phyllaries 13 or 21, green, in 1 row, hairless, tips sometimes reddish.

LEAVES: Basal, thick, long-stalked to 8 inches long (20 cm); blades oval to elliptic, ¾–1½-inches long (2–4 cm); edges entire, with rounded teeth, or lobed, surfaces hairless. Stem leaves alternate, few, stemless, smaller up the stem; edges entire to coarsely lobed.

HABITAT: Dry meadows, woodlands; foothills, montane, subalpine forests, alpine. Elevation 5,800–11,000 feet (1,768–3,352 m).

SIMILAR SPECIES: Wooton's Ragwort, *Senecio wootonii*, (SR) has thick basal leaves that sheath the stem.

Hoary Groundsel

Packera werneriifolia, Aster Family, Asteraceae; Perennial herb

QUICK ID: Look for compact rosettes with densely woolly leaves, usually 1 short leafless stem, and clusters of yellow flower heads.

RANGE: NR, MR, SR; scattered to widespread

STEM: Erect, 1 or 2–5 clustered, 5–12 inches tall (5–30 cm), woolly.

FLOWERS: June–September. Clusters of 1–8 bell-shaped flower heads with 8–13 yellow rays, 3⁄16–⅜ inch long (4–10 mm); 13 or 21 phyllaries, equally long, in 1 row, red tipped, usually hairy; conspicuous tiny, reddish bractlets underneath flower head.

LEAVES: Basal rosette, stalked and stalkless; blades narrowly lance-shaped to elliptic with a tapering base, or oval in timberline populations, ⅝–1⅝ inches long (15–40 mm); edges entire, wavy, or finely-toothed near tip. Stem has only scale-like leaves.

HABITAT: Open woods, talus slopes above treeline; foothills, montane, subalpine forests, alpine. Elevation 7,000–12,500 feet (2,133–3,810 m).

Mountain Taperleaf

Pericome caudata, Aster Family, Asteraceae; Deciduous shrub

QUICK ID: Look for a midsize scrub with yellow, tassel-like flower heads and triangular leaves with tapering tips as long as the blade.

RANGE: SR; widespread, common

STEM: Multi-branched, rounded, leafy, 5 feet tall/ wide (1.5 m).

FLOWERS: July–October. Dense clusters have up to 30 small yellow flower heads with disk flowers only; phyllaries beneath the florets are ribbed, in a single row, and hairy.

LEAVES: Opposite, stalk to 1¾ inches long (5 cm), blades to 6 inches long/wide (15 cm), triangular, tip tapering.

HABITAT: Dry rocky soils, talus slopes, cliffs, canyons; foothills, montane forests. Elevation 5,500–10,000 feet (1,676–3,048 m).

Curlyhead Goldenweed

Pyrrocoma crocea, Aster Family, Asteraceae; Perennial herb

QUICK ID: Look for thick stems with leathery leaves, slender yellow-orange ray flowers, loose rows of green phyllaries beneath the head.

RANGE: SR; widespread, common

STEM: Erect, unbranched, 12–30 inches tall (30–80 cm), reddish.

FLOWERS: July–October. Usually one head per stem, 2–3 inches wide (5–8 cm) with bright orange to bright yellow, 30–90 rays, each ½–1 ¼ inches long (12–30 mm); disk colored as rays; phyllaries oblong, in 2–3 rows in a loose stack, green often with reddish edges.

LEAVES: Basal, stalked; blades lance- or spatula-shaped to elliptic, 4–18 inches long (10–45 cm) by ¾–2⅜ inch wide (2–6 cm); edges entire, surfaces usually hairless. Stem leaves alternate, stalkless, clasping, lance-shaped, to ½ inch long (12 mm).

HABITAT: Moist meadows, open woods; foothills, montane, subalpine forests. Elevation 6,200–10,800 feet (1,890–3,200 m).

Prairie Coneflower

Ratibida columnifera, Aster Family, Asteraceae; Perennial herb

QUICK ID: Look for dense, rounded clumps of tall, slender stems topped with showy flower heads with drooping yellow-to-maroon rays around a brown, cylindrical disk.

RANGE: NR, MR, SR, Canada; widespread, common

STEM: Erect, 8–40 inches tall (20–100 cm), short-hairy.

FLOWERS: April–October. Solitary on long stalks; 4–12 rays, each ¼–1⅜ inches long (7–35 mm), yellow, maroon, to bicolored; disk brown, columnar, ½–2 inches tall (1–5 cm).

LEAVES: Basal, often wither by flowering. Stem leaves alternate, mostly on lower stem; blade compound, 2–4 inches long (5–10 cm); cut into long, narrow, opposite lobes; surfaces rough-hairy.

HABITAT: Dry to moist, coarse soils, disturbed areas; grasslands, foothills, montane forests. Elevation 4,000–9,000 feet (1,220–2,743 m).

SIMILAR SPECIES: Blackeyed Susan, *Rudbeckia hirta,* has yellow rays and a dome-shaped (not cylindrical) central disk.

Blackeyed Susan

Rudbeckia hirta, Aster Family, Asteraceae; Perennial, biennial herb

QUICK ID: Look for clumps of slender hairy stems, rough leaves, and large flower heads with yellow rays and brown disk.

RANGE: SR; widespread, common; infrequent elsewhere

STEM: Erect, upper branching, 1–3½ feet tall (30–100 cm), hairy.

FLOWERS: April–July. Flower heads bloom on 2–7¾ inch long (5–20 cm) hairy stalks; 8–16, spreading (not drooping), petal-like rays reach 1 inch long (25 mm) with strong veins, base may be reddish, tips slightly notched; domed, dark-brown central disk, ½–¾ inch wide (12–20 mm), forms "Susan's" eye.

LEAVES: Basal, long stalked. Blades 2–4 inches long (5–10 cm), lance-shaped to oval; surfaces with short, stiff hairs, edges entire to serrated. Stem leaves alternate, linear to spatula shaped.

HABITAT: Open woods, meadows, disturbed areas; grasslands to subalpine forests. Elevation 6,800–10,800 feet (2,072–3,292 m).

Cutleaf Coneflower

Rudbeckia laciniata, Aster Family, Asteraceae; Perennial herb

QUICK ID: Look for robust stems, large, pinnate leaves, showy flower heads with drooping yellow rays and yellow-to-greenish disks.

RANGE: NR, MR, SR: widespread, common; Canada: rare, introduced

STEM: Erect, branching, 2–7 feet tall (0.6–2 m), hairless, colonial.

FLOWERS: June–September. Loose arrays of flower heads have 8–12 yellow ray flowers, each ½–¾ inch long (15–20 mm), usually drooping; disk a protruding dome. Phyllaries oval to lance-shaped, often unequal in length, hairless to sparsely hairy.

LEAVES: Basal often wither by flowering. Stem leaves alternate, blades oval to lance-shaped, 4–12 inches long (10–30 cm), divided into 3–7 lobes, which may be divided again; leaves smaller upwards; edges entire or toothed, surfaces hairy or not.

HABITAT: Stream sides, meadows, open woods; montane, subalpine forests. Elevation 5,200–10,200 feet (1,583–3,109 m).

Badlands Mule's Ears

Scabrethia scabra, Aster Family, Asteraceae; Perennial herb

QUICK ID: Look for large, dense clumps with scratchy leaves and dozens of hairy, erect stems tipped with showy, yellow flower heads.

RANGE: MR, SR (CO Plateau); widespread, common

STEM: Erect, clump forming, 8–24 inches tall (20–60 cm).

FLOWERS: May–August. Flower heads 3–4 inches wide with 10–23 rays, each ⅝–2 inches long (15–50 mm); disk yellow turning brownish. Phyllaries in 3–4 rows beneath the florets, narrow, well separated, spreading, to 1 inch long (25 mm).

LEAVES: Basal and alternate stem leaves similar size. Blades stalkless (sessile), narrowly oblong to linear, 3–8 inches long (8–20 cm) to ¾ inch wide (20 mm); edges entire, surfaces rough-hairy with a prominent white midrib.

HABITAT: High desert, badlands; sagebrush, pinyon-juniper woodlands. Elevation 1,000–7,600 feet (304–2,133 m).

Showy Alpine Ragwort

Senecio amplectens, Aster Family, Asteraceae; Perennial herb

QUICK ID: Look for stalks with nodding buds and flowers, heads with yellow rays and disk, and purple or green phyllaries with tapered tips.

RANGE: MR, SR; widespread, common

STEM: Erect, single to loosely clustered, 4–24 inches tall (10–60 cm), smooth to sparsely hairy.

FLOWERS: July–August. Arrays on stem tips have 1-5 flower heads, nodding in bud and flower; 13 showy rays, each ⅝–½ inch long (15–25 mm), tips pointed, disk yellow. Phyllaries 13 or 21 in 1 row, equally long, green or black to purple, tips tapered, hairiness varies.

LEAVES: Basal, stalked, often clasping; blades broadly lance-shaped, 4–8 inches long (10–20 cm); bases tapered, edges toothed. Stem leaves alternate, surfaces smooth to sparsely hairy. Leaves mostly lower half of stem, basal withered by flowering (var. *amplectens*); leaves mostly basal and on lower half of stem (var. *holmii*).

HABITAT: Damp soil; upper subalpine forests (var. *amplectens*), alpine (var. *holmii*). Elevation 9,878–13,780 feet (2,900–4,200 m).

Tall Blacktip Ragwort

Senecio atratus, Aster Family, Asteraceae; Perennial herb

QUICK ID: Look for clumps of tall stems, broad whitish-hairy leaves, and clusters of yellow flower heads with black-tipped phyllaries.

RANGE: MR, SR; widespread, common

STEM: Erect, clumped, 14–28 inches (35–70 cm), hairy, colony forming.

FLOWERS: July–September. Elongated to rounded clusters have 20–60 heads, each with 3–5 rays, ¼–⅜ inch long (5–8 mm); disk yellow, phyllaries 5 or 8 in 1 row, equally long, tips pointed, black.

LEAVES: Basal, stalked, erect; blades oblong to egg-shaped, 4–12 inches long (10–30 cm) by ¾–1½ inches wide (2–4 cm); bases tapered, edges small-toothed, surfaces cobwebby-hairy; Stem leaves alternate, smaller, stalkless.

HABITAT: Meadows, roadsides, disturbed areas; subalpine forests, alpine. Elevation 9,000–12,800 feet (2,743–3,900 m).

Nodding Ragwort

Senecio bigelovii, Aster Family, Asteraceae; Perennial herb

QUICK ID: Look for single stems with clasping upper leaves; nodding flower heads with no rays; a yellow disk; and yellow, green, or dark-purple phyllaries.

RANGE: SR; widespread, common

STEM: Erect, single to multiple, 15–40 inches tall (40–100 cm), long-hairy to smooth.

FLOWERS: July–September. Branching arrays along upper stem have 3–12 nodding flower heads with no rays; disk yellow; phyllaries in 1 row, equally long, pointed, 13 or 21 depending on variety.

LEAVES: Basal, stalked. Blades lance-shaped to oval, 2¾–6 inches long (7–15 cm); edges entire to toothed, surfaces smooth to woolly. Stem leaves alternate, smaller upward, stemless, often clasping.

HABITAT: Meadows, slopes, open sites; foothills, montane, subalpine forests. Elevation 6,000–11,500 feet (1,828–3,505 m).

Thickleaf Groundsel

Senecio crassulus, Aster Family, Asteraceae; Perennial herb

QUICK ID: Look for basal clusters of thick, sharp-toothed, hairless leaves; flower stalks with showy flower heads with yellow rays and disk.

RANGE: NR, MR, SR; widespread, common

STEM: Erect, 6–28 inches tall (15–70 cm), hairless, rhizomatous.

FLOWERS: July–September. Open arrays have 4–12 flower heads with 8 or 13 rays, each ¼–½ inch long (5–12 mm); 13 or 21 phyllaries in 1 row, equally long, green, tips black, pointed.

LEAVES: Basal, stalked, thick; blades broadly lance-shaped to elliptic 1–6 inches long (3–15 cm); bases tapered, edges sharp-toothed to nearly entire, surfaces smooth. Stem leaves alternate, smaller, stalkless.

HABITAT: Meadows, hillsides, talus ridges, open sites; subalpine forests, alpine. Elevation 9,185–12,300 feet (2,200–3,750 m).

Desert Ragwort

Senecio eremophilus, Aster Family, Asteraceae; Perennial herb

QUICK ID: Look for leafy stems, no basal leaves at flowering, leaves deeply cut into lobes along midrib, and clusters of yellow flower heads.

RANGE: NR, MR, SR, Canada: widespread, common

STEM: Erect, branching, 12–40-inches tall (30–100 cm), hairless, often reddish.

FLOWERS: July–September. Large terminal arrays have 10–60 flower heads, each with 8 narrow yellow rays, a yellow disk, and 13 black-tipped phyllaries.

LEAVES: Basal and lower stem leaves wither by blooming. Stem leaves alternate, even-sized upward. Blades lance-shaped to oval, 2⅜–4¾ inches long (6-12 cm) by ⅝–2 inches wide (15–50 mm), margins with irregularly shaped lobes incised to the midrib; hairless.

HABITAT: Damp habitats, disturbed areas; foothills, montane, subalpine forests. Elevation 6,500–12,140 feet (1,980–3,700 m).

SIMILAR SPECIES: Notchleaf Groundsel, *Packera fendleri*, (SR) is hairy; leaves get smaller up the stem and have even-sized lobes.

Lamb's Tongue Ragwort

Senecio integerrimus, Aster Family, Asteraceae; Perennial herb

QUICK ID: Look for single, tall stems, unlobed leaves gradually smaller upward, and flattish-topped clusters of yellow flower heads.

RANGE: NR, MR, CR, Canada; widespread, common; has 4 varieties

STEM: Erect, single, 8–28 inches tall (20–70 cm); woolly, cobwebby, or smooth depending on variety.

FLOWERS: April–August. Dense arrays have 6–20 flower heads, each with 5–8 or 13 rays, ¼–⅝ inch long (6–15 mm), disk yellow; 13 or 21 phyllaries, equally long in 1 row, tips green to strongly or minutely black.

LEAVES: Basal, nearly stalkless, upright; blades elliptic to lance-shaped, 2–10 inches long (6–25 cm) by ¾–4 inches wide (1–6 cm); edges entire to toothed, surfaces smooth, woolly, or cobwebby depending on variety. Stem leaves alternate, smaller upward clasping.

HABITAT: Moist to dry meadows, hills, open woods; grasslands to upper subalpine forests. Elevation 3,000–11,000 feet (915–3,352 m).

Tall Ragwort

Senecio serra, Aster Family, Asteraceae; Perennial herb

QUICK ID: Look in moist sites for tall, hairless stems with long, serrated leaves and large clusters of showy yellow flower heads.

RANGE: NR, MR, SR; widespread, common

STEM: Erect, single or clustered, branching, 16–40 inches tall (40–100 cm), hairless.

FLOWERS: June–August. Flat-topped clusters have 30–90 flower heads, each with 5 or 8 rays, ¼–⅜ inch long (5–10 mm), disk yellow; phyllaries 8 or 13 equally long in 1 row, green, sometimes black tipped.

LEAVES: Basal often wither by blooming. Stem leaves alternate, lance-shaped to linear, 2–6 inches long (5–15 cm); base tapered, edges finely serrated. Leaves evenly spaced on stem; upper leaves smaller.

HABITAT: Moist meadows, stream banks, open woods; foothills to subalpine forests, alpine. Elevation 6,000–11,500 feet (1,000–3,200 m).

Broom-like Ragwort

Senecio spartioides, Aster Family, Asteraceae; Perennial herb

QUICK ID: Look for arching stems forming a bushy subshrub with thread-like leaves and loose clusters of yellow flower heads.

RANGE: MR, SR; widespread, common

STEM: Upright, multiple from base, freely branching, 8–48 inches tall (20–120 cm), hairless.

FLOWERS: June–October. Flat-topped to rounded arrays have 10–20 flower heads per stem; 5 ray flowers, ½ inch long (12 mm), disk yellow; 8 phyllaries in 1 row, even-sized, tips green or minutely black.

LEAVES: Alternate, same size, evenly distributed along stem. Blades linear to thread-like 2–4 inches long (5–10 cm) with lobes to ¼ inch wide (6 mm); surfaces green, hairless.

HABITAT: Coarse, dry soils, open sites, disturbed areas; grasslands, sagebrush, pinyon-juniper foothills, montane forests. Elevation 3,500–11,500 feet (1,066–3,500 m).

SIMILAR SPECIES: Riddell's Groundsel, *S. riddellii,* (SR) is hairless and usually has 13 phyllaries and 8 rays.

Arrowleaf Ragwort

Senecio triangularis, Aster Family, Asteraceae; Perennial herb

QUICK ID: Look for bushy, hairless stems; arrow-shaped, evenly spaced, toothed leaves; and showy clusters of yellow flower heads.

RANGE: NR, MR, SR, Canada; widespread, common

STEM: Erect, single or clustered, 2–5 feet tall (60–150 cm), hairless, young plants may be sparsely long-hairy.

FLOWERS: July–September. Flat-topped to rounded clusters have 10–30 flower heads per stem, each with 8 yellow rays, ⅜–⅝ inch long (9–15 mm), tips notched; disk yellow; usually 13 phyllaries in 1 row, evenly-sized, green-tipped.

LEAVES: Alternate. Blades narrowly triangular, 1½–4 inches long (4–10 cm) with a broad base, pointed tip; surfaces hairless, edges strongly saw-toothed; lower leaves long-stalked, upper short-stalked.

HABITAT: Meadows, stream banks, open woods; montane, subalpine forests. Elevation 4,000–11,500 feet (1,220–3,505 m).

SIMILAR SPECIES: Tall Ragwort, *S. serra*, has finely toothed, lance-shaped leaves, tapered bases.

Wooton's Ragwort

Senecio wootonii, Aster Family, Asteraceae; Perennial herb

QUICK ID: Look for hairless stems; smooth, oval, fleshy basal leaves with a waxy coating; and flower heads with yellow rays and disk.

RANGE: SR; widespread, common

STEM: Erect, single or clustered, 8–20 inches tall (20–50 cm), hairless.

FLOWERS: March–August. Rounded, branching arrays on stem tips have 8–24 flower heads, each with 8–10 rays, ⅜ inch long (10 mm); disk yellow; phyllaries 13 or 21, even-sized, tips green to brownish; 3 tiny bractlets, ⅛ inch long (3 mm) beneath phyllaries.

LEAVES: Mostly basal, long-stalked, fleshy; blades oval to lance-shaped, 1½–3½ inches long (4–9 cm), bases taper; edges wavy with tiny teeth, surfaces hairless with waxy coating. Stem leaves few, alternate, much smaller, stalkless.

HABITAT: Meadows, riparian, open woods; montane, subalpine forests. Elevation 4,700–11,500 feet (1,432–3,504 m).

SIMILAR SPECIES: Rocky Mt. Groundsel, *Packera streptanthifolia*, leaves, no waxy coating.

Canada Goldenrod

Solidago altissima, Aster Family, Asteraceae; Perennial herb

QUICK ID: Look in moist soils for tall stands of robust stems, scratchy leaves, and plumes with hundreds of tiny yellow flower heads.

RANGE: SR: widespread, common

STEM: Erect, upper branched, 2-6 feet tall (60–180 cm), scratchy, short hairs throughout, colony forming.

FLOWERS: August–November. Dense clusters form spreading, curving, pyramid- to club-shaped arrays. Floral stems have heads along one side, each with 8–13 rays, 1⁄16 inch long (2 mm), disk yellow.

LEAVES: Alternate, unstalked. Lower leaves whither by flowering; mid-stem blades largest, lance-shaped, 1¾–4 inches long (5–10 cm), ¼–⅝ inch wide (7–16 mm); edges entire or serrated above middle; surfaces strongly 3-nerved, bottom finely hairy, top scratchy.

HABITAT: Moist soils, stream banks, open woods; grasslands to montane forests. Elevation 2,500–8,750 feet (762–2,666 m).

SIMILAR SPECIES: Giant Goldenrod, *S. gigantea*, has smooth stems.

Missouri Goldenrod

Solidago missouriensis, Aster Family, Asteraceae; Perennial herb

QUICK ID: Look for stems often with bundles of small leaves in the leaf axils, lower leaves with winged stalks, and dense arrays of small yellow flower heads; hairless throughout.

RANGE: NR, MR, SR, Canada; widespread, common

STEM: Erect, clustered 12–32 inches tall (30–80 cm).

FLOWERS: June–October. Elongated, pyramidal clusters have 10–210 flower heads on one side of spreading, hairless floral branches; flowers have 5–14 tiny rays 1⁄16 inch long (2 mm); disk yellow.

LEAVES: Basal often present. Stem leaves alternate, stalks winged; lower blades narrow, elliptic to oblong, 2–4 inches long (5–10 cm); edges entire to serrated, surface hairless, 3-nerved, tips pointed. Upper blades stalkless, linear to lance-shaped, smaller up the stem, edges entire, lined with ciliate hairs, surfaces hairless.

HABITAT: Dry soils, prairies, open woods; grasslands, foothills, montane forests. Elevation 700–9,000 feet (213–2,743 m).

Rocky Mountain Goldenrod

Solidago multiradiata, Aster Family, Asteraceae; Perennial herb

QUICK ID: Look for short stems, lower leaves with winged stalks, and crowded, rounded clusters of flower heads with 13 small, yellow rays.

RANGE: NR, MR, SR, Canada; widespread, common

STEM: Erect, 1–10 in clusters, unbranched, 4–20 inches tall (10–50 cm), lower smooth, upper densely soft-hairy.

FLOWERS: June–September. Dense, round-topped clusters have white-hairy branches; flower heads 4–75 with 12–18 rays, each 3⁄16 inch long (5 mm); disk yellow.

LEAVES: Basal often present at flowering, stalks winged and hairy edged. Stem leaves alternate, lower and basal blades lance- to spatula-shaped, 3⁄8–7 inches long (1–17 cm) to 1 inch wide (3 cm), edges lined with tiny, ciliate hairs, toothed near tip. Upper leaves smaller, clasping.

HABITAT: Dry meadows, slopes, fellfields; upper montane, subalpine, alpine. Elevation 8,000–12,000 feet (2,438–3,660 m).

Sticky Goldenrod

Solidago simplex, Aster Family, Asteraceae; Perennial herb

QUICK ID: Look for rounded to elongated clusters blooming on all sides of stem; yellow flower heads with 8 tiny rays, sticky phyllaries.

RANGE: NR, MR, Canada: infrequent, locally common; SR: common

STEM: Erect, unbranched, 7–17 inches tall (17–44 cm), lower smooth, upper with short, flat-lying hairs.

FLOWERS: July–September. Rounded to elongated clusters, hairless or with few tiny, flat-lying hairs, have up to 150 flower heads, each with 7–16 tiny ray florets to 1⁄16 inch long (1 mm); disk yellow. Phyllaries often resinous-sticky.

LEAVES: Basal and lower leaf blades spatula-shaped, 2–4 inches long (5–10 cm) to 3⁄4 inch wide (2 cm); base tapers to a winged stalk; edges hairless, toothed. Stem leaves 5–16, lance-shaped to linear, 1⁄2–2 inches long (1–5 cm), stalkless, margins entire to toothed.

HABITAT: Dry meadows, slopes, open forests, disturbed areas; grasslands to alpine. Elevation 6,800–12,550 feet (2,072–3,825 m).

Three-nerved Goldenrod

Solidago velutina, Aster Family, Asteraceae; Perennial herb

QUICK ID: Look for slender, leafy stems, often in colonies; soft-hairy leaves; dense narrow-to-broad arrays of small, yellow flower heads.

RANGE: MR, SR; widespread, common

STEM: Erect, unbranched, 6–32 inches tall (16–80 cm), lower smooth, upper with short, flat-lying hairs, colony forming.

FLOWERS: August–October. Narrow cylindrical-to-broad or pyramidal arrays have 30–500 tiny yellow flower heads, each with 6–12 rays ⅛–¼ inch long (3–6 mm).

LEAVES: Basal present when flowering; blades linear-elliptic, 2–4¾ inches long (5–12 cm), tapering to winged stalks. Stem leaves alternate, smaller up the stem, blades ⅜–2 inches long (8–50 mm), usually with 3 strong nerves base to tip; edges entire or few teeth, surfaces sparsely to densely soft-hairy, both base and tip pointed.

HABITAT: Coarse soils, open woods, disturbed areas; grasslands to montane forests. Elevation 4,000–10,000 feet (1,220–3,048 m).

Spiny Sow Thistle

Sonchus asper, Aster Family, Asteraceae; Annual herb, introduced

QUICK ID: Look for plants with clasping prickly leaves, milky sap, and urn-shaped flower heads dense with narrow, spreading, yellow rays.

RANGE: NR, MR, SR, Canada; widespread, naturalized noxious weed

STEM: Erect, branched, 4–6 inches tall (10–55 cm), usually hairless.

FLOWERS: March–November. Loose arrays on branch tips have yellow flower heads ½–1 inch wide (12–25 mm) packed with 80–250 rays, each ⅛–¼ inch long (3–6 mm); no disk flowers. The buds resemble a vase with a fat bottom that narrows to a point.

LEAVES: Basal rosette and alternate on stem. Blades 2–12 inches long (5–30 cm), pinnate with broad, pointed lobes; edges wavy, spiny; leaf base wraps around the stem with rounded, often curled, lobes.

HABITAT: Roadsides, fields, disturbed sites. Elevation below 8,200 feet (2,500 m).

SIMILAR SPECIES: Common Sow Thistle, *S. oleraceus*, has weakly prickly leaves.

Stemless Goldenweed

Stenotus acaulis, Aster Family, Asteraceae; Perennial herb

QUICK ID: Look for mats of rigid basal leaves and clustered stems tipped with showy arrays of flower heads with yellow rays and disk; leaf edges rough-hairy.

RANGE: NR, MR, SR (absent NM); widespread, common

STEM: Erect, 1–8 inches tall (3–21 cm), mostly smooth.

FLOWERS: Terminal clusters of 1–4 flower heads, each with 5–15 oval rays, ¼–½ inch long (6–12 mm), disk yellow. Phyllaries in 2 stacked rows, outer ones lance-shaped, mostly green, tips pointed, slightly recurved.

LEAVES: Mostly basal, stalked. Blades linear to elliptic or oval, 1–4 inches long (3–10 cm) by ½ inch wide (11 mm); surfaces smooth to rough or glandular, bottom conspicuously 1–3 nerved, tips pointed.

HABITAT: Scrublands, ridges, open woods; sagebrush, foothills, montane, subalpine forests. Elevation 3,940–11,810 feet (1,200–3,600 m).

SIMILAR SPECIES: Woolly Goldenweed, *S. lanuginosus*, (NR) has densely hairy stems and leaves.

Mock Goldenweed

Stenotus armerioides, Aster Family, Asteraceae; Perennial herb

QUICK ID: Look in dry habitats for mat-forming, circular rosettes of sticky, narrow basal leaves; dead vegetation often in the center; short stalks; flower heads with yellow rays and disk; leaf edges smooth.

RANGE: MR, SR; widespread, common

STEM: Erect, low-growing, ¾–12 inches long (2–30 cm), sticky.

FLOWERS: April–August. Usually solitary heads with 5–15 elliptic to oblong, yellow rays, each to ¾ inch long (2 cm), disk yellow. Phyllaries in 3 unequal rows, whitish below, tips waxy green, blunt.

LEAVES: Mostly basal, stalked, erect, rigid; blades narrow, linear to oblong, ⅔–3½ inches long (17–90 mm) to ⅜ inch wide (1 cm); edges entire or sometimes lined with minute ciliate hairs, surfaces 3-nerved, gland dotted, sticky; points tapered. Stem leaves alternate.

HABITAT: Dry soils, canyons, badlands, rocky slopes; sagebrush, foothills, montane forests. Elevation 5,500–10,000 feet (1,676–3,048 m).

Common Tansy

Tanacetum vulgare, Aster Family, Asteraceae; Perennial herb, introduced

QUICK ID: Look for clumps of stems with fern-like leaves and flat-topped clusters of flower heads with yellow button-like disks, no rays.

RANGE: NR, MR, SR, Canada; scattered, locally common, naturalized

STEM: Erect, upper branched, 16–60 inches tall (40–150 cm), smooth to sparsely hairy, colony forming.

FLOWERS: July–September. Crowded arrays on branch tips have 20–200 flower heads about ⅜ inch wide (9 mm) with yellow disk flowers only, rays absent.

LEAVES: Basal wither by blooming. Stem leaves alternate, blades broadly elliptic in outline, 1½–8 inches long (4–20 cm) to 4 inches wide (10 cm), pinnately cut into numerous narrow, toothed lobes; surfaces smooth to sparsely hairy. Foliage poisonous.

HABITAT: Roadsides, fields, disturbed areas; grasslands, foothills, montane forests. Elevation 30–6,250 feet (10–1,900 m).

Dandelion

Taraxacum officinale, Aster Family, Asteraceae; Annual herb; introduced, invasive

QUICK ID: Look for rosettes with arrowhead-shaped lobes deeply cut along the midrib, flower heads packed with yellow rays, golf ball-size clusters of seeds with feathery tails, and milky sap.

RANGE: NR, MR, SR, Canada; widespread, naturalized weed

STEM: Flower stalks 1–10 inches tall (3–10 cm), hollow, leafless, directly from rosette.

FLOWERS: Any month. Flower heads 1–1½ inches wide (3–4 cm) with 100–200 ray flowers, no disk flowers. Fruit develops into the sphere of fluffy parachute seeds kids love to blow in the breeze. The early-blooming flowers are an important source of nectar and pollen for spring-emerging native bees and butterflies.

LEAVES: Basal rosette; blades 2–8 inches long (5–20 cm) with pointed, arrowhead-shaped lobes along the midrib.

HABITAT: Disturbed soils, lawns, roadsides; grasslands to alpine. Elevation 2,500–13,000 feet (762–3,962 m).

Stemless Four-nerve Daisy

Tetraneuris acaulis, Aster Family, Asteraceae; Perennial herb

QUICK ID: Look for dense clumps of spatula-shaped basal leaves, up to 35 flower stalks, each with a single flower head, yellow rays, disk.

RANGE: NR, MR, SR, Canada; widespread, common

STEM: Flower stalk erect, leafless, ¾–7¾ inches tall (2–20 cm).

FLOWERS: April–October. Flower stalks directly from root crown, heads have 8–15 yellow rays, each to ¾ inch long (20 mm) and tipped with 3 rounded lobes; disk yellow; phyllaries in 2 rows, hairy.

LEAVES: Basal only. Leaves linear to spatula-shaped, to 4 inches long (10 cm) by 5⁄16 inch wide (8 mm) with one distinct vein; edges entire, tips pointed; surfaces covered with silky hairs or short, stiff hairs, or shaggy, or hairless, depending on variety.

HABITAT: Meadows, forest edges, ridges, roadsides; arid grassland to alpine meadows. Elevation: 4,500–12,000 feet (1,372–3,658 m).

Navajo Tea

Thelesperma subnudum, Aster Family, Asteraceae; Perennial herb

QUICK ID: Look in dry habitats for stems with narrow lobed leaves, flower heads with or without yellow rays, broad inner phyllaries with triangular tips, and small spreading outer phyllaries.

RANGE: MR, SR: widespread, common; NR, Canada: rare

STEM: Erect, single or clumped, 4–12 inches tall (10–30 cm), smooth.

FLOWERS: May–September. Single flower heads can have 8 showy, yellow rays, each ½–¾ inch long (12–20 mm), or only yellow disk florets. Phyllaries in 2 very unequal rows: inner row broad with triangular tips, outer one narrow, much smaller.

LEAVES: Basal. Stem leaves opposite, mostly crowded on lower stem; blades ⅜–1⅜ inches long (1–4 cm); deeply cut into 3 narrow, spreading lobes.

HABITAT: Plains, open woods; arid grasslands, sagebrush, foothills, montane forests. Elevation 3,280–9,515 feet (1,000–2,900 m).

Lyall's Goldenweed

Tonestus lyallii, Aster Family, Asteraceae; Perennial herb

QUICK ID: Look at high altitudes for dense rosettes with short, clumped, leafy stems, each topped with a showy yellow flower head.

RANGE: NR, MR, SR (CO-rare), Canada; widespread, common

STEM: Erect, branched from base, leafless, 1½–6 inches tall (4–15 cm), smooth to densely sticky, glandular-hairy.

FLOWERS: July–September. Solitary on stem tips, 1–2 inches wide (25–50 mm) with 11–35 elliptic rays to ⅜ inch long (11 mm), tips have tiny teeth. Phyllaries in 3–4 rows, to ⅜ inch long (10 mm), sometimes leafy, glandular-hairy, pointed.

LEAVES: Basal, stalked, erect; blades linear to spatula-shaped, 1–3 inches long (3–8 cm). Stem leaves opposite, oblong to broadly lance-shaped, ½–1½ inches long (12–37 mm); edges entire, surfaces glandular-hairy; size gradually reduced upwards.

HABITAT: Meadows, crevices, talus slopes open woods; subalpine forests, alpine. Elevation 6,000–12,500 feet (1,828–3,800 m).

Pygmy Goldenweed

Tonestus pygmaeus, Aster Family, Asteraceae; Perennial herb

QUICK ID: Look in high altitudes for mat-forming rosettes to 1 foot wide (30 cm) and hairy stems topped with solitary, miniature sunflowers.

RANGE: SR; widespread, common

STEM: Erect, branching from base, 3½ inches tall (9 cm), densely hairy.

FLOWERS: July–August. Heads solitary with 10–35 yellow rays, elliptic, ¼–⅜ inch long (6–9 mm); disk flowers yellow. Phyllaries in 3–4 rows, leaf-like, tips pointed to rounded.

LEAVES: Basal, erect; blades linear to spatula-shaped, ⅜–2 inches long (1–5 cm), strongly veined. Alternate stem blades oblong to lance-shaped ⅜–2 inches long (1–5 cm); margins entire, lined with fine hairs; slightly smaller upward.

HABITAT: Meadows, scree slopes, rock crevices, open areas; upper subalpine, alpine. Elevation 9,000–13,000 feet (2,740–3,962 m).

Yellow Salsify

Tragopogon dubius, Aster Family, Asteraceae; Perennial herb; introduced, naturalized

QUICK ID: Look for clasping, grass-like leaves, flower heads with yellow rays, erect, dark stamens and no disk flowers, and feathery, golf ball-size seed heads much larger than a dandelion's.

RANGE: NR, RM, SR, Canada; widespread, common

STEM: Erect, branched, 15–30 inches tall (40–80 cm), milky sap.

FLOWERS: April–July. Flower heads to 1½ inches wide (4 cm) with 12 or more outer rays surrounding a dense center of small rays with erect dark stamens; no disk flowers; buds cone-shaped, tapered. Note the 2-inch-long (5 cm), narrow bracts extend far beyond the rays. Seed head a feathery puffball 3–4 inches diameter (8–10 cm).

LEAVES: Basal. Alternate on stem; blades clasping, 1–7 inches long, tapered to a long, thin point, straight, not recurved or coiled.

HABITAT: Meadows, roadsides, disturbed areas; grasslands, foothills, montane forests. Elevation 5,000–9,800 feet (1,524–2,987 m).

Golden Crownbeard, Cowpen Daisy

Verbesina encelioides, Aster Family, Asteraceae; Annual herb

QUICK ID: Look for bushy stems with large, rough leaves; yellow flower heads with notched rays; and narrow, spreading phyllaries.

RANGE: SR; widespread, common

STEM: Erect, multi-branched, 1–3 feet tall (30–90 cm), densely hairy.

FLOWERS: April–October. Long-stalked heads ¾–2 inches wide (2–5 cm) have 10–15 orange-yellow rays, each ½ inch long (12 mm), tipped with 3 teeth; disk yellow. Phyllaries in 1–2 rows, narrow, pointed, hairy, spreading to erect.

LEAVES: Leaves mostly alternate; blades triangular to lance-shaped, 1¼–3⅛ inches long (3–8 cm) by ¾–1½ inches wide (2–4 cm), coarsely toothed, gray green, short-hairy, tips pointed.

HABITAT: Dry, coarse soils, roadsides, disturbed areas; arid grasslands, sagebrush, foothills, montane forests. Elevation 3,000–8,600 feet (915–2,620 m).

Northern Mule's Ears

Wyethia amplexicaulis, Aster Family, Asteraceae; Perennial herb

QUICK ID: Look for dense basal clumps with large, elliptic, hairless, shiny green leaves; leafy stems; and yellow flower clusters with a large, central flower head and smaller side heads.

RANGE: NR, MR, SR (absent NM); widespread

STEM: Erect, branched, 10–32 inches tall (25–80 cm), smooth.

FLOWERS: May–July. Clusters on stem tips have 2–8 flower heads, each with 8–21 rays, 1–2⅜ inches long (3–6 cm). Phyllaries in loose rows, broad and leaf-like, hairless, resinous.

LEAVES: Basal, stalked; blades broadly elliptic to lance-shaped, 8–24 inches long (20–60 cm) by 2–6 inches wide (5–16 cm); base tapered, edges entire with strong white midrib, surfaces shiny, hairless, tips pointed. Stem leaves alternate, smaller, stalkless to clasping.

HABITAT: Dry meadows, open areas; grassland to montane forests. Elevation 3,000–9,850 feet (915–3,000 m).

SIMILAR SPECIES: Badlands Mule's Ear, *Scabrethia scabra*, (MR, SR) has narrow, sandpapery-rough leaves.

Yellow Spiny Daisy

Xanthisma spinulosum (Machaeranthera pinnatifida), Aster Family, Asteraceae; Perennial herb

QUICK ID: Look for sprawling clumps of bushy gray-green stems, tiny leaves with bristle-tipped lobes, and small yellow flower heads.

RANGE: NR, MR, SR, Canada; widespread, common

STEM: Spreading, clump forming with many upper branches, 8–16 inches long (20–40 cm), densely hairy.

FLOWERS: May–November. Each branch tip has a single head 1–1¼ inches wide (25–30 mm) with 14–60 bright yellow, narrow rays with pointed tips. Phyllaries in 5–6 rows, hairy with a white bristle tip.

LEAVES: Alternate, equally spaced. Blades oblong to lance-shaped, ½–1¼ inches long (12–30 mm); edges with coarse lobes or teeth with white bristle tips, surfaces hairy.

HABITAT: Coarse soils, roadsides, disturbed areas; arid grasslands, sagebrush, foothills. Elevation 3,200–7,700 feet (975–2,350 m).

SIMILAR SPECIES: Rayless Tansyaster, *X. grindelioides*, (all regions), has similar foliage, but disk flowers only, no rays.

Creeping Barberry, Oregon-grape

Berberis repens, Barberry Family, Berbericaceae; Evergreen subshrub

QUICK ID: Look for an ankle-high groundcover with holly-like leaves, clusters of small yellow flowers, and small blue-black fruit.

RANGE: NR, MR, SR, Canada; widespread, common

STEM: Woody, spreading branches, 1–8 inches tall (3–20 cm).

FLOWERS: April–June. Dense spike-like clusters 1–4 inches long (3–10 cm) have 25–50 yellow flowers, each with 6 rounded petals, ¼–⅜ inch long (6–9 mm). Fruit a rounded, ⅜-inch-diameter (10 mm), grape-like berry.

LEAVES: Alternate, pinnately compound. Blade with 5-7 opposite leaflets, each oval, ⅝–2¾ inches long (16–70 mm); margins lined with spiny teeth. The leaves turn rich shades of red in the fall.

HABITAT: Coarse soils; foothills, montane, subalpine forests. Elevation 6,900–11,200 feet (2,100–3,414 m).

Small-flower Fiddleneck

Amsinckia menziesii, Borage Family, Boraginaceae; Annual herb

QUICK ID: Look for stems and narrow leaves with bristly hairs, and coiled clusters of small yellow-orange flowers on branch tips.

RANGE: NR, MR, Canada; widespread, locally common

STEM: Erect, simple to branched, tip coiled, 4–32 inches tall (10–80 cm), stiff-bristly hairy.

FLOWERS: March–July. Clusters stiff-hairy, tightly coiled but uncoil as mature; flowers funnel-shaped, ¼ inch long (7 mm), flaring open with 5 rounded lobes. 4 nutlets, rough-bumpy.

LEAVES: Basal rosette fades by flowering. Stem leaves alternate, lance-shaped to elliptic or linear, ¾–4¾ inches long (2–12 cm) to ¾ inch wide (2 cm); edges entire, surfaces bristly hairy.

HABITAT: Dry coarse soils, disturbed areas; arid grasslands, sagebrush, montane forests. Elevation sea level to 3,000 feet (915 m).

SIMILAR SPECIES: Common Fiddleneck, *A. intermedia*, has slightly larger flowers and lobes with orange dots.

Fringed Puccoon

Lithospermum incisum, Borage Family, Boraginaceae, Perennial herb

QUICK ID: Look for hairy stems with long, narrow leaves and dense clusters of yellow, trumpet-shaped flowers with crinkly-fringed petals.

RANGE: NR, MR, SR: common; Canada: infrequent

STEM: Erect, clustered, 4–12 inches tall (10–30 cm), soft-hairy.

FLOWERS: March–August. Small clusters in upper leaf axils. Fused petals form a ½–1⅜-inch-long (12–35 mm) tube that opens ½–¾ inch wide (12–20 mm); 5 petal lobes have crinkly, ragged edges. The showy flowers are mostly infertile; tiny, self-fertilizing flowers along the stem produce abundant seeds.

LEAVES: Basal leaves whither by flowering. Stem leaves alternate, stalkless, crowded; blades linear to oblong, 1–3 inches long (3–8 cm) by ¼ inch wide (6 mm); margins entire, surfaces soft-hairy.

HABITAT: Coarse soils, open woods; grasslands, sagebrush, foothills, montane forests. Elevation 3,500–8,500 feet.

SIMILAR SPECIES: Many-flowered Puccoon, *L. multiflorum*, (MR, SR) has smooth, oval petal lobes.

Many-flowered Puccoon

Lithospermum multiflorum, Borage Family, Boraginaceae; Perennial herb

QUICK ID: Look for clumps of stems with narrow leaves and clusters of yellow, trumpet-shaped flowers with rounded petal tips.

RANGE: MR (UT), SR; widespread, common

STEM: Erect, 10–24 inches tall (25–60 cm), hairy.

FLOWERS: May–September. Clusters, often drooping, at stem ends. Flowers tubular, ⅜–½ inch (9–12 mm) long, outside hairy; 5 small flaring, rounded petal lobes. To ensure cross-pollination, some flowers have short stamens deep in the tube and a much longer style, others have long stamens that extend well above a short style.

LEAVES: Alternate. Blades linear to lance-shaped, ¾–2⅜ inches long (2–6 cm), to ⅝ inch wide (15 mm); upper surface with flat-lying hairs, lower surface and edges with spreading hairs.

HABITAT: Coarse soils, open areas; sagebrush, montane, subalpine forests. Elevation 5,900–10,000 feet (1,800–3,048 m).

SIMILAR SPECIES: Fringed Puccoon, *L. incisum*, has flowers with crinkly fringed petal lobes.

Western Stoneseed

Lithospermum ruderale, Borage Family, Boraginaceae; Perennial herb

QUICK ID: Look for clumping stems crowded with narrow leaves and small clusters of pale-yellow-to-greenish flowers with 5 rounded petals.

RANGE: NR, MR, SR (absent NM), Canada; widespread, common

STEM: Erect, leafy, 8–24 inches tall (20–60 cm), short stiff hairs.

FLOWERS: April–September. Dense clusters with leafy bracts in upper leaf axils. Flowers tubular, 3⁄16–3⁄8 inch long (4–9 mm), flaring open to ½ inch wide (12 mm) with 5 rounded petal lobes.

LEAVES: Alternate, crowded on stem. Blades linear to narrowly lance-shaped, 1–4 inches long (3–10 cm) to 3⁄8 inch wide (10 mm); edges entire, surfaces with short, rough, flat-lying hairs.

HABITAT: Dry open areas; grasslands, sagebrush, foothills, montane forests. Elevation 2,500–8,500 feet (750–2,590 m).

Yellow Cryptantha

Oreocarya flava (Cryptantha flava), Borage Family, Boraginaceae; Perennial herb

QUICK ID: Look for clumps with silvery basal leaves and leafy, hairy stems with dense, cylindrical clusters of small yellow flowers.

RANGE: MR, SR; widespread, common

STEM: Erect, branching from base, 4–16 inches tall (10–40 cm).

FLOWERS: April–June. Flower stalk lined with 5–10 ball-like clusters to form dense array. Petals united at base into a narrow tube that flares open with 5 showy, rounded lobes; the floral tube extends beyond the sharp tips of the bristly sepals beneath the flower.

LEAVES: Basal rosette; opposite on stem. Blades narrow, linear to spatula-shaped, ¾–3½ inches long (2–9 cm); edges entire, surfaces densely hairy.

HABITAT: Dry soils; sagebrush scrub, pinyon-juniper woodlands. Elevation 3,500–7,500 feet (1,065–2,195 m).

Mountain Tansymustard

Descurainia incana, Mustard Family, Brassicaceae; Perennial, biennial herb

QUICK ID: Look for leafy, branching stems, lobed leaves, small yellow flowers with 4 petals, and erect seed capsules on short stalks hugging the stem.

RANGE: NR, MR, SR, Canada; widespread, invasive

STEM: Erect, slender upper branches, to 4 feet tall (120 cm).

FLOWERS: May–September. Open clusters on stem ends with numerous small flowers, petals ⅛ inch long (3 mm). Note the seed capsule is erect, slender, ⅜–⅝ inch long (9–15 mm), slightly constricted between seeds, both ends pointed; seed stalks erect, usually shorter than capsule, often almost touching main stem.

LEAVES: Basal wither by blooming; stem leaves alternate, stemless. Blade 1-4 inches long (3–10 cm), pinnately lobed; leaflets toothed to deeply incised; upper leaves smaller, lobes narrower.

HABITAT: Disturbed areas; from sagebrush to alpine. Elevation 328–11,500 feet (100–3,500 m).

Western Tansymustard

Descurainia pinnata, Mustard Family, Brassicaceae; Annual herb

QUICK ID: Look for stems with clusters of tiny yellow flowers and gray-hairy leaves; thin seed pods with long stalks line the stem.

RANGE: NR, MR, SR, Canada; widespread, common

STEM: Erect, single or branching, 5–22 inches tall (13–56 cm).

FLOWERS: February–July. Yellow, 4 oval petals, 1⁄16–⅛ inch long (1–3 mm). Seed pods, 3⁄16–½ inch long (4–13 mm), tip slightly larger than base (club-shaped), slightly curved, angled upward; pod stalk 3⁄16–⅞ inch long (4–23 mm), horizontal to slanting upward.

LEAVES: Basal wither by flowering; alternate on stem. Blades pinnately compound, 1–6 inches long (3–15 cm), smaller towards top, covered with dense, fine grayish hairs. Note the leaflets along midrib are divided into round-tipped lobes.

HABITAT: Roadsides, disturbed areas; sagebrush, pinyon-juniper woodlands. Elevation 3,600–8,800 feet (1,100–2,685 m).

Flixweed

Descurainia sophia, Mustard Family, Brassicaceae; Annual, biennial herb; introduced

QUICK ID: Look for heads of tiny yellow flowers, 1-inch-long (25 mm) pods lining the stem, leaflets divided 2-3 times into pointed segments.

RANGE: NR, MR, SR, Canada; widespread, common, invasive

STEM: Erect, single or branching, 12-32 inches tall (30-80 cm).

FLOWERS: February-July. Clusters elongate as pods mature and line the stem below the flowers. Petals 4, oval, 1⁄16-1⁄8 inch long (2-3 mm). Seed pods thin, linear, ½-1 inch long (1-3 cm), slightly constricted between seeds, slightly curved, angled upward; stalk of pod 3⁄8-5⁄8 inch long (9-15 mm), horizontal to slanting upward.

LEAVES: Basal fern-like; alternate on stem. Blade 1-6 inches long (3-16 cm), finely hairy, divided 2-3 times into slender, linear, pointed lobes that get smaller, narrower up the stem.

HABITAT: Disturbed areas; sagebrush to alpine. Elevation 4,300-9,850 feet (1,310-3,000 m).

Golden Draba

Draba aurea, Mustard Family, Brassicaceae; Perennial herb

QUICK ID: Look for short, hairy stems with leaves that hug the stem, and dense, rounded clusters of small flowers with 4 yellow petals.

RANGE: NR, MR, SR, Canada; widespread, common

STEM: Erect, usually unbranched, 4-16 inches tall (10-40 cm).

FLOWERS: June-August. Clusters have 18-52 flowers with 4 petals ¼ inch long (6 mm). Seed pods flat, 3⁄8-¾ inch long (9-19 mm), often twisted, on short stalks angling upward.

LEAVES: Basal rosette, elliptic, to 1¼ inches long (30 mm), surfaces hairy, edges entire with ciliate hairs. Stem leaves alternate; blades lance-shaped, edges entire or toothed; bottom surface densely hairy, top less hairy. Note the vertical leaves hugging the stem.

HABITAT: Grasslands, open forests; montane, subalpine forests, alpine tundra. Elevation 2,300-13,700 feet (1,036-4,175 m).

Western Wallflower

Erysimum capitatum, Mustard Family, Brassicaceae; Biennial, perennial herb

QUICK ID: Look for dense clusters of flowers with 4 orange or yellow petals, and wire-like seed pods standing erect under the flowers.

RANGE: NR, MR, SR, Canada; widespread, common

STEM: Erect, single or branching, 15–40 inches tall (38–100 cm).

FLOWERS: April–August. Showy, dense, elongated-to-rounded clusters have flowers ¾ inch wide (2 cm) with 4 oval petals in a cross pattern. Spreading, rounded petals, ½–1 inch long (12–25 mm), range from lemon yellow to orange red, or rarely lavender or cream. Seed pods narrow, cylindrical, 1⅜–4¾ inches long (4–12 cm), angling upward.

LEAVES: Basal leaves usually whither by blooming. Alternate stem leaves, linear to spoon-shaped, to 2⅜ inches long (6 cm) by ¾ inch wide (2 cm); surfaces with short hairs, edges entire or with a few small teeth.

HABITAT: Grasslands, sagebrush, foothills, montane, subalpine conifer forests. Elevation 4,200–12,000 feet (1,220–3,658 m).

Common Twinpod

Physaria didymocarpa, Mustard Family, Brassicaceae; Perennial herb

QUICK ID: Look for basal rosettes with trailing stems and upturned clusters of small yellow flowers with 4 petals; paired, hairy seed pods.

RANGE: NR, MR, Canada; widespread, common

STEM: Prostrate, radiating, unbranched, ¾–6 inches long (2–16 cm).

FLOWERS: May–June. Rounded clusters on stem tips; flowers have 4 oblong petals, each ⅜–½ inch long (10–12 mm). Seed pods inflated, paired, ⅜–¾ inch long (1–2 cm), papery, fuzzy-hairy.

LEAVES: Basal, long stalked; blades oval-pointed, ⅝–1⅝ inches long (15–40 mm); edges slightly wavy or few-toothed, surfaces densely silvery-hairy. Stem leaves similar, smaller, alternate.

HABITAT: Gravelly flats, disturbed areas; arid grasslands to subalpine forests. Elevation 3,000–10,500 feet (915–3,200 m).

SIMILAR SPECIES: Sharpleaf Twinpod, *P. acutifolia,* (MR, SR) has erect to prostate stems and paired pods with flat-lying hairs.

Mountain Bladderpod

Physaria montana, Mustard Family, Brassicaceae; Perennial herb

QUICK ID: Look for rosettes of silvery-hairy leaves; clusters of small yellow flowers with 4 petals; single, inflated pods on S-curved stalks.

RANGE: SR; widespread, common; abundant in CO Front Range

STEM: Prostrate to erect, branched from base, 2–8 inches tall (5–20 cm), densely hairy.

FLOWERS: April–July. Rounded clusters on stem ends, flowers have 4 oblong petals, each ¼–½ inch long (6–12 mm). Single seed pod on upright S-shaped stalk ¼–¾ inch long (5–20 mm), pods inflated, oval, ¼–½ inch long (6–12 mm), densely hairy.

LEAVES: Basal rosette, stalked; blades elliptic to rounded, ¾–2 inches long (2–5 cm); edges entire to toothed, surfaces densely hairy. Stem leaves alternate, often on one side of stem, linear to diamond-shaped ⅜–1⅝ inches long (1–4 cm); edges entire to toothed.

HABITAT: Sandy flats, slopes; arid grasslands, sagebrush, foothills, montane forests. Elevation 5,000–9,500 feet (1,524–3,895 m).

Tall Tumble Mustard

Sisymbrium altissimum, Mustard Family, Brassicaceae; Annual herb, introduced, invasive

QUICK ID: Look for basal rosettes with pinnate lobes divided to the midrib, branching stems with long white hairs and narrow leaves, and clusters of small yellow to creamy flowers with 4 petals.

RANGE: NR, MR, SR, Canada; widespread, common, naturalized

STEM: Erect, tangled upper branching, 12–60 inches tall (30–150 cm), usually with conspicuous long, white hairs.

FLOWERS: March–September. Compact, branching clusters; 4 petals ¼–⅜ inch long (6–10 mm). Seed pods narrow, cylindrical 2–4 inches long (5–10 cm), stalks as thick as the pod.

LEAVES: Basal rosette, stalked; blades 2–6 inches long (5–15 cm), deeply pinnately lobed with 5–8 pairs of pointed, toothed segments. Stem leaves alternate, distinctly different, lobes linear, filament-like.

HABITAT: Disturbed areas; arid grasslands, sagebrush, foothills, montane forests. Elevation 4,200–8,900 feet (1,280–2,750 m).

False London Rocket

Sisymbrium loeselii, Mustard Family, Brassicaceae; Annual herb, introduced, invasive

QUICK ID: Look for rosettes with pinnate leaves with a large triangular terminal lobe, similar but smaller stem leaves, and dense clusters of small flowers with 4 bright-yellow petals.

RANGE: NR, MR, SR, Canada; widespread, common, naturalized

STEM: Erect, upper branched, 14–48 inches tall (35–120 cm), lower with scattered, long hairs.

FLOWERS: July–August. Clusters dense, branched, with scattered long hairs; 4 petals, rounded, ¼–⅜ inch long (6–9 mm); seed pods thin, cylindrical, ⅜–2 inches long (1–5 cm), stalk thinner than pod, erect or angled up, not overtopping flowers.

LEAVES: Basal rosette, long-stalked; blade 1–3 inches long (3–8 cm), pinnate with 2–4 triangular lobes per side and a larger terminal lobe, edges entire or toothed, surfaces hairy, tips pointed. Stem leaves alternate, similar but much smaller.

HABITAT: Disturbed areas; grasslands to montane forests. Elevation 6,000–9,000 feet (1,828–2,750 m).

Desert Prince's Plume

Stanleya pinnata, Mustard Family, Brassaceae; Perennial herb

QUICK ID: Look in arid habitats for plume-like stems, dense spikes of bright-yellow tubular flowers, and long slender pods below the flowers.

RANGE: NR, MR, SR; widespread, common

STEM: Erect, branched from base, 1–4 feet tall (30–120 cm), smooth.

FLOWERS: April–September. Spike-like plumes have flowers with 4 oblong petals to ¾ inch long (2 cm) that bloom from the bottom of the stalk upward; a dense array of drooping to ascending pods develops below flowers; pods 1¼–3½ inches long (3–9 cm), smooth, slightly constricted between seeds.

LEAVES: Basal wither by flowering. Stem leaves alternate, long stalked, narrow, lance-shaped, 1½–8 inches long (4–20 cm); lower blades pinnately lobed; upper blades lobed or not.

HABITAT: Dry soils, badlands, dunes, washes, canyons; grasslands, sagebrush, foothills. Elevation 5,000–7,000 feet (1,524–2,134 m).

Nylon Hedgehog Cactus

Echinocereus viridiflorus, Cactus Family, Cactaceae; Perennial succulent cactus

QUICK ID: Look for small, rounded stem with 10-18 nipple-like ribs lined with areoles, each with red, white, or brown multicolored spines; flower petals yellow to greenish, blooms form around sides of stem.

RANGE: SR; widespread, infrequent

STEM: Spherical or cylindrical, single or small clumps, 3-12 inches tall (8-30 cm) by 1-3 inches diameter (3-8 cm).

SPINES: Areoles have 12-38 comb-like radial spines, and 0-17 central spines 1-1½ inches long (3-4 cm), round, not flat.

FLOWERS: Funnel-shaped flowers ⅜-1¼ inches wide (1-3 cm); petals (tepals) to 1 inch long (25 mm), delicate, yellow to greenish, often with dark mid-stripe; stamens have creamy anthers.

HABITAT: Arid grasslands, sagebrush, pinyon-juniper foothills, ponderosa forests. Elevation 4,900-8,000 feet (1,495-2,438 m).

Brittle Prickly Pear Cactus

Opuntia fragilis, Cactus Family, Cactaceae; Perennial cactus

QUICK ID: Look for spreading, clumping mats of spiny, cylindrical segments, or pads, with showy yellow flowers and many stamens.

RANGE: NR, MR, SR, Canada; widespread

STEM: Joined segments 2 inches long (5 cm) by 1 inch thick (3 cm), dark green, easily detached for animal dispersal.

SPINES: Pad surface dotted with areoles, each woolly, with tiny, tan, barbed glochids in a crescent along upper edge, and 3-8 spines ¼-1 inch long (8-24 mm) with gray-to-tan tips; top spines are longest, spreading; the lower 0-3 spines short, pointing downward.

FLOWERS: May-July. Showy flowers 1¾ inches wide (5 cm), petals (tepals), yellow to yellowish green, often with a reddish base, or occasionally solid magenta; filaments white or red; anthers yellow; style white; stigma lobes green. Fruit a dry, tan, oblong capsule.

HABITAT: Coarse soils, open areas; grasslands, sagebrush, foothills, montane forests. Elevation 2,000-8,000 feet (610-2,438 m).

Plains Prickly Pear Cactus

Opuntia macrorhiza, Cactus Family, Cactaceae; Perennial cactus

QUICK ID: Look for prostrate, spreading clumps of spiny pads to 5 feet wide (1.5 m), and cup-shaped yellow flowers with reddish centers.

RANGE: MR (UT), SR; widespread, locally common

STEM: Pads round to oblong, 3-5 inches long (7.5-13 cm), often wrinkled; jointed pads spread in chains 1-2 pads high.

SPINES: Pads lined with diagonal rows of 5-7 areoles with tufts of tiny, hair-like, barbed bristles (glochids), and 1-4 white-to reddish-brown spines, mainly on upper pad and edges; spines to 2½ inches long (6 cm), straight or curved, lower pointing downward.

FLOWERS: May–June. Yellow usually with red center, 2-3 inches wide (5-8 cm), filaments and anthers pale yellow, stigmas with creamy-to-yellow-greenish lobes. Fruits fleshy, dull red, elongated, 1-1½ inches long (25-38 mm), glochids but no spines.

HABITAT: Dry, coarse soils; arid grasslands, sagebrush, pinyon-juniper foothills. Elevation 3,400-8,000 feet (1,036-2,438 m).

Many-spined Prickly Pear Cactus

Opuntia polyacantha, Cactus Family, Cactaceae; Perennial cactus

QUICK ID: Look for a low-spreading cactus to 10 inches high (25 cm) with rooting pads, solid yellow flowers, and fruit covered with spines.

RANGE: NR, MR, SR, Canada; widespread, common

STEM: Prostrate, spreading, one pad high with jointed flat, oval pads.

SPINES: Spines in most areoles: var. *hystricina* (SR) areoles have 7-18 spines, all similar but grading in length, longest 2-3⅛ inches long (5-8 cm), spreading and curling in all directions; var. *polyacantha* (all regions) has 2 types of spines: 1-3 major ones, ¾-1½ inches long (2-4 cm), and 0-5 minor ones pointing down, 3⁄16-⅜ inch long (5-10 mm).

FLOWERS: April–May. Flowers to 3½ inches wide (9 cm), tepals yellow (occasionally red); stigma lobes green. Fruit a dry, tan cylinder to 2 inches long (5 cm) with both glochids and spines.

HABITAT: Dry coarse soils; grasslands, sagebrush, pinyon-juniper foothills, montane forests. Elevation 3,800-8,200 feet (1,158-2,500 m).

Orange Honeysuckle

Lonicera ciliosa, Honeysuckle Family, Caprifoliaceae; Deciduous woody vine

QUICK ID: Look for slender, woody vines with fused, opposite leaves near dense clusters of showy orange trumpet flowers and red berries.

RANGE: NR, Canada; widespread, common

STEM: Trailing, twining, 1–10 feet long (0.3–3 m).

FLOWERS: April–July. Short, compact whorls on branch ends with up to 20 tubular flowers; tube cylindrical, 1–1⅝ inches long (3–4 cm), hairy within, opening with 5 wide-spreading lobes. Stamens and stigma protrude favoring hummingbird pollination. Fruit in clusters of round, red berries.

LEAVES: Opposite; blades oval to elliptic 2⅜–4 inches long (6–10 cm), upper 1–2 pairs fused around stem; edges ciliate-hairy, surfaces hairless, tips round to sharp.

HABITAT: Forest openings, thickets; foothills, montane forests. Elevation sea level to 6,270 feet (1,910 m).

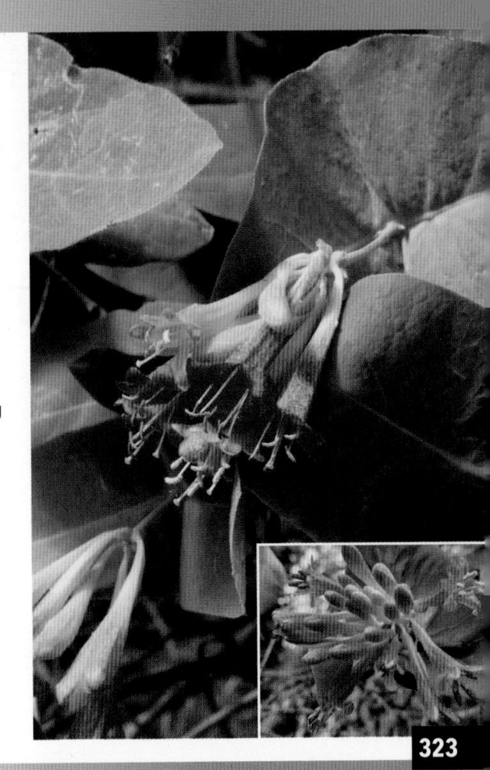

Twinberry Honeysuckle

Lonicera involucrata, Honeysuckle Family, Caprifoliaceae; Deciduous woody shrub

QUICK ID: Look for a leafy, bushy, midsize shrub with opposite leaves; twin, tubular, yellow flowers; and twin shiny, black berries.

RANGE: NR, MR, SR, Canada; widespread, common

STEM: Erect, branching, twigs 4-angled, 6 feet tall and wide (2 m).

FLOWERS: May–August. Paired flowers from leaf axils, cupped by 2 pairs of large, fused, leaf-like bracts; tube ⅜–¾ inch long (1–2 cm), with 5 small lobes slightly flaring open; outer surface densely glandular-hairy. Fruit paired black berries; bracts reddish.

LEAVES: Opposite. Blades elliptic to oblong, 1½–6 inches long (4–15 cm); top surfaces smooth, bottoms stiff-hairy, tips pointed.

HABITAT: Moist woodlands, thickets; sagebrush, foothills, montane, subalpine forests. Elevation 1,970–9,515 feet (600–2,900 m).

Spreading Nailwort

Paronychia depressa, Pink Family, Caryophyllaceae; Perennial herb

QUICK ID: Look for loosely matted, prickly plants with crowded, sharp-pointed leaves, and clusters of tiny, yellow, star-like flowers.

RANGE: MR, SR; scattered, locally common

STEM: Sprawling, branched, 1-3 inches tall (3-8 cm), 1-6 inches long (3-15 cm), short-hairy.

FLOWERS: May-August. Glandular-hairy, loose clusters have 3-7 tiny flowers; 5 minute petals; sepals yellowish green, oblong, ⅛-⅜ inch long (3-9 mm), slightly spreading, short-hairy, bristle-tipped.

LEAVES: Basal and crowded on stem, fleshy. Blades linear, ⅜-1 inch long (9-25 mm) by 1⁄16 inch wide (1 mm); edges entire, surfaces with fine, short hairs, tips abruptly sharp pointed.

HABITAT: Dry plains, rocky ridges, slopes; grasslands, sagebrush, foothills, montane forests. Elevation 2,625-9,850 feet (800-3,000 m).

SIMILAR SPECIES: The alpine Rocky Mountain Nailwort, *P. pulvinata*, (SR) forms dense cushions with tiny, oval leaves without bristle-tips.

Creeping Nailwort

Paronychia sessiliflora, Pink Family, Caryophyllaceae; Perennial herb

QUICK ID: Look for dense cushions packed with fleshy, oval leaves that nestle small, yellowish-green, star-like flowers.

RANGE: NR, MR, SR, Canada; widespread, scattered, infrequent

STEM: Sprawling, branched, 2-7 inches tall (5-18 cm), 2-10 inches long (5-25 cm), short-hairy.

FLOWERS: May-September. Usually solitary, or dense clusters of 3-6, nestled in leaves on branch tips; 5 minute petals, 5 yellowish-green sepals, ⅛-¼ inch long (3-5 mm), slightly spreading, bristle-tipped.

LEAVES: Basal and overlapping on stem. Blades linear, ⅛-⅝ inch long (4-16 mm) by 1⁄16 inch wide (1 mm), surfaces smooth to short-hairy, tips tapering to bristle-tipped.

HABITAT: Rocky hills, open slopes, plains; grasslands, sagebrush, foothills, montane forests. Elevation 2,500-9,500 feet (762-2,895 m).

SIMILAR SPECIES: Spreading Nailwort, *P. depressa*, (MR, SR) forms loose mats.

Yellow Beeplant

Peritoma lutea (Cleome lutea), Beeplant Family, Cleomaceae; Annual herb

QUICK ID: Look for bushy stem with showy clusters of yellow flowers with long protruding, spidery stamens and long dangling seed pods.

RANGE: NR, MR, SR; widespread, common

STEM: Erect, 1-5 feet tall (30-150 cm), hairless, colony forming.

FLOWERS: April-September. Dense rounded to elongated clusters have flowers with 4 petals and yellow stamens extending beyond the petals, like a pin cushion; seed pods dangle underneath the flowers.

LEAVES: Alternate with stalks 1-2 inches long (3-5 cm); blade palmately divided into 3-7 linear to elliptic segments, each to ¾-2 inches long (2-5 cm), up to ⅜ inch wide (1 cm); edges entire, surfaces hairless, tip pointed.

HABITAT: Coarse soils, roadsides; sagebrush, foothills, montane, subalpine forests. Elevation 4,000-8,000 feet (1,219-2,438 m).

Lanceleaf Stonecrop

Sedum lanceolatum, Stonecrop Family, Crassulaceae; Perennial succulent herb

QUICK ID: Look for rosettes of succulent leaves, and reddish stems topped with clusters of yellow, star-shaped flowers.

RANGE: NR, MR, SR, Canada; widespread, common

STEM: Erect, brittle, clumped, 2-8 inches tall (5-20 cm).

FLOWERS: June-August. Tight, flat-topped clusters have flowers ⅜-¾ inch wide (1-2 cm), 5 spreading petals, lance-shaped ¼-½ inch long (6-11 mm), 5 shorter sepals; anthers yellow to reddish.

LEAVES: Basal rosette; blades succulent, linear to oval, 3/16-1 3/16 inches long (5-30 mm), sharp pointed. Stem leaves alternate, oval to lance-shaped, slightly flattened, green to reddish, deciduous after flowering; erect, hugging the stem, overlapping.

HABITAT: Rocky outcrops, stream banks, meadows; grasslands to alpine. Elevation 8,500-13,280 feet (2,590-4,048 m).

SIMILAR SPECIES: Weakstem Stonecrop, *S. debile*, (NR, MR) has opposite, pinkish leaves.

Wormleaf Stonecrop

Sedum stenopetalum, Stonecrop Family, Crassulaceae; Perennial succulent herb

QUICK ID: Look for flower stalks with succulent leaves, tiny plantlets in the axils, and terminal clusters of yellow, star-shaped flowers.

RANGE: NR, MR, Canada; widespread, common

STEM: Flower stalks erect, branched, 3-8 inches tall (8-20 cm).

FLOWERS: May–August. Clusters have 9-25 flowers; petals 5, spreading, pointed, ⅜ inch long (9 mm); filaments and anthers yellow.

LEAVES: Alternate, stalkless, spreading to erect, often curved; blades linear ¼–⅝ inch long (5–15 mm) by ⅛ inch wide (3 mm), bottom has prominent midvein; offset plantlets grow in leaf axils.

HABITAT: Talus slopes, meadows, understory woods; grasslands to subalpine. Elevation 1,968–10,170 feet (600–3,100 m).

SIMILAR SPECIES: Lanceleaf Stonecrop, *S. lanceolatum*, (all regions) doesn't have offshoots in the leaf axils. Weakstem Stonecrop, *S. debile*, (NR, MR) has opposite, pinkish leaves.

Yellow Mountain Heather

Phyllodoce glanduliflora, Heath Family, Ericaceae; Evergreen shrub

QUICK ID: Look for low-growing plants with short, linear leaves and nodding, yellow, urn-shaped flowers with hairy stalks and sepals.

RANGE: NR, MR, Canada; widespread, common

STEM: Prostrate to erect, branched, 8–16 inches tall (20–40 cm).

FLOWERS: June–September. Erect clusters have nodding flowers, each on 1-inch-long (3 cm), glandular-hairy stalks on branch tips. Flowers have 5 creamy-yellow-to-greenish, hairy petals constricted at opening; stamens, style enclosed, sepals densely glandular-hairy.

LEAVES: Alternate, crowded, spreading, somewhat overlapping; blades narrow, linear ⅛–½ inch long (4–12 mm); edges glandular toothed; surfaces hairless, bottom deeply grooved.

HABITAT: Moist meadows, slopes; subalpine forests, alpine. Elevation 3,000–11,500 feet (915–3,500 m).

Yellow Milkvetch

Astragalus flavus, Legume Family, Fabaceae; Perennial herb

QUICK ID: Look for bushy clumps with loose clusters of white to yellow flowers on leafless stalks taller than the leaves.

RANGE: SR, MR; widespread, locally common

STEM: Erect, hairy, 2–16 inches tall (5–40 cm).

FLOWERS: April–June. Elongated clusters have 6–30 upward-pointing (not nodding), tubular flowers, each about ¾ inch long (20 mm), with 1 upturned banner petal, 2 small side wing petals that cup around 2 keel petals in the center; sepals beneath the flowers are woolly-hairy with tapering points. Pods oblong, spreading to erect, ½ inch long (13 mm), hairy, grooved. Flowers in MR are more yellow.

LEAVES: Alternate, pinnately compound. Leaflets 9–21, widely spaced, narrow, ¼–¾ inch long (5–20 mm), often folded along the midvein; surfaces covered with short, silvery hairs.

HABITAT: Selenium-rich soils in semi-deserts, sagebrush, pinyon-juniper foothills. Elevation 4,000 to 8,000 feet (1,220–2,440 m).

Yellow Sweetclover

Melilotus officinalis, Legume Family, Fabaceae; Biennial herb; introduced, naturalized

QUICK ID: Look in disturbed areas for bushy plants with 3 palmate leaflets and slender, erect spikes lined with pea-like, yellow flowers.

RANGE: NR, MR, SR, Canada; widespread, common on roadsides

STEM: Erect, clustered, 2–5 feet tall (60–150 cm).

FLOWERS: Spring, summer. Crowded elongated clusters have 30–70 small yellow flowers, each ¼–¾ inch long (6–8 mm); flowers droop, are pea-like with an upright banner petal, 2 side wings, and 2 keel petals. Fruit is a small, flat pod with 1–2 seeds.

LEAVES: Alternate, with ½-inch-long (12 mm) stalk. Blade has 3 palmate, elliptic leaflets, each ½–1 inch long (1–3 cm); edges entire to slightly toothed.

HABITAT: Disturbed areas, roadsides; grasslands, sagebrush, foothills, montane forests. Elevation 4,000–8,500 feet (1,220–2,590 m).

SIMILAR SPECIES: Another exotic, White Sweet-clover, *M. albus*, sometimes lumped with this species, often grows with this species.

Yellow Locoweed

Oxytropis campestris, Legume Family, Fabaceae; Perennial herb

QUICK ID: Look for basal clumps of pinnate leaves; spikes of pale-yellow, pea-like flowers; foliage greenish, short-hairy to silky.

RANGE: NR, MR, SR (absent NM), Canada; widespread, common

STEM: Flower stalk erect, 2–15 inches tall (5–38 cm), hairy.

FLOWERS: April–September. Spike to rounded head with 5–40 pea-like flowers, each ⅜–¾ inch long (1–2 cm) with 5 petals: 1 upturned banner, may have dark lines; 2 wings, beak-like keel of 2 petals may be purple tinted; calyx beneath petals has both white and black hairs. Pods erect, oblong, short-hairy, ⅜–1 inch long (10–25 mm), tips pointed.

LEAVES: Basal, pinnately compound, 7–35 leaflets, elliptic to lance-shaped, ¼–1 inch long (5–23 mm); surfaces hairy to top smooth.

HABITAT: Coarse soils, open areas; sagebrush, foothills, montane, subalpine forests, alpine. Elevation sea level to 11,000 feet (3,552 m).

SIMILAR SPECIES: White Locoweed, *O. sericea*, has white flowers and silvery, long-hairy foliage.

Mountain Golden Banner

Thermopsis montana, Legume Family, Fabaceae; Perennial herb

QUICK ID: Look in mountains for stems with palmate leaves; 3 leaflets; spikes of yellow flowers; and slender, erect, straight pods.

RANGE: NR, MR, SR; widespread, common

STEM: Erect, leafy, clustered, branched, 8–30 inches tall (20–75 cm).

FLOWERS: May–August. Spikes on branch tips have 6–25 flowers, each pea-like with an erect banner petal with 2 lobes, 2 forward-pointing side petals around 2 keel petals holding the stamens. Pods erect, straight, linear, hairy, 1¾–2½ inches long (5–6 cm).

LEAVES: Alternate, long-stalked with 3 leaflets, each elliptic to lance-shaped, ¾–3½ inches long (2–9 cm) by ¼–1½ inches wide (5–36 mm); edges entire, tip pointed rounded.

HABITAT: Mountain meadows, open woods; foothills, montane, subalpine forests. Elevation 6,200–11,600 feet (1,890–3,523 m).

SIMILAR SPECIES: Prairie Golden Banner, *T. rhombifolia*, (all regions, low elevations) has spreading, crescent-shaped pods.

Golden Currant

Ribes aureum, Current Family, Grossulariaceae; Deciduous shrub

QUICK ID: Look for an upright, thornless shrub with fan-shaped, lobed leaves; yellow, trumpet-shaped flowers; and orange-to-purple, juicy berries.

RANGE: SR: widespread, common; NR, MR: scattered, locally common

STEM: Upright, branched, 3–6 feet tall (1–2 m).

FLOWERS: March–June. Clusters have up to 15 bright-yellow, tubular flowers, ¼–⅜ inch long (6–10 mm) with 5 spreading, yellow petal-like sepals and 5 smaller erect, reddish petals; stamens as long as the petals. Fruit a round, hairless berry to ⅜ inch diameter (10 mm); red, orange, or purplish black; edible, juicy, sweet.

LEAVES: Alternate. Blade broadly oval to wedge-shaped, ¾–2 inches wide (2–5 cm), deeply dissected into 3 lobes, toothed or not; surfaces pale green, hairless with age. Leaves turn red to maroon in the fall.

HABITAT: Riparian woodlands; sagebrush, foothills, montane forests. Elevation 4,000-8,000 feet (1,220–2,438 m).

Scouler's St. Johnswort

Hypericum scouleri, St. Johnswort Family, Hypericaceae; Perennial herb

QUICK ID: Look in moist soils for colonies with rounded clusters of yellow flowers edged with black dots, and long, extended stamens.

RANGE: NR, MR, SR, Canada; widespread, common

STEM: Erect, branching, 7–27 inches tall (18–68 cm), rhizomatous.

FLOWERS: June–September. Flowers have 5 yellow petals ¼–⅝ inch long (6–15 mm) lined with tiny black dots; 75–100 showy yellow stamens radiate like a pin cushion.

LEAVES: Opposite. Blades without stalks, ⅜–1⅜ inches long (10–35 mm), oval to elliptic, tips pointed to rounded. Note the glandular black dots, especially along the edges.

HABITAT: Moist soils, meadows, open areas; foothills, montane, subalpine forests. Elevation 7,000–9,300 feet (2,133–2,835 m).

SIMILAR SPECIES: Common St. Johnswort, *H. perforatum*, a landscape plant invasive in all regions, is bushy with narrow, oblong leaves.

Glacier Lily

Erythronium grandiflorum, Lily Family, Liliaceae; Perennial herb

QUICK ID: Look for 2 blade-like leaves, a slender leafless flower stem, and one nodding yellow flower with petals curled backwards.

RANGE: NR, MR, SR, Canada; widespread, common

STEM: Erect, unbranched, 2–12 inches tall (5–30 cm), smooth.

FLOWERS: March–July. Usually 1 flower per stalk, 6 petal-like tepals, narrow, pointed, recurved exposing 6 slender dark-red, cream, or yellow anthers. Two subspecies: ssp. *grandiflorum* (all regions) has bright-yellow tepals; ssp. *candidum* (NR) has creamy-white tepals.

LEAVES: Basal from bulb. Two blades elliptic to oblong, broad, 2–8 inches long (5–20 cm); base narrow, edges entire, wavy or not; surfaces smooth, solid green.

HABITAT: Meadows, openings; sagebrush, foothills, montane, subalpine forests, alpine. Elevation 650–10,170 feet (200–3,100 m).

Spotted Fritillary

Fritillaria atropurpurea, Lily Family, Liliaceae; Perennial herb

QUICK ID: Look for stems with narrow, whorled leaves and nodding flowers that are yellowish green mottled with purplish brown.

RANGE: NR, MR, SR; widespread, locally common

STEM: Erect from bulb, unbranched, 4–24 inches tall (10–60 cm).

FLOWERS: April–August. Each stem has 1–4 flowers, nodding, bell-shaped to spreading, 1–2 inches wide (3–5 cm); 6 petal-like tepals, oblong to diamond shaped, ⅜–1 inch long (10–25 mm); tip pointed, not curved back.

LEAVES: Loose whorls of 2–3 on upper stem nodes. Blades linear, 2⅜–4¾ inches long (6–12 cm) by ⅛–⅜ inch wide (3–10 mm), angled upward.

HABITAT: Rich humus of grasslands, sagebrush, foothills, montane, subalpine forests. Elevation 4,000–9,000 feet (1,220–2,743 m).

Columbia Tiger Lily

Lilium columbianum, Lily Family, Liliaceae; Perennial herb

QUICK ID: Look for sturdy stems lined with nodding, bell-shaped, yellow-orange flowers with 6 back-curved, spotted petals.

RANGE: NR, Canada; widespread, common

STEM: Erect, unbranched, 1–4 feet tall (30–120 cm), smooth.

FLOWERS: May–August. 1–25 flowers pendent on ascending pedicel stalks from upper stem; 6 petal-like tepals, lance-shaped, 2–2½ inches long (4–6 cm), yellow orange to reddish, strongly bent back exposing 6 dangling stamens with orange or yellow pollen. Pollinated by the wings of swallowtail butterflies.

LEAVES: Whorled along mid-stem in 2–9 sets of 6–9 leaves; blades lance-shaped to elliptic, 1–4 inches long (3–10 cm), pointed; edges entire, often wavy, surfaces smooth. Upper and lower leaves scattered, alternate.

HABITAT: Sagebrush, foothills, montane, subalpine forests. Elevation sea level to 6,900 feet (2,100 m).

Wood Lily

Lilium philadelphicum, Lily Family, Liliaceae; Perennial herb

QUICK ID: Look in moist areas for this native lily with red-orange, tapering, curled-back petals with dark spots near the base.

RANGE: NR, MR, SR (rare), Canada; scattered, uncommon

STEM: Erect, 1–2 feet tall (30–60 cm), hairless.

FLOWERS: June–August. Clusters of 1–3 erect flowers on stem tips; each flower has 6 petal-like tepals, 6 protruding stamens; tepals 2–3 inches long (5–8 cm), pointed, tapering to a narrow base, lower half has dark spots. Pollinated by the wings of swallowtail butterflies.

LEAVES: Alternate on stem but whorls of 4–11 leaves near the top. Blades elliptic to linear, 1⅛–4 inches long (3–10 cm) by ⅛–1 inch wide (3–25 mm).

HABITAT: Moist open woods, stream banks, bogs; montane, subalpine forests. Elevation 6,600–9,700 feet (2,010–2,960 m).

Whitestem Blazingstar

Mentzelia albicaulis, Blazingstar Family, Loasaceae; Annual herb

QUICK ID: Look for rosettes with deeply lobed leaves, slender branching stems, scratchy leaves with hooked hairs, and small yellow flowers that open near dusk.

RANGE: NR, MR, SR, Canada; widespread, common

STEM: Erect, branched, 4–16 inches tall (10–40 cm), rough-hairy.

FLOWERS: February–July. Flowers ½–¾ inch wide (1–2 cm) with 5 petals, each ¼ inch long (6 mm), tip pointed; stamens extend beyond the throat; cylindrical, hairy calyx tube cups petals with pointed lobes. Fruiting capsules, ⅜–1⅛ inch long (8–28 mm), covered with long hairs, tipped with 5 finger-like tips.

LEAVES: Basal present at flowering; blades lobed or coarsely toothed, midvein white. Stem leaves alternate, linear to triangular, ¾–4¾ inches long (2–12 cm); edges entire, toothed, or deeply lobed along midrib; both sides rough with barbed hairs.

HABITAT: Coarse soils, disturbed areas; arid grasslands, sagebrush, foothills, montane forests. Elevation 4,000–7,000 feet (1,220–2,134 m).

Bushy Blazingstar

Mentzelia dispersa, Blazingstar Family, Loasaceae; Annual herb

QUICK ID: Look for brittle, branching stems; entire to shallow-lobed, rough leaves; and small yellow flowers that open near dusk.

RANGE: NR, MR, SR (absent NM), Canada; widespread, common

STEM: Erect, slender, branched, 4–16 inches tall (10–40 cm).

FLOWERS: May–August. Clusters on branch tips. 5 petals oval to ¼ inch long (3–6 mm), tip rounded; stamens 20–40, protruding outside throat. Fruit capsules erect to curved, narrow, cylindrical, to 1¼ inches long (30 mm).

LEAVES: Basal leaves persisting; blades elliptic to linear, edges entire to wavy or shallowly toothed, surfaces hairy. Alternate stem leaves similar, up to 4 inches long (10 cm).

HABITAT: Dry soils; grasslands, sagebrush, foothills, montane forests. Elevation 1,312–10,170 feet (400–3,100 m).

Giant Blazingstar

Mentzelia laevicaulis, Blazingstar Family, Loasaceae; Biennial or perennial herb

QUICK ID: Look for bushy stems; clinging leaves with barbed hairs; and large, showy flowers with golden-yellow petals and stamens.

RANGE: NR, MR, Canada; widespread, common

STEM: Erect, branched, 12–40 inches tall (30–100 cm), rough-hairy, aging to smooth.

FLOWERS: May–October. Compact clusters of flowers 1–3 inches across (3–8 cm) with 5 narrow, pointed petals, each 1¾–2¾ inches long (5–7 cm); up to 200 long yellow stamens; bracts linear to few-toothed, ⅜–1 inch long (9–25 mm). Capsules oblong, ¾–1 ½ inches long (2–4 cm), hairy. Flowers close by noon.

LEAVES: Basal rosette. Stem leaves alternate; blades lance-shaped to elliptic, 1⅝–6 inches long (4–15 cm); edges with wavy teeth, or pinnate with many shallow, forward-pointed lobes along midrib; surfaces dense with barbed hairs.

HABITAT: Dry, coarse soils; dunes, rocky slopes, disturbed areas. Elevation 2,000–9,845 feet (610–3,000 m).

Adonis Blazingstar

Mentzelia multiflora, Blazingstar Family, Loasaceae; Perennial herb

QUICK ID: Look for slender stems with narrow, lobed, clinging leaves, and pale-to-bright-yellow flowers that open near dusk.

RANGE: SR; widespread, common

STEM: Erect, branched from base, 6–40 inches tall (15–100 cm), rough-hairy.

FLOWERS: April–September. Flowers 1–2 inches wide (3–5 cm) with 5 spatula-shaped, pale-yellow-to-golden petals and 5 smaller petal-like modified stamens; stamens long, showy. Capsule cylindrical, hairy, ⅜–1 inch long (1–3 cm), topped with 5 spreading spikes.

LEAVES: Basal present at flowering. Stem leaves alternate. Blades narrowly linear to elliptic or lance-shaped, to 6 inches long (15 cm) by 1⅛ inches wide (3 cm); edges entire to shallow-toothed or lobed along the midrib. Bottom surface dense with barbed hairs.

HABITAT: Coarse soils, disturbed areas; arid grasslands, foothills, montane forests. Elevation 3,000–8,500 feet (915–2,590 m).

Scarlet Globemallow

Sphaeralcea coccinea, Mallow Family, Malvaceae; Perennial herb

QUICK ID: Look for a low-growing plant with palmate leaves with narrow, finger-like lobes and spikes of small, orange, cupped flowers.

RANGE: NR, MR, SR, Canada; widespread, common

STEM: Erect, branching, 1–2 feet tall (30–60 cm), densely covered with white star-shaped hairs, rhizomatous.

FLOWERS: Spring to fall. Short, dense spike-like clusters have flowers 1 inch wide (3 cm) with 5 notched orange, salmon, or scarlet petals; stamens and anthers yellow; no tiny, hair-like bractlets at base of flower.

LEAVES: Alternate; blades rough, hairy, ⅜–1½ inches long (10–38 mm) with a rounded outline about as long as wide; palmately divided with 3–5 radiating lobes, middle lobe longest, pinnately cleft into smaller lobes.

HABITAT: Open ground, disturbed areas; arid grasslands, sagebrush, foothills, montane forests. Elevation 3,500–8,700 feet (1,066–2,650 m).

Munro's Globemallow

Sphaeralcea munroana, Malvaceae, Mallow Family; Perennial herb

QUICK ID: Look in dry habitats for hairy stems; triangular leaves with shallow lobes; and spikes of small, orange, cupped flowers.

RANGE: NR, MR, Canada; widespread, common

STEM: Erect, branched, 1–3 feet tall (30–90 cm), gray-hairy.

FLOWERS: May–August. Narrow clusters along stem have few to many flowers, each 1 inch wide (3 cm) with 5 notched, red-orange petals; stamens and anthers yellow. Note the 3 tiny, hair-like bractlets at base of flower.

LEAVES: Alternate, stalked; blades triangular with 3–5 shallow lobes, ¾–2½ inches long (2–6 cm); edges coarsely toothed, surfaces gray green with star-shaped hairs.

HABITAT: Dry soils, badlands, forest openings; arid grasslands, sagebrush, foothills. Elevation 2,000–7,000 feet (610–2,134 m).

Rocky Mountain (Yellow) Pond Lily

Nuphar polysepala, Pond Lily Family, Nymphaeaceae; Perennial aquatic herb

QUICK ID: Look in shallow water for large, oval, floating leaves; showy, round, cup-shaped flowers with yellow-to-red-tinted sepals.

RANGE: NR, MR, SR (NM–rare), Canada; widespread, locally common

STEM: Thick, fleshy, submerged or emerging, 3–6 feet long (1–2 m).

FLOWERS: April–August. Solitary, floating or emerging above water, cup-shaped, 2–4 inches across (5–10 cm); sepals 6–9, outer ones green, inner ones yellow to red-tinged, 1⅜–2⅜ inches long (4–6 cm); petals 10–20, smaller; stamens yellow to reddish. Fruit capsule oval, 2–4 inches long (5–10 cm), berry-like seed mass jelly-like.

LEAVES: Floating or emerging on stalks to 6 feet long (2 m); blades leathery, broadly oval to heart-shaped, 4–16 inches long/wide (10–40 cm), with deeply cut rear lobes.

HABITAT: Aquatic, shallow ponds, sluggish streams; montane, subalpine forests. Elevation sea level to 11,000 feet (3,353 m).

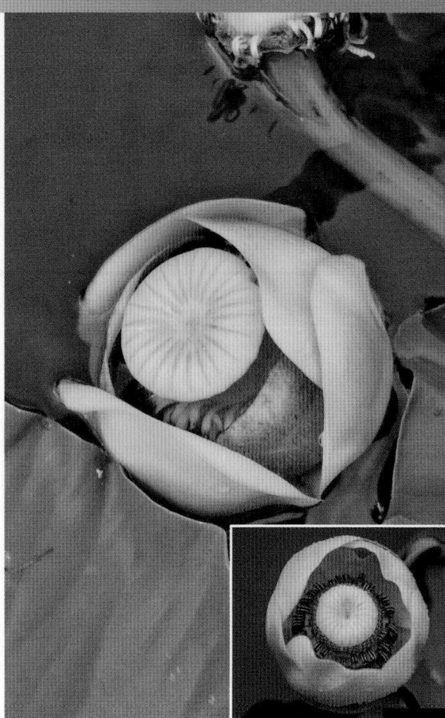

Yellow Evening Primrose

Oenothera flava, Evening Primrose Family, Onagraceae; Perennial herb

QUICK ID: Look for stemless plants with yellow flowers to 2 inches wide (5 cm) with 4 petals and long tubes rising directly from basal rosette.

RANGE: NR, MR, SR, Canada; widespread, common

STEM: None, colony forming.

FLOWERS: April–September. Petals ⅜–1⅝ inches long (1–4 cm); stamens unequal, style extends beyond the anthers and has 4 cross-like lobes; 4 sepals bend back against stem. Buds erect, angled, tipped with tiny, finger-like, spreading (not joined) tips 1/16–3/16 inch long (1–5 mm). Seed capsules sharply 4-angled.

LEAVES: Basal rosette crowded with leaves on stalks 1–3 inches long (3–8 cm). Blades oblong to linear in outline, size variable, 1–14 inches long (3–36 cm); edges toothed or deeply, irregularly lobed.

HABITAT: Seasonally moist soils, meadows, disturbed areas; grasslands, sagebrush, pinyon-juniper foothills, montane, subalpine forests. Elevation 3,600–11,000 feet (1,130–3,352 m).

Hairy Evening Primrose

Oenothera villosa, Evening Primrose Family, Onagraceae; Biennial herb

QUICK ID: Look for tall, hairy, leafy stems topped with clusters of flowers with erect buds and 4 yellow petals; hairy throughout.

RANGE: NR, MR, SR, Canada; widespread common

STEM: Erect, often reddish, branched or not, 20–78 inches tall (50–200 cm), densely hairy.

FLOWERS: June–September. Spikes from upper leaf axils; floral tube 1–2 inches long (3–5 cm), petals to ¾ inch long (2 cm); buds erect, hairy, with tiny sepal tips separate (not fused); stamens equal. Note the style with 4 cross-like lobes is equal or shorter than anthers.

LEAVES: Basal rosette; blades elliptic to lance-shaped, 4–12 inches long (10–30 cm) by ¾–2 inches wide (2–5 cm). Stem leaves alternate, smaller, edges entire, toothed, or wavy.

HABITAT: Moist soils, meadows, roadsides; grasslands to subalpine forests. Elevation 4,600–10,500 feet (1,400–3,200 m).

SIMILAR SPECIES: Another tall species, Hooker's Evening Primrose, *O. elata*, in similar habitats, has a style longer than the stamens.

Yellow Lady's Slipper Orchid

Cypripedium parviflorum, Orchid Family, Orchidaceae; Perennial herb

QUICK ID: Look for stems with broad, oval leaves and the distinctive pouch-shaped, yellow flowers.

RANGE: NR, MR, SR, Canada; scattered, rare

STEM: Erect, softly hairy, 7–24 inches tall (18–60 cm).

FLOWERS: June–July. Yellow lip pouch up to 4 inches long (10 cm); petals and sepals yellowish brown: 2 twisted petals spread to the sides; 1 yellowish-brown sepal arcs above the flower and 2 fused into 1 curl below. Lady's Slipper Orchids use "deceit pollination" to attract pollinators. They save energy by producing a sweet odor but no nectar reward.

LEAVES: Alternate with sheathing bases. Blades 4–6 per stem, broadly lance-shaped, 3½–5½ inches long (9–14 cm) by 1½–2 inches wide (4–5 cm); parallel veins run the length of leaf.

HABITAT: Moist soils, bogs, riparian; pinyon-juniper foothills, montane forests. Elevation 6,000–9,500 feet (1,828–2,895 m).

Cusick's Paintbrush

Castilleja cusickii, Broomrape Family, Orobanchaceae; Perennial herb, hemiparasitic

QUICK ID: Look for low clumps with sticky, soft-hairy foliage, and spikes of flowers with showy yellow, forked bracts.

RANGE: MR, NR, Canada; widespread, common

STEM: Erect, solitary to few, unbranched, 6–20 inches tall (15–50 cm).

FLOWERS: April–August. Spikes have hairy, pale-yellow bracts with 1–2 short lobes. The small, yellowish-tipped, beak-like flower is within or slightly protruding beyond the yellowish-green sepal tube (calyx).

LEAVES: Alternate. Blades 1–1¾ inches long (3–5 cm), broadly to narrowly lance-shaped, margins flat with 3–5 spreading lobes, upper leaves have rounded central lobe; surfaces shaggy-hairy, sometimes with red veins. Though the leaves photosynthesize, the roots are parasitic on grass roots.

HABITAT: Moist meadows; sagebrush steppes, montane forests. Elevation 1,600–8,200 feet (500–2,500 m).

SIMILAR SPECIES: Yellow Paintbrush, *C. flava*, has leaves with sharp-pointed central lobes.

Yellow Paintbrush

Castilleja flava, Broomrape Family, Orobanchaceae; Perennial herb, hemiparasitic

QUICK ID: Look for clusters with showy spikes of yellow, petal-like bracts and grayish-to-purplish leaves with 3–5 narrow, pointed lobes.

RANGE: NR, MR, SR (absent NM); widespread, common

STEM: Erect, several to many, 6–22 inches tall (15–55 cm), hairy.

FLOWERS: June–September. Dense spikes have bright- to pale-yellow, hairy bracts, sometimes orange or light red, with 3–5 slender lobes. The small, greenish, beak-like flower protrudes beyond the yellow-to-red sepal tube (calyx).

LEAVES: Alternate. Blades linear to lance-shaped, 1–2 inches long (3–5 cm), deeply cut with central lobe pointed; margins often folded along the midrib, surfaces hairy. Though the leaves photosynthesize, the roots are parasitic, usually on sagebrush, Artemisia species.

HABITAT: Dry soils; sagebrush, foothills, montane, subalpine forests. Elevation 3,000–9,850 feet (900–3,000 m).

Western Yellow Paintbrush

Castilleja occidentalis, Broomrape Family, Orobanchaceae; Perennial herb, hemiparasitic

QUICK ID: Look for short, hairy stems with 2-inch (5 cm) spikes of flowers with pale-yellow-to-greenish bracts; mostly above timberline.

RANGE: SR, NR, Canada; widespread, common

STEM: Erect, single or clustered, to 8 inches tall (20 cm).

FLOWERS: June–September. Flower clusters have sticky hairs and reach 2¾ inches long (7 cm); petal-like bracts are hairy with pointed tips, sometimes with 2 spreading side lobes; often aging dull reddish purple. The greenish beak-like flower extends fully beyond the yellow-tipped sepal tube (calyx).

LEAVES: Alternate. Blades linear to lance-shaped, ⅝–1½ inches long (15–38 mm); lower leaves flat, unlobed, with 3 distinct veins and short-hairy surfaces; upper leaves pointed or with 2 small lobes.

HABITAT: Moist meadows, slopes, talus; upper subalpine to alpine tundra. Elevation 5,000–14,100 feet (1,500–4,300 m).

SIMILAR SPECIES: Yellow Paintbrush, *C. flava*, grows to 24 inches tall (60 cm) in subalpine meadows.

Pale Paintbrush

Castilleja pallescens, Broomrape Family, Orobanchaceae; Perennial herb, hemiparasitic

QUICK ID: Look for clumps of short, erect stems with narrow, lobed leaves and spikes of yellowish-green to purplish petal-like bracts.

RANGE: NR, MR; widespread, common in grasslands and sagebrush

STEM: Erect, unbranched, 4–12 inches tall (10–30 cm), short-hairy.

FLOWERS: June–August. Flower clusters vary in colors and hues. Petal-like bracts yellow to greenish or purple-tipped with 3–5 lobes. The yellow-greenish beak-like flower is equal or slightly longer than the tips of the surrounding yellow-greenish sepal tube (calyx).

LEAVES: Alternate, green to purple-tinged or deep purple. Blades linear to narrowly lance-shaped, ⅜–1⅝ inches long (1–4 cm), edges entire to 3–5 lobed.

HABITAT: Dry slopes, open forests, meadows, fellfields; grasslands, sagebrush, montane, subalpine forests, alpine. Elevation 4,920–9,515 feet (1,500–2,900 m).

Sulphur Paintbrush

Castilleja septentrionalis (C. sulphurea), Broomrape Family, Orobanchaceae; Perennial herb, hemiparasitic

QUICK ID: Look for few to several tall stems with spikes of flowers with showy yellow bracts; leaves strongly veined, usually unlobed.

RANGE: NR, MR, SR, Canada; widespread, common

STEM: Erect, branched or not, 10-24 inches tall (25-60 cm); lower stem has few or no hairs, upper stem has long hairs.

FLOWERS: May–September. Hairy spike-like clusters. Bracts lance-shaped, pale yellow to whitish, occasionally pink-tinted; base and underside green, tips yellow to creamy with 0-5 pointed, pitchfork lobes. Flower beak green to pale-yellow, ⅝-1 inch long (15-25 mm), extends beyond sepal tube (calyx).

LEAVES: Alternate. Blades with 0-3 lobes, green to purplish, narrow to broadly lance-shaped, ¾-2¾ inches long (2-7 cm), hairless or with a few scattered short hairs.

HABITAT: Open forests, rocky slopes; montane, subalpine forests and meadows. Elevation 7,000-12,200 feet (2,133-3,700 m). This is one of the most widespread paintbrushes.

Yellow Owl's-clover

Orthocarpus luteus, Broomrape Family, Orobanchaceae; Annual herb, hemiparasitic

QUICK ID: Look for erect, yellowish-green-to-purplish, leafy stems with spikes of small yellow, club-shaped flowers; colony forming.

RANGE: NR, MR, SR, Canada; widespread, common

STEM: Erect, 4-16 inches tall (10-40 cm), dense with glandular hairs.

FLOWERS: July–September. Dense, hairy spikes with green, leaf-like, pointed bracts; flowers tubular, yellow ⅜-⅝ inch long (10-15 mm), 2 lips of equal length, upper lip hood-like enclosing anthers and style, lower lip with a slight pouch.

LEAVES: Alternate. Lower stem leaves linear to lance-shaped, ½-1⅜ inches long (1-4 cm); upper leaves have 3 deep lobes; margins entire, tips pointed, surfaces glandular-hairy.

HABITAT: Moist coarse soils, meadows, riparian areas, roadsides; grasslands, sagebrush, pinyon-juniper foothills, montane forests. Elevation: 6,000-10,000 feet (1,829-3,048 m).

Bracted Lousewort

Pedicularis bracteosa, Broomrape Family, Orobanchaceae; Perennial herb, hemiparasitic

QUICK ID: Look for tall stems with fern-like leaves and hairy spikes of yellow-to-reddish, tubular flowers with arching club-like hoods.

RANGE: NR, MR, SR, Canada; widespread, common

STEM: Erect, single or clustered, unbranched, 1–3 feet tall (30–100 cm), hairless.

FLOWERS: June–September. Clusters to 18 inches long (45 cm) with hairy, leaf-like bracts. Flowers yellow to reddish brown tinted, tubular, 1 inch long (25 mm); upper lip hood-like, arches above lower lip.

LEAVES: Basal with long stalks, may be absent at flowering. Stem leaves alternate with short stalks or stalkless; blades linear to oblong or lance-shaped, 2¾–6⅜ inches long (7–16 cm); deeply cut to midrib, lobes toothed, fern-like.

HABITAT: Stream sides, open forests, meadows; montane, subalpine forests, alpine. Elevation 4,000–12,000 feet (1,220–3,656 m).

SIMILAR SPECIES: Giant Lousewort, *P. procera*, (MR, SR) to 5 feet tall (155 cm), has pale-yellow, red-streaked flowers and fern-like leaves.

Canadian Lousewort

Pedicularis canadensis, Broomrape Family, Orobanchaceae; Perennial herb, hemiparasitic

QUICK ID: Look for dense clusters of pinnately lobed basal leaves; short stems; and spikes of yellow, tubular flowers with an upper hooded lip and lower lip with spreading lobes.

RANGE: SR; widespread, locally common

STEM: Erect, unbranched, 4–20 inches tall (10–50 cm), hairy.

FLOWERS: June–August. Elongated, spike-like, hairy clusters have 10–40 flowers ¾–1 inch long (2–3 cm); floral tube yellow, petals yellow, red-veined, or purplish; upper lip arching, hooded covering stamens, beakless; lower lip yellow or white, spreading.

LEAVES: Basal, 2–20; blades lance-shaped ¾–4 inches long (2–10 cm); shallowly cut into rounded, toothed lobes, surfaces smooth to hairy; often reddish in spring. Stem leaves 1–10, opposite, smaller.

HABITAT: Woodlands, ridges, meadows; montane, subalpine forests. Elevation 7,200–10,200 feet (2,195–3,110 m).

Parry's Lousewort

Pedicularis parryi, Broomrape Family, Orobanchaceae; Perennial herb, hemiparasitic

QUICK ID: Look for tall clustered stems, fern-like leaves, and spikes of tubular, creamy-yellow flowers with a hooded upper lip with a straight, conical beak.

RANGE: NR, MR, SR; widespread, common

STEM: Erect, clustered, 4–26 inches tall (10–65 cm), hairy or not.

FLOWERS: June–August. Dense, hairless, spike-like clusters have leaf-like bracts and 5–50 tubular flowers, each with 2 lips: upper lip forms an arching hood with a conical beak extending beyond the spreading lobes of the lower lip. The calyx cupping the petals is green with purple stripes.

LEAVES: Mostly basal, alternate on stem. Blades lance-shaped in outline, 1–8 inches long (3–20 cm), pinnately divided into coarsely toothed segments; surfaces hairy or smooth.

HABITAT: Moist, well-drained meadows; slopes; upper montane, subalpine forests, alpine. Elevation 7,875–13,125 feet (2,400–4,000 m).

SIMILAR SPECIES: *P. parryi* ssp. *purpurea*, (NR) has purple flowers.

Giant Lousewort

Pedicularis procera, Broomrape Family, Orobanchaceae; Perennial herb, hemiparasitic

QUICK ID: Look for clumps of head-high stems with fern-like leaves and dense spikes of pale-yellow, tubular flowers streaked with red.

RANGE: MR, SR; widespread, common

STEM: Erect, robust; leafy, 30–60 inches tall (75–150 cm), hairy.

FLOWERS: July–August. Dense spikes have 10–50 hairy flowers interspaced with long, narrow, hairy, leaf-like bracts. Tubular flowers, 1–1⅜ inch long (25–36 mm) with 2 red-streaked lips; upper lip with rounded hood arches over yellowish lower lip with 3 spreading lobes with red lines. Calyx cupping the petals is green and purple.

LEAVES: Basal leaves to 4–12 inches long (10–30 cm), pinnately divided into separate segments with sharp teeth, like a fern frond, hairless. Stem leaves alternate, similar, scattered, smaller upward.

HABITAT: Meadows, wooded slopes; foothills, montane, subalpine forests. Elevation 7,200–11,000 feet (2,195–3,353 m).

Golden Corydalis

Corydalis aurea, Poppy Family, Papaveraceae; Annual, biennial herb

QUICK ID: Look for low clumps with 10–50 short stems and spikes of tubular, golden flowers with rear spurs.

RANGE: NR, MR, SR, Canada; widespread, common

STEM: Erect, delicate, leafy, 8–18 inches tall (20–45 cm).

FLOWERS: May–August. Short stems with spike-like clusters of 10–20 yellow, irregular, tubular flowers, ½–⅝ inch long (13–15 mm); 4 petals: outer 2 with spreading lips are joined to form a rounded rear spur, inner 2 joined to form a hood over the stigma. Fruit a slender pod-like capsule ½–¾ inch long (12–20 mm).

LEAVES: Alternate. Blade compound, leaflets deeply cut into numerous narrow, pointed lobes; surfaces hairless.

HABITAT: Sagebrush arid grasslands, sagebrush, foothills, montane, subalpine forests. Elevation 3,500–11,100 feet (1,066–3,353 m).

Manyflowered Monkeyflower

Erythranthe floribunda (Mimilus floribundus), Lopseed Family, Phrymaceae; Annual herb

QUICK ID: Look in wet habitats for soft- to sticky-hairy stems, paired yellow flowers, and 5 petals nearly equal in shape with red dots.

RANGE: NR, MR, SR, Canada; scattered, infrequent

STEM: Erect to trailing, single or branching from base, 2–16 inches long/tall (5–40 cm), glandular-hairy, sticky to soft with age.

FLOWERS: May–July. Flowers in leaf axils, usually paired; tubular, ¼–⅝ inch long (5–15 mm), 5 lobes, mostly equal; lower lip red-dotted, hairy; stigma and filaments same length. Fruiting capsules cylindrical, ⅛–¾ inch long (3–10 mm).

LEAVES: Opposite, on stalks to ½ inch long (12 mm). Blades triangular to oval, pointed, ⅜–2 inches long (1–5 cm), 3–5 pinnate veins; edges toothed, lined with long hairs; surfaces sparsely hairy.

HABITAT: Moist slopes, meadows, muddy soils; montane, subalpine forests. Elevation 5,900–8,530 feet (1,800–2,600 m).

Roundleaf Monkeyflower

Erythranthe geyeri (Mimulus glabratus), Lopseed Family, Phrymaceae; Perennial herb

QUICK ID: Look in wet habitats for creeping, mat-forming stems and bright-yellow flowers with 2 lips and a hairy, red-dotted throat.

RANGE: SR; scattered, locally common

STEM: Sprawling, rooting, branching, 4–16 inches long (10–40 cm).

FLOWERS: March–August. Flowers tubular, throat ⅜–¾ inch long (1–2 cm) with 2 lips; upper lip has 2 lobes; lower lip with 3 lobes, the middle bearded, sparsely red-spotted or not, does not close the throat; calyx smooth to sparsely hairy. In fruit the erect calyx lobes don't fold over to close the capsule.

LEAVES: Opposite, lower with short stalks, upper stalkless. Blades oval to rounded, ¼–1 inch diameter (6–25 mm), with 3–5 palmate veins, shallow teeth, smooth to sparsely glandular-hairy.

HABITAT: Shallow water, wet soils; foothills, montane, subalpine forests. Elevation 4,600–10,500 feet (1,400–3,200 m).

SIMILAR SPECIES: Seep Monkeyflower, *E. guttata*, lower lip nearly closes the throat.

Seep Monkeyflower

Erythranthe guttata (Mimulus guttatus), Lopseed Family, Phrymaceae; Perennial herb

QUICK ID: Look in seeps and shallow water for clumping plants with small, tubular, bright-yellow flowers with hairy throats with red dots.

RANGE: NR, MR, SR, Canada; widespread, common

STEM: Erect to sprawling, reddish, hollow, 1–2 feet tall (30–60 cm).

FLOWERS: April–September. Clusters from leaf nodes have 3–20 tubular flowers, each ⅜–1 inch long (1–3 cm); 2 upper lobes, 3 lower lobes; hairy ridges almost close throat. Calyx tube smooth to hairy, ridged, tips triangular, unequal in length, fold over seed capsule.

LEAVES: Opposite. Blades oval to rounded, ⅝–2 inches long/wide (15–50 mm), hairless or nearly so, with 5–7 prominent veins, and margins with irregular teeth or lobes. Lower leaves have stalks, upper leaves clasping.

HABITAT: Wet soils, shallow water; foothills, montane, subalpine forests, alpine meadows. Elevation sea level–11,000 feet (3,353 m).

SIMILAR SPECIES: Roundleaf Monkeyflower, *E. geyeri*, (SR) has an open flower throat.

Musk Monkeyflower

Erythranthe moschata (Mimulus moschatus), Lopseed Family, Phrymaceae; Perennial herb

QUICK ID: Look for sticky, white-hairy plants, often musk-scented, and yellow flowers with lined, hairy petals nearly equal in size.

RANGE: NR, MR, SR (absent NM), Canada; widespread, common

STEM: Erect to sprawling, branching, rooting, 2–28 inches long (5–70 cm), white-hairy, rhizomatous.

FLOWERS: May–September. Flowers 1 (often 2) in leaf axils; tubular with 5 spreading, nearly equal petals, usually with dark lines or red dots in hairy throat; stigma longer than filaments.

LEAVES: Opposite, short-stalked below, unstalked upward. Blades oblong, ⅜–2⅜ inches long (1–6 cm), pinnately veined; edges coarsely toothed, surfaces smooth to glandular-hairy.

HABITAT: Moist meadows, forest openings, muddy soils; sagebrush, foothills, montane forests. Elevation 2,500–10,170 feet (400–3,100 m).

SIMILAR SPECIES: Manyflowered Muskflower, *E. floribunda*, has nearly equal, red-dotted petals, but usually paired flowers at nodes.

Miniature Monkeyflower

Erythranthe suksdorfii (Mimulus suksdorfii), Lopseed Family, Phrymaceae; Annual herb

QUICK ID: Look for low, densely branched, leafy plants with small yellow flowers, nearly equal-sized lobes, and a red-spotted throat.

RANGE: NR, MR, SR; widespread, uncommon

STEM: Erect, branching from base, ¼–4 inches tall (5–100 mm).

FLOWERS: April–August. Flowers solitary from leaf axils. Floral tube ¼ inch long (6 mm), 5 spreading petal-lobes nearly equal in size, notched or not; throat smooth to sparsely hairy, usually red spotted. Sepal tube clasping the floral tube ribbed, smooth to glandular-hairy, often purple.

LEAVES: Opposite, stalkless. Blades linear to lance-shaped or oval, pointed, ¼–¾ inch long (5–20 mm); edges entire, surfaces minutely to glandular-hairy.

HABITAT: Clay, sandy soils, open areas; sagebrush, foothills, montane, subalpine. Elevation 4,000–10,000 feet (1,220–3,048 m).

Dalmatian Toadflax

Linaria dalmatica, Plantain Family, Plantaginaceae; Perennial herb; introduced, naturalized, invasive

QUICK ID: Look for stems with oval, closely spaced, clasping, blue-green leaves and spikes of yellow, snapdragon-like flowers.

RANGE: NR, MR, SR, Canada; widespread, locally common

STEM: Erect, upper branching, 1–3 feet tall (30–90 cm), rhizomatous.

FLOWERS: April–October. Spikes of tubular flowers, each ⅝–1 inch long (15–25 mm), with 2 lips, the lower lip white to orange, densely hairy, closes the throat; rear spur to ¾ inch long (2 cm), mostly parallel to stem. One plant can produce 500,000 highly viable seeds.

LEAVES: Opposite, alternate, or whorled, crowded on stem. Blades elliptic to oval, ½–2 inches long (1–5 cm); bases clasp the stem, tips pointed to tapering.

HABITAT: Disturbed areas, roadsides; grasslands, sagebrush, foothills, montane forests. Elevation sea level to 8,500 feet (2,590 m).

Yellow Toadflax

Linaria vulgaris, Plantain Family, Plantaginaceae; Perennial herb; introduced, naturalized, invasive

QUICK ID: Look for stems with narrow linear leaves, spikes of creamy-yellow flowers with a bulging dark-yellow center, and a long rear spur.

RANGE: NR, MR, SR, Canada; widespread, locally common

STEM: Erect, upper branching, 1–3 feet tall (30–90 cm), rhizomatous.

FLOWERS: May–September. Spike-like clusters 3–6 inches long (8–15 cm); tubular flowers pale yellow, ¾–1⅜ inches long (20–35 mm); upper lip has 2 erect lobes, lower lip lobes fold downward with a dark-yellow ridge in throat; rear spur usually parallel to stem. One plant can produce 30,000 seeds and spread aggressively by rhizomes.

LEAVES: Alternate, opposite, or whorled, crowded on stem, stalkless but not clasping. Blades narrow, linear, ¾–4 inches long (2–10 cm) by 3/16 inch wide (4 mm).

HABITAT: Roadsides, waste areas; grasslands, foothills, montane, subalpine forests. Elevation 1,460–9,300 feet (445–2,835 m).

Yellow Penstemon

Penstemon confertus, Plantain Family, Plantaginaceae; Perennial herb

QUICK ID: Look for creamy-yellow, tubular flowers with 5 rounded, petal-like lobes in dense clusters separated along the stem.

RANGE: NR, Canada; widespread, common

STEM: Erect, clumped, 4–28 inches tall (10–70 cm), mostly smooth.

FLOWERS: May–August. Clusters 2–10, cylindrical, dense, the bottom one separate, each with 2-9 tubular flowers, ⅜–½ inch long (8–12 mm), with 5 spreading lobes; flower tube hairless externally, moderately woolly-hairy inside, with 2 ridges; 4 anthers brown, beardtongue has straight tip with yellow-brownish hairs.

LEAVES: Basal, on stalks, often densely clumped; blades elliptic to lance-shaped, ¾–5 inches long (2–12 cm) by 1 inch wide (25 mm); base tapered, edges entire, surfaces hairless, tip pointed. Stem leaves similar, smaller, 4–7 pairs, opposite, unstalked.

HABITAT: Dry slopes, meadows, open forests; sagebrush, foothills, montane, subalpine forests. Elevation 1,200–8,400 feet (335–2,563 m).

Brandegee's Jacob's-ladder

Polemonium brandegeei, Phlox Family, Polemoniaceae; Perennial herb

QUICK ID: Look for leafy stems with smelly, hairy leaves, and clusters of pale-yellow-to-white, funnel-shaped flowers.

RANGE: MR (WY), SR; widespread, common

STEM: Erect, branched from base, 3–12 inches tall (8–30 cm), densely glandular.

FLOWERS: May–July. Clusters erect to nodding; floral tube ¾–1⅛ inches long (2–3 cm) spreads open with 5 rounded, petal-like lobes; 5 yellow stamens in mouth of throat. White flowers more common in northern range. Flower shape adapted for hummingbird and hawk moth pollination.

LEAVES: Mostly basal, ¾–7¾ inches long (2–20 cm) with numerous oval leaflets densely covered with glandular hairs. Stem leaves similar, alternate; leaflets 3/16–⅜ inch long (4–10 mm), spaced in whorl-like clusters along midrib.

HABITAT: Rock outcrops, openings, meadows; montane, subalpine forests. Elevation 8,000–13,000 feet (2,438–3,962 m).

Winged Buckwheat

Eriogonum alatum, Buckwheat Family, Polygonaceae; Perennial herb

QUICK ID: Look for tall, hairy, slender, branching stems with tiny yellow flowers and reddish seeds with 3 small, wafer-like wings.

RANGE: MR, SR; widespread, common

STEM: Erect, open, leafless branches, 20–50 inches tall (50–127 cm).

FLOWERS: June–October. Clusters of flowers ⅛ inch wide (3 mm), yellow with 6 pointed, petal-like sepals and showy, extended stamens. Prominent greenish-yellow seeds have 3 wings and mature rusty reddish. Seeds hang on short stalks in tight, round clusters.

LEAVES: Basal rosette grows 3–7 years before blooming and dying; blades 2–7¾ inches long (5–20 cm), narrowly lance-shaped with tapering bases; edges and surfaces with long hairs. Stem leaves alternate ⅜–3½ inches long (1–8 cm), smaller up the stem.

HABITAT: Dry soils; arid grasslands, sagebrush, foothills, montane forests. Elevation 4,400–9,000 feet (1,341–2,743 m).

SIMILAR SPECIES: Annual Buckwheat, *E. annuum*, has clusters of small white flowers.

Baker's Buckwheat

Eriogonum arcuatum, Buckwheat Family, Polygonaceae; Perennial herb

QUICK ID: Look for basal leaves with cobwebby hairs and rounded, leafy clusters of small, hairy, yellow flowers on short stalks. Long- and short-stemmed varieties occur.

RANGE: SR; widespread, common

STEM: Erect, 1–3 upper branches, ¾–10 inches tall (2–25 cm), hairy.

FLOWERS: June–October. Dense umbrella-shaped clusters on 2–3 stalks rising from stem node with 3–8 leaf-like bracts; flowers about ¼ inch long (6 mm) including short stalk (stipe), yellow to reddish tinted, hairy; stamens extend beyond flower.

LEAVES: Basal, in loose to dense mat. Blades oblong to elliptical, ⅜–2 inches long (1–5 cm) including stalk; edges entire, flat; surfaces densely woolly.

HABITAT: Grasslands, sagebrush, foothills, montane, subalpine forests. Elevation 3,700–13,780 feet (1,220–4,200 m).

SIMILAR SPECIES: James Buckwheat, *E. jamesii*, (SR) differs only by having white flowers.

Matted Buckwheat

Eriogonum caespitosum, Buckwheat Family, Polygonaceae; Perennial herb

QUICK ID: Look for tight mats with hairy leaves and leafless flower stems topped with ball-like clusters of small yellow flowers.

RANGE: NR, MR, SR (WY); widespread, common.

STEM: Erect, not branching, 1-4 inches tall (3-10 cm), hairy or not.

FLOWERS: April-July. Spherical clusters to ¾ inch diameter (2 cm) with no leaf-like bracts below head. Flowers small, to ⅜ inch long (1 cm), yellow to reddish, densely hairy. Male and female flowers usually separate.

LEAVES: Basal rosette forms mats; blades elliptic to oval, ⅜ inch long (1 cm); edges entire, rolled under, both surfaces gray-hairy.

HABITAT: Grasslands, sagebrush, foothill, montane pine forests. Elevation 5,000-9,850 feet (1,500-3,000 m).

Golden Buckwheat

Eriogonum flavum, Buckwheat Family, Polygonaceae; Perennial herb

QUICK ID: Look for matted plants, leaves with densely hairy bottoms, leafless flower stalks, and dense rounded clusters of bright-yellow flowers.

RANGE: NR, MR, SR (absent NM), Canada; widespread, common

STEM: Erect, unbranched, 4-8 inches tall (10-20 cm), white-hairy.

FLOWERS: June-September. Dense umbrella-like clusters have 4-20 radiating branches tipped with tiny flowers. Note the silky hairs on the petals and 4-6 leaf-like bracts below the branching cluster.

LEAVES: Basal, stalked; blades oblong to narrowly elliptic, ¾-2¾ inches long (1-7 cm) by ⅛-⅝ inch wide (3-15 mm); edges entire; top surface green-hairless to short woolly-hairy, bottom densely white woolly-hairy. High-elevation plants are smaller.

HABITAT: Open areas; grasslands, sagebrush, foothills, montane, subalpine forests, alpine. Elevation 1,640-10,500 feet (500-3,200 m).

Sulphur Flower Buckwheat

Eriogonum umbellatum, Buckwheat Family, Polygonaceae; Perennial herb

QUICK ID: Look for basal mats, leafless flower stems, whorls of leaf-like bracts below umbrella-like branches, and clustered yellow flowers.

RANGE: NR, MR, SR, Canada; widespread, common; has 41 varieties

STEM: Erect, branching, 2–12 inches tall (5–30 cm), hairy or not.

FLOWERS: June–September. A long stem leads to a cluster of leaf-like bracts; several flower stalks rise from the whorl to a second whorl with small-to-miniscule bracts below each umbrella-like cluster. Flowers ⅛–⅜ inch long (3–10 mm), yellow fading to reddish, hairless.

LEAVES: Basal rosette loose to compact. Leaves have stalks ¼–1 inch long (6–25 mm); blades oblong to elliptic, ¼–1 inch long (6–25 mm) by 1 inch wide (3 cm); edges entire, bottom surface densely woolly, top lightly hairy, or both sides bright green.

HABITAT: Dry meadows, openings; foothills, montane, subalpine forests, alpine. Elevation 3,940–9,190 feet (1,200–2,800 m).

Common Purslane

Portulaca oleracea, Purslane Family, Portulacaceae; Annual herb; introduced, naturalized

QUICK ID: Look for fleshy, prostrate, hairless branches with tiny yellow flowers and round-tipped, succulent leaves.

RANGE: NR, MR, SR, Canada; widespread, common, invasive

STEM: Prostrate, succulent, to 24 inches long (60 cm), hairless.

FLOWERS: May–November. Flowers tiny, ⅛–⅜-inch wide (3–9 mm), 5 yellow, notched petals surrounded by clusters of leaves. Fruit capsule ⅛–¼ inch diameter (3–8 mm) with seeds.

LEAVES: Alternate. Blades numerous, oval to spoon-shaped, ¼–1 inch long (6–25 mm), flat, succulent, often reddish-purple tinged.

HABITAT: Coarse soils, yards, disturbed areas; arid grasslands to foothills. Elevation 3,700–8,500 feet (1,127–2,590 m).

NOTES: Though considered "one of the 10 most noxious weeds in the world," it's high in iron, protein, and has the "highest content of omega-3 fatty acids and antioxidants of any leafy vegetable tested" (Flora of North America).

Yellow Columbine

Aquilegia flavescens, Buttercup Family, Ranunculaceae; Perennial herb

QUICK ID: Yellow flowers have spurs pointing up; petals pointing down; and yellow, white, or pink sepals spread like outstretched wings. Lower leaflets fan shaped.

RANGE: MR, NR, Canada; widespread, common

STEM: Slender, 7–27 inches tall (18–69 cm).

FLOWERS: June–August. Flowers cylindrical; petal-like sepals yellow, white, or pink; held at right angles; petal blades yellow with rounded tips; spurs ⅜–¾ inch long (10–19 mm) with incurved tips. Note the stamens extend about ½ inch (12 mm) below petals.

LEAVES: Basal, alternate on stem. Leaves compound, divided twice in sets of 3 with fan-shaped leaflets, each with 2–3 lobes. Basal leaves 3–12 inches long (8–30 cm); stem leaves few, smaller.

HABITAT: Moist soils, meadows, open woods; montane, subalpine forests, alpine slopes. Elevation 4,000–11,500 feet (1,220–3,505 m).

Water-plantain Buttercup

Ranunculus alismifolius, Buttercup Family, Ranunculaceae; Perennial herb

QUICK ID: Look in wet areas for clumped stems with long-stalked, basal leaves and clusters with few small yellow flowers with many stamens.

RANGE: NR, MR, SR, Canada (rare); widespread, locally common; 6 varieties

STEM: Erect, upper branched, 2–16 inches tall (6–40 cm), hairy or not, colony forming.

FLOWERS: May–August. Spreading clusters on long stalks have few flowers, petals 4–6 or 5–12, oval, ¼–⅝ inch long (6–15 mm); stamens 25–90 around cone of pistils.

LEAVES: Basal, long-stalked; blades lance-shaped to elliptic, 1–6 inches long (3–15 cm); edges entire, surfaces hairy or not. Stem leaves alternate, unstalked, edges entire to minutely toothed.

HABITAT: Wet soils, meadows, stream banks; montane, subalpine forests, alpine. Elevation 4,265–11,800 feet (1,300–3,500 m).

Heartleaf Buttercup

Ranunculus cardiophyllus, Buttercup Family, Ranunculaceae; Perennial herb

QUICK ID: Look for heart-shaped basal leaves, deeply divided stem leaves, and clusters with few small yellow flowers with many stamens.

RANGE: SR: widespread, common; NR, Canada: rare

STEM: Erect, branched, 10–21 inches tall (11–53 cm), hairy or not.

FLOWERS: May–September. Open clusters have 1–5 flowers on long, soft-hairy stalks, petals 5–10, oval, ¼–⅝ inch long (6–15 mm).

LEAVES: Basal, long stalked; blades spade-shaped to elliptic, ¾–3 inches long (2–8 cm), usually undivided, sometimes 3–5 lobed, base heart-shaped; edges entire to round-toothed, surfaces soft-hairy, tips rounded to pointed. Stem leaves alternate, short-stalked, palmate, lobes narrow.

HABITAT: Wet to dry meadows, open sites; montane, subalpine forests, alpine. Elevation 8,000–11,500 feet (2,350–3,500 m).

Eschscholtz's Buttercup

Ranunculus eschscholtzii var. *eschscholtzii*, Buttercup Family, Ranunculaceae; Perennial herb

QUICK ID: Look for hairless stems each with 1–3 yellow flowers with 5 petals, and long-stalked basal leaves with 3 lobes. Features differ depending on variety.

RANGE: NR, MR, SR, Canada; widespread, common; 6 varieties

STEM: Erect to sprawling, 1½–10 inches tall (4–25 cm), hairless.

FLOWERS: June–August. Loose clusters have 1–3 flowers, 5–8 petals, oval, ¼–⅝ inch long (6–15 mm); many stamens.

LEAVES: Basal, long stalked; blade outline egg- to heart-shaped, ⅜–1⅝ inches long (1–4 cm), always 3 lobed; each lobe divided again into 1–2 segments, tips rounded or toothed; surfaces hairless. Stem leaves absent or lobed.

HABITAT: Meadows, slopes; upper montane, subalpine forests, alpine. Elevation 8,000–11,800 feet (2,438–3,600 m).

SIMILAR SPECIES: Graceful Buttercup, *R. inamoenus*, (all regions) has both lobed and unlobed basal leaves.

Sagebrush Buttercup

Ranunculus glaberrimus, Buttercup Family, Ranunculaceae; Perennial herb

QUICK ID: Look in middle elevations for low-growing stems with hairless, rounded basal leaves and small flowers with 5 yellow petals.

RANGE: NR, MR, SR, Canada; widespread, common; 2 varieties

STEM: Prostrate, clumping, 1½–6 inches tall, (4–15 cm), hairless.

FLOWERS: March–June. Loose clusters have 1–4 flowers, 5–10 petals, oval, ⅜–½ inch long (9–13 mm); stamens many; bracts beneath flower deeply 3-lobed.

LEAVES: Basal, long stalked; blades egg-shaped to elliptic, ¼–2 inches long (7–52 mm); edges entire to deeply round-lobed (var. *glaberrimus*, low-elevation shrublands), or undivided, rarely lobed (var. *ellipticus*, moist, high-elevation grasslands); tips rounded to pointed, surfaces hairless. Stem leaves similar, alternate, unstalked.

HABITAT: Moist areas, meadows, open woods; grasslands, sagebrush, foothills, montane forests. Elevation 1,640–9,000 feet (500–3,600 m).

Graceful Buttercup

Ranunculus inamoenus, Buttercup Family, Ranunculaceae; Perennial herb

QUICK ID: Look for leafy rosette of fan-shaped leaves, stalks with narrow-lobed leaves, and small flowers with 5 yellow petals.

RANGE: NR, MR, SR: widespread, common; Canada: infrequent

STEM: Erect, 1-several, 2–13 inches tall (5–33 cm), hairy or not.

FLOWERS: April–September. Loose clusters have 3–7 flowers, each ⅜–¾ inch wide (10–20 mm) with 5–7 oval petals; many stamens surround a green cone of pistils.

LEAVES: Basal, long stalked; blades oval to rounded, ⅜–1½ inches long/wide (1–4 cm), a mix of undivided, fan-shaped blades or with 2–3 lobes. Upper stem blades alternate with 3–5 narrow, linear-to-lance-shaped lobes.

HABITAT: Moist, coarse soils, meadows, slopes; foothills, montane, subalpine forests. Elevation 7,000–12,000 feet (2,134–3,658 m).

SIMILAR SPECIES: Eschscholtz's Buttercup, *R. eschscholtzii* var. *eschscholtzii* (all regions), has basal leaves always 3-lobed.

Rocky Mountain Buttercup

Ranunculus macauleyi, Buttercup Family, Ranunculaceae; Perennial herb

QUICK ID: Look in high-elevation meadows for flowers with short stems; narrow basal leaves with teeth on the tips; and cup-shaped, yellow flowers with long, black-hairy sepals under the petals.

RANGE: SR; common; endemic CO and NM

STEM: Erect, 1-several clumped, 2⅜-6 inches tall (6-15 cm), smooth or hairy.

FLOWERS: June-August. 1-2 flowers on stem tips; 5 (up to 8) petals, oval ⅜-¾ inch long (10-20 mm); stamens many around green cone of pistils; sepals under petals dense with long, black hairs.

LEAVES: Basal; blades narrowly elliptic to lance-shaped, ⅝-2 inches long (15-50 mm); undivided, ends rounded or pointed, tipped with several teeth. Stem leaves similar, alternate, clasping, long-hairy.

HABITAT: Wet meadows, slopes, often near receding snow; subalpine to alpine. Elevation 10,826-12,960 feet (3,300-3,950 m).

Roadside Agrimony

Agrimonia striata, Rose Family, Rosaceae; Perennial herb

QUICK ID: Look for narrow spikes of small yellow flowers and compound leaves with variable-sized leaflets.

RANGE: NR, MR, SR, Canada; widespread, locally common

STEM: Erect, stout, hairy, 36-40 inches tall (90-100 cm).

FLOWERS: July-September. Yellow with 5 petals, 3/16 inch long (4 mm), densely crowded on an elongated spike-like cluster blooming from bottom upward. The outer rim of the flower head is lined with tiny, hooked bristles. Seed capsule is a prickly bur.

LEAVES: Alternate. Blades hairy, pinnately compound to 8 inches long (20 cm) with a mix of 7-13 large and small leaflets, each elliptic to oval, 1 3/16-4¾ inches long (3-12 cm); margins have coarse teeth.

HABITAT: Stream sides, meadows, thickets; foothills to mixed conifer forests. Elevation 6,300-8,800 feet (1,900-2,680 m).

Shrubby Cinquefoil

Dasiphora fruticosa, Rose Family, Rosaceae; Deciduous shrub

QUICK ID: Look for a low-mounding shrub with dense branching, tiny hairy leaflets, and showy yellow flowers with oval petals.

RANGE: NR, MR, SR, Canada; widespread, common

STEM: Densely branching, 1-3 feet tall and wide (30-90 cm).

FLOWERS: June-September. Solitary or few on branch tips; flowers ¾-1¼ inches wide (2-3 cm) with 5 petals, numerous stamens.

LEAVES: Alternate. Pinnately compound with 3-7 crowded leaflets, linear to elliptic ¼-1 inch long (5-25 mm), linear to oblong; surfaces silky-hairy, edges often rolled under.

HABITAT: Foothills, montane, subalpine forests, alpine meadows. Elevation 7,500-12,500 feet (2,286-3,810 m).

Bigflower (Leafy) Cinquefoil

Drymocallis fissa, Rose Family, Rosaceae; Perennial herb

QUICK ID: Look for low clumps with hairy stems, pinnately compound leaves, and 1-inch (3 cm) flowers with 5 yellow petals and center.

RANGE: MR, SR; widespread, common, especially CO, WY

STEM: Erect, slender, 1 or more from base, 6-14 inches tall (15-35 cm), hairy.

FLOWERS: May-August. Crowded clusters have 5-15 showy flowers on upper stem; 5 oval petals are separated by 5 yellow, hairy, pointed sepals; yellow stamens surround a yellow receptacle in the center.

LEAVES: Basal, alternate on stem. Blade pinnately compound, 2¾-7½ inches long (7-19 cm) with 5-6 pairs of leaflets along the midrib and a terminal leaflet, all ½-1⅜ inches long (12-35 mm), elliptic to oval, toothed, sparsely to moderately hairy; 1-3 similar stem leaves; smaller leaflets sometimes interspersed along midrib.

HABITAT: Sagebrush, foothills, open montane forests. Elevation 5,250-9,850 feet (1,600-3,000 m).

Large-leaf Avens

Geum macrophyllum, Rose Family, Rosaceae; Perennial herb

QUICK ID: Look for a dense rosette of pinnate leaves, stems with long hairs, and clusters of 4-6 flowers with 5 oval, yellow petals.

RANGE: NR, MR, SR, Canada; widespread, common

STEM: Erect, branching, 12-40 inches tall (30-102 cm), long hairs.

FLOWERS: May-August. Flowers to ½ inch wide (12 mm) on hairy stalks with leaf-like bracts; petals ⅛-¼ inch long (3-6 mm); sepals fold back against the stem. Fruit a pincushion sphere densely packed with red, thread-like styles tipped with yellow hooks.

LEAVES: Basal blades 4-10 inches long (10-25 cm), compound with leaflets along midrib. Note the terminal leaflet has 3 lobes with the middle one by far the largest. Stem leaves alternate with 2-3 pointed lobes with serrated margins.

HABITAT: Meadows, stream sides, clearings; montane, subalpine forests. Elevation 6,600-10,200 feet (2,012-3,109 m).

SIMILAR SPECIES: The look-alike Yellow Avens, *G. aleppicum*, has basal leaves with similar-sized lobes on the terminal leaflet.

Alpine Avens

Geum rossii, Rose Family, Rosaceae; Perennial herb

QUICK ID: Look for colony-forming rosettes with fern-like leaves, slender stalks, showy flowers with 5 yellow petals, and many yellow stamens with brownish anthers.

RANGE: NR, MR, SR, Canada; widespread, locally common

STEM: Erect, 1½-11 inches tall, (4-28 cm), downy or not.

FLOWERS: June-September. Clusters have 1-4 flowers with 5 rounded petals, each ¼-½ inch long (6-12 mm); 5 sepals cup the petals, green to purple, pointed, shorter than petals.

LEAVES: Basal; blades pinnately compound, 1-5 inches long (3-13 cm), crowded with 13-26 major leaflets, elliptic with 3-5 lobes; minor leaflets 0-14 may alternate with the larger ones; surfaces smooth to silvery-hairy. Stem leaves several, alternate, small, toothed.

HABITAT: Fell fields, moist meadows; timberline, alpine tundra. Elevation 9,000-13,000 feet (2,745-3,962 m).

Alpine Ivesia

Ivesia gordonii, Rose Family, Rosaceae; Perennial herb

QUICK ID: Look for clumps of erect, fern-like basal leaves and flower stems tipped with rounded clusters with 10–20 small yellow flowers.

RANGE: NR, MR, SR (absent NM); widespread, locally common

STEM: Erect from woody base, 2–8 inches long (5–20 cm), usually hairy-glandular.

FLOWERS: June–August. Dense, rounded terminal clusters packed with tiny flowers, each to ½ inch wide (12 mm) with 5 oval petals surrounded by longer green, hairy sepals.

LEAVES: Basal, 3–20 from woody base; blades 1–3 inches long (3–8 cm), pinnately compound with 10–25 overlapping leaflets per side; leaflets deeply divided into 4–8 narrow, round-tipped lobes to ¾ inch long (19 mm); surfaces sticky with glandular hairs, with long hairs or not; 1 small stem leaf.

HABITAT: Rocky soils; grasslands, sagebrush, montane, subalpine forests, alpine. Elevation 8,000–12,000 feet (2,438–3,568 m).

Silverweed Cinquefoil

Potentilla anserina (Argentina anserina), Rose Family, Rosacea; Perennial herb

QUICK ID: Look for plants with spreading reddish runners, leaves with saw-toothed leaflets, and solitary flowers with 5 yellow petals.

RANGE: NR, MR, SR, Canada; widespread, common

STEM: Creeping, reddish, rooting stolons to 20 inches long (50 cm).

FLOWERS: May-September. Flowers solitary on long, leafless stalks from branch tips; 5 petals, oval, slightly notched, ¼–½ inch long (6–12 mm); many stamens surround bristly, conical center.

LEAVES: Mostly basal; blades pinnately compound, 3-8 inches (8-20 cm) long; 9-25 large leaflets interspaced with smaller ones; margins sharply toothed or lobed; top sides sparsely hairy, underside densely covered with silvery hair. Stem leaves alternate at stolon nodes.

HABITAT: Moist to dry soils, openings, disturbed areas; grasslands to subalpine forests. Elevation 5,000–9,842 feet (1,524–3,000 m).

Elegant Cinquefoil

Potentilla concinna, Rose Family, Rosacea; Perennial herb

QUICK ID: Look for low-growing, clumping stems with densely silky-hairy, palmate leaves, and loose clusters of yellow flowers with 5 petals and many stamens.

RANGE: MR, SR: widespread, common; NR, Canada: locally common

STEM: Prostrate, branching from base, ¾–6 inches tall (2–15 cm), densely hairy.

FLOWERS: April–June. Loose clusters on branching, hairy stalks have 3–12 flowers, ⅝ inch wide (15 mm), with 5 slightly notched petals, not overlapping, often with orange base; many stamens surround cluster of pistils; sepals beneath flower densely hairy.

LEAVES: Basal, long stalked; blades palmate with 5 radiating leaflets, each ¼–¾ inch long (6–20 mm), bottom pair may be slightly separate; edges silvery-hairy, often curled inward; top surface sparsely to densely straight-hairy, bottom silvery-woolly; tips toothed.

HABITAT: Wet meadows, open woods; sagebrush, foothills, montane, subalpine forests, alpine. Elevation 6,240–12,470 feet (1,900–3,800 m).

Fanleaf Cinquefoil

Potentilla flabellifolia, Rose Family, Rosaceae; Perennial herb

QUICK ID: Look near timberline for loose mats of basal leaves with 3 fan-shaped leaflets and bowl-shaped yellow flowers on long stalks.

RANGE: NR, MR, Canada; widespread, common

STEM: Erect, branching from base, 4–12 inches tall (10–30 cm), hairless.

FLOWERS: June–September. Terminal clusters on long stalks have 1–5 flowers with 5 notched petals, each ¼–½ inch long (6–12 mm); many stamens surround cluster of pistils.

LEAVES: Basal, long stalked; blades palmate with 3 fan-shaped-to-oval leaflets, ⅜–2 inches long (1–5 cm); edges flat with 6–14 uneven teeth near tip, usually hairless. Stem leaves 1–2, alternate, smaller.

HABITAT: Meadows, open woods, riparian; montane, subalpine forests, alpine. Elevation 3,300–12,140 feet (1,000–3,700 m).

Slender Cinquefoil

Potentilla gracilis, Rose Family, Rosaceae; Perennial herb

QUICK ID: Look for palmate basal leaves with evenly toothed leaflets and clusters of small yellow flowers with 5 petals and many stamens.

RANGE: NR, MR, SR, Canada; widespread, common; 3 varieties in RM

STEM: Erect, branching from base, 6–28 inches tall (15–70 cm).

FLOWERS: May–September. Open clusters have 10–60 flowers, each with 5 petals ¼–⅜ long/wide (6–10 mm); many stamens surround cluster of pistils; sepals beneath petals hairy.

LEAVES: Basal, long stalked; blades palmate with 5–9 elliptic to oval leaflets, ¾–4 inches long (2–10 cm); edges evenly toothed either ¼–½ way or ¾ way to midvein, depending on variety; both surfaces can be smooth and green, or bicolored with the bottom white-cottony. Stem leaves 1–4, alternate, smaller.

HABITAT: Meadows, flats; grasslands to subalpine forests. Elevation 1,000–11,450 feet (304–3,500 m).

Woolly Cinquefoil

Potentilla hippiana, Rose Family, Rosaceae; Perennial herb

QUICK ID: Look for pinnate basal leaves green on top, silvery-hairy on bottom, and loose clusters of small yellow flowers with 5 petals.

RANGE: SR: widespread, common; NR, MR, Canada: locally common

STEM: Erect, branched, 8–16 inches tall (20–40 cm), densely silky-hairy, often reddish.

FLOWERS: June–September. Open clusters have 10–30 flowers; 5 oval petals, to ⅜ inch long (10 mm), tips rounded or notched; sepals hairy, about length of petals; 20 stamens, numerous pistils.

LEAVES: Basal clumps, long stalked; blades pinnately compound with 5–13 leaflets along midrib, each ½–1½ inches long (12–40 mm), upper 3 largest; edges have shallow teeth; top gray-hairy, bottom densely silky-hairy, white. Stem leaves 1–2, alternate, smaller.

HABITAT: Dry soils, open areas, disturbed areas; grasslands to alpine tundra. Elevation 6,500–11,500 feet (2,000–3,500 m).

Norwegian Cinquefoil

Potentilla norvegica, Rose Family, Rosaceae; Annual herb

QUICK ID: Look for clumped leafy stems, leaves with 3 rough leaflets, and flowers with 5 yellow petals shorter than sepals.

RANGE: NR, MR, SR, Canada; widespread, common, circumboreal

STEM: Erect, usually upper branched, 8–28 inches tall (20–70 cm), short stiff-hairy.

FLOWERS: June–August. Compact, leafy, spreading clusters have flowers ¼–½ inch wide (6–12 mm) with 5 oval petals slightly shorter than sepals; 15–20 stamens surround pistils.

LEAVES: Basal 0–few. Stem leaves long-stalked, alternate; blade with 3 leaflets, elliptical to oblong, ⅜–3 inches long (1–8 cm), middle leaflet longest with short stalk; edges shallow-lobed to coarse-toothed; surfaces sparsely to moderately hairy; bottom paler.

HABITAT: Moist meadows, wetlands, drainages, clearings; grasslands to subalpine forests. Elevation 6,000–9,500 feet (1,800–2,900 m).

SIMILAR SPECIES: Brook Cinquefoil, *P. rivalis*, (throughout) has 3–5 leaflets, 10 stamens, and stems with short, soft hairs.

Pennsylvania Cinquefoil

Potentilla pensylvanica, Rose Family, Rosacea; Perennial herb

QUICK ID: Look for clumps of stems with pinnate leaves, deeply toothed leaflets, and crowded clusters of small yellow flowers.

RANGE: NR, MR, SR, Canada; widespread, common

STEM: Erect, upper branching, 4–32 inches tall (10–80 cm), hairy.

FLOWERS: June–September. Crowded clusters of 5–40 yellow flowers with 5 petals, each to ¼ inch long/wide (6 mm), about equal to sepals, tips rounded; numerous stamens and pistils.

LEAVES: Mostly basal, long stalked; blade pinnately compound, 2–6 inches long (5–15 cm) with 5–11 lance-shaped leaflets; surfaces sparsely to densely gray-hairy; edges with 4–8 teeth cut halfway to midvein, often rolled under. Stem leaves 1–4 alternate, smaller.

HABITAT: Rocky soils, openings, disturbed areas; grasslands to alpine. Elevation 7,000–11,000 feet (2,133–3,352 m).

SIMILAR SPECIES: Woolly Cinquefoil, *P. hippiana*, in similar habitats, has leaflets with shallow teeth and white-woolly undersides.

Beautiful Cinquefoil

Potentilla pulcherrima, Rose Family, Rosacea; Perennial herb

QUICK ID: Look for clumps of palmate leaves with 5-7 leaflets with green tops, densely white-woolly bottoms, and yellow petals often with an orange base.

RANGE: NR, MR, SR, Canada; widespread, common

STEM: Erect to sprawling, branched from base, 8-32 inches tall (20-80 cm), sparsely to densely hairy.

FLOWERS: May–August. Loose, branching clusters have 10-50 flowers, each with 5 petals ¼-⅜ inch long (6-9 mm), tip rounded to notched; sepals hairy, pointed, shorter than petals.

LEAVES: Mostly basal, long-stalked to 8 inches long (20 cm); blades palmate with 5-7 radiating leaflets 1-2⅜ inches long (3-6 cm), the center leaflet the longest; edges flat, evenly toothed, cut ¼-½ to the midvein; top surface green, bottom densely woolly-white. Stem leaves smaller, 1-3, alternate.

HABITAT: Coarse soils, meadows, openings; grasslands to alpine meadows. Elevation 7,000-12,200 feet (2,133-3,718 m).

Antelope Bitterbush

Purshia tridentata, Rose Family, Rosaceae; Semi-evergreen shrub

QUICK ID: Look for shrubs with stiff tangled branches, bundles of tiny hairy leaves with 3 lobes, and flowers with 5 creamy petals.

RANGE: NR, MR, SR, Canada; widespread, common

STEM: Bushy branches, 3-7 feet tall/wide (1-2 m); twigs brown, hairy.

FLOWERS: April–June. Solitary from branch tips; 5 petals, each ⅛-¼ inch long (3-6 mm); base narrow, tip rounded, fragrant; many long yellow stamens. Seeds oval, ¼-½ inch long (6-12 mm), densely hairy, leathery, with a pointed tip.

LEAVES: Alternate, short-stalked in bundles on side twigs; blades wedge-shaped, 3 shallow lobes, ¼-⅜ inch long (6-9 mm) by ⅛-¼ inch wide (3-6 mm), top surface green, hairy; bottom greenish white, cobwebby-hairy, edges rolled under.

HABITAT: Dry slopes, hills, flats: grasslands to subalpine forests. Elevation 1,000-9,000 feet (304-2,743 m).

Woolly Mullein

Verbascum thapsus, Figwort Family, Scrophulariaceae; Biennial herb; introduced, invasive

QUICK ID: Look for basal rosettes of large, soft, velvety basal leaves, and tall bloom stalks tipped with a dense spike of small yellow flowers.

RANGE: NR, MR, SR, Canada; widespread, common, naturalized

STEM: Erect, unbranched, 1-6 feet tall (30–182 cm), velvety-hairy.

FLOWERS: April–October. A crowded spike has yellow flowers ⅝–1 inch wide (15–25 mm) with 5 petal-lobes; blooms from the bottom up.

LEAVES: Basal rosette forms first year; blades broadly lance-shaped, 4–6 inches long (10–15 cm); edges entire, surfaces densely soft-woolly, tip pointed. Stem with alternate leaves forms second year; blades stemless, smaller upward.

HABITAT: Roadsides, disturbed areas; grasslands to subalpine forests. Elevation 4,700-9,500 feet (1,432–2,895 m).

Longleaf Groundcherry

Physalis longifolia, Nightshade Family, Solanaceae; Perennial herb

QUICK ID: Look for hairless stems and leaves; nodding greenish-yellow, bell-shaped flowers with dark center spots; and ribbed sacks holding a single berry.

RANGE: MR, SR; widespread, common

STEM: Erect, branched, 20–40 inches tall (50–100 cm), hairless, angled, rhizomatous.

FLOWERS: June–October. Solitary from leaf axils on nodding stalk, flowers bell-shaped, partially spreading open, ½–¾ inch wide (12–20 mm) with 5 fused petals, center has dark blotches, anthers yellow or purple; fruit in an oblong, pointed, papery sac with 10 ribs, berry ¼–½ inch diameter (6–12 mm), green maturing yellow.

LEAVES: Alternate, long stalked; blades lance-elliptic, 1-6 inches long (3–15 cm) by ⅜–2⅜ inches wide (1-6 cm); edges entire to wavy or coarsely toothed.

HABITAT: Disturbed areas, fields, roadsides; arid grasslands, sagebrush, foothills. Elevation 4,000–7,500 feet (1,220–2,295 m).

Buffalobur Nightshade

Solanum rostratum, Nightshade Family, Solanaceae; Annual herb

QUICK ID: Look in dry sites for a low, bushy plant with straight, yellow spines on the stems, leaves, and seed capsules; flowers have crinkly, yellow petals and protruding stamens.

RANGE: NR, MR, SR, Canada (introduced); widespread, common, invasive throughout

STEM: Erect, multi-branched, 1-3 feet tall (30-90 cm), hairy, spiny.

FLOWERS: May–October. Clusters have showy 1-inch-wide (25 mm) flowers with 5 bright-yellow, tissue-like, fused petals with 4 protruding yellow stamens and 1 dark and longer. Fruit a round berry inside a densely spiny capsule, ½ inch wide (12 mm).

LEAVES: Alternate. Blades 2–8 inches long (5–20 cm), 4 inches wide (10 cm), with 2-5 rounded, irregular lobes that cut all the way to the midrib; sharp spines grow along the midrib, veins, and stalk.

HABITAT: Dry soils, overgrazed disturbed areas; arid grasslands, sagebrush, foothills. Elevation 3,300–7,500 feet (1,005–2,286 m).

Yellow Prairie Violet

Viola nuttallii, Violet Family, Violaceae; Perennial herb

QUICK ID: Look for dense basal clumps of lance-shaped leaves and leafless stalks with deep-yellow flowers.

RANGE: NR, MR, SR, Canada; widespread, common

STEM: Mostly buried, ¾–3 inches tall (2–8 cm).

FLOWERS: April–June. Stalk 1–5 inches long (3-13 cm) with single flower; 5 petals: 2 upper petals often with backs tinged purple, 2 lateral petals with short yellow hairs and dark lines at base, lower with dark lines and a nubby rear spur 1 mm long.

LEAVES: Basal, long-stalked; blades lance-shaped to elliptic, ⅜–4 inches long (1–10 cm), about 3 times longer than wide, bases tapered; edges entire to toothed, surfaces smooth to minutely hairy. Stem leaves alternate, similar.

HABITAT: Dry open woods, plains; grasslands, sagebrush, foothills, montane forests. Elevation 1,312-8,530 feet (400–2,600 m).

SIMILAR SPECIES: Sagebrush Violet, *V. vallicola*, (all regions) has long-stalked leaves with oval to elliptic blades with rounded bases.

Goosefoot Violet

Viola purpurea, Violet Family, Violaceae; Perennial herb

QUICK ID: Look for clumps of long-stalked, rounded-to-diamond-shaped leaves, and leafless stalks with yellow flowers.

RANGE: NR, MR, Canada; widespread, common

STEM: Erect to buried, 2-6 inches tall (5–15 cm).

FLOWERS: April–September. Single flower on stalk 1-2¾ inches long (3-7 cm); 5 petals: lateral pair bearded, lower 3 purple lined, bottom petal ¼-½ inch long (6-14 mm) with a nubby rear spur.

LEAVES: Basal 1-6, on stalks ¾-2⅛ inches long (2-5 cm); blades heart- to lance-shaped, or rounded, ⅜-2 inches long (1-5 cm) by ¼-1⅝ inches wide (5-40 mm); edges coarsely few-toothed, surfaces veined, bottom purple tinted, hairy. Stem leaves alternate, similar, smaller. All features variable.

HABITAT: Gravelly soil, meadows, slopes; grasslands, montane, subalpine forests. Elevation 4,265–11,155 feet (1,300–3,400 m).

SIMILAR SPECIES: Canary Violet, *V. praemosa*, (NR, MR, SR) has tongue-shaped, elliptic to oval leaves with green bottoms.

Goathead, Puncture Vine

Tribulus terrestris, Caltrop Family, Zygophyllaceae; Annual herb; introduced, noxious weed

QUICK ID: Look for loose leafy mats, opposite pinnate leaves, and small yellow flowers followed by vicious burs with sharp spines.

RANGE: NR, MR, SR, Canada; widespread, common, naturalized

STEM: Sprawling, trailing, to 3 feet long (90 cm), hairy.

FLOWERS: May–October. Single flowers, ¼–⅜ inch wide (6–10 mm) in the axil of the smaller of the paired leaves; 5 petals, rounded to squared with notched to entire tips; 10 stamens. The seed bundle separates into 5 nutlets with stout, thorny spines.

LEAVES: Opposite, pinnately compound with one of each pair smaller; blades ¾–1¾ inches long (2–5 cm); leaflets elliptic, 3–6 pairs, points tapered; surfaces and margins have scattered hairs.

HABITAT: Coarse soils, yards, disturbed areas; arid grasslands, sagebrush, foothills. Elevation 3,200–7,800 feet (975–2,377 m).

Rocky Mountain Maple

Acer glabrum, Soapberry Family, Sapindaceae; Deciduous tree/shrub

QUICK ID: Look in moist, coniferous forests for a small tree with broad, rounded leaves with 3–5 toothed lobes that turn brilliant fall colors; seeds have 2 oval wings.

RANGE: NR, MR, SR, Canada; widespread, common

TRUNK: Single to shrubby, 3–30 feet tall (1–10 m), young twigs red.

FLOWERS: Insignificant, yellowish, blooming after leaves emerge. Seeds have 2 greenish-brown wings, each ¾–1 inch long (2–3 cm), attached in a V shape so it twirls in the wind for dispersal.

LEAVES: Opposite, long-stalked; blades rounded, 1–5 inches wide (3–12 cm) with 3–5 palmate lobes, shallow to deeply cut; edges coarsely serrated, surfaces smooth.

HABITAT: Moist, open forests, riparian; montane to lower subalpine forests. Elevation 6,600–12,700 feet (2,000–3,900 m).

SIMILAR SPECIES: Bigtooth Maple, *A. grandidentatum*, (MR) has leaves with narrow lobes with blunt teeth and fine hair on the bottoms.

Box Elder

Acer negundo, Soapberry Family, Sapindaceae; Deciduous tree

QUICK ID: Look along waterways for broad, spreading trees; leaves with 3 leaflets with teeth; and seeds with 2 oval wings.

RANGE: NR, MR, SR, Canada; widespread, locally common

TRUNK: Upright, single to multiple, 40–65 feet tall (12–20 m), canopy spreading.

FLOWERS: Insignificant, yellowish, blooming before or with leaf emergence. Seeds have 2 greenish-gray to red, red-tinted wings, each 1–1⅝ inches long (3–4 cm), attached in a V shape so it twirls in the wind for dispersal. Male and female flowers on separate trees.

LEAVES: Opposite, long stalked, reddish when young; blades pinnate with 3–7 oblong to lance-shaped leaflets, each 2–4¾ inches long (5–12 cm) by 2–3 inches wide (6–8 cm); coarsely few-toothed, bottom hairy; turns yellow in autumn.

HABITAT: Riparian woodlands; foothills, montane forests. Elevation 1,100–8,000 feet (330–2,500 m).

Gambel's Oak

Quercus gambelii, Beech Family, Fagaceae; Deciduous tree/shrub

QUICK ID: Look for thickets of shrubs or stands of small trees with gnarled limbs, deeply lobed leaves, and acorns.

RANGE: MR, SR; widespread, common

STEM: Upright tree to bushy shrub, 6–25 feet tall (2–7.6 m), bark dark, furrowed with age, thicket forming.

FLOWERS: May–June. Separate male and female catkins on same tree. Acorns 1–3, cap cup-shaped, covers ¼–½ of the nut; nut oval, light brown, to ⅝ inch long (15 mm).

LEAVES: Alternate, short stalked; blade elliptic, 2–4¾ inches long (5–12 cm), deeply cut with 5–9 rounded lobes; edges entire to coarsely toothed, top surface bright green, bottom dull, hairy, base tapered; reddish brown in autumn.

HABITAT: Dry slopes (shrub) to moist canyons (trees), disturbed areas; sagebrush, pinyon-juniper foothills, montane forests. Elevation 5,000–10,000 feet (1,500–3,000 m).

Thinleaf Alder

Alnus incana ssp. *tenuifolia*, Birch Family, Betulaceae; Deciduous tree/shrub

QUICK ID: Look along waterways for bushy shrubs/trees with smooth bark, serrated, deeply veined leaves, and small, cone-like seed capsules.

RANGE: NR, MR, SR, Canada; widespread, common

STEM: Upright to shrubby, usually 6–16 feet tall (2–5 m), bark gray, crown open, spreading.

FLOWERS: April–June. Separate clusters of male and female catkins on same twig. Cone-like capsules egg-shaped, ⅜–⅝ inch long (10–15 mm), woody, green turning brown, remain on tree after opening.

LEAVES: Alternate, stalked, thin; blade oval to elliptic, 1⅝–4 inches long (4–10 cm) by 1–3 inches wide (3–8 cm); base rounded, edges coarsely double serrated, top surface smooth, bottom sparsely hairy along veins, brown in autumn.

HABITAT: Wet soils, stream banks, shores, meadows; montane, subalpine forests. Elevation 5,000–10,770 feet (1,524–3,280 m).

Narrowleaf Cottonwood

Populus angustifolia, Willow Family, Salicaceae; Deciduous tree

QUICK ID: Look along waterways for large trees with narrow, lance-shaped leaves on short stalks; seeds cottony, leaves gold in autumn.

RANGE: NR, MR, SR, Canada; widespread, common

STEM: Erect, upper branched, to 65 feet tall (20 m), bark smooth and whitish when young, dark with furrows and ridges when old.

FLOWERS: April–June. Dangling, yellow-green catkins appear before leaves emerge; male and female flowers on separate trees. Seeds fluffy, cottony, dispersed i in the wind.

LEAVES: Alternate, stalk round, ⅜ inch long (8 mm); blades narrow, lance-shaped, 1⅝–3 inches long (4–8 cm) to 1 inch wide (3 cm); edges finely serrated, surfaces smooth, shiny green, tip pointed.

HABITAT: Stream sides, flood plains; foothills, montane forests. Elevation 5,000–9,700 feet (1,525–2,950 m).

SIMILAR SPECIES: Black Cottonwood, *P. trichocarpa*, (NR, MR) has triangular leaves with round leaf stalks about ½ blade length; Eastern Cottonwood, *P. deltoides*, has triangular leaves.

Quaking Aspen

Populus tremuloides, Willow Family, Salicaceae; Deciduous tree

QUICK ID: Look for dense stands of tall, white-trunked trees; rounded leaves with long, flat stalks that quake in the breeze; and brilliant gold colors in autumn.

RANGE: NR, MR, SR, Canada; widespread, common

STEM: Erect, upper branched, to 100 feet tall (30 m); bark white to gray, smooth, furrowed near base on old trees; forms clonal colonies.

FLOWERS: May–June. Dangling, yellow-green catkins appear before leaves emerge; male and female flowers on separate trees; cottony seeds disperse in the wind.

LEAVES: Alternate, stalk flat, about blade length; blade rounded to oval, 1–3 inches long and wide (3–7 cm); edges entire to finely serrated, surfaces smooth, tip pointed.

HABITAT: Mountain slopes, meadows, disturbed areas; montane, subalpine forests. Elevation 6,000–11,000 feet (1,828–3,352 m).

NOTES: A clonal grove in Utah with 40,000 trees is estimated to be the oldest organism on the planet, 4,855 years old.

Common Juniper

Juniperus communis, Cypress Family, Cupressaceae; Evergreen shrub groundcover

QUICK ID: Look at high elevations for low-growing, spreading shrubs with green, needle-like leaves and rounded, fleshy, berry-like cones.

RANGE: NR, MR, SR, Canada; widespread, common

STEM: Sprawling, densely branched, 2–3 feet tall (60–91 cm).

FLOWERS: May–June. Tiny, yellowish-green cones, male and female on separate plants. Seed cones fleshy, berry-like, rounded, ¼–⅜ inch long (6–9 mm), first year green, second year ripening dark blue.

LEAVES: Whorls of 2–3 per fascicule, needle-like, ¼–½ inch long (7–12 mm), spreading away from stem.

HABITAT: Dry slopes, rock slides, open woods; montane, subalpine forests, alpine. Elevation sealevel to 9,333 feet (2,845m).

Rocky Mountain Juniper

Juniperus scopulorum, Cypress Family, Cupressaceae; Evergreen tree

QUICK ID: Look for stately, conical conifers with drooping branch tips; blue-gray leaves; and blue-black, berry-like cones.

RANGE: NR, MR, SR: widespread, common; Canada: infrequent

STEM: Single, upright, 25–35 feet tall (8–10 m), branches spreading to ascending, ends drooping, crown conical, bark exfoliating in strips.

FLOWERS: March–May. Tiny, yellowish-green cones, male and female on separate plants. Seed cones juicy, berry-like, rounded, ¼–⅜ inch long (6–9 mm), first year powdery blue, second year ripening to dark blue.

LEAVES: Opposite, whorled around stem, scale-like, triangular, flat against branch, blue gray to green, not prickly except when young.

HABITAT: Rocky soils, meadows, slopes, canyons; arid grasslands, foothills, montane forests. Elevation 4,000–9,365 feet (1,220–2,854 m).

Lodgepole Pine

Pinus contorta var. *larifolia*, Pine Family, Pinaceae; Evergreen tree

QUICK ID: Look for single-trunked trees, often in dense stands; needles in pairs; and short, thick, resinous cones attached directly to the branches.

RANGE: NR, MR, SR, Canada; widespread, common

STEM: Erect, reaching 150 feet tall (45 m), shape evenly tapered, branches horizontal, crown conical.

FLOWERS: Tiny, wind pollinated, male and female cones separate. Seed cones stalkless, oval to conical, 1–2¾ inches long (3–7 cm), thick, woody with spine-tipped scales. Cones open to release winged seeds the second season or remain closed for years until fire melts the resin coating to release seeds in massive quantities.

LEAVES: Needles in bundles of 2, whorled around twig, 2–3 inches long (5–8 cm), stout.

HABITAT: Slopes, valleys; montane, subalpine forests. Elevation 8,500–11,500 feet (2,590–3,500 m).

Two-leaf Pinyon Pine

Pinus edulis, Pine Family, Pinaceae; Evergreen tree

QUICK ID: Look for small, often straggly trees with short, paired needles and small rounded cones with 8–10 nutritious, nut-like seeds.

RANGE: MR, SR; widespread, common

STEM: Single or multiple, to 50 feet tall (15 m), open, spreading branches, conical to rounded shape with age; Christmas-tree-shaped when young.

FLOWERS: Tiny, wind pollinated, male and female cones separate. Seed cones oval, 1–2 inches long (3–5 cm), with woody, thick, resinous, blunt scales. Cones open second season, then drop.

LEAVES: Needles in bundles of 2, whorled around twig, ¾–1½ inches long (2–4 cm), stout, sharp pointed.

HABITAT: Dry mesas, slopes, hills, commonly with Junipers; foothills, montane forests. Elevation 4,500–10,000 feet (1,400–3,050 m).

Limber Pine

Pinus flexilis, Pine Family, Pinaceae; Evergreen tree

QUICK ID: Look for pines with tapering trunks; low, horizontal limbs; flexible twigs; bundles of 5 needles; and large cones.

RANGE: NR, MR, SR, Canada; widespread, common

STEM: Straight to contorted, often multi-trunked, much branched, to 50 feet tall (15 m), crown pyramidal to rounded; bark thin, gray.

FLOWERS: June–July. Tiny, wind pollinated, male and female cones separate. Seed cones cylindrical, 3-6 inches long (8-15 cm), mature second season, then drop. Seeds dispersed and buried by birds, small mammals.

LEAVES: Needles in bundles of 5, dark green, 1-2 ¾ inches long (3-7 cm).

HABITAT: Poor, dry, rocky soils; grasslands, sagebrush, foothills, montane, subalpine forests. Elevation 4,000–12,500 feet (1,200–3,800 m).

Ponderosa Pine

Pinus ponderosa, Pine Family, Pinaceae; Evergreen tree

QUICK ID: Look for tall, stately pines with large scales of brownish-orange, vanilla-scented bark; long needles; and egg-shaped cones.

RANGE: NR, MR, SR, Canada; widespread, common

STEM: Erect, 65–130 feet tall (20–40 m), upper branches horizontal, crown broadly conical to rounded; bark reddish-brown in large, scaly plates.

FLOWERS: Tiny, wind pollinated, male and female cones separate. Seed cones conical to egg-shaped, 3–4 inches long (7–10 cm) with thick, woody scales and a stout prickle pointing toward base of cone. Cones shed winged seeds second season, then drop.

LEAVES: Needles mostly in bundles of 3, often 2, whorled around twig, 4–6 inches long (10–16 cm).

HABITAT: Dry slopes, canyons, mesas, open woods; foothills, montane forests. Elevation 5,600–10,000 feet (1,900–2,800 m).

Rocky Mountain Douglas-fir

Pseudotsuga menziesii var. *glauca*, Pine Family, Pineaceae; Evergreen tree

QUICK ID: Look for tall conifers with short, single needles and hanging cones with distinct, 3-lobed bracts on the cone scales.

RANGE: NR, MR, SR, Canada; widespread, common

STEM: Erect, upper branching, to 130 feet tall (40 m); bark reddish brown, deeply furrowed; young trees pyramidal, older have a narrow to broadly conical crown.

FLOWERS: Male and female cones separate. Pollen cones oval, yellow red. Seed cones greenish turning brown, 1⅝–3 inches long (4–7 cm), scales tipped with a 3-lobed bract, middle lobe narrow, longest. Cones release seeds first season, then drop.

LEAVES: Needles single, flat, radiating around stem, ¾–1 inch long (2–3 cm), bluish green to dark green, tips blunt.

HABITAT: Mountain slopes, plateaus, often co-dominate with Ponderosa Pine; foothills, montane, subalpine forests. Elevation 5,000–10,000 feet (1,500–3,000 m).

Subalpine Fir

Abies lasiocarpa, Pine Family, Pinaceae; Evergreen tree

QUICK ID: Look in coniferous forests for tall, spire-like trees; single, flat (not angled) needles; and erect, cylindrical, dark-purple cones.

RANGE: NR, MR, SR, Canada; widespread, common

STEM: Erect, single trunk to 100 feet tall (30 m); branches horizontal, whorled around trunk; bark gray, furrowed with age; shape spirelike.

FLOWERS: June–July. Pollen cones clustered, purplish at pollination. Seed cones cylindrical with rounded end, 2–4 inches long (5–10 cm), dark purple, scales not spiny. Cones mature in 1 season with winged seeds, then disintegrate.

LEAVES: Needles solitary, spiraled round twig, flat, ⅜–1 inch long (11–25 mm), curved upward, light green to bluish green, flexible; tip slightly notched to rounded.

HABITAT: Montane, subalpine forests. Elevation 4,500–12,000 feet (1,371–3,656 m); typically with Engelmann Spruce, *Picea engelmannii*.

SIMILAR SPECIES: White Fir, *A. concolor*, has a greenish cone.

Engelmann Spruce

Picea engelmannii, Pine Family, Pinaceae; Evergreen tree

QUICK ID: Look for tall, conical conifers with blue-green, angled needles (roll between fingers to test); cones dangle from branches.

RANGE: NR, MR, SR, Canada; widespread, common

STEM: Erect, to 100 feet tall (30 m), branches whorled around trunk, slender, drooping; bark furrows with age.

FLOWERS: Tiny, wind pollinated, male and female cones separate. Seed cones conical to cigar-shaped, ⅝–2¾ inches long (4–7 cm), covered with thin, woody, fan-shaped scales with papery, fringed tips; scales open to release winged seeds in 1 season, then cone drops.

LEAVES: Needles dark to blue green, spreading in all directions on branch, ¼–1¼ inches long (6–30 mm), 4 angled, square in cross section. Note the needles are flexible, tips pointed but not sharp.

HABITAT: Moist dense forests, canyons; montane, subalpine, forests. Elevation 7,000–12,000 feet (2,134–3,636 m).

SIMILAR SPECIES: Colorado Blue Spruce, *P. pungens*, has ridged, sharp-pointed needles.

Colorado Blue Spruce

Picea pungens, Pine Family, Pinaceae; Evergreen tree

QUICK ID: Look for tall conifers branched from top to bottom; short, 4-angled, dark-green-to-bluish needles; cones droop from branches.

RANGE: MR, SR; widespread, common

STEM: Upright, to 100 feet tall (30 m), branches stout, horizontal, whorled around trunk from top to bottom, crown broadly conical.

FLOWERS: Tiny, wind pollinated, male and female cones separate. Seed conical to cigar-shaped, 2¾–4½ inches (7–11 cm), covered with thin, woody, fan-shaped scales with papery, fringed tips; scales open to release winged seeds in 1 season, then cone drops.

LEAVES: Needles green to blue green, spreading in all directions from twig, ⅝–1 inch long (16–25 mm), 4 angled, square in cross section. Note the needles are rigid and sharp-pointed.

HABITAT: Moist, dense forests, riparian; foothills, montane, subalpine forests. Elevation 6,000–11,000 feet (1,828–3,352 m).

RESOURCES

Ackerfield, Jennifer. *The Flora of Colorado,* 2nd edition. 2022. BRIT Press.

Allred, Kelly, et. al. *Flora Neomexicana* III. 2020.

Beidleman, Richard, Linda Beidleman. *Plants of Rocky Mountain National Park.* 2020. Falcon Press.

Carter, Jack. *Trees and Shrubs of New Mexico.* 2012. Mimbres Publishing.

Dodson, Carolyn, William Dunmire. *Mountain Wildflowers of the Southern Rocky Mountains.* 2007. University of New Mexico Press.

Guennel, G.K. *Guide to Colorado Wildflowers, Volume 1 (Plains and Foothills) and Volume 2 (Mountains).* 1995. Westcliff Publishers.

Heil, Kenneth, D. et. al. *Flora of the Four Corners Region.* 2013. Missouri Botanical Garden Press.

Kimball, Shannon F., Peter Lesica. *Wildflowers of Glacier National Park.* 2010. Trillium Press.

Miller, George. *Wildflowers of Colorado & Southern Wyoming.* 2017. Adventure Publications.

Mammoser, Don, Stan Tekiela. *Wildflowers of Colorado Field Guide.* 2022. Adventure Publications.

Shaw, Richard, Marion Shaw. *Plants of Yellowstone and Grand Teton National Parks.* 2008. Wheelwright Publishing.

Taylor, Robert. *Sagebrush Country: A Wildflower Sanctuary.* 1992. Mountain Press Publishing.

WEB RESOURCES

The Biota of North America Program. www.BONAP.org

Intermountain Regional Herbarium Network. intermountainbiota.org

Flora of British Columbia. ibis.geog.ubc.ca/biodiversity/eflora/

Flora of North America. efloras.org

Montana Field Guide. fieldguide.mt.gov

SEINet Herbarium Consortium. swbiodiversity.org/

Southwest Colorado Wildflowers. SWColoradoWildflowers.com, webpage by Al and Betty Schneider

Wildflowers of New Mexico. WildflowersNM.com, webpage by George Oxford Miller

Wildflower Search. WiildflowerSearch.org. webpage by Steve Sullivan

GLOSSARY

acorn the fruit of an oak tree with a hard shell and large seed

acute a leaf tip that tapers to a sharp point with more or less straight sides

aerial the part of a plant above ground or water

alluvial organic or inorganic matter, such as soil, rocks, and sand, deposited by running water

alpine the high-altitude region or zone above timberline where trees cannot grow due to the short growing season

alternate indicates leaves are placed separately along stem, not in pairs (see opposite) or grouped (see whorled)

angiosperms plants that produce flowers with seeds in ovaries (compare with gymnosperms)

annual a plant that germinates from seed, flowers, sets seeds, and dies in one growing season

anther the tip of a stamen that produces pollen

apex the tip or point farthest from the point of attachment

aquatic growing in water

arboreal tree-like

areole (areola) a small protrusion or depression on a surface, such as the region of a cactus that bear spines and/or flowers

ascending growing at an angle before curving upward

asymmetric irregular in shape, not divisible into equal haves, as in some leaves and flowers

axil the upper angle of the juncture of a leaf or flower with the stem

banner the upper petal in a pea-like flower, such as in the legume family, Fabaceae

basal positioned or growing from the base, such leaves at the base of a stem

bearded bearing tufts of long hairs

berry a fleshy fruit with many small seeds (example: tomato)

biennial a plant that lives for two years, usually producing a basal rosette of leaves the first and flowers and fruit the second

bilateral arranged on two sides, as leaves on a stem

bilaterally symmetrical an object (leaf, flower) that can divided into equal, mirror-image halves when cut along only one axis (example: an ice-cream cone, lupine flower)

bipinnately compound in this text, a leaf with segments along the midrib with each segment divided into lobes or leaflets along its midrib

bisexual a flower with both male and female reproductive organs (stamens and pistils)

bladder an inflated, thin-walled seed pod

blade the flat portion of a leaf or petal

bloom a whitish, waxy, powdery coating found on some trigs, leaves, and fruit; also a flower or blossom

blossom a flower

bracts usually small, leaf-like structures below the petals and sepals of a flower. In some species the bracts are larger and more colorful than the flowers (paintbrushes, poinsettias)

branch a major division of a stem, trunk, or limb

bulb an enlarged underground bub with fleshy layers (onion, lilies)

bur a plant part armed with bristle-like, often hooked, spines

bushy densely branched with numerous limbs, twigs, leaves

calyx the collective whorl of sepals around the base of a flower

capsule a fruit that splits open when dry, releasing multiple seeds

catkin a dense, spike-lie cluster of flowers, often dangling, in a tree or shrub; the flowers usually lack petals and are unisexual

cilia small hairs, usually along the edge of a structure (leaf, petal)

circumboreal growing around the world at high northern latitudes

clasping a leaf base that partially or entirely surrounds a stem

colonial plants that form colonies, usually by interconnected underground roots

columnar shaped like a column

compound leaf a leaf divided into two or more leaflets that resemble separate leaves

conic cone shaped, conical

coniferous plants, mostly trees, that bear cones (pine, spruce, fir)

corm a short, vertical underground stem with papery leaves (compare with bulb)

corolla collectively, all the petals of a flower

creeping growing along the surface of the ground

cultivar a form of plant with characters (attractive leaves, flowers, drought tolerance) developed through cultivation

cylindric cylinder shaped, elongated with a round cross section

deciduous falling off, as with leaves in the winter

dioecious male and female flowers occurring on separate plants

disk flowers tiny, tubular flowers in the center of flower heads in the sunflower family, Asteraceae (compare with ray flower)

dentate having outward-pointed teeth along the edge of a leaf

dissected leaf leaf blade deeply cut into small segments (example: yarrow leaf)

drupe a fleshy fruit containing a seed with a stony covering (example cherry, peach)

elliptic elliptical or oval shaped

endemic occurring in a limited geographic area or soil type

entire margin a smooth leaf edge with no teeth or lobes

erect vertical stems, not declining or spreading

evergreen plants that maintain green leaves year-round, never losing them all at the same time; opposite of deciduous

exotic not native, introduced to an area but not naturalized

fascicle a tight bundle, as of leaves, on a limb or twig (example: pine needles)

filament thread-like structure, as in the stalk of a stamen that is tipped with the pollen-bearing anther

fleshy thick, pulpy, often juicy or succulent

floral tube elongated, tube formed by fused petals, often flaring open with petal-like lobes; often sized to attract pollinators with tongues of the same length

floret small flower within a dense cluster, as in disk florets in a sunflower

foliage collectively, the leaves of a plant

foothills zone the transition zone between plains and steppe zones and montane forest zones; dominated by pinyon pine, juniper, and oaks in the southern Rockies, ponderosa pine and Douglas-fir to the north

gland a structure, often on the tip of a hair, that secretes an oily or sticky substance

glaucous covered with a whitish, waxy coating

glochid a hair-like, barbed bristle usually clustered at the base of spines on Opuntia cacti

gymnosperm plants that produce seeds not in an ovary or fruit, usually in cones (pines, firs, spruce trees) ; compare with angiosperms

habitat the specific environmental conditions at the location where a plant grows

head a dense cluster of flowers, resembles a single flower in the aster family, Asteraceae (sunflowers)

hemiparasite a plant that obtains part of its food from another organism, but also photosynthesizes (paintbrushes)

herbaceous a plant without above-ground woody parts that dies back to the ground in the winter, or during summer drought

herbage the non-reproductive parts of a plant: leaves, stems, roots

hood an arched upper petal that usually encloses the stamens

inflorescence a cluster of flowers

irregularly shaped flower petals not similar in shape or arrangement

keel the two lower petals that unite to form a longitudinal ridge in the pea-shaped flowers of the legume family, Fabaceae

latex a milky sap, as in plants in the milkweed family, Apocynaceae

leaflet one of the segments of a compound leaf

legume a dry pod containing a row of seeds, as in a pea pod, in the legume or bean family, Fabaceae

linear long and narrow with parallel sides

lip the upper and lower petal projections of an irregular flower, each lip may be lobed, as in penstemons

lobe a rounded segment on the edge of a leaf or flower part

margin the edge of the blade of a leaf or leaflet

mat a dense basal or low growth of interwoven stems and leaves, as in many alpine plants

midrib the central vein of a leaf with branching side veins

monoecious male and female flowers separate but on same plant

montane forest zone the mixed pine-fir forests located between foothills and subalpine forests

native plant a plant that historically occurs in a region, not introduced or requiring human aid to survive

naturalized a plant introduced into a region that adapts, reproduces, and becomes permanently established

nectar guides lines or spots on petals that lead pollinators to the nectaries, sometimes visible only in ultraviolet light

nectary the organs or glands that produce nectar, usually within flowers near the base of the petals

nerve a prominent vein in a leaf

nodding bent downward

nut a dry, hard fruit with a single seed

opposite plant parts borne across from each other along a stem, as in paired leaves

ovary the expanded portion of the pistil that contains the immature seeds (ovules) that after fertilization ripen into the fruit with seeds

ovule immature seed within the ovary

palmate lobed, veined, or divided from a central point

palmately compound leaf all the leaflets are united at a single point and radiate out like fingers from the palm of a hand (compare with pinnately compound)

parasite an organism that obtains all its nutrients from another organism

perennial a plant that lives for more than one growing season, may day back to the roots in the winter

perfoliate a leaf base that entirely surrounds a stem

petals the part of a flower, often colorful, that surrounds the reproductive organs, collectively called the corolla (compare with sepals and tepals)

petiole the stalk or stem of a leaf

phyllary the bracts at the base of the flower head in the aster family, Asteraceae

pinnately compound leaf a leaf with leaflets, or pinna, attached along the sides of the midrib; if the leaflets are again divided into segments along their central rib, the leaf is twice pinnately compound

pistil the female part of a flower that contains the ovary (with ovules), style, and stigma (often with slender lobes)

pod a dry fruit capsule, especially a legume

pollen tiny grains produced by the anther of the stamen that when transferred to the stigma fertilize the ovules in the pistil

prostate lying or growing flat on the ground

radial symmetry a round flower that if cut through the center in any direction forms equal sections, like a pie

ray flowers petal-like flowers around a center of disk flowers on the flower head of a compound flower in the aster family, Asteraceae; often are sterile and serve only to attract pollinators

recurved bent or curving backward

rhizome a horizontal underground stem or root

root crown the head of a root at ground level where stems form

rosette a dense, radiating cluster of leaves or flowers (see basal rosette)

runner a slender prostrate stem that roots at leaf nodes or the tip

sagebrush steppe in the Rocky Mountains, the life zone below forests and foothills; dominated sagebrush species, Artemisia, shrubs, flowers, and grasses

scape a leafless flower stalk growing from ground level, usually from a basal rosette

sepals leaf-like structures in a whorl below the petals that enclose the bud; may be colorful and indistinguishable from the petals

serrate saw-like teeth along the edge of a leaf

sessile attached without a stalk, as in leaves

shrub a woody plant usually with multiple stems and branches; smaller than a tree

spike an unbranched, elongated flower cluster with the individual flowers attached without stalks directly to the central stem; buds bloom from the bottom upward

stamen the male reproductive organ of a flower, consists of a long, slender filament topped with a pollen-producing anther

staminode a modified, sterile stamen, or beardtongue, of a penstemon flower, often with tufts of hair

stigma the tip of the pistil that receives pollen for fertilization

style the narrow stem of the pistil that connects the ovary to the stigma

subalpine the zone between the montane forest zone and alpine tundra, or treeline

subshrub a small shrub

subspecies a ranking below species level that recognizes significant differences that occur in a species across the broad range of the plant

succulent juicy, fleshy, as in leaves, stems

tendril a slender, string-like organ from the tip of a leaf or stem that twists or twines around other plants for the purpose of climbing or support

tepals refers to both petals and sepals when they are indistinguishable from each other, as in cactus flowers

terminal growing at the tip of a stem or branch

trifoliate having three leaves or leaflets

variety (var.) a ranking below subspecies that recognizes minor differences across the broad range of the plant

whorl more than two plant parts, such as leaves of flowers, attached in a circle around a stem

woody plants with solid stems and branches that grow from season to season (shrubs, trees)

INDEX

Note: **Bold** indicates the **main account** for a given species.

B

D

E

F

G

H

I

J

K

N

O

P

Q

R

S

T

U

V

W

X

Y

Z

INDEX BY COMMON NAME

G

M

PHOTO CREDITS

All interior images by **George Oxford Miller** unless otherwise noted.

Interior images identified by page number followed by t-m=top main image; t-i=top inset image; b-m=bottom main image; and b-i=bottom inset image.

All images copyrighted.

Karen Eakins: 412; **Virgina Skilton:** 48t-m

Images used under license from Shutterstock.com:

Dandelion Abbey: 323t-i; **aga7ta:** 369b-iB; **ArgenLant:** 112t-i; **Brody O:** 15; **Cavan-Images:** 288t-i; **Dominic Gentilcore PhD:** 309b-i; **Ihor Hvozdetskyi:** 89t-m; **Holger Kirk:** 57b-i; **Krishna.Wu:** 4; **Brian Lasenby:** 331b-i; **Judith Lienert:** 333t-i; **LifeCollectionPhotography:** 19t-m; **Grigorii Pisotsckii:** 193b-i; **Michael Stubben:** 33b-m; **Sundry Photography:** 286b-i; **Vankich1:** 192t-m; **Jonas Vegele:** 18t-i; **Nikki Yancey:** 55t-m, 55t-i, 125b-i, 201t-i, 323t-m, 368t-iA, 370b-iB

These images are used under CC0 1.0 Universal (CC0 1.0) Public Domain Dedication license, which can be found at https://creativecommons.org/publicdomain/zero/1.0/:

aiwendil: 370b-iA; **Patrick Alexander:** 22b-m, 23t-m, 31b-m, 33b-i, 39b-i, 39b-m, 43t-i, 45b-i, 47t-i, 54t-i, 63b-i, 64b-i, 67t-m, 67t-i, 68b-m, 69b-i, 76t-m, 86t-i, 90b-m, 94b-i, 110t-i, 111b-i, 118t-i, 119t-m, 126t-i, 136b-i, 136b-m,136b-m, 141b-i, 145t-m, 145t-i, 151t-i, 160b-i, 173t-m, 177b-i, 181t-i, 181t-m, 182b-i, 187t-m, 196b-m, 200b-i, 201t-m, 208t-i, 212t-i, 213b-m, 231t-i, 213t-m, 231b-i, 233t-i, 233b-m, 234t-i, 239b-i, 239b-m, 264t-i, 265b-i, 265b-m, 267b-m, 268t-i, 270t-i, 277t-m, 287t-i, 292b-i, 298b-i, 299t-i, 299t-m, 300b-m, 300b-i, 307t-i, 317b-i, 317b-m, 318b-i, 319t-i, 319t-m, 323b-m, 324t-m, 324t-i, 324b-m, 324b-i, 330b-i, 341t-m, 341b-i, 343t-i, 347b-i, 348t-i, 356t-i, 362b-m, 362b-i, 364t-iB, 369b-iA; **AnRo0002:** 215t-i; **Nora Bales:** 286t-m; **Larry Blakely/calphotos.berkeley.edu:** 283t-i; **Mason Brock:** 231b-m; **Quinn Campbell:** 371t-m; **Kathleen Houlahan Chayer:** 156t-i; **Checkermallow:** 217t-m; **ck9000:** 41t-i; **dghjertaas:** 54b-m; **Dag Terje Filip Endresen:** 57b-m, 308t-i; **Forest Service Northern Region:** 88t-m; **Kathy Fulton:** 334b-i; **Peter Garber:** 113t-i; **GlacierNPS:** 244b-i; **John W. Hancock:** 62t-i, 318b-m; **Robb Hannawacker:** 178b-m, 244t-m, 367b-i; **Hardyplants at English Wikipedia:** 239t-m; **Allan Harris:** 49b-i; **Alex Heyman:** 44b-m, 51b-i, 194b-m, 200b-m, 273t-i, 293t-i; **Laura Holloway:** 60t-m; **Parker Hopkins:** 88t-i; **Hovenweep National Monument:** 33t-m; **Braden J. Judson:** 87b-i; **Dwight Kingsbury:** 25b-m; **lallen:** 116t-i; **Scott Loarie:** 194t-m, 196t-i; **Craig Martin:** 81t-m, 166b-m, 177b-m, 179t-m, 186t-m, 202b-i, 272b-i, 276b-i, 290t-m, 292t-i, 304b-i, 341t-i; **Bill Michalek:** 335t-m; **msieges:** 272b-m; **Daryl Nolan:** 313b-m; **NPS/Neal Herbert/Yellowstone National Park:** 78b-i, 254t-m; **NPS/Jacob W. Frank/GlacierNPS:** 112t-m, 213t-m; **NPS/Jacob W. Frank/Yellowstone National Park:** 73b-m, 78b-m, 82t-m, 172t-i, 256t-i, 315t-i, 335t-i; **NPS/Neal Herbert:** 141b-m; **NPS/Jane Olson/Yellowstone National Park:** 352t-m; **NPS/S. Zenner/Grand Teton National Park:** 81b-m; **Randal:** 185t-i, 192b-i; **Spencer Quayle:** 225t-m, 370b-m; **Gabe Schp:** 150b-i, 166b-i; **sgene:** 193b-m, 220t-i, 344t-m; **Patrick Sowers:** 63t-i, 132t-m; **Zoltán Stekkelpak:** 194b-i; **Aaron Sidder:** 210t-m; **James H. Thomas:** 263b-i, 263b-m; **USDA FS Modoc NF/Gauna:** 352t-i, 363t-i; **USDA NRCS Montana:** 40t-i, 65b-m, 119t-i, 160b-m, 264t-m, 366t-i; **USFWS Mountain-Prairie:** 41t-m; **Sean Washington:** 290b-m; **Yellowstone National Park:** 21t-i, 32t-i

These images are used under Attribution 2.0 Generic (CC BY 2.0) license, which can be found at https://creativecommons.org/licenses/by/2.0/:

Ettore Balocchi: 117b-i, no modifications, original image at https://www.flickr.com/photos/29882791@N02/8304598438/, 117b-m, no modifications, original image at https://www.flickr.com/photos/29882791@

N02/8304598768/; **Bill Bradford:** 326t-i, no modifications, original image at https://www.flickr.com/photos/42693729@N04/14375827949/; **Tom Brandt:** 18t-m, no modifications, original image at https://www.flickr.com/photos/12567713@N00/5719774189/; **Forest Service Northern Region:** 225t-i, no modifications, original image at https://commons.wikimedia.org/wiki/File:Mountain_lady%27s_slipper_(Cypripedium_montanum)_(7204162914).jpg/; **Emma Forsberg:** 98b-i, no modifications, original image at https://www.flickr.com/photos/echoforsberg/2626827067/; **Judy Gallagher:** 217b-i, no modifications, original image at https://www.flickr.com/photos/52450054@N04/24972443726/; **John Game:** 111b-m, no modifications, original image at https://www.flickr.com/photos/47945928@N02/43117381874/, 126t-m, no modifications, original image at https://www.flickr.com/photos/47945928@N02/35374195820/, 330b-m, no modifications, original image at https://www.flickr.com/photos/47945928@N02/5992054052/; **Jason Hollinger:** 139b-i, no modifications, original image at https://www.flickr.com/photos/7147684@N03/15740047499/, 190t-i, no modifications, original image at https://www.flickr.com/photos/7147684@N03/3817688461/, 217t-i, no modifications, original image at https://www.flickr.com/photos/7147684@N03/910358856/, 233b-i, no modifications, original image at https://www.flickr.com/photos/7147684@N03/15738673299/, 351b-m, no modifications, original image at https://www.flickr.com/photos/7147684@N03/3817484515/; **Joost J. Bakker IJmuiden:** 89t-i, no modifications, original image at https://www.flickr.com/photos/joostjbakkerijmuiden/51874004540/, 174t-m, no modifications, original image at https://www.flickr.com/photos/joostjbakkerijmuiden/52169475080/; **James St. John:** 228b-i, no modifications, original image at https://www.flickr.com/photos/jsjgeology/19283239043/; **Jim Kravitz:** 86t-m, no modifications, original image at https://www.flickr.com/photos/jimmypk/3816626594/; **Don Loarie:** 313b-i, no modifications, original image at https://www.flickr.com/photos/loarie/16738134785/; **Doug McGrady:** 90b-i, no modifications, original image at https://www.flickr.com/photos/douglas_mcgrady/28691299277/, 183t-i, no modifications, original image at https://www.flickr.com/photos/douglas_mcgrady/31324729574/, 183t-m, no modifications, original image at https://www.flickr.com/photos/douglas_mcgrady/32047940281/, 224t-m, no modifications, original image at https://www.flickr.com/photos/douglas_mcgrady/42246297265/; **NPS/Jacob W. Frank/Denali National Park and Preserve:** 115t-i, no modifications, original image at https://www.flickr.com/photos/denalinps/7833397820/, 195b-m, no modifications, original image at https://www.flickr.com/photos/denalinps/7833183330/; **Brian Saunders:** 295bm & i, no modifications, original image at https://www.flickr.com/photos/btsaunders/859875817/; **Katja Schulz:** 123b-i, no modifications, original image at https://www.flickr.com/photos/treegrow/14891662378/, 210t-i, no modifications, original image at https://www.flickr.com/photos/treegrow/14891595600/; **Forest and Kim Starr:** 128b-i, no modifications, original image at https://www.flickr.com/photos/starr-environmental/24515229383/; **Peter Stevens:** 54t-m, no modifications, original image at https://www.flickr.com/photos/nordique/5701550012/, 114t-i, no modifications, original image at https://www.flickr.com/photos/nordique/7562414040/, 187b-i, no modifications, original image at https://www.flickr.com/photos/nordique/19738286394/, 254t-i, no modifications, original image at https://www.flickr.com/photos/nordique/6909542642/; **Sam Thomas:** 195b-i, no modifications, original image at https://www.flickr.com/photos/sjthomasbotany2/52376061651/; **Amy Washuta:** 105b-i, no modifications, original image at https://www.flickr.com/photos/150025895@N04/49903116947/; **Ruurd Zeinstra:** 98b-m, no modifications, original image at https://www.flickr.com/photos/ruurdz/3597526563/; **Andrey Zharkikh:** 24b-i, no modifications, original image at https://www.flickr.com

/photos/zharkikh/28435572360/, 24b-m, no modifications, original image at https://www.flickr.com/photos/zharkikh/28719923655/, 25t-i, no modifications, original image at https://www.flickr.com/photos/zharkikh/6951282563/, 25t-m, no modifications, original image at https://www.flickr.com/photos/zharkikh/7627790912/, 35t-m, no modifications, original image at https://www.flickr.com/photos/zharkikh/6794338373/, 35t-i, no modifications, original image at https://www.flickr.com/photos/zharkikh/6840461418/, 47t-m, no modifications, original image at https://www.flickr.com/photos/zharkikh/48209815606/, 51b-m, no modifications, original image at https://www.flickr.com/photos/zharkikh/14812678805/, 64b-m, no modifications, original image at https://www.flickr.com/photos/zharkikh/6853922224/, 68t-m, no modifications, original image at https://www.flickr.com/photos/zharkikh/48549178257/, 69t-m, no modifications, original image at https://www.flickr.com/photos/zharkikh/8193614141/, 69t-i, no modifications, original image at https://www.flickr.com/photos/zharkikh/8193615563/, 86b-i, no modifications, original image at https://www.flickr.com/photos/zharkikh/6327751645/, 96b-i, no modifications, original image at https://www.flickr.com/photos/zharkikh/29688707921/, 96b-m, no modifications, original image at https://www.flickr.com/photos/zharkikh/6812753983/, 104t-m, no modifications, original image at https://www.flickr.com/photos/zharkikh/6659623229/, 105b-m, no modifications, original image at https://www.flickr.com/photos/zharkikh/49947261452/, 116t-m, no modifications, original image at https://www.flickr.com/photos/zharkikh/36111819795/, 118t-m, no modifications, original image at https://www.flickr.com/photos/zharkikh/35383846465/, 123b-m, no modifications, original image at https://www.flickr.com/photos/zharkikh/6427330683/, 149b-i, no modifications, original image at https://www.flickr.com/photos/zharkikh/14755884621/, 149b-m, no modifications, original image at https://www.flickr.com/photos/zharkikh/37253343535/, 150b-m, no modifications, original image at https://www.flickr.com/photos/zharkikh/48579841342/, 159t-i, no modifications, original image at https://www.flickr.com/photos/zharkikh/35927506015/, 159t-m, no modifications, original image at https://www.flickr.com/photos/zharkikh/48759021688/, 159b-m, no modifications, original image at https://www.flickr.com/photos/zharkikh/48183641392/, 159b-i, no modifications, original image at https://www.flickr.com/photos/zharkikh/49982478941/, 162b-m, no modifications, original image at https://www.flickr.com/photos/zharkikh/6427634459/, 163b-m, no modifications, original image at https://www.flickr.com/photos/zharkikh/35725253915/, 163b-i, no modifications, original image at https://www.flickr.com/photos/zharkikh/6805130376/, 168t-m, no modifications, original image at https://www.flickr.com/photos/zharkikh/51392760060/, 168t-i, no modifications, original image at https://www.flickr.com/photos/zharkikh/6425134885/, 212b-m, no modifications, original image at https://www.flickr.com/photos/zharkikh/6537918891/, 212b-i, no modifications, original image at https://www.flickr.com/photos/zharkikh/6946466501/, 220t-m, no modifications, original image at https://www.flickr.com/photos/zharkikh/50011845187/, 299t-i, no modifications, original image at https://www.flickr.com/photos/zharkikh/14639706125/, 230t-m, no modifications, original image at https://www.flickr.com/photos/zharkikh/6886318540/, 232b-i, no modifications, original image at https://www.flickr.com/photos/zharkikh/35437791161/, 235t-i, no modifications, original image at https://www.flickr.com/photos/zharkikh/35862447050/, 235t-m, no modifications, original image at https://www.flickr.com/photos/zharkikh/42440886335/, 244t-i, no modifications, original image at https://www.flickr.com/photos/zharkikh/6566982837/, 264b-m, no modifications, original image at https://www.flickr.com/photos/zharkikh/15903212810/, 264b-i, no modifications, original image at https://www.flickr.com/photos/zharkikh/51186083526/, 276t-i, no modifications, original image at https://www.flickr.com/photos

/zharkikh/6710463761/, 283t-m, no modifications, original image at https://www.flickr.com/photos/zharkikh/32021603980/, 286t-i, no modifications, original image at https://www.flickr.com/photos/zharkikh/50296026558/, 309b-m, no modifications, original image at https://www.flickr.com/photos/zharkikh/35272491035/, 327t-i, no modifications, original image at https://www.flickr.com/photos/zharkikh/14295670494/, 332b-m, no modifications, original image at https://www.flickr.com/photos/zharkikh/43584744952/, 333t-m, no modifications, original image at https://www.flickr.com/photos/zharkikh/30818109308/, 337t-i, no modifications, original image at https://www.flickr.com/photos/zharkikh/28338001867/, 348t-m, no modifications, original image at https://www.flickr.com/photos/zharkikh/46806757465/, 356t-m, no modifications, original image at https://www.flickr.com/photos/zharkikh/9391465319/, 365t-i, no modifications, original image at https://www.flickr.com/photos/zharkikh/6660441597/, 366t-m, no modifications, original image at https://www.flickr.com/photos/zharkikh/6855165765/, 371t-iB, no modifications, original image at https://www.flickr.com/photos/zharkikh/6592935317/, 371b-m, o modifications, original image at https://www.flickr.com/photos/zharkikh/32114897525/

These images are used under Attribution-NoDervis 2.0 Generic (CC BY-ND 2.0) license, which can be found at https://creativecommons.org/licenses/by-nd/2.0/:

Jacob W. Frank/Rocky Mountain National Park: 55b-m, no modifications, original image at https://www.flickr.com/photos/rockynps/14989936135/; 58b-i, no modifications, original image at https://www.flickr.com/photos/rockynps/14987013871/, 60b-i, no modifications, original image at https://www.flickr.com/photos/rockynps/14987037261/

These images are used under Attribution 3.0 Unported (CC BY 3.0) license, which can be found at https://creativecommons.org/licenses/by/3.0/deed.en/:

Dave Powell, USDA Forest Service (retired), Bugwood.org: 66b-m, no modifications, original image at https://commons.wikimedia.org/wiki/File:Penstemon_glaber_var_alpinus_1216053_3x2.jpg, 71b-m, no modifications, original image at https://www.forestryimages.org/browse/detail.cfm?imgnum=1216032; **Dcrjsr:** 226b-i, no modifications, original image at https://commons.wikimedia.org/wiki/Spiranthes_romanzoffiana#/media/File:Ladies_tresses_Spiranthes_romanzoffiana_flower_detail.jpg

These images are used under Attribution 4.0 International (CC BY 4.0) license, which can be found at https://creativecommons.org/licenses/by/4.0/:

aarongunnar: 241b-m, no modifications, original image at https://www.inaturalist.org/photos/75874106/; **Peter L Achuff:** 222b-m, no modifications, original image at https://www.inaturalist.org/photos/174423424/, 348b-i, no modifications, original image at https://www.inaturalist.org/photos/175224416/; **Matt Berger:** 30b-m, no modifications, original image at https://www.inaturalist.org/photos/141192302/, 63b-m, no modifications, original image at https://www.inaturalist.org/photos/53216643/, 68t-i, no modifications, original image at https://www.inaturalist.org/photos/145293507/, 118b-i, no modifications, original image at https://www.inaturalist.org/photos/141560030/, 118b-m, no modifications, original image at https://www.inaturalist.org/photos/141560051/, 172t-m, no modifications, original image at https://www.inaturalist.org/photos/140178519/, 188b-i, no modifications, original image at https://www.inaturalist.org/photos/145307314/, 188b-m, no modifications, original image at https://www.inaturalist.org/photos/148760930/, 196t-m, no modifications, original image at https://www.inaturalist.org/photos/145276906/, 211b-i, no modifications, original image at https://www.inaturalist.org/photos/51855069/, 222b-i, no modifications, original image at https://www.inaturalist.org/photos/145258494/, 227t-m, no modifications, original image at https://www.inaturalist.org/photos/50021952/, 229t-m, no modifications, original image at https://www.inaturalist.org/photos /122743630/, 263t-i, no modifications, original image at https://www .inaturalist.org/photos/120744949/, 263t-m, no modifications, original image at https://www.inaturalist.org/photos/122268171/, 310t-i, no modifications, original image at https://www.inaturalist.org/photos /232844215/, 315t-m, no modifications, original image at https://www .inaturalist.org/photos/121822493/, 326b-m, no modifications, original image at https://www.inaturalist.org/photos/47153906/, 332b-i, no modifications, original image at https://www.inaturalist.org/photos/139869689/, 335b-m, no modifications, original image at https://www.inaturalist.org /photos/139853982/, 337t-m, no modifications, original image at https: //www.inaturalist.org/photos/145410446/, 363t-m, no modifications, original image at https://www.inaturalist.org/photos/191207531/, 371b-i, no modifications, original image at https://www.inaturalist.org/photos /148762938/; **Don Boucher:** 255b-m, no modifications, original image at https://www.inaturalist.org/photos/16376840/; **John Brew:** 60t-i, no modifications, original image at https://www.inaturalist.org/photos /43415828/; **Daniel Cahen:** 209t-i, no modifications, original image at https://www.inaturalist.org/photos/20620241/; **Caleb Catto:** 36t-m, no modifications, original image at https://www.inaturalist.org/photos/147278593/, 68b-i, no modifications, original image at https://www.inaturalist.org /photos/133972135/, 161t-m, no modifications, original image at https: //www.inaturalist.org/photos/88629017/, 173t-i, no modifications, original image at https://www.inaturalist.org/photos/133832590/, 178t-i, no modifications, original image at https://www.inaturalist.org/photos /138832229/, 364t-iA, no modifications, original image at https://www .inaturalist.org/photos/63739824/; **Peter Chen 2.0:** 241b-i, no modifications, original image at https://www.inaturalist.org/photos/65278162/; **Alan Covington:** 310t-m, no modifications, original image at https://www .inaturalist.org/photos/149515268/; **Daniel:** 44b-i, no modifications, original image at https://www.inaturalist.org/photos/196141473/, 334b-m, no modifications, original image at https://www.inaturalist.org/photos /207590552/; **Ryan Durand:** 18b-m, no modifications, original image at https://www.inaturalist.org/photos/113030283/, 25b-i, no modifications, original image at https://www.inaturalist.org/photos/146473165/, 66t-m, no modifications, original image at https://www.inaturalist.org/photos /113034398/, 211b-m, no modifications, original image at https://www .inaturalist.org/photos/78257032/, 262b-i, no modifications, original image at https://www.inaturalist.org/photos/122294781/; **Nolan Exe:** 132t-i, no modifications, original image at https://www.inaturalist.org/photos /119888599/, 157b-i, no modifications, original image at https://www .inaturalist.org/photos/44456150/, 227t-i, no modifications, original image at https://www.inaturalist.org/photos/84223430/, 230t-i, no modifications, original image at https://www.inaturalist.org/photos/80377287/, 326b-i, no modifications, original image at https://www.inaturalist.org/photos /143002200/, 338b-i, no modifications, original image at https://www .inaturalist.org/photos/84213127/; **Robert Flogaus Faust:** 199t-m, no modifications, original image at https://commons.wikimedia.org/wiki /File:Lathyrus_ochroleucus_RF.jpg/, 205b-m, no modifications, original image at https://commons.wikimedia.org/wiki/File:Philadelphus_lewisii_RF .jpg/, 331t-m, no modifications, original image at https://commons .wikimedia.org/wiki/File:Lilium_columbianum_RF.jpg/; **Rob Foster:** 185t-m, no modifications, original image at https://www.inaturalist.org/photos /31326534/; **Laura Gaudette:** 60b-m, no modifications, original image at https://www.inaturalist.org/photos/142063811/; **Darrin Gobble:** 106t-m, no modifications, original image at https://www.inaturalist.org/photos /137036583/, 186t-i, no modifications, original image at https://www

.inaturalist.org/photos/204533887/; **Jason Grant:** 257b-m, no modifications, original image at https://www.inaturalist.org/photos/44157833/; **joergmlpts:** 342b-i, no modifications, original image at https://www.inaturalist.org/photos/34054710/; **kara_white:** 213b-i, no modifications, original image at https://www.inaturalist.org/photos/186094754/; **Kate:** 326t-m, no modifications, original image at https://www.inaturalist.org/photos/84204344/; **Ben Keen:** 21t-m, no modifications, original image at https://www.inaturalist.org/photos/80044119/, 262b-m, no modifications, original image at https://www.inaturalist.org/photos/198409325/; **John Krampl:** 371t-iA, no modifications, original image at https://www.inaturalist.org/photos/216582069/; **Katie Kucera:** 199t-i, no modifications, original image at https://www.inaturalist.org/photos/204120648/; **Eric Lamb:** 27t-i, no modifications, original image at https://www.inaturalist.org/photos/84916642/; **Don Loarie:** 258b-i, no modifications, original image at https://www.inaturalist.org/photos/170533670/, 344t-i, no modifications, original image at https://www.inaturalist.org/photos/84885517/; **marek:** 18b-i, no modifications, original image at https://www.inaturalist.org/photos/39941595/, 63t-m, no modifications, original image at https://www.inaturalist.org/photos/39941571/, 73t-i, no modifications, original image at https://www.inaturalist.org/photos/133724364/; **Whitney Brook Matson:** 69b-m, no modifications, original image at https://www.inaturalist.org/photos/208198971/, 73b-i, no modifications, original image at https://www.inaturalist.org/photos/127879546/; **Wendy McCrady:** 40t-m, no modifications, original image at https://www.inaturalist.org/photos/179247648/; **Erin McKittrick:** 36t-i, no modifications, original image at https://www.inaturalist.org/photos/75834195/; **mfeaver:** 30b-i, no modifications, original image at https://www.inaturalist.org/photos/207771120, 54b-i, no modifications, original image at https://www.inaturalist.org/photos/20056389/; **mister_bumble:** 174t-i, no modifications, original image at https://www.inaturalist.org/photos/70916596/; **Attila Oláh:** 258t-i, no modifications, original image at https://www.inaturalist.org/photos/212874659/, 258t-m, no modifications, original image at https://www.inaturalist.org/photos/213466985/; **Harry Podschwit:** 290t-i, no modifications, original image at https://www.inaturalist.org/photos/45580577/; **John Powers:** 49b-m, no modifications, original image at https://www.inaturalist.org/photos/98553510/; **Evan M. Raskin:** 66t-i, no modifications, original image at https://www.inaturalist.org/photos/1177340/; **Katja Schulz:** 73t-m, no modifications, original image at https://www.inaturalist.org/photos/1081678/; **Jared Shorma:** 290b-i, no modifications, original image at https://www.inaturalist.org/photos/195836226/; **Michelle Smith:** 338b-m, no modifications, original image at https://www.inaturalist.org/photos/63254853/; **Donovan Roberts:** 113t-m, no modifications, original image at https://www.inaturalist.org/photos/231593058; **Ryan Sorrells:** 85b-m, no modifications, original image at https://www.inaturalist.org/photos/196670685/; **J Straka:** 187b-m, no modifications, original image at https://www.inaturalist.org/photos/172003535/; **Rachel Stringham:** 335b-i, no modifications, original image at https://www.inaturalist.org/photo/211988404/; **Ken-ichi Ueda:** 184b-m, no modifications, original image at https://www.inaturalist.org/photos/447058/, 184b-i, no modifications, original image at https://www.inaturalist.org/photos/88154123/, 255b-i, no modifications, original image at https://www.inaturalist.org/photos/151563/; **Tom Wainwright:** 48t-i, no modifications, original image at https://www.inaturalist.org/photos/45056092/

ABOUT THE AUTHOR

George Oxford Miller is a botanist, an environmental photojournalist, and a past president and lifetime member of the Albuquerque Chapter of the Native Plant Society of New Mexico. After graduating from The University of Texas at Austin with a master's degree in botany and zoology, George pursued a career as an environmental journalist specializing in nature recreation and travel, in addition to environmental issues. He is a frequent contributor to *New Mexico Magazine* and has written 25 nature guides, including *Wildflowers of Colorado and Southern Wyoming* and *Backyard Science & Discovery Workbook: Rocky Mountains*. He is also the author of *Native Plant Gardening for Birds, Bees, and Butterflies* for the Southwest, Southern California, and Northern California, as well as *A Guide to Wildflowers, Trees, and Shrubs of Texas*. His website WildflowersNM.com has descriptions, photos, and identification tips for 700 wildflowers of the Southwest and southern Rocky Mountains.